SELECTED LETTERS
OF
WILLIAM MAKEPEACE THACKERAY

Also by Edgar F. Harden

THE EMERGENCE OF THACKERAY'S SERIAL FICTION

THACKERAY'S 'ENGLISH HUMOURISTS' AND 'FOUR GEORGES'

W. M. THACKERAY: *HENRY ESMOND* (*editor*)

ANNOTATIONS FOR THE SELECTED WORKS OF
W. M. THACKERAY: The Complete Novels, the Major Non-Fictional
Prose and Selected Shorter Pieces (*editor*)

THE LETTERS AND PRIVATE PAPERS OF WILLIAM MAKEPEACE
THACKERAY: A Supplement (*editor*)

Selected Letters of William Makepeace Thackeray

Edited by
Edgar F. Harden

Selection and editorial matter © Edgar F. Harden 1996

All rights reserved. No reproduction, copy or transmission of this publication may be made without written permission.

No paragraph of this publication may be reproduced, copied or transmitted save with written permission or in accordance with the provisions of the Copyright, Designs and Patents Act 1988, or under the terms of any licence permitting limited copying issued by the Copyright Licensing Agency, 90 Tottenham Court Road, London W1P 9HE.

Any person who does any unauthorised act in relation to this publication may be liable to criminal prosecution and civil claims for damages.

First published 1996 by
MACMILLAN PRESS LTD
Houndmills, Basingstoke, Hampshire RG21 6XS
and London
Companies and representatives
throughout the world

ISBN 0–333–66073–0

A catalogue record for this book is available from the British Library.

10 9 8 7 6 5 4 3 2 1
05 04 03 02 01 00 99 98 97 96

Printed in Great Britain by
The Ipswich Book Company Ltd
Ipswich, Suffolk

For Belinda Norman-Butler

Contents

Preface	ix
Chronology	xi
Introduction	xv
List of Letters	xxiii
List of Repositories	xxxiii
The Letters	1
Further Reading	377
Index	379

PREFACE

These letters have been selected according to two principles: their ability to convey the essential biographical developments of a very interesting life, and their ability to represent highly characteristic verbal and pictorial expressions of a great man of letters. Therefore I shall include not only written utterances addressed to other identifiable human beings, but also those addressed to the partly externalized, and therefore of course partly imagined, audiences of his diaries, which include a memorably expressive prayer to mankind's most important imagined audience: God. In this wish to convey to readers Thackeray in his most revealing forms of personal expression, I have occasionally omitted portions of early journal letters and diaries, though always with clear indication of doing so (#2-5, 14, 17, 28, 33). Those readers wishing to to go on and read the complete correspondence should consult *The Letters and Private Papers of William Makepeace Thackeray,* four volumes of which, edited by the late Gordon N. Ray, appeared in 1945-46, and two supplementary volumes of which, edited by myself, appeared in 1994.

Letters that were published in the Ray volumes have been newly edited for their appearance here; such letters and those taken from my two volumes have also been newly annotated for a different reading public. Since this edition is addressed to a general audience, most of Thackeray's professional letters to his publishers have been omitted, but a number of them have necessarily been included to remind the reader of the extraordinary energies of Thackeray's engagement with the profession of writing, and of his sometimes desperate and endlessly prolonged need to support himself financially, and to leave an inheritance for the adequate maintenance of his insane wife, who ultimately outlived him by over thirty years, and of his young daughters.

The letters are transcribed literally, with the exception of unintended repetitions (e. g. "to to"), cancelled matter, and superscript portions of words. All editorial insertions appear within square brackets. When Thackeray misspells a proper name, the correct form appears in an annotation and in the index. All of Thackeray's postscripts appear at the foot of the text after the signature, even though they may be squeezed in at the top and side of the original letter. Manuscript addresses, postmarks, and endorsements are ignored; specialist readers can find them in the six volumes of collected letters.

    For permission to publish letters in their possession I should like gratefully to acknowledge the following: Armstrong Browning Library, Baylor University; Special Collections, Mugar Library, Boston University; Brigham Young University Library; the British Library; Syndics of the Cambridge University Library; Archives, Charterhouse School, and the kind permission of the Governing Body; Chatsworth Settlement Trustees; Dartmouth College Library; Detroit Public Library; Fitzwilliam Museum; Houghton Library, Harvard University; Hertfordshire Record Office; Huntington Library; Hugh Walpole Collection, King's School, Canterbury; Brotherton Collection, Leeds University Library; Pierpont Morgan Library; National Library of Scotland; Henry W. and Albert A. Berg Collection, New York Public Library, Astor, Lenox, and Tilden Foundations; Fales Library, New York University; Bodleian Library, University of Oxford; University of Pittsburgh Library; Parrish and Taylor Collections, Princeton University Library; Department of Rare Books and Special Collections, University of Rochester Library; Rosenbach Museum and Library; South Caroliniana Library, University of South Carolina; A. H. Stirling; Strathclyde Regional Archives; Harry Ransom Humanities Research Center, University of Texas at Austin; The Master and Fellows, Trinity College, Cambridge University; Alexander Turnbull Library, Wellington, New Zealand; Alderman Library, University of Virginia; and Beinecke Library, Yale University.

    For vital assistance with this project, I wish to express my appreciation to the predecessors who have published Thackeray correspondence, notably of course the late Gordon N. Ray; to the many librarians and curators who have helped me over the years; to individual scholars who have provided me with specific information and who have supported my application for the grant support that has enabled this volume to come into being; to my research assistant, Susan MacFarlane; to Margaret Sharon, Computing Services, Simon Fraser University, and to Anita Mahoney, Dean of Arts Office, Simon Fraser University, for computing assistance; to the National Endowment for the Humanities, which furnished funds that made possible the editing of two final volumes of the collected letters, on which this selection partly draws; to the Social Sciences and Humanities Research Council of Canada, which provided funds for the preparation of this volume; and to Mrs. Edward Norman-Butler, whose continuing support over many years has prompted the dedication of this volume to her.

CHRONOLOGY

1811	Born in Calcutta, the only child of Richmond Thackeray, a prosperous official of the British East India Company, and Anne Becher Thackeray.
1815	Father dies, leaving a large estate.
1817	Comes to England. Mother, still in India, marries Captain Henry Carmichael-Smyth.
1817-21	Attends school in Southampton, then in Chiswick.
1820	Mother and step-father come to England.
1822-28	Attends Charterhouse School.
1829-30	Attends Trinity College Cambridge; has notable gambling losses; leaves without a degree.
1830-31	In Weimar.
1831-33	In London as law student and later as journalist.
1833	Loses most of his inheritance in the failure of an Indian bank.
1833-37	In Paris as art student and journalist.
1836	Publishes *Flore et Zéphyr,* a collection of eight captioned lithographs. Marries Isabella Shawe, member of an Anglo-Irish family.
1837	Settles in London writing reviews, articles, and short comic fiction for magazines. Birth of daughter Anne.
1837-38	Publishes *The Yellowplush Papers* serially with authorial illustrations in *Fraser's Magazine*.
1838	Birth of daughter Jane (who dies in 1839).

1839-40	Publishes *Catherine* serially with authorial illustrations in *Fraser's Magazine*.
1840	Birth of daughter Harriet. Publishes *A Shabby Genteel Story* in *Fraser's Magazine*. Publishes *The Paris Sketch Book,* a two-volume collection of earlier magazine pieces and new work, with authorial illustrations. Wife becomes permanently insane.
1841	Publishes *Comic Tales and Sketches,* a two-volume collection of earlier magazine pieces, with authorial illustrations.
1842	Begins contributions to *Punch.* Travels in Ireland.
1843	Publishes *The Irish Sketch Book* in two volumes with authorial illustrations.
1844	Publishes *Barry Lyndon* serially in *Fraser's Magazine*.
1844-45	Travels through the Mediterranean to the Near East.
1846	Publishes *Notes of a Journey from Cornhill to Grand Cairo* in one volume.
1846-47	Publishes *The Book of Snobs* serially with authorial illustrations in *Punch*.
1847-48	Publishes *Vanity Fair* serially with authorial illustrations in monthly parts.
1848-50	Publishes *Pendennis* serially with authorial illustrations in monthly parts.
1851-53	Lectures in England, Scotland, and America on the English humorists of the eighteenth century.
1852	Publishes *Henry Esmond* in three volumes.
1853	Publishes *The English Humourists of the Eighteenth Century* in one volume.
1853-55	Publishes *The Newcomes* serially with illustrations by Richard Doyle in monthly parts.

1855-57	Lectures in America, Scotland, and England on the four Georges.
1857-59	Publishes *The Virginians* serially with authorial illustrations in monthly parts.
1860	Becomes first editor of *The Cornhill Magazine,* where he publishes *Lovel the Widower* and *The Four Georges* serially with authorial illustrations.
1860-63	Publishes *Roundabout Papers* serially with authorial illustrations in *The Cornhill Magazine.*
1861-62	Publishes *Philip* serially with authorial illustrations and illustrations by Frederick Walker in *The Cornhill Magazine.*
1862	Resigns editorship of *The Cornhill Magazine.*
1863	Dies.
1864	Unfinished *Denis Duval* published serially with authorial illustrations in *The Cornhill Magazine.*

INTRODUCTION

Since Thackeray's father died in Calcutta when Thackeray was only four, his mother became the sole center of his emotional life as a child and continued to be a major presence ever afterwards, outliving him by a year. One can therefore readily imagine the trauma caused by the boy's separation from her when, fifteen months after the death of his father, he was sent to England to escape the dangers of the Indian climate, while she remained behind to marry a military officer with whom she had been in love before her marriage. The boy's pain intensified in England when a long sequence of unhappy educational experiences began with a year spent at a school run by a tyrannical master at Southampton (#141). Although Thackeray was then transferred to a less brutal school at Chiswick, his separation from his mother lasted for three and one-half years, ending with her return to England with her husband, Henry Carmichael-Smyth, in July 1820, shortly before Thackeray's ninth birthday.

Eighteen months later he was transferred to his stepfather's school, Charterhouse, in London, where he spent six largely unhappy years learning "a little Latin & a very little Greek" (#10), being "lulled into indolence" and later "bullied into despair" (#5) by overbearing masters, and finding his chief outlets in the enjoyments provided by his own drawing, by contemporary magazines and comical prints, and by occasional visits to the theatre (#2). When he entered Trinity College, Cambridge, in early 1829, the educational bullying he had experienced had produced uncertainty about his abilities and a hostility to the systematic learning endorsed by his mother. A loving and supportive woman whom he later called his "best friend & his greatest consolation" (#20), she was also a challenging figure who repeatedly communicated her melancholy Evangelicalism, her numerous anxieties, and her disapproval when his behavior failed to meet her rigorous standards.

Thackeray's performance during his years at Charterhouse and during his first term at Cambridge fell into that category, as did his behavior during a summer trip to Paris in 1829, where at Frascati's he discovered in himself a mania for gambling (#6) that he exhibited on his return to Cambridge and later in London (#14). After five terms of poor academic performance at Cambridge, and indulgence in the "expensive habits" (#9) that he learned there, as well as the one that he had brought back from Paris, Thackeray left the university and received permission to make a trip to Germany before determining upon a profession. Passing a pleasant nine months of freedom there, chiefly at Weimar (#8-10, 199), Thackeray learned German, enjoyed the Weimar society, agitatedly responded to his mother's dissatisfaction with his past conduct (#10), and—having to choose some profession—reluctantly entertained the idea of law: an obviously inappropriate choice for anyone of his undisciplined temperament.

Although he made arrangements in June 1831 to begin legal studies in London, and struggled to overcome the "succession of idleness & dissipation" (#11) that seemed to him to characterize his past life, he resisted the idea of ever practising law, and before another year had elapsed was giving up his studies (#14) in favor of a life of pleasure, repentance, and more pleasure: widespread reading, especially of novels, and visits to theatres, art galleries, restaurants, taverns, gambling saloons, and wherever he apparently contracted a venereal disease that caused the urethral stricture that intermittently troubled him for the rest of his life. A similar life of pleasure and ineffectual but nagging repentance ensued in Paris, where he went for four months after coming of age in July 1832. Finally in May 1833, deciding to take up journalism, he bought, edited, and wrote for a small two-penny weekly London newspaper, *The National Standard*, which reported on literature, science, music, theatricals, and the fine arts.

Here at last his career as a writer had begun, but not for long, since he was drawn again in July 1833 to Paris, where he tried to reconcile his duties to the newspaper with the thought of studying art in Paris (#15). A return to London did not resolve the conflict (#16), and by October Thackeray was studying in a Paris atelier (#17). By the end of that month, however, he seems to have received notice that most of the remainder of his patrimony—over £10,000—had been lost because of the failure of an Indian bank in which it had been invested. Although he tried to keep *The National Standard* alive, he gave up in February 1834, returning to Paris later that year with financial support from his maternal grandmother to study art (#18). Here he passed what he described as "a very jolly time" (#122) in spite of his poverty, but one that was succeeded by a dreary sense of failure to master the techniques of professional drawing and painting (#19-20).

He found a second emotional center for his life during the summer of 1835, however, when he met and fell in love (#21) with the eighteen-year-old daughter of a deceased Irish army officer, Isabella Shawe, who was living with her domineering mother in a Parisian boarding-house. Here was a disaster in the making. Thackeray, who had previously longed to be married (#14, 16), was attracted by Isabella's innocence and simplicity, but these very qualities ultimately proved to be major deficiencies, revealing in her an inability to mature and to overcome the difficulties of life—an inability that evidently helped to cause her later depression and psychic collapse. She brought him the burden of dependency, but he loved her for being "so good & so gentle" (#48), and for possessing "more nobleness and simplicity . . . than I've seen in most people in this world" (#60). Although he later called it an absurdly imprudent marriage, he seems never to have regretted it, and told her in 1838: "Here have we been nearly 2 years married & not a single unhappy day" (#28).

That happiness gave him an important inner stability, but the marriage was not achieved without the necessity of his overcoming both her mother's opposition and also, of course, his own lack of a profession and income. Brief employment with an English language newspaper in Paris seems to have ended in early 1836, while publication, apparently during April, in London and Paris of his first separate work, a collection of eight lithographs entitled *Flore et Zéphyr,* subsidized by his friend John Bowes Bowes, failed to bring income. Another newspaper venture seemed more promising, however, when Thackeray's stepfather, Major Carmichael-Smyth, invested in a London newspaper, *The Constitutional and Public Ledger,* and secured Thackeray employment as Paris correspondent. Here Thackeray thought he had finally found the opportunity to escape the prospect of "a doubtful future, a precarious profession, and a long and trying probation" (#22), but the opportunity proved to be only short-lived, and for years afterwards he had to face what he thought he had escaped.

With the apparent prospect of steady employment, however, Thackeray married Isabella in August 1836 (#23), living in Paris until March 1837, when they moved to London, where Major Carmichael-Smyth had become the chief financial support for the faltering *Constitutional*. With its collapse on 1 July 1837, Thackeray was forced to begin a career as an independent writer free of familial subsidy. Accordingly, he became a reviewer and a writer of imaginative fiction for magazines, beginning with a review of Carlyle's *The French Revolution* for *The Times* in August, "The Professor. A Tale" for *Bentley's Miscellany* in September, the first installment of "The Yellowplush Correspondence" for *Fraser's Magazine* in November, and "A Word on the Annuals" for *Fraser's* in December. Thirty pieces appeared during 1838, testifying to the accuracy of Carlyle's observation that Thackeray was writing for his life. It was a professional life of writing for newspapers and magazines that continued for ten years until novel-writing began to be his chief activity, with the successful appearance of *Vanity Fair* (1847-48).

During that decade, his personal life underwent significant changes, beginning with the birth of his daughter, Anne, in June 1837, who was followed in July 1838 by Jane (#29), and in May 1840 by Harriet (#38). Meanwhile, the straitened financial circumstances of his mother and step-father had forced them to move to Paris, where they could live more cheaply—a move that resulted in the writing of many of Thackeray's surviving letters. The demands of running a household, the death of Jane (#31), and post-partum depression following the birth of Harriet (#42-43) contributed significantly to Isabella's permanent psychic breakdown in September 1840 (#45-46)—a multiple trauma for Thackeray, since he not only lost his wife and was unable thereafter to remarry, but also was separated from his two young children, who had to live in Paris, where his mother could take care of them. Since he tried to give his wife the best possible sanatorium treatment (#47), his financial burdens also increased, as we can see in several moving letters that he wrote in attempting to secure acceptances for magazine work (#48-49). Although he had previously described writing for magazines as "work wh. wd. kill any writer in 6 years" (#41), he had no alternative, faced as he was (he wrote in August 1841) with "the horrible care and fear of want wh. has been hanging over me in the past year since my wife's affliction" (#57).

As always, however, he was in part buoyed by the irrepressible bubbling up of what he called "a great fund of animal spirits that want to break out in the shape of argument or jollification" (#43)—whether in the form of comic or satirical writing, in the discussion of pictures or books, in travel and the enjoyable experience of landscapes and architecture, or in the convivial society of other people. Indeed, for all his misery, one thinks of Thackeray as one of the great enjoyers of life. As he wrote, even while expressing admiration of a saintly friend, "yet the world would not be so good a world as it is were all men like him: it would be but a timid ascetic place in wh. many of the finest faculties of the soul would not dare to exercise themselves" (#34). For Thackeray, joviality is a spiritual virtue (#42).

He found stimulation in public places, not just as an arena of human conduct to be observed, but as an atmosphere condusive to the act of writing itself: "there is so much stir, bustle and blood flowing, that the work is done in 1/2 the time" (#60). "Solitude creates a muzziness and incoherency in me . . .—I am never thinking of what I am writing about" (#62). Going out to dinner every night in the week might be immersing oneself in a bustling "racket," he acknowledges to his mother, but "this racket agrees better with me than a quieter life and I have managed to write a good deal" (#65). "It agrees with me wonderfully the ceaseless racket," he writes with consistent conviction thirteen years later (#217). His "great faculty of enjoyment" (#114) expresses itself with equal fervor in work and play, and if he sometimes regrets what the jollification takes out of him, a truly jolly life means to Thackeray "plenty of work . . . and plenty of fun" (#70). If he "wallow[s]in turtle and swim[s] in claret and Shampang" (#125), the "Champagne & . . . laugh[ter]" (#94) bubble over as well into the gusto of writing.

In reading his comical writing, one is intermittently struck by its extraordinary exuberance, which expresses itself from the beginning of his career in extravaganzas like "The Professor" (1837), whose hero is a manic oyster eater ("Why, then, the world's mine oyster"), and "The Tremendous Adventures of Major Gahagan" (1838-39), an uproarious burlesque of Anglo-Indian military narratives. Among his correspondence, the pretended letter from New York to Mrs. Brookfield offers the most extended example of comic extravagance (#110), but his "sudden humours" (#122) bubble forth in a variety of other situations as well, most frequently in his amusing drawings, 75 of which occur in these letters, but also when he sends out invitations (#68, 108, 121), responds to an uneventful few days (#70), lapses into comic doggerel (#58, 217), dashes off an impromptu (#123, 137), or engages in some other form of nonsense (e.g. #157).

If writing nonsense is a sign of health (#131), so too is the writing of satire. For Thackeray, satire, like criticism, had to be free from loyalty to political parties or to snobbish values. Since we live in "a world of humbug," the writing of satire is "capital fun," expressing "a good scornful kind" of laughter without ceasing to be "good natured" (#34). "What I want is strong government and social equality" (#46), he wrote, instead of the insolent and arbitrary domination over a "lickspittle" (#77) public by a few titled individuals who all too often are "scum" (#46). At times he felt, "I fail by sneering too much" (#36), but he sought to check that excess in his satire. If he welcomed the opportunity to write for *Punch* because it provided not only good pay but "a great opportunity for unrestrained laughing sneering kicking and gambadoing" (#60), his most famous *Punch* series, *The Book of Snobs* (1846-47), ended with a notable statement of the need for restraint (#90); moreover, as the word "gambadoing" indicates, his "kicking" was typically the cutting of amusing capers.

Being very much aware of how human beings *perform* to one another (#107), especially when they are people whose professional occupation requires it of them (#111), Thackeray made endless efforts in his letters to preserve naturalness. Therefore even the slightest awareness of his beginning to "compose" brings him to halt, and to start in a new direction (e. g. #166). Consequently, his letters are not literary "compositions," but attempts at relaxed sincerity of human expression or, alternatively, outbursts of extravagant buffoonery that no one could mistake for the deceits of posturing. If he humbly apologizes for the "grumbling" or "stupidity" that he feels accompanies his relaxed mode of expression, his readers can understand that he is not primarily seeking to "entertain." Given the range and diversity of his activities and moods, he tells a correspondent that "I am never content." One can understand, therefore, why he admires someone who is consistently "cheerful . . . honest . . . kind and artless" (#189), for he finds nobility in such integrity of character—that is, in such unity and coherence.

Hence his love of simplicity, whether he found it in children (#91), in his wife and other women (#38, 41), in other men like his stepfather (#60), in architecture (#193), or even in food (#89). "Manliness and simplicity of manner go a great way with me" (#53) he wrote, implying his tastes in literary as well as social behavior. Their opposite, dandiacal posturing, of course provoked his satire. Whereas Goldsmith had "a charming simplicity" (#102), Bulwer seemed to Thackeray to indulge in egoistical posturing, as exemplified by his love of "very eloquent clap-trap" (#14). "Fine writing" was therefore an anathema to Thackeray, who praised Dickens for having "simplified his style" in *David Copperfield* and "kept out of the fine words" (#125). Thackeray described the dedication he wrote for *Vanity Fair* as "very simple" (#106). Mary Graham Carmichael, his cousin, came to appal him precisely because, although she began as "a very simple generous creature," she underwent a transformation that made her capable of outdoing Becky Sharp herself—in conversation as well as in a letter that was "a miracle of deception." Thackeray's response was: "Pray God to keep us simple" (#122).

For a complex human being like Thackeray, however, simplicity had constantly to be sought, as we see in a letter to Mrs. Brookfield, for example, where, after a burst of extravagant humor, he writes: "I suppose one only gets to simplicity à force d'artifice—and gradually casts off the skin of fine-writing—Is it honesty or only consummate roguery? both I think" (#130). Here we see the typical working of his psyche in the rhythm of utterance and counter-response. Beneath his attempts to achieve simplicity lies artful purpose. Even letter writing to a friend reveals itself to be always partly a strategem as well as an effort to communicate honestly. Hence Thackeray constantly tries to subdue pride with humility, as he fights off the wish to achieve fame with the wish to write only for fortune (#50), constantly apologizes for his egoism, characterizes his grief as selfish (#59), tries to think of himself as a tradesman rather than an artist (#75), resists the flattery that comes when he has achieved fame with *Vanity Fair* (#101), but knows that he has now become someone whose letters will be saved and will be read by later generations: "I think it is impossible for literary men to write natural letters any more: I was just going to say something, but thinks I in future ages when this letter comes to be &c—they will say 'he was in embarrassed circumstances he was reckless and laughed at his prodigality he was &c[']" (#111).

The extravagances were only too true ("I spend as much money as I get" [#140]) and were quite in character, but the expenses were not merely personal, for his generosity increasingly responded to the needs of indigent friends and acquaintances (#225, 229, 230). He also had a household to support, for his children had come to live with him in September 1846, causing grief to his mother at parting with them in Paris, but giving him a profoundly happy emotional center for the rest of his life (#84). A more turbulent love expressed itself in his growing attachment to Mrs. William Brookfield (#67, 79, 88), who was married to an old college friend of Thackeray's. She responded only very limitedly, however, and by September 1851 her husband's angry jealousy of Thackeray's intense feelings had caused a permanent break between them and Thackeray, who felt that he had suffered an "amputation" (#155) of a part of himself. His chief confidantes were two ladies who became like sisters to him, Kate Perry and Jane Perry Elliot (#155-156), and of course his mother (#158).

Difficult as it was for Thackeray to restrain expenditures, whether emotional or financial, his sense of responsibility to his daughters and to his insane wife, who was now being cared for privately in England, was deepened by a serious gastric illness (#131, 134, 140) that occurred during the writing of *Pendennis* (1848-50). Accordingly, he came to seek an additional source of income: writing and giving public lectures, which he did in England, Scotland, and America in 1851-53 and in 1855-57 with great success. In America he enlarged his circle of friends still further, especially with the wife and daughters of the George Baxter family, notably with the oldest daughter, Sarah, who played the role of Beatrix Esmond to his role as an aging Henry Esmond (#178). The financial success of these lectures finally allowed him to make a major provision for the future well-being of his own family members. He completed these efforts with income from his later writings and from his editorship (1859-62) of *The Cornhill Magazine,* which enabled him to build "Vanity Fair House" (#253), "the Palazzo" (#266), a fine, well-furnished home with an excellent wine cellar on Palace Green, Kensington, where he entertained generously and felt, he wrote, "like the hero at the end of a Story!" (#266).

The exuberance of Thackeray's spirits, however, was significantly circumscribed by two factors: a deep-seated melancholy persisting from childhood, and a state of health that increasingly worsened after 1853. As his remarks about grumbling help to indicate, he frequently felt profoundly dissatisfied "with what I do either as a man or a lit[er]ary man" (#134). One can readily understand how the personal insecurity caused by his early loss of a father, his ensuing separation from his mother, his harsh schooling, and his inability to control his prodigality and to find a meaningful, satisfying course of life was deepened by his mother's Evangelicalism, with her relentless articulation of human depravity and the terrors of Hell, and by her gloomy disapproval of his youthful conduct. Readers can therefore be moved by his epistolary challenges to her dogmatism and especially to the darkness of her outlook, for we can see how he was battling against a similar gloom in himself, one that arose from a sense of his unworthiness that was one of his most enduring legacies from her. At the same time, however, one must acknowledge the power of the love they felt for one another and the comfort that they continually sought to give each other. Since, after their first parting, Thackeray never could bear to part for a lengthy time with anyone of whom he was fond, one can see in his extended correspondence with his mother, whom he visited every day when she moved late in life from Paris to a residence in London, a continual reassertion of his closeness to her. We can see, with a similar understanding, how this need for her companionship is mirrored in a series of unusually close and self-revealing relationships with other female confidantes: Mrs. Procter, Mrs. Brookfield, Miss Perry, Mrs. Elliot, and Mrs. Baxter—who also offered him alternatives to his mother's concerns; as he wrote to Mrs. Elliot, "didactic friendship I dont value" (#208).

  In spite of all the pains as well as pleasures that Thackeray experienced, the care that came most to oppress him was ill-health. Aside from occasional pain from his early urethral stricture, and the experience of his dangerous illness in 1849, Thackeray enjoyed "sheer roaring good health" (#114) until he contracted a malarial fever in Italy in late 1853. Thereafter he had frequent attacks of "spasms" (#227), accompanied by vomiting, diarrhea, purgation, pain, chills, and fever—attacks made worse by overindulgence in the food and drink that accompanied genial socializing, especially with male friends (#229). Difficulty with his "water pipes cistern &c" (#211) became more troublesome as well, causing pain, instrumentation, and frequent visits to the urinary specialist, Henry Thompson. Although his spirits returned with the temporary departure of his illnesses, their increasing freqency inhibited his work, made lecturing impossible, and told him of a shortened life expectancy. When he died on the evening of 23/24 December 1863 of the rupture of a cerebral blood vessel brought on by a violent attack of spasms and vomiting, he had lived a full life but was only 52.

LIST OF LETTERS

Correspondent   *Date*

1. Mrs. Henry Carmichael-Smyth — 11 June 1818
2. Mrs. Henry Carmichael-Smyth — 13-18 February 1828
3. Mrs. Henry Carmichael-Smyth — 28 February 1829
4. Mrs. Henry Carmichael-Smyth — 23 March 1829
5. Mrs. Henry Carmichael-Smyth — 16 April 1829
6. Mrs. Henry Carmichael-Smyth — 21 August 1829
7. Mrs. Henry Carmichael-Smyth — 31 July 1830
8. Mrs. Henry Carmichael-Smyth — 28 September 1830
9. Mrs. Henry Carmichael-Smyth — 3 December 1830
10. Mrs. Henry Carmichael-Smyth — 31 December 1830
11. Edward FitzGerald — 18 July 1831
12. John Mitchell Kemble — January 1832
13. Edward FitzGerald — April? 1832
14. Diary — April - November 1832
15. Mrs. Henry Carmichael-Smyth — 6 July 1833
16. Mrs. Henry Carmichael-Smyth — 6 September 1833
17. Mrs. Henry Carmichael-Smyth — 22-29 October 1833
18. Edward FitzGerald — 8 October 1834
19. Frank Stone — 17 April 1835
20. Mrs. Henry Carmichael-Smyth — 18-23 July 1835
21. William Ritchie — September 1835
22. Isabella Shawe — 14-15 April 1836
23. Mrs. John Ritchie — 25 August 1836
24. Edward FitzGerald — 7 October 1836

25.	John Mitchell Kemble	13 December 1836
26.	Frank Stone	20 January 1837
27.	James Fraser	5 March 1838
28.	Mrs. William Makepeace Thackeray	11 March 1838
29.	Mrs. Matthew Shawe	12 July 1838
30.	Richard Bentley	19 November 1838
31.	Mrs. Henry Carmichael-Smyth	March 1839
32.	Mrs. Henry Carmichael-Smyth	1-2 December 1839
33.	Mrs. Henry Carmichael-Smyth	23-30 December 1839
34.	Mrs. Henry Carmichael-Smyth	18 January 1840
35.	Mrs. Bryan Waller Procter	16 February 1840
36.	Mrs. Henry Carmichael-Smyth	April 1840
37.	Mrs. Bryan Waller Procter	22 May 1840
38.	Mrs. Henry Carmichael-Smyth	1 June 1840
39.	Mrs. Bryan Waller Procter	7 July 1840
40.	Bryan Waller Procter	July 1840
41.	Mrs. Henry Carmichael-Smyth	30 July 1840
42.	Mrs. Henry Carmichael-Smyth	20-21 August 1840
43.	Mrs. Henry Carmichael-Smyth	Aug. - 1 Sept. 1840
44.	Mrs. Henry Carmichael-Smyth	10 September 1840
45.	Mrs. Henry Carmichael-Smyth	17 September 1840
46.	Mrs. Henry Carmichael-Smyth	4-5 October 1840
47.	Edward FitzGerald	10 January 1841
48.	James Fraser	25 February 1841
49.	Mrs. Thomas Carlyle	25 February 1841
50.	Mrs. Bryan Waller Procter	19 March 1841
51.	Mrs. Thomas Carlyle	20 March 1841
52.	Mrs. Bryan Waller Procter	5 April 1841
53.	Mrs. Bryan Waller Procter	28 May - 5 June 1841
54.	Richard Bentley	1 June 1841

LIST OF LETTERS

55.	Diary	27 July - 11 Aug. 1841
56.	George William Nickisson	7 August 1841
57.	Mrs. John Ritchie	19 August 1841
58.	Edward FitzGerald	13 Sept. - Oct. 1841
59.	Edward FitzGerald	9 March 1842
60.	Mrs. Henry Carmichael-Smyth	11 - ? June 1842
61.	Edward FitzGerald	4 July 1842
62.	Mrs. Henry Carmichael-Smyth	? - 16 October 1842
63.	Antonio Panizzi	December 1842
64.	Anne Thackeray	1842?
65.	Mrs. Henry Carmichael-Smyth	March? 1843
66.	George William Nickisson	8 April 1843
67.	Mrs. William Makepeace Thackeray	3? May 1843
68.	The Rev. William Henry Brookfield	26 May 1843
69.	Mrs. Bryan Waller Procter	August 1843
70.	His family	17-18 December 1843
71.	Peter Purcell	25 December 1843
72.	Mrs. Henry Carmichael-Smyth	21-22 August 1844
73.	Mrs. William Makepeace Thackeray	17 September 1844
74.	Chapman and Hall	10 January 1845
75.	Richard Bedingfield	1 June 1845
76.	Mrs. Henry Carmichael-Smyth	2 August 1845
77.	Mrs. Henry Carmichael-Smyth	28 November 1845
78.	Alexander William Kinglake	24 February 1846
79.	Mrs. Henry Carmichael-Smyth	6 March 1846
80.	Mrs. Henry Carmichael-Smyth	March 1846
81.	Mrs. Bryan Waller Procter	26 April 1846
82.	Richard Monckton Milnes	29 May 1846
83.	Henry Vizetelly	13 September 1846
84.	Mrs. Henry Carmichael-Smyth	4 December 1846

85. Bradbury and Evans   December 1846
86. Mrs. Bryan Waller Procter   1846?
87. Mrs. Bryan Waller Procter   January 1847
88. The Rev. William Henry Brookfield   3 February 1847
89. Henry Reeve   23 February 1847
90. Mark Lemon   24 February 1847
91. George William Nickisson   1 March 1847
92. Mrs. Henry Carmichael-Smyth   15 April 1847
93. Edward Chapman   29 May 1847
94. Mrs. Henry Carmichael-Smyth   2 July 1847
95. William Smith Williams   23 October 1847
96. Leigh Hunt   3 January 1848
97. William Smith Williams   January 1848
98. Mrs. Edward Marlborough Fitzgerald   31 January 1848
99. Mrs. John Ritchie   5 February 1848
100. George Henry Lewes   6 March 1848
101. Edward FitzGerald   March - May 1848
102. John Forster   14 April 1848
103. The Duke of Devonshire   1 May 1848
104. Mrs. William Henry Brookfield   June 1848
105. Mrs. Henry Carmichael-Smyth   29 June 1848
106. Mrs. Bryan Waller Procter   29 June 1848
107. Mrs. William Henry Brookfield   10 July 1848
108. Mr. & Mrs. Edward John Sartoris   July 1848
109. Robert Bell   3 September 1848
110. Mrs. William Henry Brookfield   5 September 1848
111. Mrs. Bryan Waller Procter   13 September 1848
112. Lady Cullum   4 October 1848
113. Mrs. William Henry Brookfield   7-9 October 1848
114. Mrs. William Henry Brookfield   1 November 1848

115. Edward Chapman — 22 November 1848
116. Arthur Hugh Clough — 26 November 1848
117. Mrs. William Henry Brookfield — 29 November 1848
118. Mrs. William Henry Brookfield — December? 1848
119. Edward FitzGerald — 19 December 1848
120. Lady Blessington — 1848
121. Mrs. Eyre Evans Crowe — 1848?
122. Mrs. William Henry Brookfield — 4-5 February 1849
123. Mrs. Charles Arthur Gore — March 1849?
124. Adelaide Ann Procter — April 1849
125. Lady Blessington — 6 May 1849
126. Mrs. William Henry Brookfield — 17-19 May 1849
127. Mrs. Grantham Munton Yorke — 1 June 1849
128. Mrs. T. F. Elliot and Kate Perry — 29 June 1849
129. Adelaide Ann Procter — 5? August 1849
130. Mrs. William Henry Brookfield — 18 September 1849
131. Mrs. Bryan Waller Procter — 17 October 1849
132. Tom Taylor — 29-30 December 1849
133. Lady Castlereagh — 3 January 1850
134. James Spedding — 5 January 1850
135. Abraham Hayward — 1 February 1850
136. Magdalene Brookfield — 26 February 1850
137. Mrs Charles S. Fanshawe — March? 1850
138. John Forster — 3 April 1850
139. The Rev. William Henry Brookfield — April? 1850
140. Eliot Warburton — 13 April 1850
141. Anne and Harriet Thackeray — 26 May 1850
142. Mrs. William Henry Brookfield — 21 August 1850
143. Mrs. William Henry Brookfield — 23 December 1850
144. Anne Thackeray — 24 December 1850

145. Robert Smith Surtees	29 December 1850
146. Lady Eastlake	7 January 1851
147. The Rev. William Henry Brookfield	18 March 1851
148. Thomas John Mazzinghi	April? 1851
149. Mrs. William Henry Brookfield	29 April 1851
150. Mrs. William Henry Brookfield	1 May 1851
151. David Masson	6? May 1851
152. Mr. and Mrs. Thomas Carlyle	23? May 1851
153. Leigh Hunt	29-30 May 1851
154. John Forster	June 1851
155. Kate Perry	September 1851
156. Mrs. T. F. Elliot and Kate Perry	26 September 1851
157. Lady Stanley	28? October 1851
158. Mrs. Henry Carmichael-Smyth	10 November 1851
159. George Smith	26 December 1851
160. Mrs. John Brown	5 January 1852
161. Mrs. T. F. Elliot and Kate Perry	7? January 1852
162. Lady Pollock	January 1852
163. Mrs. Henry Carmichael-Smyth	15 March 1852
164. Anne and Harriet Thackeray	22 April 1852
165. Anne and Harriet Thackeray	18-20 June 1852
166. Mrs. T. F. Elliot and Kate Perry	21 June 1852
167. William Allingham	6 August 1852
168. Mary Holmes	10 August 1852
169. Dr. John Brown	6 October 1852
170. Anne Thackeray	October 1852
171. Edward FitzGerald	27 October 1852
172. Mrs. Bryan Waller Procter	29 October 1852
173. Anne and Harriet Thackeray	4-11 November 1852
174. George Smith	26 November 1852

175. Mrs. T. F. Elliot and Kate Perry	7 December 1852
176. Sarah Baxter	22 December 1852
177. Mrs. Bryan Waller Procter	22 December 1852
178. Mrs. George Baxter	2 January 1853
179. Henry Marie Brackenridge	19 February 1853
180. Albany Fonblanque	4 March 1853
181. Lucy Baxter	April 1853
182. Mrs. Henry Carmichael-Smyth	19 April 1853
183. Mrs. George Ticknor	20 April 1853
184. Mrs. George Baxter	May? 1853
185. The George Baxters	18-19 May 1853
186. Sir Edward Bulwer-Lytton	21 June 1853
187. Sarah Baxter	4-5 July 1853
188. Mrs. T. F. Elliot and Kate Perry	13-15 July 1853
189. Sarah Baxter	26 July-7 August 1853
190. Bryan Waller Procter	September 1853
191. Mrs. T. F. Elliot and Kate Perry	October 1853
192. Elizabeth Strong and Lucy Baxter	17 Oct. - 3 Nov. 1853
193. Mrs. Henry Carmichael-Smyth	5 December 1853
194. Mrs. Bryan Waller Procter	Jan. - 4 Feb. 1854
195. Kate Perry	19? March 1854
196. Paul Émile Daurand Forgues	16 September 1854
197. Dr. and Mrs. John Brown	31 December 1854
198. The Rev. John Allen	7 February 1855
199. George Henry Lewes	28 April 1855
200. S. N. Rowland	2 May 1855
201. William Ritchie	25 May 1855
202. Mrs. T. F. Elliot and Kate Perry	2 July 1855
203. His family	30-31 October 1855
204. Mrs. Henry Carmichael-Smyth	16?-20 November 1855

205. Mrs. George Baxter and Sarah Baxter — 11 December 1855
206. Anne Thackeray — 18 December 1855
207. Mrs. George Ticknor — 13 January 1856
208. Kate Perry — 14-16 February 1856
209. Mrs. T. F. Elliot and Kate Perry — 10 March 1856
210. Mrs. Thomas Frederick Elliot — 24-26 March 1856
211. William Duer Robinson — 7-9 May 1856
212. Mrs. Frank Hampton — 12-13 July 1856
213. Mrs. T. F. Elliot and Kate Perry — 10 September 1856
214. Bradbury and Evans — 18 November 1856
215. Amy Crowe — November 1856
216. Mrs. T. F. Elliot and Kate Perry — November 1856
217. Mrs. T. F. Elliot and Kate Perry — 2 December 1856
218. Mrs. T. F. Elliot and Kate Perry — 6-7 December 1856
219. Mrs. Frank Hampton — 10-12 December 1856
220. Mrs. John Blackwood — 14 December 1856
221. Mrs. Henry Carmichael-Smyth — 9-12 January 1857
222. Frederick Cozzens — 8 Feb.- 5 April 1857
223. Mrs. T. F. Elliot and Kate Perry — 21-22 February 1857
224. John Everett Millais — 26 February 1857
225. The George Baxters — 31 Oct. - 27 Nov. 1857
226. John Blackwood — 21 December 1857
227. William Duer Robinson — 23 Jan. - 25 Feb. 1858
228. John Reuben Thompson — 25 February 1858
229. Mrs. George Baxter — 10-23 April 1858
230. Mrs. Henry Carmichael-Smyth — May 1858
231. Adelaide Ann Procter — 4 June 1858
232. The George Baxters — 25 August 1858
233. Lady Pollock — 20 September 1858
234. Dr. John Brown — 4 November 1858

LIST OF LETTERS

235.	Captain Atkinson	27 December 1858
236.	Lady Hardinge	13 March 1859
237.	Mrs. Maria Haas	15 May 1859
238.	Mrs. John Blackwood	28 May 1859
239.	Anne and Harriet Thackeray	23 August 1859
240.	Alfred Tennyson	Sept. - 16 Oct. 1859
241.	Mrs. George Baxter	21 Sept. - 18 Oct. 1859
242.	Anthony Trollope	28 October 1859
243.	John H. Bewley	31 October 1859
244.	A Contributor	1 November 1859
245.	The Rev. Samuel Reynolds Hole	26 January 1860
246.	Sir Henry Davison	4 May 1860
247.	The George Baxters	25 December 1860
248.	Thomas Frederick Elliot	11 January 1861
249.	Frederick Locker	22 January 1861
250.	John Frederick Boyes	10-19 March 1861
251.	William Stirling	1 May? 1861
252.	Henry Holland	17 May 1861
253.	Mrs. George Baxter	24 May 1861
254.	George Smith	May 1861
255.	The Rev. Whitwell Elwin	24-31 May 1861
256.	Mrs. Thomas Milner Gibson	21-26 July 1861
257.	George Smith	30 September 1861
258.	John Frederick Boyes	1 October 1861
259.	George Virtue	13 December 1861
260.	William Stirling	1861
261.	Edward Fordham Flower	7 January 1862
262.	Contributors and Correspondents	25 March 1862
263.	Mr. and Mrs. George Baxter	6?-9 May 1862
264.	Robert Bell	May 1862

265. George Smith   1 July 1862
266. Mrs. Henry Carmichael-Smyth   5 July 1862
267. The George Baxters   25 December 1862
268. Dr. John Brown   23 September 1863
269. Dr. Henry Thompson   15 December 1863
270. Joseph Parkes   [1844-50]
271. Lady Morley   [1846-55]
272. The Misses Power?   [1847?-49?]
273. Lady Louisa de Rothschild   [1848-49]
274. Sir Jonathan Frederick Pollock   [1848-54]
275. Lady Olliffe   [1853-63]
276. William Makepeace Thackeray Synge   [1860-63]
277. Dr. James Reeves Traer   [1862-63]

LIST OF REPOSITORIES

Baylor University: Armstrong Browning Library
Letter 249

Boston University: Special Collections, Mugar Library
Letter 21

Brigham Young University Library
Letter 93

British Library
Letters 1–11, 14–17, 20, 22, 24, 28, 31–4, 36, 38, 41–7, 55, 58–60, 63, 65, 67, 70, 72–3, 76–7, 79–80, 84, 92, 94, 104–5, 141, 144, 153, 158, 163–4, 170, 173, 193, 203–4, 206, 221, 230, 239

Cambridge University Library
Letter 78

Cambridge University: Trinity College
Letters 82, 112, 198, 256

Charterhouse School: Archives
Letter 91

Chatsworth House
Letter 103

Dartmouth College Library
Letters 25, 183, 207

Detroit Public Library
Letter 215

Fitzwilliam Museum
Letter 252

LIST OF REPOSITORIES

Harvard University: Houghton Library
Letters 57, 119, 135, 137, 152, 176, 201, 210, 222, 228–9, 232, 237, 275 (all bMS Eng 881)

Hertfordshire Record Office
Letter 186

Huntington Library
Letters 29 (HM 15332), 99 (HM 15275), 120 (HM 15259), 125 (HM 15252), 128 (HM 15323), 157 (HM 6980), 192 (HM 6990), 245 (HM 6995)

King's School: Hugh Walpole Collection
Letters 180, 202

Leeds University Library: Brotherton Collection
Letters 19, 30, 51

Pierpont Morgan Library
Letters 26, 47, 123, 264 (all MA 4500), 85 (MA 2011), 98, 107, 110, 113–15, 117, 118, 122, 126, 139, 143, 147, 149–50 (all MA 469-470), 159, 174, 254, 257, 265 (all MA 4724), 220, 226 (both MA 1418), 247 (MA 3306), 250 (MA 472)

National Library of Scotland
Letters 35, 37, 39, 40, 50, 52, 53, 69, 81, 86, 87, 106, 111, 124, 129, 131, 169, 172, 177, 190, 194, 231 (all Acc 10625, on long-term loan), 154, 160, 169, 197, 234, 268 (all Acc 6134)

New York Public Library: Berg Collection
Letters 61, 66, 74, 89, 90, 95, 96, 97, 100, 101, 108, 124, 133, 136, 138, 151, 166, 168, 171, 178, 185, 205, 209, 211–13, 225, 227, 235, 253, 258, 263, 270

New York University: Fales Library
Letters 27, 48, 54, 71, 146, 238, 261, 276–7

University of Oxford: Bodleian Library
Letter 116

University of Pittsburgh Library
Letter 179

LIST OF REPOSITORIES

Princeton University Library: Parrish Collection
Letters 56, 134, 145, 246

Princeton University Library: Taylor Collection
Letters 18, 27, 242, 272

University of Rochester Library: Special Collections
Letters 216, 236

Rosenbach Museum and Library
Letters 88, 130, 142, 155–6, 161, 175, 188, 191, 195, 208, 217–18

University of South Carolina: South Caroliniana Library
Letters 184, 187, 189, 219, 241, 267

Strathclyde Regional Archives
Letters 251, 260

University of Texas at Austin: Humanities Research Center
Letters 121, 214, 269

Turnbull Library
Letter 140

University of Virginia: Alderman Library
Letters 182, 243

Yale University: Beinecke Library
Letter 240

THE LETTERS

1. TO MRS. HENRY CARMICHAEL-SMYTH
11 June 1818

My dearest of all dear Mamas
  I have much pleasure in writing to you again from Fareham to tell how happy I am. I went to Roche Court to see Mr & Mrs Thresher. I saw a birds nest with young ones in it in a beautiful Honeysuckle bush, and a Robbins in another place. This has been Neptune day with me I call it so becase I go into the water & am like Neptune Your old acquaintances are very kind to me & give me a great many Cakes, & great many Kisses but I do not let Charles Becher kiss me I only take those from the Ladies. I dont have many from Grandmama. Miss English gives her very kind love to you, and begs you will soon come home Pray give my kindest love to Pappa. Aunt Becher bought me a Caliduscope, it is a very nice one.
  I have spent a very pleaseant day at Catesfie[l]d, Miss O'Bryen gave me a very pretty jest Book. I should like you to have such another pretty house as Mrs O'Bryens there is such a beautiful Garden. I am grown a great Boy I am three feet 11 inches and a quarter high I have got a nice boat. I learn some poems which you was very fond of such as the Ode on Music &c I shall go on Monday to Chiswick to see my Aunt Turner & heare the Boys speak. I intend to be one of those heroes in time. I am very glad I am not to go to Mrs Arthurs. I have lost my Cough and am quite well, strong, saucy, & hearty; & can eat Granmamas Goosberry pyes famously after which I drink yours & my Papas Good health & a speedy return.
  believe me my dear Mama
    Your dutiful Son
    W Thackeray

            Fareham. June 11th
             Hants.

Mama: Mrs. Henry Carmichael-Smyth (1792-1864), the former Anne Becher, who in 1810 had married Thackeray's father, Richmond Thackeray (1781-1815). She married her second husband, Henry Carmichael-Smyth (1780-1861) in 1817. *Charles Becher:* a maternal uncle. *Grandmama:* Mrs. John Becher (1735-1825), the former Anne Fleyeham, Thackeray's great-grandmother, who lived at Fareham with her unmarried daughter Anne, Thackeray's great-aunt. *Ode on Music:* presumably William Collins's "The Passions: An Ode to Music." *Aunt Turner:* Mrs. John Turner, Thackeray's great-aunt. She and her husband kept a school for boys at Chiswick. *Mrs. Arthur:* proprietor, with her husband, of a harsh school in Southampton that Thackeray attended 1817-18.

2. TO MRS. HENRY CARMICHAEL-SMYTH
13-18 February 1828

[. . .]
Feb. 13. I have not been out of the house all day. I have got a headache, but do not like to stay out of school for the Doctor would tell me that it was a disgraceful shuffle, and a lie and all that sort of thing: so I think it better to bear the pain—I have been to see a ventriloquist at Charter-House to day. Such nonsense! I came away before it was over. I did not see Charles there. I hope he was there, for it would have entertained him, and varied the monotony of Charter-House Life—I feel ever[y] day, as if one link were taken from my chain, I have a consolation in thinking there are not many links more—I have not procured any Valentines for exportation, indeed I dont know that I shall. I have been working all the evening, and must be up by seven to work again tomorrow morning—So good night dear Mother.
[. . .]
Monday—Nothing written on Friday, Saturday, or Sunday—Friday I was so hard at work—Saturday I went to Southampton Row, and they dined at two—Sunday ditto—I went to the Adelphi on Saturday night, and fell in love with Mrs. Yates—I have thought of nothing but Mrs. Yates, since then—Mrs. Yates, Mrs. Yates, Mrs. Yates! She is so pretty, and so fascinating and so ladylike and so—I need not go on with her good qualities—I am glad I did not write before now for I should not have got your nice long letter—Alfred Huyshe never called on me, but I suppose he had plenty to do without it—Mrs. Dick called on Mrs. Ritchie in the Christmas holy days; she said she had been taken ill the first day she got to town, and was laid up for a month, so that accounts for my not seeing or hearing of her—I have got four hours of delightful Doctor Russell to day before me, is it not felicitous? Every day he begins at me—Thackeray Thackeray! you are an idle profligate shuffling boy, (because) your friends are going to take you away in May &c &c—I have not stopped out of school once this term—These five weeks have passed away very quick methinks! There goes the big bell and I must have done for the present;

but we will have a little more chat, before night. I hope to send this off this evening—Good bye till School is all over for the day—
[. . .]

the Doctor: Dr. John Russell (1787-1863), Headmaster of Charterhouse School 1811-32. *Charles:* Charles Smyth, presumably a relative of Major Carmichael-Smyth. *Southampton Row:* the residence of John Ritchie (d. 1849), who had married Thackeray's paternal aunt, Charlotte Thackeray (1786-1854). *Mrs. Yates:* Mrs. Elizabeth Yates (1799-1860), who was performing at the Adelphi Theatre in James Robinson Planché's burletta, *Paris and London: Or, A Trip across the Herring Pond.* *Mrs. Dick:* Mrs. William Flemming Dick, the former Emily Thackeray (b. 1804?), a paternal cousin.

3. TO MRS. HENRY CARMICHAEL-SMYTH
28 February 1829

Trinity. College. Cambridge—
Saturday 28 February. 1829.
I am now about to begin my first journal, my dearest Mother, which will I hope be always sent, with the regularity with which it is now my full purpose to give to it—After Father left me I went in rather low spirits to my rooms, & found myself just too late for lecture; I was employed all the morning in nailing and hammering and such like delectable occupations; about one o'clock I went to Hine's of Corpus, & with him strayed about among the groves or rather fields wh. skirt the Colleges of Kings Trinity &c &—afterwards I walked with Young up to Chesterton, & ran half the way home again (Chesterton is two miles from Trinity) You may wonder what could have inspired my legs with such unusual activity—There was a boat race, at wh. it is the duty of all the Under-Graduates to attend, & shout for their various Colleges. Next I did devour a vast dinner in Hall, next I went to Chapel in my new surplice, & my new cap, & got an old greasy wretched thing in its stead and finally had Carne & Hine to tea with me who are now gone, & have left me to write these few lines to my dearest Mother, to remind her of her affectionate Son. W M T.
[. . .]

Hine: James Hine (b. 1808), who had come to Trinity College from Merchant Taylor's School. *Young:* James Reynolds Young (1807-84), whom Thackeray had known at Charterhouse. *Carne:* Joseph Carne (1809-36), whom Thackeray had also known at Charterhouse.

4. TO MRS. HENRY CARMICHAEL-SMYTH
23 March 1829

[. . .]

Monday—I have made a fool of myself!—I have rendered myself a public character, I have exposed myself—how? I spouted at the Union! I do not know what evil star reigns to day or what malignant dæmon could prompt me to such an act of folly—but however up I got, & blustered & blundered, & retracted, & stuttered upon the character of Napoleon—Carne had just been speaking before me and went on in a fluent & easy manner but it was all flam—as for me I got up & stuck in the mud at the first footstep then in endeavoring to extract myself from my dilemma, I went deeper and deeper still, till at last with one desperate sentence to wit that "Napoleon as a Captain, a Lawgiver, and a King merited & recieved the esteem & gratitude & affection of the French Nation." I rushed out of the quagmire into wh. I had so foolishly plunged myself & sat down like Lucifer never to rise again with open mouth in that august assembly—So much for the Union—I read from 8 o'clock till 1 this morning, & considerably more in the evening—So tho' I have been foolish to day I have not been idle—Tomorrow I must I fear cut one of the Lectures, for going to the Union quite put out of my head that there was a preparation requisite before I cd. attend at Lecture; I mean reading over the lecture beforehand—I shd. look rather foolish if I did not. I must read 2 books of Euclid for my examination on Friday—So till tomorrow Fare-thee well—WT.

[. . .]

a fool: the first of Thackeray's many uncomfortable experiences as a public speaker. *the Union:* the undergraduate debating society, the Cambridge Union. *like Lucifer:* i. e. in his fall from Heaven (Isaiah 14: 12).

5. TO MRS. HENRY CARMICHAEL-SMYTH
16 April 1829

[. . .]

Thursday—This day last year (as I just called to mind) did I leave Charter-House, and now I am sitting at Cambridge writing a letter home with a mind perfectly contented with the change the year has wrought in my situation. I have just had two men here who from 8 to 12 have been talking over Old Charterhouse doings, telling for the hundredth time old Charter-House Stories wh. possessed but little interest at their first broaching, & a great deal less at this their

hundredth repetition   I have not that gratitude and affection for that respectable seminary near Smithfield—which I am told good scholars always have for the place of their education; I can not think that school to be a good one, when as a child, I was lulled into indolence & when I grew older & could think for myself was abused into sulkiness and bullied into despair—But this must be a very ungrateful theme to you, I can readily fancy that the out-pourings of my but[t] of indignation will be but a bitter dose for you, I will not therefore proceed in my Philippic—To day has been with me an idle day rather—But a little idleness doth one good. I had my hair cut yesterday, and the comfort I feel in losing some pounds of superfl[u]ous hair (or delapillated manhood, as Griffin The Tonsor hath it.) is extraordinary—It can certainly rain at Cambridge—I dined out at a man's rooms to day but retired at seven o'clock as I thought I saw movements predicating a rubber at whist, wh. is my aversion—I have been going about in my walks lately drawing churches here is one but I forget whether Coton or Granchester.—
What I drew it for I cannot say, only I think to see whether I had lost the acquirement or not. This country is of course ugly in the extreme but there are a number of quaint old buildings, and
pretty bits scattered about. I think I shall take solitary walks and see how I get on in this way of drawing—I called yesterday at one o'clock on a man to walk & found him in bed!—Men are here very fond of going to bed late, & getting up late—The former of these I like not, nor I hope the latter. Good night—
[. . .]

6. TO MRS. HENRY CARMICHAEL-SMYTH
21 August 1829

[Paris]

I have this moment read your letter, my dear Mother, wh. surprised me, and I confess hurt me, for I did not think I deserved those strong terms of reproof in which it was couched—I mentioned that I had been to Frascati's—but for what went I? to gain? No—It was a sight wh. I perhaps might never have another opportunity of seeing, it was a curious chapter in the book of life, the perusal of wh.

has done me the greatest good—it has taught me not to trust so much in myself as before my pride or my ignorance would have led me to do; it has shewn me that I could not, (as few could) resist the temptation of gambling, & it therefore has taught me—to keep away from it—The same motive which would have led me to a Theatre led me to Frascati's—I was obliged if I went to stake my ten francs at the table instead of paying at the door—If I had not done so *I should never have arrived at a piece of self knowledge, which I can conscientiously thank God for giving me.* I might have thought, as I did during the 1st. quarter of an hour I was there, that it was a pleasant play, into which men merely entered for amusement and gain—I should not have known that it was only for the *latter*. I might at another time [have] been induced to enter a gaming-house with more money than I had then in my pocket & *I should have as certainly staked it*—I have learnt the full extent of the evil, I have discovered my temperament & inclination with regard to it, and the necessity wh. I did not then know of avoiding it—In what then am I so blameable? I went with *no* bad motive, no desire for gain. Mother, I came out with a knowledge of my own weakness of my own utter inability to resist a crime on wh. I could before descant with all the knowledge of ignorance; I might have thanked God as the Pharisee did because I was "not such as the Publican"—"I do not rush into destruction blindly & wilfully as this gamester, I do not hazard my family's welfare & my own, by throwing my money to the winds, or what is worse by seeking for gain in dishonest & ungodly wise—" I could not say this but I may say with the Publican, "Lord have mercy on me a Sinner"—"Grant me strength to resist what Thou hast given me opportunity to see; it is not because I am weak, that Thou wilt desert me."

  I will weary your patience no more my dear Mother by such a subject—Had it not been for the letter of this morning, you should have had a longer and a more amusing epistle than this—as it is I have no spirit to proceed, I will begin my journal for you to night, & will dispatch it this day week—Good bye till tonight my dearest Mother; & may God grant that you never again call me avaricious and mean when I am but curious, that you never again think because I before was ignorant that therefore I was good; or that because I am now aware of my own weakness I must be wicked—

Yr. affectionate Son—
William M. Thackeray

  I said in my last letter I think, that I should go into one of the low gaming houses—this of course unless I receive permission from you—I shall not now do.

Frascati's: a gambling establishment on the Rue de Richelieu.   *book of life:* a term originally used in Revelation 22: 19.   *as the Pharisee:* Luke 18: 11.   *say with the Publican:* Luke 18: 13.

7. TO MRS. HENRY CARMICHAEL-SMYTH
31 July 1830

Coblentz. July 31. 1830.

I had written a long letter to you, my dearest Mother, from various places where I had stopped, but have with my usual carelessness lost it—it will I suppose fall into the hands of some German waiter who may instruct himself if he can with its contents.

After a passage of four & twenty hours we arrived at Rotterdam, not having had occasion on the way to part with any of the precious meats wh. you know I am such an adept at swallowing—I saw Robert Frith, he has grown a great deal & has learnt to talk English like a Dutchman.—The town of Rotterdam is the finest I ever saw in point of comfort & cleanliness—the houses are magnificently well built and the people are—but you can read all about the people & town in that entertaining book the Encyclopædia. The next morning Tuesday at five I set off for Cologne, & we were six and thirty hours on our voyage—There were no beds lots of passengers who were strewed over the cabin on stools & sofas on tables & under tables; I was out all the night, but managed to sleep snugly on the top of some coals wh. were placed on the deck—The Rhine to Cologne is not as pretty as a Dutch Canal. There is nothing to see on it, except here & there a town, & a little church almost every hundred yards. These are the prevailing fashions of churches—We had on board almost all our London passengers—who are in the most desperate hurry to get on—We arrived at 3 at Cologne & many of them were off again by five—

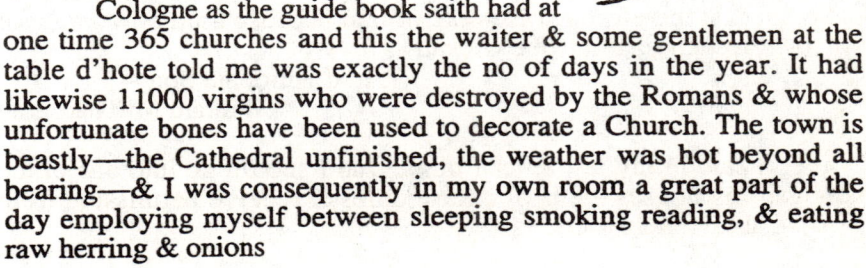

Cologne as the guide book saith had at one time 365 churches and this the waiter & some gentlemen at the table d'hote told me was exactly the no of days in the year. It had likewise 11000 virgins who were destroyed by the Romans & whose unfortunate bones have been used to decorate a Church. The town is beastly—the Cathedral unfinished, the weather was hot beyond all bearing—& I was consequently in my own room a great part of the day employing myself between sleeping smoking reading, & eating raw herring & onions

Yesterday the beauties of the journey began, & I really think the Rhine is almost equal to the Thames. One or two views were of course magnificent—The ladies had got their Byrons to read when they arrived at "the castled crag of Drachenfels"—here is something like unto it

There was a pretty little girl on board to whom I talked the most delicious sentiment and quoted Shelley & Moore to her great edification & delight. I really did feel rather sentimental, & intended to have made some pathetic verses on her & the Rhine but she came from a boarding school at Boulogne, & that staggered my sentiment; & dinner was ordered & that entirely destroyed it—Last night we arrived here, tomorrow I go on to Francfort—A gentleman of the name of Balfour a fellow passenger is going with me presently to Ems about nine miles from Coblentz.

This is a beautiful place, magnificent old houses, old turrets old bridges &c—I have got one or two sketches; the Moselle & the Rhine here join; the grand fortress of Ehrenbreitstein looks over the town & here you must fill up the description from your imagination—There are some thousand of Prussian Soldiers in the town I walked a mile with a regiment of them this morning at 5. (I went out to sketch) the band is the most beautiful I ever heard, far superi[or to] the band of the horse Guards. The men are noble looking fellows in short blue jackets & black crop belts—I have met with some good figures among the people here are two who were on board the steamer

The boy with the pipe was exactly like Raphael & the man would have made a good study for a Buccaneer—We had on board 2 artists with one of whom I have made acquaintance the Duc de Fitzjames the old Russian Admiral Tchelchagoff—I have been writing with seppia as I could get no Ink. Good bye Dearest Mother till next week when I will write again.

  I wish I could say something better than the stale & formal Remember me to all at home & believe me your affte Son

W. M. Thackeray.

Frith: Robert William Frith (b. ca. 1811), whom Thackeray had known at Charterhouse. *"the castled crag of Drachenfels":* Byron, *Childe Harold's Pilgrimage,* Canto III, lyric following stanza 55. *Moore:* Thomas Moore (1779-1852), Irish poet.

8. TO MRS. HENRY CARMICHAEL-SMYTH
28 September 1830

Weimar Tuesday. Septr. 2[8].

My promises, dearest Mother, have been faithfully kept; and if you have received my letters as regularly as I have written them, you must have received every fortnight those gems epistolary poetical & graphical wh. I have punctually sent you; for this time I have delayed my letter a week in order to see, if I could have anything to answer in the letters I expected from England—This is the ninth or tenth week of my stay in Germany, & in all that time I have not been blessed with a single line from home!—

You see the direction to my letter, wh. will with your good leave be my direction while I remain in Germany On arriving here I found an old Schoolfellow who is staying with a German family here, & who said that the place was exactly suited for me; I made every inquiry & found he was in the right for without letters of introduction I have got into the best Society of the place. There is an excellent German Master, & a respectable family with whom I live, wh. I think were the three things you wished me to have while in Germany

It seems the old Grand Duke had a great love for English manners & English men, & tho' the present Duke is not quite so prepossessed in our favor yet he is happy to see all the Englishmen who come here, (& there are generally three or four residing) at his Court I have accordingly had a pair of trowsers cut into breeches, & have had the honor of making my appearance in his august presence; and in order to become a complete courtier have taken a Master in the art of Waltzing & Gallopading—There is a capital library here wh. is open to me, & an excellent theatre wh. costs a shilling per night, & a charming petite societé wh. costs nothing.

Goethe the great lion of Weimar I have not yet seen, but his daughter in law has promised to introduce me.

So much for Weimar wh. I think you will agree with me, is as good a place as I could possibly select for my stay in this country— The day after I wrote to you from Elberfeldt I went by diligence to Cassel, & a dull journey it was! I don't know whether the journey or its destination was the most interesting—at Cassel I was obliged to stay three days, there being no diligence, & any other conveyance was beyond my means. All the papers said there was a revolution there, during my stay, I saw nothing of it; the same was the case at Cologne so you may suppose that these German revolutions or "Spectacles" as they call them are no very dreadful things.

Everybody who goes to Cassel sees Wilhelmshöhe; which is I think far superior to Versailles, the water works are very refreshing there is a new Castle a l'antique with some tolerable pictures, a beautiful Chapel, & a delightful armory—I went in company with a German Student, & a Herr Professor, with whom I afterwards proceeded by diligence to Gotha by way of Eisenach. at Eisenach we staid two hours, I had time to see Luthers hiding place in the old castle of Worzburg, where while all the world were seeking him he was quietly lodged, translating the Bible & having occasional tiffs with the Author of Evil. They shew you a place in his study where in the height of his wrath he discharged an inkstand at the Devil, who had long tormented him in the shape of [a] blue-bottle fly—In performing this pilgrimage to the Worzburg I lost my dinner & got thoroughly wet through, in this unhappy state I had to proceed to Gotha, under the racking pains of hunger & rheumatism, which I am sorry to say has been my constant companion since I left Elberfeld; I have had it [in] my shoulder & my face for some time I could not use my arms, & afterwards for a considerable period I could not use my teeth!—

I slept at Gotha & came on here, & here I trust will end my travels; for though the Society is small it is remarkably good, & tho' the court is absurdly ceremonious, I think it will rub off a little of the rust wh. School & College have given me.

Now I am going to ask a very absurd favor; I want a cornetcy in Sir John Kennaways yeomanry!—the men here are all in some yeomanry uniform, & if hereafter I go to other courts in Germany or in any other part of Europe, some thing of this sort is necessary as a court-dress—It is true that here I can do without it, but in case of my going elsewhere I must have some dress or other; & a yeomanry dress is always a handsome & respectable one; as it is I have to air my legs in black breeches, & to sport a black coat, black waistcoat & Cock-hat; looking something like a cross between a footman & a Methodist parson.

I dont know whether the dress is expensive if so, of course I must give it up.

I am making rapid progress in Gallopading & my natural grace & symmetry of person greatly contribute to my advancement in that Science.

Last night we had at the theatre a translation of Hernani, the tragedy by Victor Hugo which made so much noise in Paris; I would recommend you to read it if possible—we have had 3 operas Medea, & the Barber of Seville & Flauto Magico; Hummel conducts the Orchestra her[e] is a picture wh is somewhat like him for Mary—The Orchestra is excellent but the Singers are not first rate.

I have got a book into wh. I paste the play bills, & any costumes or groups or remarks wh. strike me— I have fallen in love with the Princess of Weimar, who is unluckily married to Prince Charles of Prussia; I must get over this unfortunate passion, wh. will otherwise I fear bring me to an untimely end.

There are several very charming young persons of the female sex here. Miss v. Spiegel & ditto v. Pappenheim, are the evening belles—As I have delayed my letter a week, I must write again next week—I will send you a couple of translations from Körner, wh. will I think amuse you; they ought were they any thing like the original—

How do you like my new plan of folding letters; I have written them so that you may have a book full of them if you wish to keep them. Good bye dearest Mother, pray write now you know my direction for a certainty—There are no letters from yo[u] at Dresden for I have written twice [to] the post office; & there were none at

Bo[nn] write to me bei Madame Melos at Wei[mar] & I trust you will write soon—Love [to] Father; tell Mary I am thinking of having a fiddle Master—God bless you dearest Mother write soon to your affectionate Son.

W. M. Thackeray.

Schoolfellow: apparently William Garrow Lettsom (1804-87), whom Thackeray had known at Cambridge. *German Master:* Dr. Friedrich Weissenborn (d. 1852). *old Grand Duke . . . present Duke:* Karl August (1757-1828) and his successor, Karl Friedrich (1783-1853). *Goethe . . . daughter in law:* Thackeray did, in fact, come to meet the eighty-one year old Goethe, whose daughter-in-law was Frau August von Goethe (1786-1859). *Sir John Kennaway:* Kennaway (d. 1836), first Baronet, was the Carmichael-Smyth's landlord in Devon. *Hernani:* Hugo's verse drama had had a tumultuous premiere on 25 February 1830 in Paris, during which the applause of his partisans had overcome the boos of the play's opponents. *Medea:* presumably *Medée* (1797) by Luigi Cerubini (1760-1842). *Hummel:* Johann Hummell (1778-1837), pianist, composer, and conductor. *Mary:* Mary Graham (1815-71), later Carmichael, an orphaned niece of Thackeray's mother, who had adopted her in 1820. Thackeray sometimes referred to her as "Polly." *Princess . . . Prince Charles of Prussia:* Maria of Weimar (1808-77), wife of Prince Friedrich Karl of Prussia. *Spiegel . . . Pappenheim:* Melanie von Spiegel and Jenny von Papenheim (1811-90). *Körner:* Karl Theodor Körner (1791-1813), dramatist and critic.

9. TO MRS. HENRY CARMICHAEL-SMYTH
3 December 1830

Friday December 3.

This is the only night in the week, dearest Mother, in wh. there is not a court or a play, & wisely is it ordained inasmuch as the Post to England goeth out on this unoccupied night—Here is Christmas coming & I for the first time these ten years not at home to participate in the turkey & ham—be it so—I must fast on kraut & beef, while, you ye happy natives of England, luxuriate on mince pies & lozenges plumpudding & cherry-brandy!—I firmly belie[ve] (& as an experienced traveller my belief ought to be of some weight) that my fatherland is the only place for being comfortable in—there all the delights of life, here schnaps & stoves & rheumatism!—two months ago I was in love with two young ladies—but the day dream hath passed away, & I am left here without a flame (for as I said we have only stoves) & without a being who cares twopence whether I stay or go—I tried an experiment the other day, hinting that I was going to have £15000 a year, & the respect I received was wonderful, but I have undeceived the natives, & am treated sans respect & ceremony.

The old ladies here seem to be bent on marrying their daughters, two have told me that they did not wish *much* money for their Melanies or their Eugenies, but merely a competency—but I did not speak on the hint and as the respectable dowagers find they can make nothing of me they almost cut me. You will think I am talking scandal, but in this little place, as soon as an Englishman arrives inquiries are made whether he is an eldest or only Son, and as all Englishmen are rich or supposed to be so, the round of mothers offer the round of daughters who are as you may suppose by this time rather stale.

I lament my trusty blue coat in England, it would be of amazing comfort to me here—We have had no snow yet, but the weather is awfully cold, so that a complete casing of flannel has been requisite—Old Goethe the Glory of Weimar & of Germany was very nearly carried off by the bursting a blood vessel—but the old man has recovered in an amazing manner, & now at 83 writes as hard, & drinks as gaily as he did twenty years ago.

I have read a good deal of Goethe and Schiller, the latter is by far the favorite here—Goethe is by practice & profession a libertine, Schiller was on the contrary a man whose religion & morals were unexceptionable—It must have been a fine sight twenty years ago, this little court, with Goethe Schiller & Wieland & the old Grand Duke & Duchess to ornament it—The present Duke is I believe good natured, but he is imprudent & proud for he never will condescend to speak with any of his subjects who have not a von tacked to their names—He has got a big valet with whom he boxes occasionally, the valet as in duty bound, falls under the vigorous "coups" of his Königliche Hoheit; an officer told me that he saw him one day roaring on the ground, & the simple Grand Duke said, "Get up Fritz, have I hurt thee, here is a gulden to console thee"—The man must make a good thing of it if he does it with proper discretion—   Did not I tell you how cheap fur is here? You may have a pelisse for a guinea—

The more I see of it, the more I am sure that if I could in any way procure an attachéship, I could work my way in the profession—Most of the men are rich & idle: (I speak of the Berlin and Paris ones) & if a poor man [would] but be industrious—he would have a double spur & a [double] advantage—Of the four men at Berlin 2 have been in the guards & got tired, & now they are in the corps diplomatique and are tired—they say the profession is interesting enough but the town is so dull—I have been taking a little recreation in the fields of civil-law, & as I expected have not found the Pandects of Justinian much to my taste. I suppose however it must be—a clergyman I cannot be, nor a physician so I must drudge up poor & miserable the first part of my life, & just reach the pinnacle (or somewhere near it I trust[)], when my eyes will hardly be able to see the prospect I have been striving all my life to arrive at—These are the pleasures of the law—& to these I must I fear dedicate myself—As I have thought a great deal on the profession I *must* take; & the more I think of it the less I like it—However I believe it is the best among the positive professions & as such I must take it, for better or worse. I thought a little time ago the army would have done, but now I suppose there will be no war & no advancement In this country, I could live & have a reasonable family upon the income I have that is if I can mend the expensive habits, wh. that blessed University Cambridge has taught me—Don't suppose I lament not reading Mathematics, but I am sorry I ever was at the University—I do not regret my employment of time there, but of money—I am glad I have come here, for I am a good deal by myself, & read & think a little—and in learning German, I acquire a tangible money-getting advantage—This letter has been filled with I's, but they will interest my dear Mother, as they will shew her the state of mind & feelings of her affectionate son—W. M. Thackeray.

Best love for father, & "best wishes" for his farm—I have commenced a letter for Mary in the shape of a song of Goethe wh. shall soon appear.

speak on the hint: see *Othello*, I, iii, 166.   *Wieland:* Christoph Wieland (1733-1813), writer and translator.   *Königliche Hoheit:* (Ger.) Kingly Highness. *Pandects of Justinian:* a lengthy compilation of excerpts from the writings of Roman jurists, made for the Emperor Justinian and published in 533.

10. TO MRS. HENRY CARMICHAEL-SMYTH
31 December 1830

[Weimar]

Your letters always make me sorrowful, dearest Mother, for there seems some hidden cause of dissatisfaction, some distrust which you do not confess & cannot conceal & for which on looking into myself I can find no grounds or reason—Idleness irresolution & extravagance are charges wh. have been long laid against me, & to which I know I am still but too open—but I can say that tho' still idle & extravagant I am not so much so as when in England, for here I have more inducement to industry & less temptation to expense.

You seem to take it so much to heart, that I gave up trying for Academical honors—perhaps Mother I was too young to form opinions but I did form them—& these told me that there was little use in studying what could after a certain point be of no earthly use to me—they told me that subtle reasonings & deep meditations on angles & parallelograms might be much better employed on other subjects—

that three years industrious waste of time might obtain for me mediocre honors wh. I did not value at a straw, is it because I have unfortunately fallen into this state of thinking that you are so dissatisfied with me[?]—

At school it was the same thing I never obtained anything like an honor there—I was not stupid—when I left school I had read as much of other subjects as any boy of my age—Do not lay it all to my wilful idleness—Mother mother would it not have been better to have consulted my inclinations & have fostered them than to have persevered in a system which was determined on long before the object of it had manifested any talents or desires for or against it—For ten years of my life I was at school, it was thought that this discipline of misery was necessary to improve & instruct me; with all the power I had I struggled against it—the system was persevered in—& the benefit of ten years schooling was a little Latin & a very little Greek—which a year at any other time would have given me—I know that the system you pursued you considered was the best—it might be that any other would have been attended with the same result—but I who was the object of it because now I am old enough to think & to act a little for myself am *thought* idle & ungrateful—because I consider it unsuited to me, & do what I can to pursue a different one—Do not fancy me dearest Mother, angry or undutiful in writing what I have done—all my purpose in it is to beg & entreat you not to form wishes for my entering on pursuits wh. if you thought as I do you wd. think it my duty to avoid—You will think me ungrateful, because I set myself so resolutely against what I know to be your wish, I am very young but if I have had any experience at all it has been in the system of education which you wish me to adopt—I wish to God that I could so alter or smother my feelings as to be able to adopt it—for then I should have at any rate the satisfaction of knowing that I acted according to yr. wishes—but I can not smother them, I can not alter them—tho I have struggled long, much longer than you believe, mother, to do so. In my reading & my pursuits here I have had a freedom which I never enjoyed in England—& I hope you will feel the benefit it has done me.

I will not alter or look again at a word I have written. it may be badly written but it is strongly felt. It may give you some idea of the misery wh. every letter I have had from home has given me—for they have all more or less spoken of the same subject—they have all told me that you are angry & discontented with me—& instead of looking forward with pleasure to the time of receiving your letter—I have been almost afraid to open them knowing the reproaches & the misery which not the words but the tenor of them conveys—Do not dearest Mother suppose anything ungrateful or undutiful in what I here have said—but I do trust you will feel more confidence in me—that you will not fancy that I can do nothing in life because I believe that study at the

University is almost waste of time—that you will hope with me that I may be able to exert myself successfully or not as soon as age or circumstance may bring me to a worthier object & a nobler sphere.

The questions you wish answered I will to the best of my power the next time I write—There is no English chaplain here—but the Germans are very good & I can now understand them pretty well—In the shape of writing I have translated several things of Goethes a play of Kotzebues—& am going to commence on a short history of Germany which will instruct me both in history & German—When I first came here I did not go to Church very regularly as my attendance there was productive but of small profit—as I begin to comprehend the language of course I shall attend more regularly— The doctrine here is not near so strict as in England—many of the dogmas by wh. we hold are here disregarded as allegories or parables—or I fear by most people as fictions altogether. They call our Religion in England too "objective" & not refined enough for their more mature understandings—But more of this another time, till then dearest Mother believe me in spite of what may be after all only a conceited rhapsody believe me dearest Mother your affectionate Son W. M. Thackeray
Dec 31—

Kotzebue: August von Kotzebue (1761-1819), German dramatist. *history of Germany:* Kompendium der deutschen Reichsgeschichte by Konrad Mannert (1756-1834).

11. TO EDWARD FITZGERALD
18 July 1831

Bridgewater July 18. 1831.
I must have a half hour's talk with you tonight, dear Fitzgerald, for I am quite alone & in no mood to pursue the very unpleasant task wh. I have taken on myself to perform—Have you been botanizing, or poetizing, or talking with your friend Mr. Nursey about Rembrandt & Elizabethan houses, or sailing on your river with your sister?—I dont know what should put me in so sentimental a mood, but do you know I have been for the last half-hour drinking tea, & thinking about you & your sister—you must find it very pleasant having a sister whom you can talk to & love as much as you will   I am staying here alone doing that stupid book at the rate of about 3 pages a day, Schulte is here to be sure, but we have had 2 rows already, one about Matthew who lives a little way from here & who has been to see me—he is improved in mind, & appearance for he

does not look the rake he used—& has met with some very sad & trying experience since last I saw him—all that I hope for him is that he may get through every other difficulty as honorably as he has his late one.

 I left London a very few days after you, for I felt very miserable & solitary there I used to go & walk in Regent Street but the place was a desert without your fashionable form I tried the Divans, & felt just as I used to do at School, on going into the "Strangers' Room" where I had last seen my parents so I did the wisest thing I could do paid my bill, & hastened home to an expecting family circle—Departing thence to Bridgewater I hied—German my object bold resolve my guide I purpose here three days or more to stay—Whence to the Mansion of the Reverend J- Matthew's at Kilve near Bridgewater away Where if you wish to write to me you may, & this is all that I in rhyme can say—

 Do write to me, old fellow, for a letter from you will do me good & make me happy—though I am tolerably happy at present, for I feel proud in thinking that my dinner only costs me eighteen pence & that in four days I have only drunk half a bottle of wine—The paper on wh. I write cost me sixpence a quire & I have no doubt you will be a little angry with my economy that is if you read my letter—Now the answer I expect from you must be prompt & full the lines of it must be as close at least as these on this page, & the matter of it infinitely more amusing—Some fool has remarked in the Latin Grammar the blessed source of all my quotations that Gens humana novitatis avida est—at the present moment I most respectfully though decidedly deny the truth of the assertion as regards me—for lo! I am surrounded by novelty & I regard it [not]—Balls routs & races I pass them by with scorn, & had rather receive a letter from you without a particle of news than any earthly blessing wh. I can call to mind—but I have got a headache & am going to bed—God bless you

 I am twenty years old to day, & I don't know why this birthday has awakened a number of solemn & unpleasant feelings, wh. such an anniversary never raised before—But I was looking back yesterday, & I cannot find a single day in the course of my life which has been properly employed—I can only behold a melancholy succession of idleness & dissipation, which now leaves me without mental satisfaction, & I fear without proper repentance—I looked by chance at the opposite page after I wrote the word repentance, & do you know seeing that account of my dinners & wine drinking has quite gladdened me, & made me think there is some chance for me after all. Of one thing I am determined that I never will practise the law, or at least will retire from it, before my business should occupy me too much—This perhaps is not very likely, & leaves me just in my old place in spite of what "I have determined"—Write to me very soon—

how I do long for the time when we may roam through Regent Street, & drink fat chocolate as heretofore—And now I am come to a phrase, wh. I find wonderous puzzling to construct properly—Believe me your—fill it up as you think old fellow—In the whole catalogue of yours truly sincerely affectionately &c—I can't find one half warm enough.

W. M. Thackeray—

Write to me at Budleigh Salterton Devon.

FitzGerald: Edward FitzGerald (1809-93), whom Thackeray had known at Cambridge, the closest friend of Thackeray's young manhood, and the future translator of *The Rubáiyát of Omar Khayyám* (1859). *Mr. Nursey:* Perry Nursey, an artist and musician. *your sister:* apparently Andalusia FitzGerald, later Soyres. *that stupid book:* Mannert's *Kompendium*. *Schulte:* Franz Schulte, a German whom Thackeray had apparently met in Cambridge and then again in Frankfurt. *Matthew:* Henry Matthew (1807-61), whom Thackeray had known at Cambridge. *the Divans:* places of resort for enjoying cigars, coffee, magazines, and newspapers. *the Reverend J- Matthew:* the Reverend John Matthew, father of Henry Matthew. *Gens humana novitatis avida est:* (Lat.) humankind longs for novelty.

12. TO JOHN MITCHELL KEMBLE
January 1832

A plain statement of
a most unhappy case—

In re Thackeray }
a lunatic

Hilary Term. 2 Wm. IV.

Last Sunday night at nine, unhappy Thack-
-eray in velvet vest & breeches black
Sat sweetly musing in his easy chair
With a snug fire & half an hour to spare
Now he surveyed his handsome Sunday clo'es
Now he the bellows blew & now his nose—
He thought how blest in half an hour he'd be
Hearing sweet music drinking sweeter tea
When lo! oblivion on his senses crept

He dozed, he snoozed, he dreamt, he snored, he slept.
Ponderous & brazen tongued the bell then broke
His placid sleep—the lovely youth awoke!—
With startled ears & fears he hears, o Grimes!
Half past eleven by the Temple chimes!!!—

Kemble: John Mitchell Kemble (1807-57), whom Thackeray had met at Trinity College, Cambridge. He became a notable Old English scholar, and also served 1835-44 as editor of *The British and Foreign Review*, a journal to which Thackeray contributed.   *Hilary Term:* from 11 to 31 January at the Inns of Court in 1832.

13. TO EDWARD FITZGERALD
April? 1832

[. . .]
Here am I on my high stool with an action agst. Noah Thornley for debauching Martha Dewsnap whereby she became big & sick with child & whereby her father lost the services of her his daughter & servant so that you see Law is not altogether so dry a study as you wd. imagine it to be—This letter will be sent by a Mr. Drury a friend of Martineau's, who goes to Cambridge at 3 o'clock by the Times—Martineau I like immensely & learn a good deal from him he is a very well read man & withal very modest as all well read men ought to be—On Tuesday I dined at Kembles, where there was a very splendid spread. C. Kemble is I think an excellent fellow & no humbug about him
[. . .]

Here is a scene at the Spotted dog a publick house near the Strand where you pay tuppence to hear singing &c—The faces are not at all caricatured not even the eyebrows—The poor devil to the right hof the picter sung a solo about rosy Bacchus—the other two & a youth whose face I cannot draw sung a glee the one eyed man base. Now you must give [...]

[...]: the hiatuses occur in the original.   *Drury:* Henry Drury (1812-63), whom Thackeray had known at Cambridge.   *Martineau:* Arthur Martineau (1807-72), whom Thackeray had also known at Cambridge.   *Kemble:* Charles Kemble (1775-1854), actor.

14. DIARY
April - November 1832

[London. 3 April 1832:] Despatched my verses to Charlotte—dined at Woods, was all day with Mother—went to the Adelphi but found no room, also to No 60 where I lost 6/6.

[4 April:] Had a pleasant letter from Fitz-Gerald; Edwards and Caldwell breakfasted & ate 8 eggs between them besides meat. went to Mother & in the evening to Woods' leaving them at the Oratorio. Then to 60 *for the last time, so help me God* where I won back the exact sum I had lost the day before. [...]

[5 April:] [...] Took a lesson in dancing, & dined in chambers with Caldwell played ecarté till four o'clock in the morning & lost eight pound 7 shillings—before I knew where I was, so much for reform. [. . .]

[11 April:] [. . .] Was not at Taprell's, & have not read a syllable of anything for 3 days. I must mend, or else I shall be poor idle & wicked most likely in a couple more years. [. . .]

[29 April:] [. . .] Found Kinderley tipsy with a common beast of the town, & took him away from her, & home to bed—much to the Lady's disgust & Kinderley's advantage—She threatens to set her bully on me. [. . .]

[2 May:] Dr. Maginn called & took me to the Standard shewing me the mysteries of printing & writing leading articles, with him all day till 4—called on Goldshede—dined at the Sabloniere broke my vow & one five pounds at play at 60 Quadrant—[. . .]

[3 May:] At Taprells—dined here at Caldwell's expence with 2 sporting men Mr. Monro & Mr. Kay—the last an excellent fellow but poor went to Dobb's in the evening & played whist lost of course.

[6 May:] [. . .] Read Eugene Aram but was much disappointed (as usual) It is a very forced & absurd taste to elevate a murderer for money into a hero—The sentiments are very eloquent clap-trap. There is no new character (except perhaps the Corporal) & no incident at all—Arams confession is disgusting, it would have been better, more romantick at least, to have made him actuated by revenge hatred jealousy or any passion except avarice, which is at more variance with the character given him in the Novel, than wd. have been a hotter & (as we suppose) a nobler passion—The book is in fact humbug; when my novel is written it will be something better I trust—One must however allow Bulwer wit & industry I think unless his quotations were for his book & not from his memory: enough of Aram. Wrote yesterday to F. G. with a letter as from Herrick—It might have been made pretty but was poor enough—How can a man know his own capabilities or his inferiority?—Not by reading—one acquires thoughts of others & gives one's self the credit of them. Bulwer has a high reputation for talent & yet I always find myself competing with him—This I suppose must be vanity—If it is truth why am I idle?—Here is enough conceit for to night—

[9 May:] [. . .] went to see Der Freyschütz very good—Miss Schneider sung & acted very sweetly, the orchestra was admirable & the house crammed—nevertheless I went to sleep at the end of the second act, from the debauch of last night. Bought a big stick wherewithal to resist all parties in case of attack.

[11 May:] Idle all day dined with Maginn Gent & others at the Keans head—spielte und verlierte acht pfund.

[5 June:] The day spent in seediness repentance & novel reading—[. . .] I did nothing else all day except eat biscuits, a very excellent amusement & not so expensive as some others—

[17 June:] breakfasted at home & spent the morning reading novels & writing hymns!—went to Maginn dined at the Barly-Mow & drank Sherry with him till ten—he then took me to a common brothel where I left him, very much disgusted & sickened to see a clever & good man disgrace himself in that way. His money matters press upon him I suppose & make him reckless—Thank God that idle & vicious as I am, I have no taste for scenes such as that of last night—There was an old bawd & a young whore both of them with child—The old woman seemed au reste a good natured beast enough with a countenance almost amiable—The young one was very repulsive in manner & face—Came home sickened & fell asleep instead of going to Kembles.

[Paris. 18 August:] [. . .] May Almighty God give me strength of mind to resist the temptation of play, & to keep my vow that from this day I will never again enter a gaming house—[. . .]

[19 August:] I broke the vow I solemnly made yesterday—& thank God lost the last halfpenny I possessed by doing so—At first I had won back nearly all my losings & went away but the money lay like sin in my pocket & I am thank heaven rid of it—[. . .]

[22 August:] Read Cousins history of Philosophy—went to the Louvre read at Galignani's & at the Palais Royal—am much pleased with Cousin his style & his spirit—The excitement of metaphysics must equal almost that of gambling at least I found myself giving utterance to a great number of fine speeches & imagining many wild theories wh. I found it impossible to express on paper—[. . .]

[9 September:] [. . .] spielte und winnte 14 stücken gold—bezahlte zehn davon—

[19 September:] have just come from talking of debauchery & it's consequences—wh. have made me long for a good wife, & a happy home—[. . .]

[20 September:] read the 15th. chapter of Gibbon played all the morning at "tonneaux" with Gerard & Jones for dinner & operas & perigord pies—[. . .]

[21 September:] [. . .] find myself growing loving on every pleasant married woman I see.—

[8 October:] [. . .] spielte und fegelte—[. . .]

[9 November:] [. . .] habe meine schlechte Bucher verbrannte—Dank sey Gott—[. . .]

[17 November:] [. . .] saw a poor opera of Bellini's Il Pirata—then for a minute to Frascati's where I lost all I had—

[3 April] *Charlotte:* Charlotte Shakespear (d. 1849), later Crawford, a paternal cousin.   *No 60:* a gambling establishment at 60 Regent's Quadrant.   [11 April] *Taprell:* William Taprell, a special pleader with whom Thackeray studied law 1831-32.   [2 May] *Dr. Maginn:* William Maginn (1793-1842), L.L.D., a prominent Tory journalist who helped found *Fraser's Magazine* in 1830 and served as one of its major contributors.   *the Sabloniere:* a hotel in Leicester Square. [6 May] *Eugene Aram:* Bulwer's recently-published criminal romance, one of his "Newgate novels."   [9 May] *Der Freyschütz:* Weber's opera had its English premiere on 9 May 1832.   [11 May] *spielte und verlierte acht pfund:* (Ger.) gambled and lost eight pounds.   [17 June] *au reste:* (Fr.) moreover.   [22 Aug.] *Cousins history: Cours de l'histoire de la philosophie* (1829), by Victor Cousin (1792-1867).   [9 Sept.] *spielte . . . davon:* (Ger.) gambled and won 14 pieces of gold—paid ten of them.   [20 Sept.] *15th. chapter of Gibbon:* Chapter 15 of *The Decline and Fall of the Roman Empire,* in which Gibbon subjects "the progress and establishment of Christianity" to a "candid but rational inquiry." *"tonneaux":* a game in which discs are aimed at openings in a barrel (Fr.: *tonneau*). [8 Oct.] *spielte und fegelte:* (Ger.) gambled and fornicated.   [9 Nov.] *habe . . . Gott:* (Ger.) I have burned my wicked books—Thank God.

15. TO MRS. HENRY CARMICHAEL-SMYTH
6 July 1833

Meurice's. Rue Rivoli.
Saturday July 6.

I have just found your letter dear Mother lying under a heap of papers, where to guess from the date it must have been for the last 2 days;—however it was very welcome at last, for I had been expecting news from you for a week or more, & am glad that it was so good when it came—I am here in my old quarters comfortable enough except for the weather wh. is burning hot, & for the bore of packing up for a short visit to my friend Lemann's house at Brie; where I shall be much ennuyeed I expect—there is however to be a fete, & some other gaieties wh. will relieve us a trifle—I have likewise been for some days to Choisy le Roi, & once to Versailles, where I passed a pleasant day enough, & shall return some day next week I think—Here every thing goes on as usual, & except that I have only once caught a sight of la belle Duvernay, everything is gay and merry—I dont know how long I shall stay here, not long I think, but I hate settling long beforehand, & I dont much like the prospect of returning to town; but I must try & make this paper worth something, & I suppose, that to obtain that end, my presence will be necessary on the other side of the water—It goes on very flourishingly as I hear, but I cant get subscribers for it here, the postage being so enormous that it quite overbalances the cheapness of the paper—It looks well however to have a Parisian correspondent; & I think that in a month more I may get together stuff enough for the next ten months.—I have been thinking very seriously of turning artist—I think I can draw better than do any thing else & certainly like it better than any other occupation why shouldn't I?—It requires a three years apprenticeship however, wh. is not agreeable—but afterwards the way is clear & pleasant enough; & doubly so for an independent man who is not obliged to look to his brush for his livelihood;—an artist here has been counselling me very strongly to make the trial at least & here it can be done cheap, there are ateliers where one can work at a pound a month; & there are all other necessary means & appurtenances—An artist in this town is by far a more distinguished personage than a lawyer & a great deal more so than a clergyman—I went yesterday to call on one; who received me quite en prince; he had an atelier twenty feet high, & fifty long, covered with all sorts of tapestry, old arms, china, carved chairs, & cabinets; he is a second rate man a little better than a drawing master, but I envy him his chairs & cabinets—

I have been a good deal with my aunt, she lives very much alone & is glad of someone to talk to of evenings; about all I have seen I refer you to the National Standard: to wh. I have written a great letter this morning, wh. must be my excuse for such a short one to you—God bless you dear Mother, give my Papa a thousand kisses for me & embrace Mary & James.   ever your affte Son.

W. M. T.

Mrs. Ritchie shewed me a long letter from Charlotte Shakespear full of "her James"; & one from Mrs. Halliday, a most sour haughty & ill tempered epistle—

Meurice's: a fashionable hotel.   *ennuyeed:* (Angl. Fr.) bored.   *Duvernay:* Marie-Louise Duvernay (b. 1810), ballet dancer.   *this paper: The National Standard,* a minor London weekly newspaper that Thackeray had purchased in May 1833, and that he edited until February 1834, when it ceased publication.   *en prince:* (Fr.) royally.   *my aunt:* Mrs. John Ritchie.   *James:* James (later Sir James) Carmichael (1817-83), nephew of Major Carmichael-Smyth.   *her James:* James H. Crawford, whom Thackeray's cousin, Charlotte Shakespear, had recently married.   *Mrs. Halliday:* the former Augusta Thackeray (1785-1849), a paternal aunt.

16. TO MRS. HENRY CARMICHAEL-SMYTH
6 September 1833

Garrick Club. September 6.
I am wanting very much to leave this dismal city dear Mother, but I must stay for some time longer, being occupied in writing puffing & other delightful employments for the N Standard—I have had an offer made for a partner, wh. I think I shall accept, but the business cannot be settled for a week or ten days—In the mean time I get on as well as I can, spending my mornings in St. Pauls Churchyard, & my evenings in this Club, wh. is a pleasant & cheap place of resort—We have thanks to me & some other individuals established a smoking room, another great comfort—I am writing on a fine frosty day, wh., considering this is the heat of the Summer, or ought to be, is the more to be appreciated—   I find a great change between this & Paris, where one makes friends, & here though for the last three years I have lived, I have not positively a single female acquaintance—I shall go back to Paris I think, & marry somebody—There is another evil wh. I complain of, that this system of newspaper writing spoils one for every other kind of writing; I am unwilling now more than ever, to write letters to my friends, & always find myself attempting to make a pert critical point, at the end of a sentence—   I have just had occasion to bid adieu to Regulus; he has been breaking bottles of wine, & abstracting liquor therefrom; & this after I had given him a coat a hat & a half crown to go to Bartholomew Fair—he lied stoutly, wept much, & contradicted himself more than once, so I have been obliged to give him his Congé, & am now clerkless. This is I think the only adventure wh. has occurred to me, I have been talking of going out of town, but les affaires!—as for the theatres they are tedious beyond all bearing; & a solitary evening in Chambers is more dismal still—one has no resource but this Club; where however there is a tolerably good library of reviews, and a pleasant enough society—of artistes of all kinds, & gentlemen who drop their absurd English

aristocratical notions. You see by this what I am thinking of. I wish we were all in a snug apartment in the Rue de Provence. Fitz-Gerald has been in town for a day or two, & I have p[lenty] of h[is] acquaintances, there are a number of litterateurs who frequent this Club, & the National Standard, is I am happy to say growing into repute—though I know it is poor stuff—

A friend of mine just come from the Country says he shot ten brace on the 1st September, may Father have had as good sport; there are lots of partridges here for four shillings a pair.

Goodbye dear Mother, I hope the law business is blowing over, & the storm wh. you must have heard, & wh. is not yet lulled in London—I am going to make a play about the loss of the Amphitrite—God bless you, & all at Larkbeare   ever yr. affte Son
W M Thackeray.

Here is a letter full of I's, dear Mother, but there is nothing to say: these are some of the characters of the Club—Smith is very like.

Mr. Poole.   Don Telesforo   James Smith
(a of Paul Pry)   de Trueba   Rejected Addresses

Garrick Club: in June 1833 Thackeray had joined the Garrick Club, which became a life-long favorite.   *St Pauls Churchyard:* the location of *The National Standard*'s publication office.   *Congé:* (Fr.) dismissal.   *les affaires:* (Fr.) business.   *the Amphitrite:* a ship carrying 125 female convicts bound for Botany Bay broke up off Boulogne in a gale on 31 August 1833, with an almost total loss of life.   *Poole:* John Poole (1786?-1872), dramatist, author of *Paul Pry* (1825).   *Telesforo:* Don Telesforo de Trueba y Cozio (1805?-35), miscellaneous writer.   *Smith:* James Smith (1775-1839), joint author, with his brother, Horace (1779-1849), of *Rejected Addresses* (1812), a series of poetic parodies.

17. TO MRS. HENRY CARMICHAEL-SMYTH
22-29 October 1833

Monday—22. Monday. 29.

I spend all day now dear Mother at the Atelier & am very well satisfied with the progress wh. I make; I think that in a year were I to work hard I might paint something worth looking at, but it requires at least that time before one can gain any readiness with the brush. The other men in the Atelier are merry fellows enough, always singing, smoking, fencing, & painting very industriously besides. Most of them have skill in painting but no hand for drawing—little Le Poittevin himself is a wonderful fellow—I never knew so young a man paint so well & so rapidly & in so many different lines. He has now gone to Brussels with a picture wh. he painted in eight days; wh. would take most men as many months; I want him to go to England for the exhibition of May, where if he would choose a striking subject he would make I think a great figure.

The weather has set in very cold and rainy, I fortify myself with bischoff and segars at the Atelier, & pass the evening generally with my aunt or Mrs Pattle—not going much to the theatres wh. are not very brilliant—I get tickets for the Italian Opera—where the company is very good, & where there is a beautiful creature called Grisi—I saw my ancient flame Duvernay at the French Opera the other day, & wondered how I could have ever been smitten—Now this would be an awkward circumstance in marrying a wife: it will be better I think not to be in love with her at all—only to have a kind of respect, & esteem for the sharer of one's couch, & the payer of the baker's-bills.

I dine to day with the Pattles & shall meet pretty Theodosia—I wish she had £11325 in the 3 per Cts—I would not hesitate above two minutes in popping that question wh. was to decide the happiness of my future life—Goodbye. Must go to my work shop—

The artists with their wild ways & their poverty are the happiest fellows in the world—I wish you could see the scene every day in the Atelier. Yesterday we had a breakfast for five consisting of 5 sausages 3 loaves & a bottle of wine for 15 sous; there were no plates or knives accordingly the meat was carved by the fingers—afterwards pipes succeeded & then songs imitations of all the singers in Paris they are admirable musicians—all this obstreperous gaiety grew out of the sum of three pence wh. had been expended by each man—

[. . .]

Le Poittevin: Edmond le Poittevin (1806-70), French landscape painter. *bischoff:* (Ger.) mulled wine. *Mrs. Pattle:* Mrs. James Pattle, whose husband was in the Bengal Civil Service. *Grisi:* Giulia Grisi (1811-69), Italian soprano. *£11325:* the precision of the figure suggests that it identifies Thackeray's loss of capital in an Indian bank failure, where the greater part of his inheritance had recently disappeared.

18. TO EDWARD FITZGERALD
8 October 1834

Here is the third letter I have begun, dear Edward, in reply to that noble one wh. I have just received from you—the two first were full of thanks, but I think I had better leave you to fancy these, finding it myself so difficult to describe them.—What I like to think of better than your generosity or the cause of it, is the noble & brotherly love, wh. I believe unites us together; my dear friend & brother, may God grant that no time or circumstance ever should diminish this love between us; it seems to me a thing wh. one should cultivate & preserve as a virtue, or as a kind of religion, of wh. it seems to have usurped the place & I hope to exercise this power,—I might fill sheets with this kind of talk as I have done before; but I find when I look at what has been written that I have not expressed what I wanted—I wonder how sentimental writers manage to clothe fine thoughts in fine sentences—I suppose because they only act them—when they come to feel them they must be tongue-tied as I am.—

I am here in a boarding house with my Grandmother and a

Miss Langford, who acts as the old lady's companion; this girl is very rich—she wears rouges & sticks little bits of sticking-plaister about her face by way of ornament, and drops all her h's—the people of the boarding house have settled that I am going to marry her—her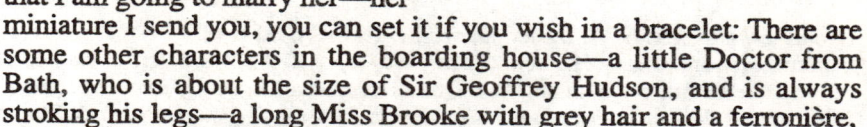
miniature I send you, you can set it if you wish in a bracelet: There are some other characters in the boarding house—a little Doctor from Bath, who is about the size of Sir Geoffrey Hudson, and is always stroking his legs—a long Miss Brooke with grey hair and a ferronière, who looks as if she had committed a murder. I wish you were here to see them all, & to follow me on long walks to the Louvre—I am writing I know in a most rambling & unsatisfactory manner for I am obliged to keep up a conversation with me grandma—

I have copied at the Louvre two Titian portraits Leonardo's Charles VII. Interior by deHoog, & woman playing on the harpsicalls by Terburg—They are all of them very bad, but I dont despair—To night I begin at the life academy; I will make the drawings you wish—I made two failures of the Sheriff, & the Gamekeeper otherwise you would have had them with the others—wh. I fear you praise too much—at present I have on me a strange longing to paint Christ in the tomb with the 2 Angels—a young man has sent an admirable painting from Rome on this subject, in the Eastlake School, only broader & bolder.—

Yesterday at the Luxembourg I was astonished to see how bad every thing was—there is not I think a single good picture among all the elite of modern French Art—but then in return, the sketches in the novels, the penny magazines &c are full of talent—Delaroche's famous Jane Grey is poor I think judging from the prints—

At the theatres there is plenty of good fun I [have] not yet seen the Juif errant,—or the Tempest, though I have a strange longing to see Duvernay as Miranda—Therese looks most Madonna like & lovely, she has got a child after 4 years marriage—I don't think I am in love with her any more—

God bless you dear Edward—

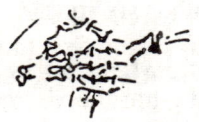

wh. means true to deth.

if you write (as you must) before the 19th. October direct No 8 Rue Louis le Grand. after 22. Rue de Provence, where we have taken a very pretty little apartment—
  This letter is I see as unfit to send as the others—
  I will write again immediately

Grandmother: Mrs. E. W. Butler, the former Harriet Becher (d. 1847), Thackeray's maternal grandmother.   *Hudson:* Jeffrey Hudson (1619-82), a dwarf in the service of the Duke of Buckingham and later Queen Henrietta Maria.   *ferronière:* (Fr.) a fillet around the head with a precious stone in front.   *de Hoog:* Pieter de Hooch (1629-77?), Dutch genre painter.   *Leonardo's Charles VII:* no such da Vinci work exists.   *Terburg:* Gerard Ter Borch (1617-81), Dutch genre painter.   *Christ . . . 2 angels:* John 20: 12.   *Eastlake:* Charles (later Sir Charles) Lock Eastlake (1793-1865), genre and religious painter.   *Delaroche:* Paul Delaroche (1797-1856), French portrait and historical painter.   *Juif errant:* (Fr.) The Wandering Jew.

19. TO FRANK STONE
17 April 1835

Your letter was the first of the batch my dear Stone, & was more welcome to me even than the hot-cross buns, wh. on this day, our religion ordains that we should devour:—I have been a little spooney ever since the perusal of the letters, but my tears (& there were one or two upon my honour) were those of a pleasant content, when I thought of the half-dozen good fellows, who felt so kindly for me. God bless all the boys, & watch over the liquors they drink & the pictures they draw—as for myself I am in a state of despair—I have got enough torn up pictures to roast an ox by—the sun riseth upon my efforts & goeth down on my failures, and I have become latterly so disgusted with myself, and art & every thing belonging to it, that for a month past I have been lying on sofas reading novels, & never touching a pencil.
  —In these six months, I have not done a thing worth looking at—o God, when will thy light enable my fingers to work, & my colours to shine?—if in another six mos. I can do no better, I will arise & go out & hang myself.
  We have an exhibition here with 2500 pictures in it, of wh. about a dozen are very good—but there is no body near Wilkie or Etty, or Landseer—lots of history pieces or what they call here 'ecole anecdotique'—little facts cut [out] of history, & dressed in correct

costumes—battles murders & adulteries are the subjects preferred—Of costumes I have amassed an awful collection, and this in truth is all I have done, except some infamous water-colour copies perpetrated at the Louvre when it was open—Now the old pictures are covered up until June, by the performances of the modern men. there are lots of six & thirty feet canvasses, but not a good one among them—here is as good a portrait painter as ever I saw, one Champmartin who has been abused by the Athenæum man. No good water colours this year—though I have seen some by Roqueplan (who is a little snob, who condescended to do me out of a five franc piece) that are as fine as Reynolds—most noble in point of colour sentiment force & so forth.

I wish you would tell me how, you used to make that nice *grain*. I have tried all ways in vain.—I had hoped to have gone into Germany for this summer, & on to Italy in autumn, but my governors & the rest of our tribe are to come here in a month & I shall not be sorry to stay, & have a little more copying at the Louvre.—have you been asked to a tea-party by my Mamma? I wish you would call there some day, for you are a great favorite, & if you talk about the son of the house, you cant talk too much or stay too long.

Mahony gives me great accounts of you & Mac. o happy men, you are on the high road to fame & fortune. et Moi, moi, pauvre jouet de la fortune, voyant, jour par jour les esperances du matin moqués par les horribles realités du soir, je n'ai qu'a lutter, a me resigner, a me consoler de mes propres malheurs, dans les succes de mes amis— With this flare up in the French tongue for the grammar of wh. I do not vouch, I must conclude my letter. God bless you, my dear fellow—I thank you very much for your letter, & for your feelings towards 1 who is most sincerely your friend.

W. M. T.

Stone: Frank Stone (1800-59), water-colorist and oil painter. *the sun riseth . . . & goeth down:* see Ecclesiastes 1: 5. *Wilkie:* David (later Sir David) Wilkie (1785-1841), genre painter. *Etty:* William Etty (1787-1849), subject painter famous for his nudes. *Landseer:* Edwin (later Sir Edwin) Landseer (1802-73), genre painter. *Champmartin:* Charles Émile Callande de Champmartin (1797-1883), French portrait painter. *Roqueplan:* Joseph Etienne Roqueplan (1802-55), French landscape, marine, and genre painter. *grain:* (Fr.) texture. *Mahony:* Francis Sylvester Mahony (1804-66), "Father Prout," a writer for London periodicals like *Fraser's Magazine,* who spent much of his life in Paris. *Mac:* Daniel Maclise (1806-70), portraitist and genre painter. *et Moi . . . mes amis:* (Fr.) and I, I, poor plaything of fortune, seeing day by day the hopes of the morning mocked by the horrible realities of the evening, I can only struggle, resign myself, console myself for my own misfortunes with the successes of my friends.

20. TO MRS. HENRY CARMICHAEL-SMYTH
18-23 July 1835

I don't know dearest Mother why you have deprived me of my usual birth-day privilege whether it is because you intend to come so soon to Paris that a letter would be unnecessary; or whether you wish to punish me for my own remissness wh. I confess & deplore—if it is for the first reason I can only say that G. M & I have been looking out every day for I don't know how many months, and if for the last that my hand is at work from morning till night, and that I have got a strange antipathy for letter-writing—au reste you know very well that I don't think about you the less, because I don't write, for a man does not forget his best friend & his greatest consolation, when he is alone, and neither very well nor very cheerful.—not after a bitter & fruitless day's work, such as is every day's work now, or a scene with a certain old lady, you may suppose that I think about home and the dear Mother who would sympathize with my failures and hasten, I think, my successes, and would not hurt me with bad words, such as with a wonderful eloquence and ingenuity are rung into my ears by G. M.

Still it hurt me very much to be obliged to leave her, as I have done, and to reject the stipend wh. she made me for a while—but I am sure I was right in quitting her, and giving up the pitiful money.—however I made the separation as smooth as possible—did not hurt her feelings and I believe we are better friends now than when we were together—She comes to see me very often—and I walk stoutly up three times a week to be scolded—now that we are parted nobody can be more anxious than she about my health & so on—she has employed every kind of entreaty to get me back—but I have stood firm—I dont think

—but I wont talk any more about this business, for it has vexed me a good deal & you more I fear.

I have likewise been laid up with a little spirt of sore throat & fever; wh. is over long since, leaving the inconvenience only of a Doctors bill—likewise you heard how I fell from a horse at Montmorency—another doctor's bill—I asked G. M six times for the money to pay it and really could not find it in my heart to ask her again.

—Luckily Frank sent me £25 but it was well nigh swallowed up and I must by hook or crook get 10 more wh. will last me till September when comes his next Divd. of 25—I must begin on the poor little capital that's flat—the deuce is in it if I can't make my own livelihood in a couple of years—I have at this moment a good offer—a publisher here will give me a good deal to do—for I have been highly recommended to him, but he wants views of cities wh. are out of my line. I have made five drawings of one place here in Paris, and have cut them up one after another for they were too bad to shew him, these repeated disappointments make me ready to hang myself. in fact I am as thoroughly disheartened as a man need be—for I can do nothing—and yet I know I have got the stuff to make as good a painter as the very best of them. but I wont brag or grumble any more—you shall have this scrap of a letter as it is—only do do dear Father & Mother, set out on your journey, & bring a little consolation to your uncomfortable & affectionate Son.

W. M. T.

1 Rue des Beaux Arts.
   Faubourg St. Germain
  Thursday I think—I wish you would send a note & ask FitzGerald to dine—he you know is my crony next to you—and you needn't mind the expense for he only eats potatoes & drinks water.
    God bless you.

G. M: Grandmother—i. e. Mrs. Butler.   *au reste:* (Fr.) moreover.   *leave her:* during June Thackeray had moved to 1 Rue des Beaux Arts.   *Frank:* Francis Thackeray (1793-1842), Thackeray's uncle, who helped to administer the remainder of his inheritance.

21. TO WILLIAM RITCHIE
September 1835

My dear William
  The thing is impossible—I am tied to my Mamma's tail, & must maintain myself in this position for some weeks longer.—We are going I believe to Strasburg, whence it is my intent to voyage viâ Munich across the Tyrol into Ittaly—Besides this I am arrived at such a pitch of sentimentality (for a plain girl without a penny in the world) that my whole seyn, être, or being, is bouleversé or capsized.—I sleep not neither do I eat, only smoke a little & build castles in the clouds; thinking all day of the propriety of a sixieme, boiled beef & soup for dinner, & the possession of the gal of my art.—This must acct. for my neglect of Jane wh. has been shameful, the fact is I have been so busy of evenings uttering the tenderest sentiments in the most appropriate language, that I never had the heart to disturb her, among her virgin companions.—God knows how it will end, I will, if I can, bolt before I have committed myself for better or worser,—but I don't think I shall have the power. My mamma has given me a five franc piece to amuse myself and stop away for a day, but like the foolish fascinated moth I flickers round the candle of my love.

I suppose you go *up* in October—I would write you some very delightful moral sentiments on the occasion only you see that I am in such a state of mental exhaustion that it is impossible to form connected sentences, much more to pour into your astonished ear the sound & sonorous moralities wh. are likely to have an influence on yr heart.—only, my dear Fellow, in the name of the Saints, of your Mother, of your amiable family, & the unfortunate cousin who writes this—keep yourself out of DEBT.—and to do this you must avoid the dinner-parties & the rowing (boating) men.—however you will see John Kemble, who (particularly when he is drunk) will give you the finest advice on these & other moral & religious points.

I look forward with a good deal of pleasure to my trip—I am sure it wd. do you much more good to come with me, than you can get from all the universities in Christendom. I purpose going from Munich to Venice by what I hear is the most magnificent road in the world—then from Venice if I can effect the thing, I will pass over for a week or so into Turkey. Just to be able to say, in a book wh. I am going to make, that I have been there—after wh. I will go to Rome, Naples, Florence &c, and if possible pay a visit to dear Mr. Langslow; who considering all things will I am sure be charmed to see me.—then I will go to England book in hand, I will get three hundred guineas for my book—then I will exhibit at the Water Colour Society, and sell my ten drawings forthwith, then I will mar . — —

You recollect the picture of Jeannette on the Boulevards, as likewise the [. . .] of Alnaschar in the A. Nights—if you don't Zonny will tell it you.

Give my love to him, & my aunt & every body—I am going to write to Frank, (for whom I have bought a plan of the battle of Wynendael) so I need not impart to you any of the affectionate remarks, wh. I intend making him. God bless you my dear William, I will write to you sometimes on my travels, and when I am settled my wife will always be happy to see you at tea.

Your loving Cousin,
W. M. Thackeray.

1. Rue des Beaux Arts. Fbg. St. Gm.
(I think [I wi]ll be off in the [begin]ning of Septem[ber.)]

William: William Ritchie (1817-62), a cousin of Thackeray's, the elder son of John Ritchie.   *a plain girl:* Isabella Shawe (1818-93).   *sixieme:* (Fr.) sixth-floor lodging, a garret.   *Jane:* William Ritchie's sister (1822?-65).   *go up:* to Trinity College, Cambridge.   *Kemble:* John Mitchell Kemble.   *Langslow:* Robert Langslow (d. 1853), the husband of one of Thackeray's aunts, Sarah

Thackeray (1797-1847). He helped to administer the remainder of Thackeray's inheritance, along with Francis Thackeray.   *Jeannette:* evidently a girl who counted her chickens before they were hatched; see Letter 162. Her tale is an apparent variation on that of Perrette in La Fontaine's "The Milkmaid and Her Milk-Pot" (*Fables,* VII, x).   *Alnaschar:* a day-dreaming beggar in the *Arabian Nights'* tale of "The Barber's Fifth Brother."   *Wynendael:* a town near Ostend, Belgium, where the English, commanded by a distant relative of Thackeray's, John Richmond Webb (1667?-1724), defeated the French in 1708.

22. TO ISABELLA SHAWE
14-15 April 1836

18 Albion Street. Hyde Park.
Thursday 14 April.

My dear Trot, I passed the ocean in safety, and have been in Mother's arms ever since Monday night at nine o'clock. We had a very pleasant passage from Calais, & I fell in love with a pretty French girl with whom I talked the whole way—you may fancy what were my feelings on again revisiting my country, and how much ale I drank to welcome my return—I am at this moment under the effects of some—finding myself stupid & I am ashamed to say somewhat sleepy under the baneful effect of the essence of Malt & hops. Everybody is very well here, my Father grown quite young under the Homœopathic system, and my Grand Mother fully determined on revisiting Paris. I have not yet been with your Uncle, but I shall see him tomorrow probably, or at least once before he comes here to dinner next Tuesday.

The Newspaper affair goes on very well, all the Shares were taken and many more applied for; yesterday was a grand dinner [at] the Sollicitor's Mr Nokes; and I was introduced to the directors, and the Editors of the new journal. The head man is a very clever fellow I think, and I have no doubt that the Paper must flourish—But it is agreed that I am to be the Paris Correspondent, and not to go to Brussels; and they will give me three or four hundred a year—Think upon this dear Puss, et puis!—My father says I could not do better than to marry, my mother says the same—I need not say that I agree with the opinion of my parents—so, dearest, make the little shifts ready, and the pretty night caps; and we will in a few few months, go & hear Bishop Luscombe read, and be married, and have children, & be happy ever after, as they are in the Story books—Does this news please you as it does me?. Are you ready and willing to give up your home, & your bedfellow, and your kind mother, to share the fate of a sulky grey headed old fellow with a small income, & a broken nose?—Dear little woman, think a great deal on this now, for it seems to me that up to the present time (& considering the small chance of our union you were wise) you have avoided any thoughts as to the change of your condition, & the change of sentiments & of duties, wh. your marriage with me must entail—

—At this point dear Puss, I fell asleep last night, and on reading over what I wrote it seems to me that the matter and style fully shew to what a pitch of dullness I had arrived.—but I did not sleep much in the night, for I was awake thinking of this lucky change in my affairs, and of the chance it gives me of speedily returning to you—In a very few more weeks I shall be with you, and in a few months joined to you never please God to separate from you. Is it not a great blessing for me, who had a week ago only a doubtful future, a precarious profession, and a long and trying probation, to see competence & reputation so near me as they now seem to be.

I have been telling my Mother of your ills and your thinness, and she earnestly begs that you will go to one of the Homœopaths in Paris, and explain to him the whole state of your case. *Now I ask it as an especial favor, that you should do this*—for the system if it be true will cure you, and if false can do you no possible harm, for the hundredth part of a grain of medicine is all wh. they will give you to take.

I hear a sad account of John Stirling, he spits blood they say and must go very soon, but I will see the Colonel to day I hope, and hear more. I am going on a series of visits, and dear old Mother is making as much of me as possible—Mary wrote fifty invitations yesterday for a grand tea party and hop in honor of my arrival: She fancies that all the world is eager to see me. I have seen FitzGerald who has promised to come to Paris and see *us*. I was very glad to see my old friend again. My father's conduct to me in this Paper business has been very noble, he was offered a very handsome remuneration for his services as Director (£200 a year)—but he refused, all he wanted was he said that I should be employed on the Journal. God bless him for a good fellow as he is.

Here you have the whole of my budget of news, and I am as you may suppose longing for a sight of your little hand writing. I think tomorrow's bag, somehow, will have in it a letter for me. Be very happy dearest, and grow well and fat, and hope for the day when we shall meet again, and for the long long days wh. please God we shall pass together. Every body here sends you their love. I feel very happy to see them all so fond of you, and to know how much more they will love you, when they know you more. God bless you, dear woman, give a kiss to your dear Mother & to Jane for me, and ask either of them to give you a thousand for my part. I am off now with Mother avisiting.—

W. M. T.

your Uncle: Lieutenant-Colonel Merrick Shawe (d. 1843).   *Nokes:* John Nokes, attorney.   *new journal: The Constitutional,* a radical newspaper issued by a newly-formed publishing company headed by Major Carmichael-Smyth.   *head man:* Samuel Laman Blanchard (1804-45), editor of *The Constitutional.   et puis!:* (Fr.) and then!   *Bishop Luscombe:* Michael Henry Luscombe (1776-1846), who was Chaplain of the British Embassy in Paris, and did in fact marry Thackeray and Isabella on 20 August 1836.   *your kind mother:* Mrs. Matthew Shawe, the former Isabella Creagh.   *Stirling:* John Sterling (1806-44), periodical writer and central figure in the Sterling Club (1838ff.), whose members included Carlyle, Tennyson, J. S. Mill, and R. M. Milnes.   *Jane:* Isabella's sister, Jane Shawe.

23. TO MRS. JOHN RITCHIE
25 August 1836

Versailles. 25 August. 1836.

My dear Aunt.
  Mrs. Shawe who has just come to pay us a visit of condolence, brings a kind message from you, wh. Mrs. Mills in a conference of four hours imparted to her.
  WE, (does it not sound very magnificent?) shall be delighted to come and occupy your pretty little rooms, and stay with you a few or a great many days—for this place has a certain dulness, in spite of my peculiar situation, and I shall be too glad to pass a little time in your pleasant country villa.
  So that, on Saturday, my dear Aunt, I hope you will receive me & that diminutive individual, who bears the name of your affte. Nephew.

W. M. Thackeray.

24. TO EDWARD FITZGERALD
7 October 1836

15 bis Rue Neuve St. Augustin.
Friday 7. [October].

  My dear Edward. Your two letters arrived a day after each other, the first coming last in the order of Scripture.—As for the money, you have made me so used to these kinds of obligations, that I dont say a word more, but I feel very much your kind and affectionate letter, and long to have you with me.

As for the little wife it does not change one in the least it is only a new quality that one discovers in ones'self, a new happiness if you will, for my dear old friend, any thing so happy, so quiet, so calm you can't fancy; at this moment I am smoking a segar (wh. my little woman has got for me) in the very drawing room—the state apartment of the race of Tackeray! I intend with your money to b[u]y chairs and tables, to decorate this chamber, for as yet I have only hired them; and I have got your portrait and further more as the comble of sentiment I shall make Mrs. Tack write to you on this very sheet of paper.

I am sorry to say that I like the newspaper-work very much, it is a continual excitement, and I fancy I do it very well, that is very sarcastically, and though as we agreed about literature, sarcasm does no good either to reader or writer, I think in politics where all are rogues to deal with (yr. hble Servt. among them) a man cannot sneer and scorn too much, and bring the profession into disrepute—but the poor picture-painting is altogether neglected; and for this neglect I can give you no better illustration, than to tell you that it seems like quitting a beautiful innocent wife (like Mrs. T. for instance) to take up with a tawdry brazen whore.

But you don't know how happy it is (to return to the marriage business) to sit at home of evenings, and pass pleasant long nights lolling on sofas smoking & making merry: dear Edward do come and see me, it wd. do your heart good to see how happy I am.

See here is a fine picture of a clock wh. decorates the room where I am sitting, and is moreover my property—underneath it is a piano, & on the piano is a little straw bonnet, and altogether it is the comfortablest little picture wh. can be conceived it has taken me half an hour to draw for I have been painting the clock up so dexterously.

—I had a very handsome commission of £50 to make some etchings but I have tried & made such miserable work that I must give them up I find. It is a sad disappointment, for I had hoped to have done much in that line. I am surprised you have not got the Sir Rogers—Two English Artists, a Mr. Elmore and a Mr. Johnson [took] charge of them, one of them he who was to deliver them lives close to Portland Place, his father is a Doctor Elmore, and in the C. Guide you will find the address. Warwick Street I think—Cavendish Street Mrs. Thackeray says with her compliments—

I have become a woful bad scribe since I have begun to sell my pen at so much a line, and so you must not expect as many letters as of old, but if you will take the Constitutional you may have the pleasure of hearing of me every day or if you will but trip across to Paris (and who can do it more easily or has promised it more often?) my wife will give [you] the best of vegetables and the warmest of welcomes—I have got a snug little room called majestically Le Cabinet de Monsieur where I smoke all day and enlighten the L[. . .] about [. . .]

first . . . Scripture: Matthew 19: 30; 20: 16; Mark 10: 31; Luke 13: 30. *comble:* (Fr.) height. *the Sir Rogers:* Thackeray's illustrations of Sir Roger de Coverley, whom Addison had created in *The Spectator*. *Mr. Elmore . . . Dr. Elmore:* Alfred Elmore (1815-81). His father lived at 9 New Cavendish Street. *Mr. Johnson:* possibly John Johnson (1801-78). *the best of vegetables:* FitzGerald was a vegetarian. *[. . .]:* the final portion of the letter has been torn off.

25. TO JOHN MITCHELL KEMBLE
13 December 1836

15 bis Rue Neuve St. Augustin.
Paris. December 13. 1836.

My dear Kemble.

I write from the most interested motives—Mr. Beaumont is about to bring forth an Evening Paper I hear; and you must be aware how much he will need a Paris Correspondent.—Pray give me your vote and Interest, should the worthy Member for Northumberland persist in his intention.

I suppose you know how I exercise the same office for a Radical Morning Paper 'The Constitutional'—who in fact has not heard of T. T.? but I have plenty of time for another similar duty; and plenty of employment for the additional weekly—guiness it might bring—My dear fellow, do your best for me, for our friendship is old, our life is short, and our fortune uncertain: also as you know I am a married man (and you can understand my situation)—and have an alarming prospect before me of many additions to the race of Roaldus de Richmond—You also are probably in a similar state—wife, children coming, and nothing in three per cents—Why do we take wives?, why do we make children? Thou knowest as well as I, Beowulf, *we must be hammering at the head of the spear.*

Seriously (or as Joe Hume says seriatim) do your best for me: if you encourage me perhaps I will send an article for the review, (wh. wants lightness to my thinking); So that you see this note is, as all letters from married men should be, entirely about my own pocket and interest, wh. I want you to support.

I have nothing to tell you, except that I am grown strangely fat, and am the happiest man in this neighbourhood; I have a good wife, good dinners, plenty of work, and good pay—Can a man want more?—

I suppose I may offer my kindest regards to Mrs. Kemble, as, having seen a letter & a lock of her hair, I may be considered as an old acquaintance. Remember me too to all the rest of your family, father, mother and sister, they were very good to me as you know.

Can I do any thing here for you?. M. Leon Faucher spoke to me of you the other night; he is a dull prig I think, but very good at his specialité. Goodbye my dear Kemble

ever yours
W. M. Thackeray

Write to me if you have got any thing good to give me in the review, or what style of article you want or if you have not and are disposed to write

Beaumont: Thomas Wentworth Beaumont (1792-1848), a wealthy Philosophical Radical who helped to found *The Westminster Review,* but not an evening newspaper. *Roaldus de Richmond:* the alleged founder of Thackeray's family. *Beowulf:* Kemble had edited *The Anglo-Saxon Poems of Beowulf* (1833). *Hume:* Joseph Hume (1777-1855), Philosophical Radical. *the review: The British and Foreign Review,* which J. M. Kemble edited 1835-44. *Mrs. Kemble:* John Mitchell Kemble's wife, the former Natalie Wendt. *father, mother and sister:* Charles Kemble, who was married to the former Marie Thérèse Decamp (1774-1854), and their daughter, Frances Anne Kemble (1809-93). *Faucher:* Léon Faucher (1803-54), French journalist and politician.

26. TO FRANK STONE
20 January 1837

15 bis Rue Neuve St. Augustin. Paris.
20 Jany. 1837.

My dear Stone
    I have sent some drawings to London, wh. I want to be submitted to your Committee; and for wh. I hope you will act as the God-Father or Patron—I fear very much that my skill in the art is not sufficiently great to entitle me to a place in yr. Society, but I will work hard & please God improve—perhaps also the waggish line wh. I have adopted in the drawings may render them acceptable, for variety's sakes; there is no man I think, except Hunt, who amuses himself with such subjects. I hope you and Cattermole will say a good word for an old friend, and here I leave the business; confiding in friendship, trusting in Heaven; and pretty indifferent about failure, because I don't think I deserve success as yet.
    I have sent the drawings to my Mother in Albion Street, will you like a bold fellow take them under your charge and present them on the 1st. Wednesday in Feb[r]u[a]ry before the astonished Board?—I wish I had had more time to work, but the Newspaper work takes up most part of my time, and carries off a great deal of my enthusiasm. Mahony, who brings me news of the boys, says that you are all flourishing & rich: MacClise with a fine house in Fitzroy Square, and Cattermole in possession of Windsor Castle I think. Cannot you manage a trip here? only twenty five shillings and I promise you dinners breakfasteses and eve[r]y delicate attention on Mrs. T's part & mine. Lewis was here and very much to my disappointment I never knew of it until his departure. My letter is very incoherent, and yet I am sober, but the fact is three women are chattering at my elbow, and I can scarcely write or think.

I hope you go and see my Mother sometimes, though I am sure you don't; you are a great favorite with that old lady, and Miss Turner (my eldest daughter, Sir) is always asking about you.

Goodbye my dear Stone—here is a very short letter all about my own interests; but I have to write so hard for money, that I can't write for love—Send me a line about the lads and yourself, and salute them all for the sake of your old friend

W. M. Thackeray.

your Committee: the Committee of the Society of Painters in Watercolour. *Hunt:* William Henry Hunt (1790-1864), watercolorist known for his humorous pictures. *Cattermole:* George Cattermole (1800-68), watercolorist. *Lewis:* John Frederick Lewis (1805-76), watercolorist known for his Near Eastern subjects.

27. TO JAMES FRASER
5 March 1838

Boulogne. Monday.—[March].

My dear Fraser

I have seen the Doctor who has given me his commands about the hundredth number,—I shall send him my share from Paris in a day or two, and hope I shall do a good deal in the diligence tomorrow.

He reiterates his determination to write monthly for you, and to deliver *over the whole proceeds to* me. Will you therefore have the goodness to give the bearer a cheque (in my wife's name) for the amount of his contributions for the 2 last months—Mrs. Thackeray will give you a receipt for the same—you have already Maginn's authority.

Now comes another, and not a very pleasant point on wh. I must speak—I hereby give notice *that I strike for wages*.

You pay more to others, I find, than to me; and so I intend to make some fresh conditions about Yellowplush. I shall write no more of that gentleman's memoirs except at the rate of 12 guineas a sheet—and with a drawing for each number in wh. his story appears—the drawing 2 guineas.—Pray do not be angry at this decision on my part—it is simply a bargain, wh. it is my duty to make. Bad as he is, Mr. Yellowplush is the most popular contributor to your Magazine, and ought to be paid accordingly—if he does not deserve more than the Monthly Nurse or the Blue Friars I am a Dutchman.

I have been at work upon his adventures to day, and will send them to you or not as you like: but in common regard for myself I won't work at under-prices.

Well—I daresay you will be very indignant, and swear I am the most mercenary of individuals—not so; but I am a better workman than most in your crew and deserve a better price. You must not I repeat be angry, or because we differ as tradesmen break off our connexion as friends. Believe me that whether I write for you or not, I always shall be glad of your friendship, and anxious to have your good opinion.

I am ever my dear Fraser
(independent of £. S. D)
very truly yours
W. M. Thackeray—

Write me a line at Meurice's. Rue de Rivoli—I can send off Y. P. 24 hours after getting yours, drawing & all.

the Doctor: Maginn. *the hundredth number:* the April 1838 number of *Fraser's Magazine.* *the Monthly Nurse or the Blue Friars:* two series appearing in *Fraser's Magazine,* written by Harriet Downing and George Wightwick, respectively. *I can send off Y. P.:* Fraser evidently came to terms with Thackeray, for "The Yellowplush Papers" continued to appear in the magazine.

28. TO MRS. WILLIAM MAKEPEACE THACKERAY
11 March 1838

Sunday 11 March.

My dearest Dobbs. I have only 2 words to say to night, being very sleepy and tired, though I dont know with what. Last night the Crowes took me to a swarry, after wh. as I had eaten no dinner and was monstrous hungry, I went to the Café Anglais & ate a wing of cold fowl. There I found 2 old Charterhouse friends, & there I sate until 3 o'clock, so did not get up till 12, & wrote all day in my room till 6 when I went to dine with Thackeray—it is a great pity that his wife is no better than she should be. She is a kind ladylike pretty woman, with a very charming manner wh. only can belong to a good woman. Yesterday I dined at M. A's, who far from being uncomfortable was as gracious as possible; we were very happy for we talked all night of my dearest wife, till I longed to be home, and with her. It is almost a blessing that I came away, for I see now more strongly than ever, how much I love her, and how my whole heart & bowels go with her. Here have we been nearly 2 years married & not a single unhappy day. Oh I do bless God for all this great happiness wh. he has given us. It is so great that I almost tremble for the future, except that I humbly hope (for what man is certain about his own weakness and wickedness) our Love is strong enough to stand any pressure from without, and as it is a gift greater than any fortune, is likewise one superior to poverty or sickness or any other worldly evil with wh. Providence may visit us. Let us pray, as I trust there is no harm, that none of these may come upon us, as the best and wisest man in the world prayed that he might not be led into temptation. My dear dear wife may God preserve you to me & me to you.—I have been sitting for ten minutes pen in hand thinking about this last sentence, & not being able to write more on the same subject—I think happiness is as good as prayers, and I feel in my heart a kind of overflowing thanksgiving, wh. is quite too great to describe in writing—This kind of happiness is like a fine picture, you only see a little bit of it, when you are close to the canvass,—go a little distance & then you see how beautiful it is. God bless my dearest wife, & mother, & little Tomkins—I dont know whether I shall have done much good by coming away except to be so awfully glad to come back.

[. . .]

the Crowes: Eyre Evans Crowe (1799-1868), Paris correspondent of *The Morning Chronicle,* and his wife, the former Margaret Archer (d. 1853).   *Thackeray . . . his wife:* Thackeray's uncle, Martin Thackeray (1783-1864), Vice-Provost of King's College, Cambridge, and his wife, the former Augusta Yenn (d. 1869). *M. A:* Isabella's mother, Mrs. Shawe.   *bowels:* used in the Biblical sense—the seat of one's affections.   *not be led into temptation:* Matthew 6: 13; Luke 11: 4. *Tomkins:* an apparent reference to Anne Thackeray, who had been born on 9 June 1837.

29. TO MRS. MATTHEW SHAWE
12 July 1838

13 Great Coram Street Brunswick Sqre.
Thursday. 12. July. 1838.

My dear Mrs. Shawe.

We had intended to keep profoundly secret an event wh. has just occurred. Mrs. Thack after walking to Piccadilly on Monday, and eating a tolerable dinner requested me to fetch a medical gentleman wh. I did, and on my return had the pleasure to find another Miss Thackeray arrived in my family, and her mother just as unconcerned as if nothing had happened. the child is hideous of course, but when I left home in the morning I left Isabella perfectly happy, giving her a nice milk breakfast: and as cool and as comfortable as any woman possibly could be. I sent in the pride of my heart the announcement of her delivery to some of the papers the day after the event occurred; but on returning home it was resolved that the advertisement should be withdrawn, and that neither you nor my mother shd. be written to, until 3 or 4 days were over and all anxiety at an end. Fancy my disgust at finding that, after all, the announcement had got into an evening paper on Tuesday: though the Editor had promised me solemnly to withdraw it. I only learned the news ten minutes ago, and hope in heaven you may not have seen it, for you might be anxious about dear Isabella's condition, and think there were some painful reasons for our withholding the news. No such things thank God! She produces children with a remarkable facility. She is as happy and as comfortable as any woman can be.

We have got a new nurse a very good one, and a most excellent, watchful, tender nurse in Mary: who is about her, and keeps the house for me, and performs all the kind offices for her and the baby á merveille. We have been [none] the worse I assure you for being alone: th[e last] time there were too many cooks to our [broth,] all excellent ones: but I make a vow that for the 15 next confinements there shall not be more than *one*. I am now going home to write to my mother and my grandmother and Mrs. Sterling and the Colonel and Mrs. Buller, and to carry to Isabella a nice copy of the Pickwick Papers wh. my friend FitzGerald has just given me for her.

Miss Thackeray on seeing her new sister wanted to poke one of her eyes out and said teedle deedle, wh. is considered very clever. The Doctor in attendance is no less a person than Sir Charles Herbert the very pink of accoucheurs.

I find everything perfectly as well on coming home as I left; there is no symptom to occasion the least anxiety, she is perfectly well without any fever, and sound asleep: so sound that I don't like to wake her: but I think I may send you her love without.

Yours in the greatest possible haste
W M T.

another Miss Thackeray: Jane Thackeray, who had been born on 9 July 1838. *Mary:* Mary Graham.   *á merveille:* (Fr.) wonderfully.   *Mrs. Sterling:* Mrs. Edward Sterling (d. 1843), the former Harriet Coningham, whose husband (1773-1847), a staff writer for *The Times,* helped to get Thackeray employment as a book reviewer for the newspaper.   *the Colonel:* Lieutenant-Colonel Merrick Shawe. *Mrs. Buller:* Mrs. Charles Buller, Senior, the former Barbara Kirkpatrick (d. 1849). *Herbert:* Sir Charles Lyon Herbert (d. 1855).   *accoucheur:* (Fr.) obstetrician.

30. TO RICHARD BENTLEY
19 November 1838

Dear Bentley.

I am going to review all the late works on St. Petersburg for the F. Quarterly Review and should be glad if you could spare me copies of Raikes and Ld. Londonderry for such purpose.—Raikes I deserve having puffed it as you know: Londonderry more so having not mentioned it at all.

Also for Fraser I am about to make general review of literary ladies (this is of course entre nous) Mrs. Trollope I don't want having read her already but pray send me any others you have in your publishing harem. Novel writers I mean.

The last part of O Twist is I think as fine as anything in any story ancient or modern. With my best respects and wishes for Barnaby Rudge

I am yours ever
W. M. Thackeray.

13 Gt. Coram St.
Monday 19 Novr.
Send the books (if you do send) as quick as poss:

copies of Raikes and Ld. Londonderry: The City of the Czar: A Visit to St. Petersburg, in the Winter of 1829-30 (1838), by Thomas Raikes (1777-1848), and Recollections of a Tour in the North of Europe in 1836-1837, 2 vols. (1838), by Charles William Stewart (1778-1854), 3rd Marquess of Londonderry. Thackeray's article, "Manners and Society in St. Petersburg," did not appear in *The Foreign Quarterly Review* but in the January 1839 issue of *The British and Foreign Review.*   *having puffed it:* in a review of *The City of the Czar* that had appeared in *The Times* on 30 August and 7 September 1838.   *general review of literary ladies:* the article never appeared.   *entre nous:* (Fr.) confidential.   *having read her already:* Thackeray had reviewed her novel, *The Vicar of Wrexhill,* in "Our Batch of Novels for Christmas, 1837," in the January 1838 issue of *Fraser's Magazine.*   *O Twist . . . Barnaby Rudge:* Bentley (1794-1871) had just published the three-volume edition of *Oliver Twist,* which was still appearing serially in *Bentley's Miscellany,* and he had already announced the forthcoming appearance in his magazine of *Barnaby Rudge.*

31. TO MRS. HENRY CARMICHAEL-SMYTH
March 1839

My dearest Mother. The India Bill, wh. had 3 months to run, I sent to Lubbock's to get accepted, for it would have required 2 visits on my part to the City and is better done by them—Young Price was to carry sundry letters and the map of India, and was to set off the week before last—we have been so careless as never to ask whether he *has* set off but I will send tomorrow and learn particulars. Isabella will tell you how we have been gadding to Gravesend, and how dear little Pussy enjoyed the trip: it was delightful & the wind and the sunshine have made me pleasantly tipsy as it were, for I am not used to them in London wh. generates sluggishness of body and often mind too—I wish I could afford more frequent trips one to Paris above all for profit as well as for pleasure but it is not unprobable that something may turn up to keep me in London for the whole of the summer or at least within reach of it—

What shall I say to you about our little darling who is gone?—I don't feel sorrow for her, and think of her only as something charming that for a season we were allowed to enjoy: when Anny was very ill dying as I almost thought, it seemed to me wrong to pray for her life, for specific requests to God are impertinencies I think, and all we should ask from him is to learn how to acquiesce and now I would be almost sorry—No that is not true—but I would not ask to have the dear little Jane back again and subject her to the degradation of life and pain. O God watch over us too, and as we may think that Your Great heart yearns towards the innocent charms of these little infants, let us try and think that it will have tenderness for us likewise who have been innocent once, and have, in the midst of corruption, some remembrances of good still. Sometimes I fancy that at the judgement time the little one would come out and put away the sword of the angry angel I think her love for us and her beautiful purity would melt the Devil himself—Nonsense, you know what I mean. We have sent to Heaven a little angel who came from us, & loved us and God will understand her language & visit us mildly—Why write you this mad stuff dearest Mother?—God bless you and all besides I shall write G. M: and thank her for her money & use it too—

Your affte W M T.

Lubbock's: Lubbock, Forster, and Company, Thackeray's bankers.   *our little darling who is gone:* Jane Thackeray, who had died on 14 March 1839 at the age of eight months.

32. TO MRS. HENRY CARMICHAEL-SMYTH
1-2 December 1839

Sunday. Monday. December 1. 2.

My dearest Mammy. Isabella seems to have written an enormous letter to Mary, and I suppose in all those pages and crosses has given you the whole news from Great Coram Street, wh. amounts exactly to 0. We have had a succession of pleasant yellow fogs: one to day so bad that we can hardly see. We have led a tolerably sober and regular life, always up before nine breakfast over by ten books books books all day until night when to my great consolation FitzGerald has been here to smoke a segar and keep me company until one or so. Otherwise like affectionate people Mrs. Thack and I fall asleep straightway after dinner—and no bad amusement either. I find the beef and mutton lies plaguy heavy on the stomach, and causes this propensity to dozing. I can't drink either Port or Sherry and long for a little wholesome claret to enable me to perform the gradations of functions.

We have seen nothing and no one: I once to the play where I was very much bored by Bulwer's new piece: and yesterday, after working here from 10 o'clock until 10 with 1/2 an hour's dinner fancy that, I indulged in a smoking match until 2 wh. did the greatest possible good. This is interesting news, isn't it?

Well, what else is there? Mrs. Brody has gone to visit her relatives at Wapping—from six o'clock until ten last night Miss Thackeray roared incessantly in a hearty furious fit of passion wh. wd. have done your heart good to hear. I don't know what it was that appeased her but at the expiration of these four hours the yowling stopped and Miss began to prattle as quietly and gaily as if nothing had happened. What are the mysteries of children? how are they moved I wonder?—I have made Missy lots of pictures, and really am growing quite a domestic character. Kemble's child can sing twelve tunes but is as ugly as sin in revenge. However we must n't brag: for every body who comes into the house remarks Missy's squint that strange to say has grown quite imperceptible to me.

The little child is perpetually prattling about you all: and walks in the Shondileasy, with Ganny and Aunty and Polie just as if she were in France instead of here. There is a grand power of imagination about these little creatures, and a creative fancy and belief that is very curious to watch: it fades away in the light of common day: I am sure that the horrid matter-of-fact childrearers Miss Edgeworth and the like, with their cursed twopenny-halfpenny realities do away with the child's most beautiful privilege. I am determined that Anny shall have a very extensive and instructive store of learning in Tom Thumbs,

Jack-the-Giant-Killers &c[;] what use is there in the paltry store of small facts that are stowed into these poor little creatures' brains?

 I have just turned off a thundering article against Bulwer: and yesterday had the misfortune to read the Comic Almanack—any thing worse or more paltry cannot well be imagined—it is as bad, very nearly, as the prints wh. illustrate it: and these are odious. Cruikshank I suppose is tired of the thing and bends all his energies to the illustration of Jack Shepherd &c—I have not read this latter romance but one or two extracts are good: it is acted at *four* theatres, and they say that at the Cobourg people are waiting about the lobbies, selling *Shepherd-bags*—a bag containing a few picklocks that is, a screw driver, and iron levers; one or two young gentlemen have already confessed how much they were indebted to Jack Sheppard who gave them ideas of pocket-picking and thieving wh. they never would have had but for the play. Such facts must greatly delight an author who aims at popularity.

 Since writing the above I have been out to take what they call fresh air here: and am come home half choked with the fog: the darkness visible of Great Queen Street was the most ghastly thing I have seen for a long time. O for smiling Paris and sunshine!. if I can make some decent engagement with a bookseller I will pack off my traps, let the house again, and come somewhere at a decent distance from my dear old mother. I have been reading a power of old newspapers and reviews concerning Napoleon, and very curious the abuse is of that character. old Southey is one of the chief mud-flingers and it is good to read the Quarterly Review that settles he was 'no gentleman'. What are the Tories about[?] any such truculent Inquisitionism as the Times preaches now, such wilful lying and injustice never was—the Times is angry with the Queen for not having said anything about the Protestant Religion in her marriage-declaration, wh. was very modestly nay piously worded. The swindling blasphemer! it is frightful this dragging of God into the question, & hideous Pharisaical assumption of superior piety.

 I wish you could get Carlyle's Miscellaneous Criticisms, now just published in America. I have read a little in the book, a nobler one does not live in our language I am sure, and one that will have such an effect on our ways of thought and prejudices. Criticism has been a party matter with us till now, and literature a poor political Lackey— please God we shall begin ere long to love art for art's sake. It is Carlyle who has worked more than any other to give it it's independence.

 Here are 3 pages of nothing as I promised: we propose to get up at eight tomorrow and are at this very minute in the act of going to

bed. God bless my dearest Mother. Missy particularly told me to send her love, & had proposed to write too but is now snoring. Love to all
W M T.

Bulwer's new piece: The Sea Captain. *Brody:* Jessie Brodie, Anny's nurse. *Kemble's child:* J. M. Kemble's daughter, Gertrude (1837-82), later Lady Santley. *Ganny and Aunty and Polie:* Mrs. Carmichael-Smyth, Mrs. John Ritchie, and Mary Graham. *fades . . . common day:* Wordsworth, "Ode. Intimations of Immortality from Recollections of Early Childhood," l. 76. *Miss Edgeworth:* Maria Edgeworth (1767-1849), author of *The Parent's Assistant* (1796-1801) and other didactic stories for children. *article against Bulwer:* Thackeray's final Yellowplush Paper, "Epistles to the Literati. No. XIII," which appeared in the January 1840 issue of *Fraser's Magazine,* satirizing Bulwer's *The Sea Captain. Jack Shepherd: Jack Sheppard,* a "Newgate novel" by William Harrison Ainsworth (1805-82), which first appeared serially in *Bentley's Miscellany* 1839-40, with illustrations by George Cruikshank (1792-1878). Thackeray's mock-Newgate novel, *Catherine,* was appearing in *Fraser's Magazine* 1839-40. *darkness visible:* characterizing Hell in *Paradise Lost,* I, 62. *concerning Napoleon:* in connection with the writing of "Napoleon and His System," which appeared in *The Paris Sketch Book* (1840).

33. TO MRS. HENRY CARMICHAEL-SMYTH
23-30 December 1839

My dearest Mammy. I found your melancholy letter about poor Madame Vaudricourt on returning from Leatherhead to day: what a dismal blow for the survivors poor things—as for the person dying I don't think one need pity them & am not sure on the contrary that I don't envy them. It is surely the best way, if one might choose, to go off at once thus, without dismal delays and partings from relatives and fierce bodily pains. Along with your letter was one from poor Salt—all but a dead man, he writes that he is in bed with consumption wh. the Doctors pronounce incurable. Fancy such a death-bed as that, my God, cold, want, wretchedness, starvation, indifference—all these to bear along with the death-pang that is common to rich and poor. I feel ashamed of my own comfort and happiness in thinking of this dreadful grovelling misery—it seems like a reflection upon God who has bestowed his gifts so partially. Look at these unequal lots in the fortunes of men, and see how completely circumstance (of personal disposition or outward fortune) masters all—and one begins to think of Vice and Virtue as here practised, with profound scorn or else with bitter humiliation and debasement;—you orthodox people say there is no Virtue among men, and too that there is no Vice: Both are Lies as far as the world is concerned—Which is which? a hideous phantasmagorial jumble it seems, & not a reality. One has however the conviction or hope that a state of things may be when there shall reign an Abstract Good—I mean that the whole Universe may go to shivers & that still Good must remain, serene and eternal, and superior to all conditions of matter—whereas with matter Evil dies too. Lust and Hunger make evil, but these die with the body. There is to be sure the horrible Hell-Fire, wh. declares Pain to be eternal and obliges God thus perpetually to sanction Evil: just fancy it—we who know how intolerable a minute's pain of body or a single stroke of sorrow is, we who, the worst of us, have *some* good in us—fancy a scream of agony through eternal ages, and an ever present sorrow to be our ultimate boon from God or the ultimate condition of any single brother man! Judas Iscariot came into the world with diseases from his mother, and phrenological bumps—who shall visit the sins of his carcass upon his immortal soul?—By all wh. I want to argue that Good is of necessity Eternal, independent of matter & existing in spite of it—that evil is material only—and that that future state wh. we all look for when our bodies are dead (as for the resurrection of the body that can't be—our bodies crawl away into worms, or bud into daisys & buttercups, or explode into Gas all wh. again undergo modifications)—our bodies then being dead, our souls if they live cannot but be happy.

To wh. you will say: that a person holding such notions may murder thieve slander and commit every possible crime—and so he may. But are you and I prevented from committing murder from fear of Hell? not a whit. A child leaves the bread & butter for fear of a whipping, but that *is* certain and the child's intelligence only half-formed[;] our plan surely is or should be, not to keep from doing wrong from fear of punishment but to try & do right out of love of Good. I hope the latter part of the fable of Lazarus & Dives was intended for children—persons that is who had but indistinct notions of morals—there is nothing moral to us in the notion of Dives howling in flames, and begging for dear pity's sake for a drink of water wh. the other cannot give him. Punishment with us among each other in the world is very well—or rather very ill—a war between wrong and us: for we have no means of keeping Wrong in order but by belabouring and bullying it—But this is a bad imperfect means: as are all systems of Terror & Revenge. They do not prove themselves. One act of violence is not right because it has been preceded by another. For instance suppose a man is making faces at me & I give him a box on the ear; or suppose I am mistaken & fancy that the man is making faces at me and so give him the box—in either case the box is bad, philosophically & religiously we have no right to retaliate but we are obliged to make such bargains & compromises for peace & quietness' sake. However all this has been beautifully said by our Saviour two thousand years ago—the question then comes why should God exercise reprisals? reprisals wh. are morally wrong and unphilosophical?—it can't be—but the God believed in by all rude nations, the Jews as much as any other, has been material—Hell-fire is material, the conception & the bargain of the Atonement material, Heaven, harps, angels fluttering to & fro &c material &c &c &c

What can have been the occasion of the above rhapsody I don't know—it was written a week ago, and since then Anny has had the paper & I have trampled it under foot, & now I can't conceive what has been the cause of the tirade. My compassion for Salt I think but since a week my compassion has diminished, for would you believe it? the monster and his family are starving and have the impertinence to send to us every second day the impolite rogues, what do they mean by plaguing gentlemen thus? I thought myself a very fine fellow t'other day (Friday) when I gave him a shoulder of mutton minus 3 slices, a loaf & a bottle of wine & a brace of shillings—but now am most cruelly plagued by the poor wretch's importunity—and begin gravely to say 'We cant be always giving' &c What a lie! If I fancy a bottle of wine or a dinner at the Garrick I can always find a reason why it shd. be not only pardonable but necessary—& so the world wags. [. . .]

Lazarus & Dives: Luke 16: 19-26. The rich man is called Dives in the Vulgate version.   & . . . *wags:* As You Like It, II, vii, 23.

34. TO MRS. HENRY CARMICHAEL-SMYTH
18 January 1840

1[8] Jany. 1840.

My dearest Mammy. This great boon of the penny-postage has brought only bad-luck to us for the Foreign Bags are abolished for all private letters & Lettsom who was here the other day says that he and all his brethren are denied the privilege as well. We are getting on as usual I always behind hand & floundering in my business and having something particularly pressing to do just at that moment when I am writing to you. At this moment Madam you may console yourself by knowing that I ought to be at some other work, wh. is boiling and bubbling up in my brains in spite of me.—I am very much alarmed about the state of the country—not alarmed that is, for what can I lose?—but quite certain that a certain part of us are going to the deuce and that a tremendous revolution is preparing. There will be no end to it when it comes, and you will have barricading again at Paris, and there will be similar work all through Europe. The orthodox say it will be the battle of Armageddon after wh. the Millennium. There are a million and a half of chartists armed banded & corresponding closely with one another—their plan is not to meet in large bodies at all but their officers meet, and their officers' officers and these have corresponding delegates who direct the operations: had it not been for a rainy night and the cowardice of that scoundrel Frost we might have been now the British Republic for what I know and Queen Victoria in her uncle's dominions of Hanover. What have we got to resist these fellows?—ten thousand men in the 3 kingdoms who might be swallowed up body and bone before this great devouring monster of Chartism. Ten thousand stand of arms were seized upon in the city the other day—this seems all gôbe-moucherie doesn't it? And yet I do believe it to be all true I have had it from very good authority indeed—and thank God that the Chartists have not a man at their head who might set the kingdom in a blaze. With their views about equalizing property and robbery in fact of course a revolution effected by them could not last long: and the fit would soon be over: but the deuce is that one must take it and bear it and be in a fever for a couple of years until a deal of blood-letting ha[s] brought the disease down.

Our dear little woman is wonderfully well thank God and improves daily shewing I think a fine frankness and generosity of character. She has the best nurse in the world—fancy the poor woman giving away two pounds of her wages the other day to a poor Scotchwoman to bury her father-in-law with—a very silly gift for the man ought to have been buried by the Parish who begin to demur now on account of this very sum of money. It appears to be a great Superstition among the Scotch however to bury their dead respectably and at their own charges—people are known to starve and die and yet to have a little stock of shillings to bury themselves withal: wh. provision they will not touch—no not to save their lives. FitzGerald is in London the sight of him always makes me happy and idle too I am sorry to say: but he is off again on Monday to wait on his sick sisters at Hastings. You must not be too angry with Isabella for in your situation you have not experienced the rage wh. the receipt of an unpaid letter puts us into. By paying 1d. people would prevent us from paying 2d. and this 2d. sticks in our throats more than any other sum. What a strange meanness! I feel it myself and stamp and fume as if ruin were at hand. I am writing this at the British Museum waiting until my books come. I have finished Catherine and now am casting about for some other subject: it is not generally liked and I think people are quite right. A new Yellowplush addressed to Bulwer has made a great noise and has hit the Baronet pretty smartly. it is very good natured however: but you won't like that either: and it is better that ladies should not relish such grotesque humour: Rabelais, Fielding & so forth (apart the indecencies) are not good reading for women, & only for a small race of men—I don't mean to compare myself to one or the other mind—but the style of humour is the same. There is a story called Ten thousand a year in Blackwood that all the world attributes to me, but it is not mine—only better: it is capital fun: of a good scornful kind. Here come my books & so adieu for an hour or 2.

  Will you present my humble compliments to Mrs Butler and tell her that the wages of Mr. Goldsworthy have just fallen due: and that that gentleman having an extra claim of £4 agst me for board wages I presented him with a sum of 7.18.6. remaining exactly 5£ in his debt. I wd. have paid all but for a very good reason having such a heap of bills to discharge at Xmas that my purse was bled most cruelly. He is a very honest old fellow and would not charge me for his lodging at all.

  We met Lady Rodd tother day in the Park; fancy the woman sending to us the next day an immense black card with 'Lady Rodd & family return thanks &c' a year & a half after Rodd's demise!—The Ritchies have got a very pretty house in Albany Street overlooking Regent's Park, and came to us (the younger 1's) one night when Mrs. Buller did us the honor to dine. The poor old soul saw Missy and wondered that we did not give her medicine *twice a week:* pray God, she may never want it. She has a charming place at Leatherhead, and that little girl whom she has adopted so strangely—she is ruining her and killing her with physic—it was really melancholy to see the airs and selfishness of the child.

  Isabella goes tonight to the play with the Kembles; Mrs. K wrote to her the other day enjoining her to appear in *mourning*—in mourning O ye gods for the Landgravine of Hesse Homburg! What a world of humbug it is. Tuesday I have promised to go to Tennyson's out of town near Epping: in a month have a notion of paying a visit to Lettsom at Ramsgate & altogether have a most earnest longing after fresh air. I have written the kindest of letters to Frank Thack: & Mr. Langslow and am glad to be reconciled with the former. Mrs. Dick is going they say to lose a seventh child by water in the brain. We have been on a sweet trip to Clapham to see my friend Cattermole who has married a charming little wife and has a beautiful place, and on another to Chelsea to see Carlyle and Mrs. C— pleasanter more high-minded people I don't know. If you were here and could be intimate with John Allen my how you would respect him—the man is just a perfect Saint nor more nor less: & not the least dogmatical or presumptuous: but working striving yearning, day & night in the most intense efforts to gain Christian perfection—and yet the world would not be so good a world as it is were all men like him: it would be but a timid ascetic place in wh. many of the finest faculties of the soul would not dare to exercise themselves—no man however can escape from his influence wh. is perfectly magnetic.   Dearest Mammy I have no more to say—yes, we have invited Jane Shawe to come and her mother has accepted not for herself but her daughter—this however *is* all and so God bless you and all at the Havenue, and may we have a merry meeting in the summer somewhere: and don't be too eager for my letters and I promise you not to be so remiss as I have been: and will always love you, about 10000000000 times less than you love me, but as much as ever I can. I have eaten many bumbums as Missy calls them, and the little thing prattles ceaselessly about her Granny. God bless both of you.   —I hear from Mr. Salt about 4 times a week, the poor wretch is most profuse in his expressions of gratitude.

penny postage: established on 10 January 1840. *Frost:* John Frost (d. 1877), who on 4 November 1839 in Newport had led an armed Chartist uprising that was inhibited by heavy rain and dispersed by soldiers. *uncle's dominions of Hanover:* Ernest (1771-1851), Duke of Cumberland and King of Hanover. *gôbemoucherie:* (Fr.) foolishness.   *Ten thousand a year:* a novel by Samuel Warren that appeared serially in *Blackwood's Edinburgh Magazine* from October 1839 to August 1841. *Goldsworthy:* Thackeray's servant, John Goldsworthy (d. 1845). *Lady Rodd:* the former Jane Rennell (1777-1863), widow of Sir John Rodd (d. 1838).   *little girl:* Theresa Reviss (b. ca. 1832), Mrs. Buller's adopted daughter. *John Allen:* (1810-86), later Archdeacon, whom Thackeray had known at Trinity College, Cambridge.

35. TO MRS. BRYAN WALLER PROCTER
16 February 1840

13 Great Coram St.
1[6] Feb. 1840.

My dear Mrs. Procter.
   On receiving the famous Valentine I determined to send back the most witty, graceful, gallant reply that ever was written; and have been sitting almost ever since at my desk, brooding for

hours and hours upon this wonderful piece of wit.

Well, here is Sunday night, and not one single piece of fun has been conjured up, nor any 'miracle' instead of it. all I can say is that the buttons are beautiful, and that I shall be proud to wear them—but beautiful as they are (my soul, Madam, being above buttons) I hope you will allow me to take higher ground, and value the present not so much for itself, as on account of the quarter from wh. it came.

Your faithful subject
Orson

This represents Orson going to Court, after having been conquered enslaved & finally polished & presented to the world by *Valentine*

'miracle': an allusion to Edward Young's epigram written with the pencil of Lord Stanhope: "Accept a miracle instead of wit; / See two dull lines, with Stanhope's pencil writ.—" *Orson:* an allusion to the story of Valentine and Orson, two brothers brought up respectively as a knight and a wild man. Valentine conquers Orson, brings him to court, and tames him. Originally an early French romance, it was translated into English and later became the subject of a ballad in Thomas Percy's *Reliques of Ancient English Poetry* (1765).

36. TO MRS. HENRY CARMICHAEL-SMYTH
April 1840

My dearest Mammy. Look at the stamp and you will see to what a pitch of enjoyment I have been elevated. I came down here solely to have the pleasure of dating my letter from Whitehall, and of knowing the day of the month, wh. is before me on a great card that these luxurious reformers alter with the day. Missy & I begun a letter to you yesterday her's was. ["]Granny, Here is a letter. I wish my love some day to her. I been Zoologilan gardens, see eflums, and camels leopards, and monkeys and ostriches, & every thing."—this is all Miss Thackeray's letter: thank God she is very well this bright weather, as is her Mamma who is grown to a decent size and who will want consolation earlier than June as I fancy. Why won't my dearest Mammy come over for a month or so? She would be a great comfort to us, and who knows but we might at the end of the time take her back to Boulogne & there pass a summer month or two? Lettsom told me that you talked of coming and surely it is wrong not to come from the mere dread of parting—a wise old lady of forty seven ought to be more philosophical.

My book has not got on much since I wrote last nor indeed have I done much, but I am in a ceaseless whirl and whizz from morning to night, now with the book, now with the drawings now with articles for Times, Fraser, here and there: and though it's such a long time since I did write, indeed & indeed I've nothing to say, the days pass away to me like half-hours, or rather like no time at all, clean forgotten as soon as spent; one being exactly like the other and passed in a kind of delirium. The chief news is that the hot weather has brought the bugs: and these do lead me a pretty life sureloi: poor Isabella wakes too with my tossing and jumping out of bed, and cursing and swearing: I do believe this is the greatest annoyance I have. Arthur Shawe killed *fifteen* in his bed last night and to day the whole house stinks with a compound of camphor & turpentine, that we are applying to the bedding and floor.

This was begun on Sunday: since when your long letter has just come in: and Colonel Shawe's remonstrance about Arthur: of a certy my Mammy when she has determined on a point is mighty resolute—the poor lad does not cost us ten shillings a week that's a fact. We never drink wine now, and never have since he made his appearance: a bottle of gin serves us for a week nearly: and he is happy and contented. We give no dinner-parties: the only person I have had in the house is an honest fellow who wd. have been puzzled to get a dinner elsewhere: & economy is the order of the day. Let the poor lad alone until G M. comes when there will be an excellent excuse for sending him about his business. His Mother writes yesterday that Jane has refused her Somerville for *the eighth time:* they are going to leave Ireland or Doneraile now, & thank heaven the arrangement with G M. precludes the possibility of my offering them a gête. I read your article about Jack Sheppard, and such is the difference of taste, thought it poor stuff: quite below the mark, & inferior to the remarks on the same subject with wh. Catherine was concluded; & wh. are to my notion—but never mind what. I have just done a huge article on G. Cruikshank for the L. & W. wh. I will send you when it appears. And furthermore am bringing out on my own account a weekly paper called the Foolscap Library. I think it will take: and the profits of it are so enormous if successful that I dont like to share them with a bookseller: there is no reason why I should not make a big lump of money by it.

The new Boz is dull but somehow gives one a very pleasing impression of the man: a noble tender-hearted creature, who sympathizes with all the human race. You will see in the Cruikshank article, some remarks against myself: I fail by sneering too much: but I think Foolscap will succeed[;] it begins with the adventures of Dionysius Diddler all in pictures like M. Vieuxbois—quite fabulous: but a good likeness of Lardner & Bulwer introduced. I have read the whole of the latter's procès and feel much pity for him: his wife is the most graceless, drunken, lying, debauched &c possible, and if you could see his letter & the documents in support of it you would say so.

And now pray dearest Mammy, spite of lame foot think of our back-drawing room, and how useful you would be. I'm afraid of G M. and the nurses rowing. When the confinement comes I shall certainly apply to Mrs. Shawe. She has no business to be ordering fallals & leave her daughter without her allowance.

John if you please has got a new coat & weskit, and is as deaf as a stone. I borrowed 20£ to get into the Reform[+]: a man to whom I lent 30 once, sent to offer me this: it was very kind and I was glad to be under the compliment to him. I don't know that I shan't have to borrow from P A. for the Foolscap:—the thing is a fortune: but wants abt. £30 to start it: however I have some, and shan't want yet. 1000 gives 8£ profit Why shouldn't I sell 5000, 10000 copies? they will pay me 40 or 80 a week: 80 a week is 4000 a year of wh. I would put by 3 at the very least &c &c: see Alnaschar in the Arabian Nights. And so God bless my dearest Mammy: and all at number 4: how bright it must look now. My dear old Paris!

W. M. T.

+ There was no use in keeping this awful circumstance from you you'd have found it out. My other debts dont amount to 20 more.

the stamp: the embossed stamp of The Reform Club, located in Whitehall. *My book:* *The Paris Sketch Book.* *Arthur Shawe:* Isabella's brother. *Somerville:* Jane Shawe's suitor. *gête:* (Fr.) gesture. *huge article . . . the L. & W.:* "George Cruikshank's Works," which appeared in the June 1840 issue of *The London and Westminster Review,* and was republished as a separate work later that year. *Foolscap Library:* the paper was never published. *new Boz:* Dickens' *Master Humphrey's Clock,* which began its serial appearance in April 1840. *Lardner:* Dr. Dionysius Lardner (1793-1859), editor of *The Cabinet Cyclopedia* 1829-46. *procès:* (Fr.) proceedings at law. Bulwer's estranged wife, the former Rosina Doyle Wheeler, was engaged in a bitter dispute with him. *John:* Thackeray's servant, John Goldsworthy. *number 4:* the Carmichael-Smyths lived at 4 Avenue St. Marie, Faubourg du Roule, Paris.

37. TO MRS. BRYAN WALLER PROCTER
22 May 1840

Leamington.
Friday. 2[2] May.

My dear Mrs. Procter

You have just seen the last of Carlyle's lectures and are fealed with a tander peaty for the human race, pray forgive me for my trespasses, for the fact is that I am at this minute at Leamington—a hundred miles away from a good dinner that I know will be ready at six o'clock on Sunday. If you could but see how wonderful the country is—the country of Shakspeare—THE OLD HOMES OF ENGLAND standing pleasantly in smiling cowslipped lawns whence spring lofty elms through or rather I should say amidst wh. the breeze whispers melodious, the birds singing ravishing concerts, the sheep browsing here and there and waddling among the fresh pastures like walking door-mats, the tender lambs trotting about on thick legs, the cows, bullocks or kine looking solemnly with large eyes from betwixt their crooked horns, the lusty rustics sauntering round about, whistling,

the fat yeomanry cavalry

swaggering through the green lanes,—I am sure you would excuse me for asking permission to pass a few days in this paradise of a place. How I wish for Leigh Hunt or any friend who really loves the country!—

Truly yours dear Mrs. Procter
W M Thackeray

Carlyle's lectures: On Heroes, Hero Worship, and the Heroic in History, delivered in London 5-22 May 1840.   OLD HOMES: a burlesque of "The Homes of

England" by Felicia Hemans (1793-1835).   *Leigh Hunt:*   Hunt (1784-1859), a friend of Byron, Keats, and Shelley, was a poet and essayist.

38. TO MRS. HENRY CARMICHAEL-SMYTH
1 June 1840

My dearest Mammy. The two small patients are getting on very well: and very much against my will (for I have grown to hate letter-paper as Somebody does holy-water) I sit down to inform you of this circumstance. I think we have been all the better for quiet in the house: and find that the professional nurse does the business quite satisfactorily. It is Mrs. Allen's woman, a quiet cheap body. The horrible book is at last done—all but the last page: this page has taken me 3 days I have such an unnatural slowness upon me. And think of my pleasure with 7/6 in my pocket when I sent to Cunningham for the £50 to find that I was not to have it until the book was *published* wh. mayn't be for months. What was I to do? to curse to stamp to rage to meditate pawning my watch but blessed be fate. Celestial Fraser owes me £20 or near it and so I shall perhaps be all the better for the delay of the 50 being obliged to make a dreadful scuffle of work all next month instead of idling. The time at Warwick was delightful, only not quite easy in mind enough, for I was always afraid of Isabellas being confined in my absence: and the dear little woman is so good and uncomplaining that I can't bear to think of any neglect—any positive neglect I mean—as for jollifying after a day's work I cant help that, and shd. be good for nothing without it.

Arthur Shawe sets off on Tuesday, and I will if I can write to Mrs. Halliday, and Marian Irving about him—Charlotte we met at Mrs. Ritchie's as I suppose Isabella told you, a charming amiable simple creature with just enough sense to be agreeable why is it that one does not like women to be too smart?—Jealousy I suppose: a pretty selfish race we are truly, and Lady Morgan has shown how cruelly the ladies are kept down.

Indeed and indeed my dearest Mammy I can't write—I have got no ideas. This paper has been before me for an hour and I sit stupidly pondering. With it goes a letter for Tom Thackeray wh. has been owing 2 months at least. Don't be angry with me or frightened. I am well in health, fat in body, easy in mind tolerably well to do in purse: but so intolerably stupid that I had better at once shut up this letter, and pack it off to Mr. Bidwell. Never mind that but God bless my dearest Mother and all with her. Missy is delightful she is very kind to me, and comes to see me in bed. The little baby is very like the dear little one we lost—strangely like in voice. Brodie has made the mother some new night-caps wh. vastly become her, with flies to the ears much prettier than Mary's charity caps. I am inclined to think it is the bugs that make me so dull. Up stairs & down stairs & in my lady's chamber equally buggy. I'm now in the back drawing Room that is I sleep there being at this writing at the Reform Club—hang them they are at work as bad as ever. No signs however of them in the day, no remedies available, but in the night weeping, tossing, groaning, cursing, and a great deal of expectoration upon the bumps that rise here and there—You can't get at some of the places. the beasts how I hate them.

My dearest Mammy.   The immortal Paris Sketch Book is this instant concluded: after unheard of throes and pangs of labour, wh. have been going on at intervals ever since the last desperate sentence of this letter was written.

My dear Granny I have a number of play-toys, and have pleasure pleasure's happy. Little Sister only but sucks and sleeps and it cries out wa wa wa. I send Granny my loves, my loving loves. I'll come over & spend the day with her. I would be most happy to come. I can't spare [. . .] love becau[se . . .] going to send it to Somebody, I'm going to send it [. . .] but I [. . .] 2 loves, and send the old one to Granny.—With [these] declarations [on] Missy's part I had better close this letter dearest Mo[ther.] Your's has just come to hand, and G. M's maid must as you say take [up] her abode with the cook: for I occupy the other spare bed in the back drawing room. I am not surprized that Marriott shd. commence his attack,—won't it be better for you all to take a trip quietly to Brussels or Nice on the road to Italy?—at least to have some legal advice as to Marriott's power to annoy you. His creditors are the people I suppose who press for the firm is bankrupt.   God bless you—all quite well—

W M T.

The two small patients: Mrs. Thackeray, who was diminutive in size, and their infant daughter, Harriet, who had been born on 27 May 1840.   *book . . . Cunningham: The Paris Sketch Book*, published by Hugh Cunningham.   *Marian Irving:* Mrs. Archibald Irvine, the former Marianne Shakespear.   *Charlotte:* Charlotte Ritchie (d. 1878), eldest daughter of John Ritchie.   *Lady Morgan:* Lady Thomas Charles Morgan, the former Sydney Owenson (d. 1859), author of *Woman and Her Master* (1840).   *Tom:* Thomas James Thackeray (1796-1877), a cousin.   *Up stairs . . . chamber:* see the nursery rhyme, "Goosey, goosey gander."   *[. . .]:* the hiatuses are caused by two holes in the leaf.

39. TO MRS. BRYAN WALLER PROCTER
7 July 1840

Gt. Coram St.
Tuesday.

My dear Mrs. Procter
    I shall be very glad indeed to dine on Wednesday. My friend Morton and I called one evening about a fortnight since: but you were engaged in giving one of those many feasts, for wh. your house is famous, and we were obliged very disconsolately to walk away.

    The greatest poet in the House of Commons came here yesterday morning at 1/2 past 3, and we drove together in his famous fly (wh. had been sitting up all night) to Newgate to see Courvoisier killed. It was a horrible sight indeed, and I can't help mentioning it for the poor wretch's face will keep itself before my eyes, and the scene mixes itself up with all my occupations. Notes, however small, are not even exempt from it; and I expect to be very agreeable and lively tomorrow with long full particular descriptions of it.

                Most truly yrs dear Mrs. Procter
                          W M T.

Morton: Saville Morton (d. 1852), who had graduated from Trinity College, Cambridge, was a journalist friend of Thackeray's. *greatest poet in the House of Commons:* Richard Monckton Milnes (1809-95), later first Baron Houghton, poet and politician, whom Thackeray had known at Cambridge. *Courvoisier:* François Courvoisier was hanged on 6 July 1840 for murdering his employer, Lord William Russell (1767-1840). In response to the public execution, Thackeray wrote "On Going to See a Man Hanged," which appeared in the August 1840 issue of *Fraser's Magazine.*

40. TO BRYAN WALLER PROCTER
July 1840

Sir
    I have to acknowledge the receipt of a dozen bottles of Bordeaux Wine from yourself, and of a small packet of sweet cakes from your lady.

    The wine is not of the first growth but I do not for that reason propose to send it back. I am not proud, although author of the most popular work that has appeared in the present day.

    As a friend of your's, a gentleman by the name of Chorley quarrels with the book in question on account of it's lack of gentility. I have determined to curb in future that laissez-aller wh. appears to have offended him, & to write only in the genteel style—

Accept then my impressed compliments for your wine, and with them the assurances of my distinguished consideration.

Baron de Titmarsh

Great Coram Street.
Grosvenor Square.

This is particularly genteel.

T. O.

On the other side, I could not, writing in the genteel manner, express my feelings more strongly. My dear Procter, it was very good of you to think of such a present, & my wife and I enjoy it I assure you heartily— Chorley's is a capital notice I think, and the sly reproach for ungentility a compliment. I'm afraid Forster is right about the badness of the drawings; every one agrees with him but the Spectator & The Author

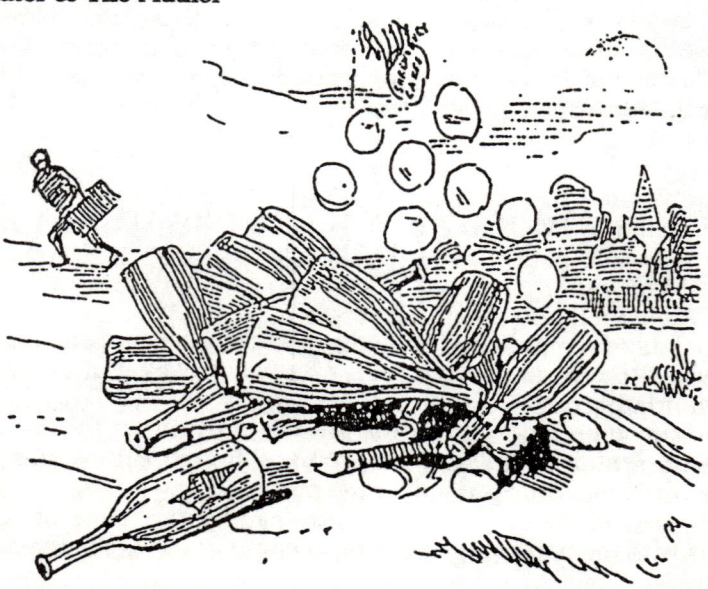

the most popular work . . . *Chorley:* Henry Fothergill Chorley (1808-72) reviewed Thackeray's *The Paris Sketch Book* in the 25 July 1840 issue of *The Athenæum*. *laissez-aller:* (Fr.) unconstraint. *This . . . genteel:* writtten vertically alongside the pointing finger. *Forster:* John Forster (1812-76), a journalist and sometime friend of Thackeray's. *the Spectator: The Spectator's* review of *The Paris Sketch Book* had appeared on 18 July 1840.

41. TO MRS. HENRY CARMICHAEL-SMYTH
30 July 1840

July 30. 1840.

Why I have not written to my dearest Mammy is indeed hard to say—not from excessive occupation certainly for I've done nothing these 10 days except pass 3 very pleasantly in the midst of the rain at Leatherhead. I think Durham's death is a piece of good fortune for Chas Buller, who has been weighed down by the corpse as it were of that man. What the Times says of him is very just I think, as far as the appreciation of character goes—not so as to the Canada failure, the rascally Whigs & Tories swamped that between them[;] when is the day to come when those 2 humbugs are to disappear from among us?. Don't be astonished. I'm not a Chartist, only a republican. I would like to see all men equal, and this bloated aristocracy blasted to the wings of all the winds. It has been good & useful up to the present time—nay for a little time longer perhaps—just up to the minute when the great lion shall shake his mane, and scatter all these absurd insects out of it. What stuff to write to be sure. But I see how in every point of morals the aristocracy is cursing the country—O for a few enlightened republicans[,] men to say their say honestly, and dare to do and say the truth. We are living in wonderful times, Madam, and who knows may see great things done: but no physical force—the bigotry of that & of the present Chartist leaders is greater than the bigotry we suffer under.—Well this is a way indeed of filling a letter to one's Mamma.

I must tell you about the carriage, that I forgot, and ought to have spoken of a month ago. It is bad news. The carriage owes £25. and won't fetch anything—not 10, not 5 in fact nothing: for there is no demand for carriages of this make, new sorts have sprung up pilentums & such like, and the machine was at first a fancy machine &c. There are 4 sales a year, shall Marks sell? that is if he can. Persons might possibly buy, by hearing of a wonderful cheap carriage in the Papers.

My dearest Mammy I want to send you the book, about wh. you have no business to speak in such terms. It has been very much puffed—eight or nine good puffs at least, and is selling very well about 400 have been got off already. Enough to pay all the expenses of authorship printing &c. and to leave 500£ profit to the publisher if the rest are sold. Longman the great publisher and Chapman & Hall Dickens's publishers with whom I have opened negociations seem to be very willing to enter into treaty with me: & I hope that something good will come out of it all—something better than that odious magazine-work wh. wd. kill any writer in 6 years. What do you think of Titmarsh in Ireland that is my next plan—I could make a good thing of it I think, and get 300£ for my 3 months work instead of 120 wh. the Magazines wd. pay me. We shall see whether any of the Publishers can be brought to pay. I make fine Alnaschar visions on the subject: but they all begin with 150£. as thus. With 150 I write a book worth 300, pay 150 off, have 150 to go on with while writing another book worth 400—and so at the end of the year there I am ready to begin a new work and with 400 in my pocket—all this is quite feasible reasonable possible probable—and if I can catch Longman or Chapman will I hope come to pass. Fancy having 500 Ye Gods what a treasure! Let us pray for this consummation. I will break from the Magazines that's flat. I sent to Fraser for money tother day whom I never overdrew 10£ & whose best man I am—he refused me & not because I had overdrawn my account, but because he had not had leisure to make it up, & thought I might have overdrawn it. There's a pretty liberal fellow for you. perhaps Grantley Berkely was not so very wrong in beating him. Such pens ink and paper I've on hand: that's why I write generally at the Reform Club: and not here in the drawing room with G M opposite reading Humphrey's Clock & much puzzled, and Isabella on the sofa. She is all but well thank God, & the baby a dear little fat flourishing podge of flesh as one says. Another blot. Missy I have just left lying on her stomach. It is inordinately hot: we are all in the most melting condition possible, and all well. I think I have a touch of the gout really & truly, for 3 months there has been a regular ceaseless pain in my great to, not sewere but steady & he looks red, this is the beginning of gout all my friends inform me, & I suppose that 1 day or other I must look for the completion of it.

  I went to Dorking from Leatherhead & saw my pretty Charlotte Crawford. There is nothing about her but simplicity: I like this milk-&-water in women—perhaps too much, undervaluing your ladyships' heads, and caring only for the heart part of the business. I have taken a fine advantage of one of the blots, & shall clap my seal on the space it occupies. Thus it is in human life that we make our failings as serviceable to us as our virtues can be. I have been reading Allan Ramsay's Poems, the Banantyne Controversy wh. proves Scott to be a rogue—and a noble article in the British Critic on Pauperism wh. has affected me extraordinarily, likewise some French novels—noble occupation for grey headed fathers of families: how happy are those who read to instruct themselves—yes, besides I have read Ranke's History of the Popes (in the way of business) with much pleasure. It is a great book, and may be read with profit by some persons who wonder how other persons can talk about the 'beautiful Roman Catholic church in whose bosom repose so many saints & sages.' Saints & sages do sleep there, and everywhere under God's sun, I think & hope. God bless my dearest Mammy, & Good night. Don't fancy I want money. I have lots.

WMT.

Durham's death: John George Lambton (1792-1840), first Earl of Durham, had died on 28 July. Charles Buller (1806-48) had been his Chief Secretary.   *the wings of all the winds:* Psalms 104: 3.   *Longman:* Thomas Norton Longman (1771-1842), publisher.   *Chapman & Hall:* a publishing house owned by Edward Chapman (1804-80) and William Hall.   *Berkely:* Grantley Berkeley (1800-81), a novelist who had horsewhipped Fraser in 1836 because of an unfavorable review in *Fraser's Magazine.   Ban[n]antyne Controversy:* a controversy in July 1840 regarding Scott's financial dealings.   *article in the British Critic:* "Pauperism and Alms-giving," which had appeared in the July 1840 issue of *The British Critic, and Quarterly Theological Review.   Ranke's . . . business:* Thackeray published a three-part review of Leopold von Ranke's (1795-1886) book in *The Times* on 10 June, 11 August, and 18 August 1840.

42. TO MRS. HENRY CARMICHAEL-SMYTH
20-21 August 1840

1 Bridge Terrace
Margate. August 20. 21.

My dearest Mammy. It seems to me that now is the first time since many weeks that I have had the time to write to you: for while on the Belgian trip, all I did was for money & with sight-seeing and sketching and having good dinners and sleeping on benches of afternoons and writing between times the day was completely spent. Indeed it was a delightful trip, pleasure & Sunshine the whole way— & more absence of care than I have enjoyed for many a long day—not that I am very careful. But it seemed a sin to be unhappy in that wonderful blue sky, and so I was as virtuous as possible I mean as jovial.   When I came back having spent 14£ I sold my mss. to Chapman & Hall for 70—that is a little book on Belgium & the Rhine to come out as a guide-book next year.   I have made an agreement with them for Ireland. £100 down, £100 on publication £100 more by degrees up to 1200 copies the end of the edition. Indeed my luck stands me wonderfully in stead: for I was beginning to have a scuffle for money. G. M. like a trump advanced 25 part of wh. enabled me to make the Belgian tour, the rest remaining with Mrs. Thack. in my absence.

That young woman I am sorry to tell you I found in such an extraordinary state of languor and depression when I came home that old Powell counselled me to bring her immediately to the sea side, and here we are arrived this very night. She has got the better of her first complaint but this was succeeded by excessive lowness of spirits that came on in my absence: nor did G. M & she as I fancy get on very merrily together[.] I have had a sad battle to fight since Sunday when I came home: but this is our marriage day & thank God the fresh air & the sunshine & the little excitement of travel have done wonders for her, & she has gone to bed tired and happy. Don't allude to it at all, or only to say that you are charmed to hear she has got round. Indeed the air & bustle acted on her like a charm. There can be nothing the matter with her (but indigestion), for she has plenty of milk, and the infant is as fat & smiling as babe can be. It is always at her, & this pulls her down of course very much. We have got a charming green little lodging here, but very dear 2 1/2 guineas a week, every body else asked 3 or 4 for rooms not so good. All our windows look to the sea, if you call this sea. A queer little sitting-room with a glass door that walks straight into the street and two neat smart bed rooms 1 on the top of the other. We dined at the Inn, and sent Missy & Brody & the baby on before. Missy I found lying on her stomach, a great deal more than half asleep. She said to Brodie 'I have come a long long way, but I wish to kiss Papa & Mamma before I go to bed.' God bless her. She is a noble little girl. Your big heart would have thumped to see her toddling about the deck, embracing in her fine innocent warmth every little child about her. I find myself growing much more sentimental as I grow older. This world is not near such a bad one as some of your orthodox pretend. We are not desperately wicked but good & loving many of us: our arms reach up to heaven, though the Devil to be sure is tugging at our heels. My dearest old Mammy I think of you often & always indeed I do: and know I shall never go to Hell for if I went you in Heaven wd. be miserable, & there you know people must be happy. I told G M. to send you a puff out of the Glasgow Argus the biggest & strongest of all. Mrs. Procter sent me a letter from her mother t'other day almost as strong: it was good of her to send it, though I know really how much this sort of flummery is worth. In spite of the puffs they have only sold 500: but this is many more than I expected. Where I have been bad is about the drawings. 1 paper the Spectator that I have no connexion with, and is seriously the only paper that understands matters of art (I swear I always said so before) says that Titmarsh is the best designer going: by Jove he is right, tho I can't get any body to think so.   How delightfully quiet this night is! The ripple of the water is most melodious, the gas lamps round the little bay look as if they were sticking flaming swords into it. What is it that sets one's spirits chirping so, on getting out from London?. poor old Gran is there alone she would not come with us, & has got a crotchet that Isabella dislikes her—indeed she doesn't, but old Gran is a sad pestering old body for all that. She is very kind.

I see the people walking about in slippers and get the most strange recollections of this place from the old time when we were here. I remember a dingy little bed-room where you used to come and wake me of mornings. I remember running for the Steamer and Pa giving me 10/—I remember going with Col. Forrest that night to see 'The two Gentlemen of Verona' Why the deuce should these things remain so clear? I have forgotten a number more important.

We have been out to walk on the Sands Missy famous. Baby ditto. My wife better in health but very low. For the last 4 days I have not been able to write one line in consequence of her. I must work now double tides. God bless my dearest Mother, and I hope I shall have a more cheerful letter to write the next time I do so. I shall take Isabella to Ramsgate & see if Mrs. Lettsom will invite us. To crown my joys I am bitten to pieces by bugs. Sweet home indeed!

We have the lodgings for a week.

a little book: the work was never published.   *desperately wicked:* Jeremiah 17: 9.   *her mother:* the third wife of Basil Montagu (1770-1851), miscellaneous writer.   *Forrest:* Lieutenant-Colonel William Forrest, husband of Major Carmichael-Smyth's sister, Georgiana.

43. TO MRS. HENRY CARMICHAEL-SMYTH
August-1 September 1840

1 Bridge Terrace. Margate.
Tuesday. 1 September I think.

My dearest Mammy. As the Poet observes, you have got hold of the wrong end of the stick about Catholicism—those obnoxious remarks wh. have been setting my dear old Mammy in such a fidget being written by Mrs. Sand, and not by Titmarsh who is only answerable for the omission of the inverted commas wh. wd. have made them over to their right owner. Concerning Judaism, I believe it is pretty generally allowed that the doctrine of a future state did not obtain among the Jews till they learned it in the Babylonish captivity.

Except that passage in Job, wh. has nothing to do with the matter, being applied by J to his own bodily condition find another in the O.T.—one that says expressly there is a Heaven for the good & something else for us wicked ones. Such a doctrine of such importance ought to be taught by something more than implication, & should not be left to honest persons to decide whether it is so or no. Who were the Sadducees who denied the resurrection?. Your book does not prove it as clearly as you say. As for Catholicism you may have your fling at it: but I am sure that the Xtian church has existed in it in all ages—it would be an insult to God to say it had not. Recollect who you are a woman with intense organs of love & respect born in Church-of-Englandism—do you think you would not have had the same love for Catholicism if you had been bred to it? Indeed you would, as I fancy, or any other creed. God forbid you should not: a woman reasons with her heart that you do Madam for all you fancy that you are unprejudiced, & I should like to show you how the assertion that every word of the Bible from Genesis to Malachi proves Jewish belief in the immortality of the Soul cant be supported, and the argument about Moses Montefiore is beside the question. But by Jupiter-Ammon, as I go through the world it seems to me that I am the single person in it, who am always right. People will not look dispassionately, but never mind God's sun shines over us all Jews, Heathen Turks, Methodists Catholics, Church-of-England men, but this is an old story that I have often told. It seems to me blasphemy to say that out of a certain sect there is no salvation, Heaven forbid say you: well then one sect is as good as another, and as men have different eyes noses and we shd. be monstrously bigotted if we were to say that such and such a hook or such and such a swivel shd be damned—in like manner let us accord the same charity to men's minds wh. are all different & must all worship God their own way. Indeed it is something noble I think to think even of this difference: that God has a responding face for every one of these myriad intelligences, and a sympathy with all. Why then be anxious that those we love should cast their religious thoughts precisely in our mould? This is the meaning of that article abt. Mrs. Sand;—let people leave others alone in religious matters; that's all I argue.

  I am or fancy I am growing more serious upon these matters—especially now that my poor little woman is so low. Indeed it is a hard matter to resist catching the infection for I am always with her: nor can I get much work done with the pitiful looks always fixed on me—and I am so unused to living alone keeping back perforce a great fund of animal spirits that want to break out in the shape of argument or jollification that the bottling of them in is annoying to me. Without my favorite talk about pictures or books I am good for nothing—yes for a little to be a nurse, and I pray God many times a day to keep me stiff to my duty—The 2 duties are very hard however—to work & to act as nurse too, but they get lighter daily 1st. from habit, and next because Mrs. Thack is improving though slowly indeed—for of mornings especially her spirits are curiously low, she is so absent then that I don't like to trust her. It is all stomach I believe I was such a fool as to take only 1 sitting room, and rue that silly piece of economy heartily. as for Miss Thackeray she as you may fancy does not disturb me the least—never asks questions, never tumbles down & hurts her nose, never begins to roar: but she is the life & soul of the house with her tantrums—

This next part of the letter is addressed to my dear Miss Graham as she is the only Capitalist of our family. Chapman & Hall before they give me the £100 want the security of some solvent person that their money should be reimbursed in case of my death or nonfulfilment of my contract. I asked G. M, but the old lady refused in a fright, fancying I wanted her money &c.—Now if Mary will write me a letter saying My dear William I have —— in the funds, and I shall be happy to be your security with Messrs. Chapman & Hall, in any manner they like: and if this letter is sufficient without any further documents I promise hereby to honour their draft for 100£ in case of your death, or on receiving proof of the nonfulfilment of the contract—'Messrs. C. & H may refer to Messrs. Lubbock & Co as to my respectability—' Such a document as this I say will get me 100£ in a jiffy, and please God Mary's money will not be wanted & I shan't die until the book is completed. As soon as I see myself decently in the way of making money & have had my stricture cured I will insure my life.

We have I trust escaped from a pretty kettle of fish. Mrs. Shawe who had not heard from her daughter for a month, threatened unless she were answered by return of Post to set off from Ireland and come to see her. The best of it is that her letter was delayed a couple of days in London before it was sent hither, and I am not yet certain that we shan't see her in one of the steamers—if so there will be scenes, and more nervousness on poor Isabella's part: wh[o is] low still, but has no flights such as she had during my absence, & on m[y] arrival. G. M. is angry with her for not answering when spoken [to—the poor] thing did not do this from sulkiness but from sheer absence & depression. You & Polly must not in the future be so open in your talk to Mrs. Parker, Mrs. P. repeated to Isabella just before her confinement every word you said, about her faults not doing her duty & so on, & in the course of her depression the poor thing had worked up these charges so as to fancy herself a perfect demon of wickedness—God abandoned & the juice knows what: so that all the good of your reproof was that she became perfectly miserable, & did her duty less than ever. It was an unlucky time to lecture her that's all: when she is better talk away and amen.—This is of course a secret.

Dearest Mammy this is stupid stuff & has taken several days writing. God knows I have enough on my brains just now if I do it properly. Thank God I thrive under it though, and have managed to do about £20 worth of work for the Times this fortnight, and am now deep in a Shabby Genteel Story for Fraser. I have not sent you the former numbers, because I want them to refer to. God bless you. We are all prospering. Missy as brown as a berry. Mamma well, & I just on the point of setting out to a little quiet Inn two miles off, where I have quiet, & a tea-garden to myself, as for writing here except when the folks are in bed it is impossible.

P.S. Dont you go for to take any of Mrs. Shawe's freaks & come off out of pity for me. I shd. be glad to see my dear Mammy but she wd. do more harm than good here
Direct to London

that passage in Job: Job 19: 25-27.   *Montefiore:* Sir Moses Montefiore (1784-1885), later first Baronet.   *that article abt. Mrs. Sand:* "Madame Sand and the New Apocalypse," which had appeared in the 14 and 21 September 1839 issues of *The Corsair* [New York], and was reprinted in *The Paris Sketch Book* (1840).   *my stricture:* a urethral stricture, presumably caused by a venereal infection some years earlier, that became a permanently recurring source of physical pain.   *work for the Times:* Thackeray's review, "Fielding's Works," which appeared in *The Times* on 2 September 1840.   *former numbers:* serial installments of Thackeray's "A Shabby Genteel Story" had appeared in the June, July, and August 1840 issues of *Fraser's Magazine;* the final installment was published in the October issue.

44. TO MRS. HENRY CARMICHAEL-SMYTH
10 September 1840

My dearest Mammy. Your letter arrived this morning, and dear Polly's voucher, of wh. there is however no need. I have made my arrangements with C & H, who have given me £120 down, & with this I shall be able to clear off some small scores, and carry the whole race to boot. A boat leaves London every Saturday: 3 days on the voyage, but it will do Isabella good I think, and so please God we shall all be at Cork on Tuesday. Cook goes. John remains behind to take care of the house, & let it if possible—a difficulty this dull season. When the book is done dearest Mammy we may talk about Italy or what you will: I tried C & H very hard to take an Italian book now but they would not. So we must wait.

Poor Isabella's lowness of spirits came back directly on returning to London: I think it would drive me mad to be much longer alone with it, and I am sure female companionship wd. be the best thing for her. I was thinking of writing to you, and sending my wife & bab[e]s to Boulogne but she will be well with her mother, while she is unwell—a ball: but I mean there will be no scenes and quarrels. A couple of months please God will set her up somewhat, and will suffice or nearly so for my Irish tour. The children are in famous health: and so am I only my rogue of a wife makes me melancholy. God bless you all, & thank my dear [Polly] for her letter—I'm going to send the *plate-chest* to C & H's—a kind of genteel pawn, but they seem manly straight forward people: & liberal rather than otherwise. We were not 3 weeks at Margate, & it cost £32—o Titmarsh Titmarsh why did you marry?—why for better or for worse. Let us pray God to enable us to bear either. I have lots of letters to write, & am just as dismal as possible. God bless all: the next letter please God will be from the beautiful city called Cork. I trust your India mail has brought you good news.

45. TO MRS. HENRY CARMICHAEL-SMYTH
17 September 1840

Grattan's Hill. Lower Glanmire Road. Cork.
17 September 1840.

My dearest Mother. We arrived here on Tuesday after a long horrible journey of three days and four nights that I can't think of now without shuddering. My dear wife's melancholy augmented to absolute insanity during the voyage, and I had to watch her for 3 nights (when she was positively making attempts to destroy herself,) and brought her here quite demented. She is better—a little better—just now, and the Doctor a very eminent & experienced man of these parts gives me the strongest hopes of her, and narrates 500 instances of similar maladies wh. he has cured. Mrs. Shawe says that she was herself affected with melancholy when she nursed, and a Lady has just this minute left her who was mad herself & tried to destroy herself in the same way. Jane & her mother have done my poor patient a great deal of good, We have lodgings next door, the children with their grandmother sometimes, sometimes with an old Irish nurse here who tends a number of brats of the house, fine rosy respectable children. I write this by my dear little woman's bedside, who won't permit me to leave her: but I bear up very well. Indeed & upon my honour I find myself rather relieved than otherwise now that the matter has come to a point, I can see what I never did till now that she has been deranged for several weeks past. On the day I went to Belgium she began to laugh as I went away,—she has been in this mood more or less since her confinement. Every single medical man I have met has told the same story. They say she must be treated with calmers, restoratives, plenty of food & quiet & very little diet—the dear baby thrives on the bottle as well as ever.

What my plans will be, of course I can't say—they will depend upon the recovery of the dear little woman. I am not the least cast down, or uncomfortable in mind or body.—This seems a sort of heartlessness in me, but when a matter has come to a head I feel little more anxiety concerning it—and what do you think I'm about at this minute? busy making a play wh. Charles Mathews promises to give particular attention to for Covent Garden. This I can do as I want no books for the purpose—as for Chapman & Hall they must wait. God bless all.

W M T.

Charles Mathews: (1803-78), comedian. The unidentified play was not produced.

46. TO MRS. HENRY CARMICHAEL-SMYTH
4-5 October 1840

My dearest Mammy. Your dear kind letter was of great comfort to me, for though I knew very well that you would sell your smock if need were to help me in my want, yet it is pleasant to have the testimony of it, & I have been half tempted to fling it in Mrs. Shawe's face, and say there Madam you who prate about self-sacrifices, you bragging old humbug see the way in wh. my mother welcomes your daughter, & think how you have received her yourself. But the woman is mad that is the fact or so monstrously unreasonable that it is in vain to talk reason to her, she never speaks but to brag and to lie, and doesn't know truth from falsehood.

—Alas I can't tell you that my dear woman is better—better she is in bodily health certainly, sleeping, eating, digesting better, and better she was in mind for 3 days past, but to day she has been clouded & rambling again. However when I look back to her worst days 3 weeks ago and her worst day this week, I see confidently the progress she has made and gratefully thank God for it.

Dearest Mother you don't know what she did this day 3 weeks: but as Mrs. Shawe has told it to Miss Carry Spencer, & Miss Spencer to her sister and all the gossips at Paris you must hear it. On this Sabbath day, on board the boat, the poor thing flung herself into the water (from the water-closet) & was twenty minutes floating in the sea, before the ship's boat even *saw* her. O my God what a dream it is! I hardly believe it now I write. She was found floating on her back, paddling with her hands, and had never sunk at all. This it was that told me her condition. I see now she had been ill for weeks before, and yet I was obstinately blind to her state, and Powell & the surgeons must tell me that there was not the slightest reason to call a physician, that nothing was the matter with her, that change of air wd. cure her & so on. O God what a mercy this was! I hardly remember the thing now—so sudden was it: it did not shock me at the time either. I don't know why: but it is better you should know it from me, than from any of Mrs. Spencer's gossips who might suddenly pour it out upon you at Paris.

In the next night she made fresh attempts at destruction and the first week here was always attempting to quit the bed: You may fancy what rest I had. I had a riband round her waist, & to my waist, and this always woke me if she moved. But lately she has made no sort of similar attempt, and only yesterday spoke of it in terms of the greatest remorse and sorrow, nor will she I do believe fall again into the same frightful mania. But she has for the present the greatest dread of steamers, & I fear for some time to come putting her to the risk of a voyage. There is a little boat to Cove 7 miles off. When she is better I may practice her on that: and then I must get her to Dublin, from Dublin to Liverpool by night with a dose of opium from L to London, from London to Dover, & so on. It will cost me £40 to bring them all that way: nor dare I separate her from the children: for though she does not care for them when near, she is wretched if away from them Indeed & indeed I hardly see my way at all just now. We must wait until she is [muc]h better before we venture on a move.

Monday 5: We are a little better this morning as is always the case on a sunny day. I have been for a little walk into Cork. Dan O'Connell is coming in state, a great occasion but I dare not allow myself to go from home for so long a time as 3 hours. My wife won't sit still, wont employ herself, wont do anything that she is asked & vice versâ. Mong Jew what a time of it, from four o'clock till nine this morning—as soon as ever I was asleep my lady woke me. She had had a decent slumber herself from eight until four, & when awake herself will give me no rest. Never mind as Anny says when she breaks the tumblers. The discipline is good for one's disposition if not very improving to the mind, and my health thank God is famous. The country round about is delicious: how I wish I had the time to draw some of it!: but my work now that the woman is better is just ten times more harassing than before. Poor PA must look out for a draw some day or other.   I have nearly done the 4th. act of my play—it is by no means a masterpiece, but has some good lively stuff in it I think. Three acts are already with the C. Garden people: how I shall jump if it be accepted, but that is too much luck!. I write this day to old John concerning tbe house, putting it into the hands of Messrs. Pearsall & Jorden from whom I got it. I could entertain you with some more troubles if I liked, but for this time you have enough.

I have been reading the Court Martial of poor Captain Reynolds, and that scoundrel Lord Cardigan. When are we to get rid of this insolent scum of lords altogether?—such a republican as I am becoming! but not in your way—What I want is strong government and social equality. This is stuff to write. I wish you could see Missy in the bath, such a picture of health and beauty, and our dear dear little Harriet, that I love more than the last even—the sweetest tempered little thing God ever made surely. The mother notices them but seldom. God bless you dearest Mother and all in Paris: how I wish the sea did not divide us! but pray God it won't long. Farewell: I'm in famous health & condition.

Captain Reynolds . . . Cardigan: Richard Anthony Reynolds (b. 1807), whom Thackeray had known at Charterhouse, was court-martialed in October 1840 and found guilty of insubordination because he had protested against a public slur on his character uttered by James Thomas Brudenell (1797-1868), seventh Earl of Cardigan.

47. TO EDWARD FITZGERALD
10 January 1841

Avenue Ste. Marie. Faubourg du Roule
10. January. 1841.

My dear old Edward. Your letter though it has not been answered till now gave me a great pleasure—I think your's are the only letters that were always welcome to me, for they always contain something hearty wh. makes me happier when I am happy, and consoles me when I am dull. This blow that has come upon me has played the deuce with me that is the fact, and I don't care to write to my friends and pour out lamentations wh. are all the news I have to tell. I saw my dear little woman yesterday for the first time for six weeks, since wh. time she has been at Esquirol's famous Maison de Santé. Esquirol is dead since she went there, & the place [is] conducted by his nephew, who is likewise a famous man in his profession. He says *Elle doit guérir,* and I think so too: at first she was in a fever and violent, then she was indifferent, now she is melancholy & silent and we are glad of it. She bemoans her condition and that is a great step to cure. She knows everybody and recollects things but in a stunned confused sort of way. She kissed me at first very warmly and with tears in her eyes, then she went away from me, as if she felt she was unworthy of having such a God of a husband. God help her.

My father mother and cousin are all going off to Italy in this dreadful weather, to meet a brother of the Governor's who has just come after 20 years from India—a noble fellow who adores my mother, and thinks my father the best man in the world, and has fallen in love with my cousin whom he knew when she was 4 years old, and who has fallen in love with him too as young ladies will do who are five and twenty and love letter writing. There is something very affecting in his simple admiration of her—Miss Mary writes him verses forsooth and he says 'they are the finest verses I ever read in my life' and that she must not with all her talents & accomplishments look down upon a poor illiterate soldier *grey headed* (grey headed with a dash) & 50 years' old. Then he grieves because a pair of diamond earrings that he had ordered at Delhi were not ready when he came away. Mary is a capital girl, and quite ready to jump down his throat, and so it will be a match. My poor mother is going though it breaks her heart to part with the children—and my Grandmother & I are to keep house: that is she keeps house & I live in it. Since my calamity, I have learned to love all these people a great deal more—my mother especially God bless her who has such a tender yearning big heart that I begin to cry when I think of her: and when I see her with the children, cleaving to them, am obliged to walk off for the sight is too much for me. When you read Titmarsh's letters to Miss Smith wh. I trust you will buy, as 7 1/2d out of the 2/6 will come to me—you will read a pretty incident about her and the children apropos of the Napoleon procession, I don't know what the rest of the book is scarcely for I saw no proofs and wrote as hard as I could.

Dicky Milnes is here—and I have got to like him very much almost. He is amazingly clever, and very kind-hearted he does not talk big, and if he affects to take an extraordinary degree of interest in the person before him, why it's a good affectation at any rate, and better than the common cursed indifference.

A couple of months hence I shall ask you to pay my wife's pension for a month, a heavy sum £20: but it is a comfort to have her at the very best place, and after giving her a trial there of 6 or 7 months or so, we may look out for a cheaper abode for her if it please God to keep her still ill.

As soon as I am alone with my Grandmother I intend to flare up and write a novel—about something, I don't know what yet but have a fancy for the reign of Henry V.

You must remember me very kindly to Kerrich an[d] your sister who has been so good as to like her brother['s] old friend. God bless you my dear Edward I'm writing this at the club, where a score of bawling Frenchmen are smoking and playing billiards—I don't know or speak to 1 of them, but it is very amusing to come here from time to time, and watch their ways. [. . .]

[signature cut away]

Esquirol: Jean Esquirol (1772-1840).   *Maison de Santé:* (Fr.) insane asylum. *Elle doit guérir:* (Fr.) she must be cured.   *brother:* Colonel Charles Carmichael-Smyth (1790-1870), who changed his name to Carmichael in 1842.   *Titmarsh's letters to Miss Smith:* Thackeray's *The Second Funeral of Napoleon,* which had been published in January 1841; the "pretty incident" occurs in Letter 3.   *novel . . . reign of Henry V:* Thackeray wrote almost eight chapters of "The Knights of Borsellen," which was set in fifteenth century England, but remained unfinished at his death.   *Kerrich and your sister:* John Kerrich (1798-1871), husband of the former Mary-Eleanor FitzGerald (1805-63). Edward FitzGerald was living with them in Norfolk.   *[. . .]:* the signature has been cut away.

48. TO JAMES FRASER
25 February 1841

4 Avenue Ste. Marie. Faubourg du Roule.
Paris. 25 [February] 1841.

My dear Fraser.
When I left London I was so puffed up with the success of Titmarsh, and the fine agreement I had made with Chapman & Hall, as to scorn all minor pay & thought of nothing but writing books & if I occasionally wrote for a magazine, having some immense reward for my labours.   I find however that the publishers can do without me much better than I without them, & indeed just in the midst of my pride a terrible misfortune overtook me of wh. I daresay you may have heard something, and wh., God knows, is enough to make me humble.

My little wife whom you remember so good & so gentle has lost her senses—for a while only please God for the Doctors give me strong assurances of her recovery, but in the meantime I cannot quit the neighbourhood of the place where she is, and am obliged to pay monthly very heavy sums for her care. For the first 3 months I was with her constantly myself, during that time I was so wretched that I had not the heart to write but have done something during the last 2 months, & am anxious to dispose of what I have done.

My first venture was a very unsuccessful one in the shape of the Napoleon Funeral, wh. every body has praised but nobody has bought, and I must go back to my old trade again, if my old masters have not filled up my place.

Will you receive 2 articles of mine for next month—they are both I believe very good—One on gormandizing already advertized, and another on the memoirs of Gisquet[+]—a history of Conspiracies in France during the last 10 years? If you have no fancy for me, think of my dear little wife so wretched yonder and I am sure you will lend a hand to save her. I want £20 (500 francs the price of her board) by next April. I am just going to pay my last 20£ note for her board during the month of March

Let us have a line from you immediately & burn this.

Yrs truly
W M T.

[+] the first part of this was sent to the Times, & precisely because I wanted money & because the article cost me more thought & trouble than any I had done for a long time was rejected. I am sure it is very interesting & curious

agreement . . . with Chapman & Hall: for The Irish Sketch Book. the Napoleon Funeral: The Second Funeral of Napoleon. articles: Fraser accepted both articles, "Gisquet's *Memoirs*" appearing in the May 1841 issue of *Fraser's Magazine*, and "Memorials of Gormandizing" in the June issue.

49. TO MRS. THOMAS CARLYLE
25 February 1841

4 Avenue Ste. Marie. 25 Feb

My dear Mrs. Carlyle. What shall I say to you for your kind letter? I have not had any thing so pleasant for many dismal months back, and by way of return politely enclose you three little billets for the 1d. post, begging & imploring you to stick a 1d. stamp on that for the Times. That is all my gratitude—in actions that is. I assure you in my heart I have much more. Even though you & Carlyle praise me in that outrageous way I can't help liking it, and your kind-heartedness & sympathy I love still better. A poor fellow in my case clings to such: and is glad of all the pity and good will that his friends can give him.

I left Carlyle's monstrous puff at Cavaignac's. He has not had time to take notice of it, or has been most likely carnivalizing as all Frenchmen will at this season; how your Diogenes would laugh at the rogues if he saw their mad ways of going on!.

I am very much concerned to see the death of a Captain Sterling in the paper:—is it Antony? I heartily trust not, for the sake of his good parents. Pray give my love to Mrs. Sterling when you see her. I have been hoping and praying to have good news of my own to send her, but my wife still continues in much the same state, and I am fain to look forward to the Spring, wh. will it is to be hoped bring about some change in her lamentable malady. She is not with me: but I go often to see her.

This is what I want to tell you about. The expence of her pension is exceedingly heavy, and I am casting about in all ways to raise the necessary sums. Now you have that within you Madam wh. surpasses money: viz. You can incite Sterling to get me a great puff of the reprint of the YPlush in the Times. 2 vols are fast coming out with illustrations. You can do the same with Uglo Forstero as somebody calls him. Think of nothing but puffing the book: Incite everybody: and then my dear little woman will have her pension secure.

Do not if you please now imagine that I want anything out of any body's pocket: but puffs puffs are what I desire. There has been a slight coolness between me & Fraser. I write to him with a bundle of MS.—and if Carlyle chooses to say that he hears I am in a very wretched plight wanting all the aid my friends can give me & so on, and if he adds something in the pufficatory line to poor James, I doubt not the latter will accept my bundle of papers. Another bundle goes to Bentley: and I have been occupied tooth & nail etching plates, and am inclined to do more in the same way. When Monsieur Titmarsh works in this way, be sure there is a reason for it. Confound the Times that treated him very shabbily. Amen. Dear Mrs. Carlyle, Ponder over these things in your heart, and pardon me for sending you so much about Ego: but you can do great good to Ego just now, and will I know. Soon when my work is done I will write you a letter till when believe me always gratefully yr.

W M T.

Cavaignac: Carlyle's friend Godefroy Cavaignac (1801-45), a French writer, editor, and revolutionary republican. *Diogenes:* allusion to the fourth century B. C. Greek philosopher known for his austerity and for his hostility to theorizing that was dissociated from practicality. *Antony:* Anthony Coningham Sterling (b. 1805), who actually died in 1871. He was the brother of John Sterling. *Mrs. Sterling:* Mrs. Edward Sterling. *her pension:* at Jean Esquirol's Maison de Santé at Ivry, near Paris. *reprint of the YPlush: Comic Tales and Sketches*, which included "The Yellowplush Papers," appeared in two volumes during April 1841. *Uglo Forstero:* A play on Ugolino de' Gherardeschi (d. 1289), a treacherous Italian Guelph leader who was finally overthrown, locked up in a tower with two sons and grandsons, and starved to death (see Dante's "Inferno," canto XXXIII). Forster was ugly ("Uglo") and epicurean. *Bentley:* Richard Bentley published nothing of Thackeray's during 1841. *Confound the Times:* a rather negative review of *The Second Funeral of Napoleon* had appeared in *The Times* of 19 January 1841. *Ponder . . . heart:* "But Mary kept all these things, and pondered them in her heart" *Luke* 2: 19.

50. TO MRS. BRYAN WALLER PROCTER
19 March 1841

Avenue Ste. Marie
Paris. March 19. 1841.

My dear Mrs. Procter.
 I fell into the arms of our lusty Reeve Yesterday at the Exhibition, and we agreed to dine together on Sunday—and we talked about our friends in London, and he told me how Chorley had compelled him Reeve to give up the wearing of waistcoats, and then we talked of you and Procter and I determined to send you off a little note immediately by way of apology for my last one wh. you must have thought written by a madman. Indeed it was written by a very miserable fellow who was quite unaccustomed to that kind of mood and is not a whit happier now: only he bears his little griefs more composedly. What won't a man bear with a little practice! Ruin, blindness, his legs off, dishonour, death of dearest friends, and what not. As the cares multiply + + + + , don't know whether this sentence is left unfinished because I don't know how to finish it or because it is a shame to begin such dissertations to a lady who merits more grateful treatment from one.
 What shall I tell you? last night there were at the least two hundred thousand persons of both sexes disguised in various costumes, dancing madly from ten until five this morning—as I suppose the Bishop of London did at Drury Lane when he cried out so against the French rabble. Did his Lordship dance with his apron on? It would have been a fine sight and a pretty subject for a picture. Odry says in one of the farces 'I saw a beautiful carp in the market to day and when I go next week I am determined to buy it.' I was just on the point of covering this paper with a picture of the Bishop dancing, but have put it off till next week, or till the next exhibition, or till the next time that I venture to send you a letter—Indeed I have hardly the impertinence to despatch such nonsense as this. Part of the nonsense must be laid to the account of my Grandmamma, for whom I have been cutting slices of plum-cake all the morning apropos of the marriage of my cousin, who has just taken a husband at Naples: and a very good one too: but it is very hard for a man of my dignity to be obliged to cut up plum cake, and pack it in bits of paper, and eat little

crumbs of it slyly every now & then, and to know for a certainty that I shall be unwell for having eaten it—All these things press on my mind and prevent me from writing as sensibly as otherwise under more favorable circumstances I m[ig]ht.

[Re]eve says the whole town is talking of me, & my new book—'Oho thought I they *have* found it out have they? that ballad about the Drum inspite of poor Chorley is beginning to be liked; and those Napoleon letters—well they have been a long time finding out the merit of them.' No such thing: it appears the whole town is talking about my new novel of Cecil—O just punishment of vanity!—how I wish I had written it—not for the book's sake but the filthy money's: wh. I love better than fame. The fact is I am about a wonderful romance, and oh I long for the day when the 3 volumes shall be completed. Not for the fame's sake again but for the disgusting before-mentioned consideration.

Dear Mrs. Procter, please not to read any of the foregoing part of this, but to light at once upon this conclusion wh. contains the whole cream and gist of my note, & that is I hope you are very well, I hope your husband is very well, & all the little people: and I am always

Yours most truly
W M Thackeray.

What a shame it is that I shd. send such stuff as this in answer to your letter that I keep & have read at least 10 times.

Reeve: Henry Reeve (1813-95), journalist and civil servant.   *the Bishop of London:* Charles James Blomfield (1786-1857), Bishop of London 1828-56.   *Odry:* the French actor Jacques Charles Odry (1781-1853).   *marriage of my cousin:* Mary Graham, who married Colonel Charles Carmichael-Smyth in Naples on 4 March 1841.   *ballad about the Drum:* "The Chronicle of the Drum," which was appended to *The Second Funeral of Napoleon.*   *my new novel of Cecil:* a recent novel published anonymously by Mrs. Catherine Gore (1799-1861).   *a wonderful romance:* "The Knights of Borsellen."

51. TO MRS. THOMAS CARLYLE
20 March 1841

Paris March 20. 1841.

My dear Mrs. Carlyle.
       Yesterday I was at the French Exhibition where I met honest Reeve with a budget of news from London, and saw a huge picture

say 60 feet by 80 representing a subject with wh. Mr. Carlyle is familiar, namely the Sinking of the Vengeur a French ship wh. went down with colours flying and guns roaring in the teeth of the English fleet under the command of the Duke of Clarence. Captain Renaudin is not represented eating mutton-pie as some disgusting envious English writers have hinted he did: but as the picture has not been purchased by the Govt., I thought it best to lay out a small sum and have it for Carlyle. Be good enough to build a house in your garden for its reception.

I told some Frenchmen (it is pleasant to vex the scoundrels) that the Vengeur business was what a mediocre English historian has vulgarly denominated a blague: and that Renaudins letters & what not had been published. And what do you think was the reply of the Frenchmen? They laughed at me with good-humoured incredulity, & said that I must pardon them for declining upon my simple word to believe a fact consecrated in history and that as for Renaudin's letter that was easily disposed of—it was a forgery. Present my compliments to your husband upon this, wh. may appear in a third edition of the F. R.

Your republican friend has never taken a bit of notice of Carlyle's recommendatory letter. I think he was right the praise was so powerful, that he must have wondered at a man having the face to present himself with such a document in his hand. Well, somehow, in spite of this neglect the world wags & your humble Servt. is neither more happy nor more miserable than before.

Please to give my love to Mrs. Sterling and tell her that my dear little wife is only very very little better. It will be a long long while I fear ere she be restored to me. Pray God for the time for I am a great deal more unhappy without her, than I ever thought it was in my nature to be. The illness greatly disarranges my plans, or rather prevents me from forming any until it shall settle one way or another. She is not near bad enough for me to suppose that cure is impossible nor well enough that I may have her with the children. Poor Fraser wrote me a most kind affectionate letter in reply to the 1 I sent through you: and I have furnished him & Bentley with stuff enough to keep my dear little woman where she is for 3 months to come. Meanwhile I am working at something that I hope will turn out better than poor Napoleon a sad failure; and live in clover royally with a good old grand mother who keeps me & the children. What a blessing it is in these distresses to find how many friends one has!—Every body has a kind word & a helping hand for me: so God bless every body say I.

O Donnel wrote me word that you had been good to him, and that he met at your house a Mr. Forster whom he thought 'a heavy man' Good heavens to think that light airy graceful fantastical creature a heavy man!. My friend O'D is one of the sort: but a noble high-principled fellow of a sumptuous generosity of disposition that I value much more than brains. You will have found out the first part of his character, this is to warn you of the rest.

  Yellowplush's republication has been delayed by the accursed dilatoriness & clumsiness of the copper-plate printers here, who spoiled half the work that I was obliged to do again. You will recognize that is I hope you will among the pictures in the book the dear image of Bullwig; wh fond Memory has traced. I hope successfully. Good bye dear Mrs. Carlyle. It is very pleasant to me to think of such good friends as you and your husband are to me. How I wish I could put you to the test of keeping or breaking your promise about that pipe in the garden.

W M T.

Sinking of the Vengeur: the captain and crew of the *Vengeur,* a French ship sunk by the British, had been glorified by the French press for choosing to go down with their ship instead of surrendering. Accordingly Carlyle, in the first edition of *The French Revolution* (1837), had used the incident to symbolize the unconquerable in man, only to discover that the reports of a heroic refusal to surrender were false. Accordingly, Carlyle had to modify his account in the second edition (1839). *Duke of Clarence:* William Henry, Duke of Clarence, later William IV (1830-37). *blague:* (Fr.) humbug—Carlyle's term for the French glorification. *Your republican friend:* Godefroy Cavaignac. *O'Donnel:* Arnout O'Donnel (b. 1804), Irish journalist. *Bullwig:* Bulwer, a frequent subject of Thackeray's satire, who appears as one of "The two celebrated literary characters at Sir John's," in "Mr. Yellowplush's Ajew," *Comic Tales and Sketches,* opposite 1: 245.

52. TO MRS. BRYAN WALLER PROCTER
5 April 1841

Avenue Ste. Marie 4. Fbg du Roule.
April 5. 1841.

My dear Mrs. Procter. All this week I have been thinking of your kind letter: and indeed last Monday it was a very near chance indeed that I did not bounce off by the Coach and take you and Procter at your word, and absorb ink and other liquors wh. he tempts me with—Indeed it would have been very pleasant to look out in that little green garden of yours, and see how Miss Nanny has grown, and admire the pear-blossoms (Leigh-Huntish this) and then admire Procter asleep on the Sofa, and then think what a wonderful good dinner I had had, and then talk in a certain agreeable jocose, sneering, good-humoured, scandalous, sentimental sort of way, with a certain lady that makes the best tea and the best jokes in the world—O but it would have been a pleasant holiday for a poor devil, like your humble Servant, who nevertheless heartily thanks God that he never took any such thing.

For instead of going to London, I went to see my dear little patient at Ivry, and as the Doctors there honestly confessed that they could do nothing for her, determined to try—what? the medicine that is administered in the Opera of the Elisire d'Amore: and off I took the little woman a pleasant walk across the fields to a pleasant little gudgeon house on the river, where we had a dinner and she took 2 glasses of the Elixir wh. I devoted myself to finish. It did her a great deal of good & made her eyes sparkle, and actually for the first time these 6 months the poor little woman, flung herself into my arms with all her heart and gave me a kiss

At wh. moment of course the waiter burst in.

This only served to mend matters for the lady went off in a peal of laughter the first these six months again; and since then I have had her at home not well, nor nearly well, but a hundred times better than she was this day week: when I got your letter, wh. made me think of going to London, wh. proved to me that I ought to go to Ivry, wh. induced me to try the experiment of the champagne, wh. caused my wife to give me a kiss, wh. brought the waiter into the room, wh. made my wife laugh, like the Princess Badroulboudour and so on—I told the waiter the circumstances of the case: and that the caress to wh. he had been privy was one that although it would not probably have been given had I been aware that his eye was at the keyhole, was still an embrace authorized nay enjoined by the strictest regulations of morality. The beast did not believe a word of the story but what care I?. Only let her get well, and I shall be the happiest man in the world. Ye Gods how I will venerate Champagne—I always did.

You see now dear Mr. & Mrs. P. why it is impossible that I should accept your polite invitation—Indeed it was a great deal more than polite it was very [. . .] and kind and friendly; and there is a remark Madam wh. you will allow me to intrude upon you wh. is that it is almost worth a man's while to be downcast and unhappy for a time that he may get his friends' kindness & sympathy. He relishes it so; and I think the liking for it remains afterwards: at least now I feel 100 Per cent happier than when I got your offer, and enjoy it really as much almost as if I had accepted it—

Goodbye dear Mrs. Procter and believe me always

Most truly yours & Procter's
W M T.

As economy is the order of the day, and it is always cheap to spunge on one's friends will you please to put a 1d. stamp on the enclosed and send it on its way? It seems a sin to tempt Providence and throw away 1/7d for the benefit of two rascally Governments that we cannot care a farthing for.

Miss Nanny: Adelaide Ann Procter (1825-64), their daughter, later a poetess.
Elisire d'Amore: The Elixir of Love (1832), by Gaetano Donizetti (1797-1848).
Princess Badroulboudour: daughter of the Sultan of China and wife of Aladdin in the *Arabian Nights' Entertainment.*

53. TO MRS. BRYAN WALLER PROCTER
28 May - 5 June 1841

Avenue Ste. Marie—Fbg du Roule.
28 May. 41 that is 5 June.

My dear Mrs. Procter.
   Please when you write not to give me any accounts whatever of any gaieties in wh. you indulge, or of any sort of happiness falling to the share of you or any one else. But if any body meets with an accident: is arrested, ruined, has a wife run away with, if Chorley falls ill and is marked with the small pox, do be so kind as to write me off word immediately, and I will pay the post cheerfully. The only welcome intelligence in your letter is that the Austins have lost a good deal of money, and Procter 1100£. Ah say I he takes guinea-stalls and buys water-colours does he? Well well, we shall have him down as one of us soon: in the slough of despair—Despair Madam is the word—Byronism—I hate mankind, and wear my shirt collars turned down.
   Now absurd as this seems on the part of a man naturally I believe kind-hearted: there is upon my word & honour a kind of truth in it. When I hear of bad luck happening to people I *am* glad that's the fact: and I am sure that the generosity or kindness with wh. one endeavours sometimes [to] relieve a man that has fallen into misfortune, is often the result of one's own personal good spirits and gratification at the contrast between the sufferer and ones' self.
   Is not that a turning down of shirt-collars with a vengeance? and a pretty return of for what I know is sincere sympathy and good will on your part? But let me declare solemnly and with my hand on my waistcoat (it is a great deal too hot to wear one by the way, so let us say at once like Knowles 'on me hearrrrt[']) That I dont mean to accuse the bo sex of any unworthy feeling of the sort. You are not selfish like us brutes but always kind and feeling for poor fellows in the days of their ill luck. As a proof, did not 2 old ladies toil up to this

distant quarter the other day, two old ladies one of them lame, and the thermometer at 85 for both of them, out of sheer kindness and pity for my situation? Men will not perform any such sacrifices—only 1 has called upon me in the eight months we have been here: and he came for some purpose of his own.   As for my misfortunes they are not so great as they seem: no man can afford to be miserable for nine months together at the illness of a person ever so dear to him. We get indifferent that's certain: & if bound to remain with the sick person constantly, profoundly ennuyé. For abt. six weeks I was my wife's sole attendant, and almost broke down under the slavery:—well, a woman whom I have hired to do that work, does it with the utmost cheerfulness for 10 francs a week, and never thinks about being miserable at all.

My wife will get well I hope and believe: perhaps not for a year perhaps in a month. There is nothing the matter with her except perfect indifference silence & sluggishness. She cares for nothing except for me a little. her general health has greatly improved: her ideas are quite distinct when she chooses to wake from her lethargy. She is not unhappy, and looks fresh, smiling and about 16 years old. to day is her little baby's birth-day. She kissed the child when I told her of the circumstance, but does not care for it.

You have seen a great deal more of Maddle Rachel in a week than I have often as I have been here: the only time I ever saw [her] was once with Milnes in an atrocious piece called Marie Stuart: She made the most however of that unfortunate but deservedly decapitated Sovereign.   this week (for the first time these 6 months[)] I determined to try and amuse myself at the play, and paid twenty five sous like a man to the pit, to see Madlle. Dejazet.

This young creature who is neither so innocent nor so good looking as Vestris, but on the other hand incomparably older & cleverer chose to act the part of a young girl of sixteen, in a little muslin frock & pinafore, with trowsers and long braided hair like the Misses Kenwigs; when this hideous leering grinning withered old painted simpering wretch came forward, do you know I was seized with such a qualm as to shout out 'Why—she is too ugly,' and I was obliged to stride over 10000 people in a most crowded pit in order to get rid of the sight of her. Is it that one is growing moral? par hazard in one's declining years, or only more difficult? There were hundreds of people in the house perfectly satisfied and charmed: nay many young wicked fellows casting I have no doubt eyes of fire towards this hideous old grinning wretch. Ah happy days of Youth! I once knew a man who was in love with Mrs. Vedy:—that female Methusalem or let one say at once that Methusalemess, who leads the festive dance at Covent Garden—

What delights me beyond measure is the Controversy between Macready and Heraud in the Monthly Magazine. It is a wonderful Magazine: and the Editor a man of a noble madness and dullness.

Thank you about Peter Priggins. O but a man has a good lesson sometimes for his naughty pride and vanity. I read the book the other day: and I declare was quite awe stricken by the immense vulgarity of it. I know I am not very genteel—indeed Fraser's head shopman says 'Mr. T is a man of talent but every thing he does is so atrociously vulgar'—very good, but is it as vulgar as Peter Priggins? I declare I don't think so.—I fancy I could not be if I tried: from lack of a great quality that Peter has like his Editor Theodore Hook, of admiring certain things that are essentially mean & low. There is one sentiment in Priggins that I cant express sufft. admiration of. It is said of Some young fellow who has been drunk all night and all the morning and all the day before (indeed the book is filled from beginning to end with drunkenness)—As for Tom, says Peter 'GOOD beer *always* made him sober.' Do you see the immensity of the sentiment? I never can hope to think about beer in that way, that awful, respectful way. BEER what an immense word, what a grand coarseness about it! Ah but I should like to drink some—some Hodson's pale ale, in neat little frisky bottles, uncorked by a neat-handed Phillis in a sunshiny parlour, where I have had before this some of the pleasantest gayest comfortablest dinners in the world. the parlor I mean, belongs to a Gothic Cottage near the Roman-Catholic chapel in the Regent's Park—and the master of the house often goes to sleep after dinner. Well, I am really sorry now that he has lost his money: having arrived at good humour by writing six pages of nonsense, and thinking about all the kindness and pleasure I have had from you. (I find I have been writing on a torn 1/2 sheet of paper) Will you pardon me for taking such liberties in writing on torn smoke-smelling paper, and not addressing you in a more respectuous and well-bred way?. A genteeler soul wd. never have dared to allude to Hodson's ale, in writing a letter to a lady: at the very most I know Chorley would not have hinted at anything beyond Maraschino, or allowed that he cared for aught except a pleasant conversation, & a dish of green tea

I have to ask another pardon too for introducing my friend O'Donnel to you. He is one of the best friends I have but a man extremely uncouth, and matteroffactish and going to your house I think that both you & he will feel that he is out of place, so indeed I had no business to take such a liberty as to give him credentials. But he heard me discoursing about the pleasantness of your hospitality, and asked me for a letter, as he is going to be quite alone in London. You won't like him, and I knew it when I wrote: but did not dare say so to him, and so committed upon you who have no means of resisting or resenting a still greater *bévue*. He has a thousand of the very best qualities but not the most necessary one of being pleasant. Why had I not the sense to say No to him at once?. Alfred Tennyson if he can't make you like him will make you admire him—he seems to me to have the cachet of a great man, his conversation is often delightful I think, full of breadth, manliness and humour: he reads all sorts of things, swallows them and digests them like a great poetical boa-constrictor as he is. Now I hope Mrs. Procter you will recollect that if your humble servant sneers at small geniuses, he has on the contrary a huge respect for big ones: or those he fancies to be such. Perhaps it is Alfred Tennyson's great big yellow face, and growling voice that has had an impression upon me. Manliness and simplicity of manner go a great way with me I fancy: there is a man here for instance, whom on the strength of a great pair of eyebrows and a good manner, and a dexterous silence, I have persisted in considering as a man of genius or near it, for these ten years past, and am only and with a great deal of pain beginning to be undeceived.

Was ever such a dirty piece of paper seen: or such a stupid letter full of nonsensical egotisms?. The fact is for the dingy state of the paper: I have only got a little table 3 feet by 2: and on this are a bundle of manuscripts a bottle of ink that will upset, a paint box, and water: several dry lumps of bread for rubbing out with: portfolios, drawings segars, sealing-wax the whole of my menage—and so sure as this letter is discontinued for a moment, so sure does it tumble into a puddle of ink, or another of water, or into a heap of ashes. Well I have not the courage to clean the table nor indeed to do any thing else, for I have had 10 months of wretchedness, and truth to tell am quite beaten down. I don't know when I shall come round again—not until I get a holiday, and that mayn't be for months to come: my father and mother being away in Italy, and who knows when they will come back. Meanwhile I can't work, nor write even amusing letters, nor talk of anything else but myself wh. is bearable sometimes when Ego is in very good health and spirits, but odious beyond measure when he has only to entertain you with his woes.

Yesterday I had a delightful walk with a painter from [. . .] to Saint Germain, through charming smiling countries that seem to be hundreds of leagues away from cities:—psha—this sentence was begun with a laudable intent of relieving you from the wearisome complaints of the last paragraphs but it is in vain. Allow me then dear Mrs. Procter to shut up the scrawl altogether, and to give a loose to dullness in privacy—it cant be enjoyed properly in company. In spite of wh. I am always yours and Procter's most truly,

W M T.

Knowles: the actor and playwright James Sheridan Knowles (1784-1862). *ennuyé:* (Fr.) bored. *Rachel:* the stage name of the tragedienne, Eliza Félix (1821-58). *Marie Stuart:* a French version of Schiller's *Maria Stuart*. *Dejazet:* the actress, Pauline Virginie Déjazet (1797-1875). *Vestris:* the operatic contralto Lucia Elizabeth (née Mathews) Vestris (1797-1856). *the Misses Kenwigs:* in Chapter 14 of Dickens' *Nicholas Nickleby* (1838-39). *par hazard:* (Fr.) by chance. *Macready:* William Charles Macready (1793-1873), actor and stage-manager. *Heraud:* John Abraham Heraud (1799-1887), editor of *The New Monthly Magazine* 1839-42. *Peter Priggins:* a novel written by J. T. J. Hewlett and edited by Theodore Hook (1788-1841) that appeared in 1841. *neat-handed Phyllis:* Milton, *L'Allegro*, ll. 84-85: "Of herbs, and other country messes, / Which the neat-handed Phyllis dresses." *bévue:* (Fr.) blunder. *[. . .]:* the original is torn at this point.

54. TO RICHARD BENTLEY
1 June 1841

Dear Bentley.
      Have the goodness to give my MS. of the Diamond to my friend Mr. Cunningham—I can't get any answer about it from you good bad or indifferent, & next time your obedient Servant sends you an article you may set him down without fail to be you understand what

Yrs & whatdyecallem
W M Thackeray.

the Diamond: "The History of Samuel Titmarsh and the Great Hoggarty Diamond" was written during January and February 1841 and was published in the September-December 1841 issues of *Fraser's Magazine*. *Cunningham:* Hugh Cunningham, who published Thackeray's *The Paris Sketch Book* (under the imprint of the deceased John Macrone) in July 1840, *The Second Funeral of Napoleon* in January 1841, and *Comic Tales and Sketches* in April 1841.

55. DIARY
27 July - 11 August 1841

Oh Lord God—there is not one of the sorrows or disappointments of my life, that as I fancy I cannot trace to some error crime or weakness of my disposition. Strengthen me then with your help, to maintain my good resolutions—not to yield to lust or sloth that beset me: or at least to combat with them & overcome them sometimes.

Above all O Gracious Father, please to have mercy upon those whose well-being depends upon me. O empower me to give them good and honest example: keep them out of misfortunes wh. result from my fault: and towards them enable me to discharge the private duties of life—to be interested in their ways & amusements, to be cheerful & constant at home: frugal & orderly if possible. O give me your help strenuously to work out the vices of character wh. have born such bitter fruits already:

July 27. Arrived this morng from Boulogne outside very crowded & uncomfortable. Found the wife very glad to see me, and the dear little ones very well & happy. Thank God for the kindness of those who have stood in such good stead by them. Mother's letter about Graeffenberg came wh. I answered, and after going in quest of diligence fares &c found a hydropathic physician who spoke very well indeed abt. Isabella's case. She passed the evening at the Spencer's whither I went in search of her, after paying a visit to our friends upstairs. My heart feels very humble & thankful for God's kindness towards these beautiful children, and I do heartily pray that I may be kept in a mood for seriously considering & trying to act up to my duty. How much would my powers of mind alone gain from something like regularity, & how determinedly ought I to strive to win it!

July 28. My wife I fancy a little better—certainly better—very little feeling, but a little memory and justness of speech. Drew all the morning or else read Marriotts Joseph Rushbrook a good natured manly sort of book—walked with I to the Rue de Londres & back again, by the Parc of Monsieaux that looks green & pretty, & on the plain of Menceaux, hearing the steam-engines.

After dinner talked to her, and read article on Bowes' election—found in my portfolio an article written 2 months ago, of wh. the existence was completely forgotten, & so saw more & more the utility of keeping some memorandum. Wrote till 12: and thought of a good plan for some weekly-paper articles—skits on newspaper paragraphs for the week.

Mem. remember Punch's Parliament.

The children all day delightful. O God, O God give me strength to do my duty

Thursday 29. Did nothing all day until 3 except try to make a burlesque sonnet. Recd. Dr. Reich & a gentleman who came about Eliza's character. Anny went with Mrs. Spencer to see the fête. At 2 went to read the papers, and at 3 by the railroad to St. Germains where the good Crowes had a kind dinner for us.   Read Mathilde, the extreme fashionableness of wh. will form a good subject for imitation. In the Gazette des Tribunaux an excellent acct. of a man converted from Protestantism recd. with open arms by all sorts of monk-houses and robbing each. O'D at St. Germains much better than in London— came back with him at 10/11,—the lamps of the Arc d'Etoile seen flaring bright most part of the way.

August 6. The first two or three of these days past in writing or idling of a morning, & carousing of an evening with Stevens. More letters from my mother relative to the Sudopathic plan: and I have had a couple of interviews with Dr. Weincke a clever personable man, but whose system is frightfully complicated. We began it on Thursday morning my wife sweating for 4 hours. The same to day, and baths and walks afterwards occupying the greater part of the day. On Tuesday she was pretty well, the next day exceedingly violent so much so that I was compelled to remain with her from then until now.

Read in the paper the news of Mrs. Blechynden's death. It is the sorest point I have on my conscience never to have taken notice of her.

Read a novel of Emile Souvestre; no good except in the beginning, and sent off to day Friday the article on the S. D. Election. The Morning Post very flattering to Men & Coats.

11. My mother's letters have at last had their effect and we are now bound for Germany. These days have been spent in passport-hunting & other such preparations: pray Heaven that the treatment may be beneficial.

After her violence my wife is considerably better—Looked over in these days the letters from Belgium that I had written last year at this time—& found as usual, that I had clean forgotten them. They came upon me quite as strange compositions, and seemed clever and amusing. Such a complete want of memory have I, that even an election-squib written at Bowes's had passed clean out of my mind— The more necessity then for keeping a journal of all doings, writings, & readings. [. . .]

[27 July] *Graeffenberg:* site of a Silesian hydrotherapic sanatorium.   [28 July] *Marriott:* Captain Frederick Marryat (1792-1848), whose novel, *Joseph Rushbrook or the Poacher* had recently been published.   *Bowes:* John Bowes Bowes (1815-85), whom Thackeray had met at Trinity College, Cambridge, and whom he assisted during the general election of July 1841, when Bowes was returned as M. P. for South Durham.   [29 July] *Mathilde:* a recent novel by Eugène Sue (1804-75).   [6 Aug.] *Stevens:* Augustus Stevens, a Parisian dentist.   *Mrs. Blechynden:* Richmond Thackeray's illegitimate daughter (b. 1804), who had died in India on 15 May 1841.   *Souvestre:* Émile Souvestre (1806-54), whose most recent novel was *Mémoires d'un sans-culotte bas-breton.*   *article on the S. D. Election:* Thackeray's "Notes on the North What-d'ye-callem Election," which appeared in the September and October 1841 issues of *Fraser's Magazine.*   *Men & Coats:* an article of Thackeray's published in the August 1841 issue of *Fraser's Magazine* .   [11 Aug.] *election-squib:* Thackeray's "The Firebrand Correspondence."

56. TO GEORGE WILLIAM NICKISSON
7 August 1841

Sunday 7. August.

Dear Nickison

I sent a parcel to you yesterday per Coach containing an article that will go into 2 Nos of the Magazine.

Will you send the proofs of it and the Hoggarty Diamond to my friend Chas Cole Esqre. Record Officer WhiteHall, & beg him to correct the proofs, for my sake.

My wife is in a shocking state of health, and I am going in a sort of desperation to a German Quack on the Rhine, who says he thinks he can help her. My father & mother are there and will give me some comfort.—God knows I want it.

I have just received Fraser's letter—wh. has very much affected me. Send my kindest remembrances to him. I do heartily hope and pray to see the kind-hearted fellow once again, and trust that he may yet rally.

Truly yrs
W M Thackeray.

I go tomorrow Monday
My address next week will be
Marienburg
Boppard

Nickison: George William Nickisson, who did editorial work for *Fraser's Magazine.* *an article:* "Notes on the North What-d'ye-callem Election." *Cole:* Charles Augustus Cole (1819-87), a clerk in the Public Record Office. He was the youngest brother of Henry Cole.   *Fraser ... rally:* Fraser died in October 1841.

57. TO MRS. JOHN RITCHIE
19 August 1841

Thursday. 19 August.

My dear Aunt.
       You will see by this address to what an out of the way place I have brought my poor little patient. It is however one of the most beautiful places in the world, a fine air, and a kind of genteel hospital set up for the cure of almost all complaints by means of sweating & cold water. Gouts & rheumatisms & other inflammatory ills go off here as if by magic. People begin at four o'clock in the morning to be wrapped up in blankets, where they lie & melt for four hours, then come Shower-baths, plunging baths, hip-baths, all sorts of water taken within & without, and at the end of a certain number of months: they rise up & walk. I have a strong hope that under this strange regimen my dear little patient will recover her reason.   My mother is here whose presence is the greatest possible comfort to me, and with her for a short time my cousin with her husband Charles Smyth. They are 2 of the noblest people God ever made: and are as generous as I ever knew people—they have given me 500£, wh. with 500£ more that just falls into me through the death of poor Mrs. Blechynden, puts me out of the reach of fortune for some years to come, and removes the horrible care and fear of want wh. has been hanging over me in the past year since my wife's affliction.
       When I wrote to you about money matters last September, you may remember I said I never should have applied to Mr. Ritchie, except at the last extremity, and here thank God that extremity is removed, and with it, not the least painful of the many painful necessities that have oppressed me in this unhappy year: so that now at any rate I shall be able when I come to London, not to sneak away from the dearest friends I have in it. God bless them all. What a deal of care has this generosity of Mary Smyth's removed from me!
       My uncle Charles Thackeray wrote me from Calcutta, begging me to continue if possible the annuity Mrs. Blechynden had. I shall make arrangement; but it is not fair I think that the daughter shd. have as much as was allotted for the support of daughter & mother, and I hope my Aunt Halliday will help in supporting her brothers

grandchild. She is rich I believe, at least has a handsome income—and no one at any rate can say as much for me—

My dear little wife is just stepped out of half an hour's ice-cold hip bath, and is smiling and looking very comfortable, *warm & sensible*. She says I am to remember her most kindly to you, and sends her love to Charlotte & Jane—and now as it's time to take her half an hour's brisk walk wh. always follows the bath, I shall shut this letter up, and am always dear Aunt, yours most affectionately

W M Thackeray.

this address: Thackeray provides no address. He was writing from a sanatorium near Boppard on the Rhine. *uncle Charles Thackeray:* (1794-1846?), a Calcutta barrister.

58. TO EDWARD FITZGERALD
13 September-October 1841

Heidelberg. October something. 1841.
My dear Edward I wonder whether I shall ever be able to fill this enormous sheet of paper. You must know it has just been brought to me by a fat landlord in a conical cap, along with a pint of very sour  wine, and if I have made his eyebrows very queer, it is not because I wish to persist in that old wicked trick of making queer eyebrows but because nature has given him such a pair, and how can I help it?. I wonder where my dear old Edward is at this writing—it's half a year nearly since I heard from you. I am writing in an arbour of an inn at Boppart on the Rhine, where I have been for a month with my poor little woman, under the care of a famous water-doctor in these parts, who cures everything by means of sweating, & bathing. At five o'clock in the morning Mrs. Thack begins to sweat in blankets, at eight they pour buckets of water over her, at twelve she takes an enormous douche for five minutes, at five sweating again, and more buckets of ice-cold water. Well, she has been doing this for a month and the upshot is that she is so extraordinarily better, that I do begin to think we are at last to have her well. She *is* in fact all but well, and at last, thank God for it, laughs talks and is happy. It is this day year that her malady declared itself first: and though she is not yet quite like other people, yet when I remember how bad she has been, and was but a month ago, my dear

old fellow I am ready to jump for joy. The first days she would not stand the immense sluicing of the water-pipe, and I was obliged to go in with her. It would have made a fine picture—Mrs. Thack in the condition of our first parins, before they took to eating apples, and the great Titmarsh with nothing on but a petticoat lent him by his mother, and far too scanty to cover that immense posterior protuberance with wh. nature has furnished him. I'm the contrary of a cherubim that's the fact. This is rare witty stuff to write isn't it?—Well I have nothing else to say—and am really with all the year's sufferings quite used up. When my wife is well she must set to work & take care of me I think. My father & mother are here, and the latter as you may fancy an immense comfort to me. God bless the dear old tender loving soul—it's worth while to be unhappy for a time, to find how such admirable creatures tend and suffer with one. The Governor though by Heaven's blessing perfectly well, nevertheless for the love of science gets up every morning at four, sweats for 4 hours, douches, forswears wine at dinner, douches again, and concludes the day's amusements by sitting for nearly an hour in a tub of icy-cold water. In the last twenty years he has been successively a convert to Abernethy's blue-pills, of wh. he swallowed pounds—to Morison's ditto, wh. he flung in by spoonsful to St John Long to whom he paid 100 guineas for rubbing an immense sore on & then off his back, to Homeopathy wh. put the nose of all other systems of medicine out of joint, and finally to Hydrosudopathy—agst wh. dont let me say a word. It has been the means of setting my dear little wife in her senses again.

Here comes the landlord with his eyebrows, and his two daughters to take their supper in the arbour—I wish that my Ned, were here in his stead reposing his head, underneath the grape vine; and in spite of the fleas (most annoying are these) here taking his ease, on the Banks of the Rhine. Here are gardens and bowers, here are churches & towers, wh. I copy for hours, in a sketchbook so fine—Thick orchards one sees, & Plantations of Peas, But be hanged to the fleas on the Banks of the Rhine. You can't though you try, see a cloud in the sky, but only can spy the sun in his shine, or the moon through the trees, like a round Cheshire cheese, illumines the fleas on the Banks of the Rhine. Ah here could I spend, a time without end, by the side of my friend that best friend of mine.

I forget what it was that stopped the impromptu—I couldn't get on with it most likely, and it was written in grand summer weather near a month ago. Since then I haven't been fit to write: my wife not so well: quite as reasonable but excessively violent & passionate wh. the Doctors say is a good sign. Well it worked upon me very much, & a week ago I was obliged to go away, thinking that a tour might do me good, but no such thing: I am now on the tour, as miserable as the deuce and if I write to you it's because I want to take refuge from cursed loneliness & low spirits Thanks for your letter my dear old man, the sight of your hand writing is always a comfort to me—My God, how I wish I had you to be with me. Will you go to Italy with me & my wife this winter?. If you will, I'll go: if not I must go back to Paris, and shall set upon a novel of wh. I have an idea: a famous good plan if I can but keep my tail sufficiently up: but I have no amusement at Paris, nobody to talk to, and home, I am very ashamed to confess bores me. There is that stupid old Governor of mine: we are always on the point of quarreling, though we never do. He is a worthy man however, & the dear old Mother an angel of a woman.

I have written the first act of—a tragedy, of all things in the world: and in blank verse too for Macready [to] spout. I wish I might put it in prose the subject is very good.[. . .]

Ah what a pleasure it would be to have you & old Morton, and jaw about the Fine Arts. I wanted to go to Munich, and see the modern Germans, for the purpose of exposing them; but haven't the heart, & am just going back again, to the poor little wife. If you won't come to Italy will you come to Paris for the winter?. I have another long weary winter before me. Pish. Psha. Fiddledeedee & nonsense. I've made much improvement in sketching: & have done 1 or 2 walnut trees to admiration—it's nothing but practice, and care. This is the very last model of my favorite German Student He has adopted a little of the

French fashions of late as I see with pain. I'm quite of your opinion about Farquhar, he's the only fellow among them. [He was] something more than a mere comic tradesman: and has a grand drunken diabolical fire in him.

What I have seen of the German illuminated School is donkeyism —poor *precieuse* stuff, with a sickening sanctified air. Here's the paper filled up, & it still wants 1/2 an hour of the coach. What shall I say?— Yes—I saw Fanny Buttler, & Adelaide K at Frankfurt A. looking very well: but Fanny I did not even know, she was changed so—as dirty as a housemaid, and in a housemaid's costume. She won't forgive me for not knowing her, & would hardly speak to me in consquints. Ah Yellowplush! where are the days when you lived & laughed. If I don't mind I shall be setting up for an unacknowledged genius, & turn as morbid as Bulwer. God bless you.

Direct if within a fortnight to Marienberg. Boppart. Rhine.

this day year: 13 September 1840. *St John Long:* a fashionable quack doctor who treated patients by rubbing them. *a novel:* presumably *Barry Lyndon*.

[. . .]: a portion of the letter is missing.   *Farquhar:* George Farquhar (1678-1707), dramatist.   *German illuminated School:* the "Nazarenes," notably Johann Friedrich Overbeck (1789-1869) and Peter von Cornelius (1783-1867).   *Adelaide K:* Adelaide Kemble (1814?-79), later Sartoris, soprano, the sister of Fanny Kemble Butler.

59. TO EDWARD FITZGERALD
9 March 1842

9 March. 1842

My dear Edward. Indeed I ought to have written long ago: but have been hard at work ever since I came back, and out of working times hating the sight of a pen—Thank you for your letter. The poor little woman is getting better & better—much better since I parted from her, wh. I was obliged to do on returning for she was past my management. She is close by at Chaillot, perfectly happy, obedient and reasonable. I see her of course continually—but it makes my heart sick to be parted from her; and every now and then turns up something, some reminiscence of old times or some simple thing wh. she says, & wh. knocks me quite down; and makes me cry like a child. I get melancholy too being with the children, they are not half the children without their mother—A man's grief is very selfish certainly, and it's our comforts we mourn.

Well it is probable I should have talked to you of something more amusing, but for a cursed headache wh. prevents me from working to any advantage, and so you get the refuse. I began a letter some time back that was lugubrious too, for I was very much shocked with reading in an old Galignani the result of that fatal Niger Expedition, and thought of that kind gentle sister of your's suffering & being unhappy. By Jove what a lucky fellow Kerrich is to have a wife and a great family and a chance to give all his affections full play. I hope your sister will be with him a good deal, his cheerful house will be the best consoler

What have I been doing—writing articles &c and have been to the play a good deal: it is always sure to be pleasant here. It is a great comfort to be able to like the theatre once again, and be amused by little sparkling frisky pieces. Yesterday I had a ticket to hear what they call a Stabat Mater by Rossini wh. is here making a great noise. It is very beautiful, there are 10 concerted pieces, Tamburini especially admirable, and to crown all a very good box. So I stayed away and dined off cold beef & soupe maigre, with my friend Collignon the artist, & his wife who is charming. Such a little active innocent smiling kindly creature. He a very clever fellow out of his profession, and sometimes in it, but not often. Au reste the loyalest stanchest man possible: it is quite fine to see him and his wife breasting poverty together, and indeed their soupe maigre is admirable.   What stuff and nonsense this is to write to you. I have read no novels or good books to talk of, but scores of volumes of history, in the most owllike solemn way, and by way of amusement Victor Hugo's new book on the Rhine. He is very great, and writes like a God Almighty.—about this book I've been trying to write to day & only squeezed out one lousy page.

   He says some fine things—wiz looking at the stars, he says that the night is as it were the normal colour of heaven—There is something awful in it—a dark-blue eternity glittering all over with silent watchful stars. Is it nonsense or the contrary?. I know what Venables wd. say: that the dark blue is all gammon, being an optical effect & so on—but still it's rather awful, and I feel certain that time & space are dark blue. Of course calling to mind the well-known passage of the Sacred Writer of Putney—'the old bl— b—b—y, the old pl— th—ric & w—nt—n st—r.['] What you say of the Scoundrel Yates, next, naturally comes into my thoughts—there is something awful about him too. Gracious God what a stupendous impudence! He is a fellow who would put his hands up the petticoats of an angel. I have had several distinct laughs over the Cyprian Courtezans & the pas seductif. One can see it, and that enormous Yates leering at the side-scene. I wish I had known it last month, when in a very dull paper about a piece called Nicholas Nickl[eby] of course I fell to thinking of him as Mantalini.—This was written (that is not this, but the last sentence) full ten minutes ago—ever since I have been thinking of Yates—are you doing so now at the present moment?. Tis midnight, the wind is banging and bursting doors and shutters open—I pity the poor mariner &c.—Well the thoughts of our friend have put me into a good humour: the first fit of the sort to day. Let's go to bed, and excuse me dear old fellow for writing this stupid letter, perhaps I won't send it—but I'm glad to have had a talk with you, even though about nonsense— Mon Dieu, en avons nous déja parlé dans notre temps?

Niger Expedition . . . sister . . . unhappy: Captain Bird Allen, fiancé of FitzGerald's sister, Andalusia, had been a member of the English colonizing expedition that went to the Niger on 20 August 1841, but was soon overcome by fever; Allen died on 25 October.   *Tamburini:* Antonio Tamburini (1800-76), basso.   *soupe maigre:* (Fr.) vegetable soup.   *Collignon:* several French painters during Thackeray's time had this name.   *Hugo's new book: Le Rhin,* which Thackeray reviewed in the April 1842 issue of *The Foreign Quarterly Review.*   *Sacred Writer of Putney:* Athanasius Gasker, a character created by Edward William Clarke in *The Library of Useless Knowledge* (1837), who refers to himself as "Old Blue Baby!" "the old plethoric and wanton star."   *Yates:* Frederick Henry Yates (1797-1842), actor.   *pas seductif:* (Fr.) seductive step.   *paper about . . . Nicholas Nickl[eby]:* Thackeray's "Dickens in France," which had appeared in the March 1842 issue of *Fraser's Magazine.*   *Mon Dieu . . . temps?:* (Fr.) My Lord, haven't we already spoken of it in our time?

60. TO MRS. HENRY CARMICHAEL-SMYTH
11-? June 1842

Southborough nr. Tunbridge Wells.
11 June 1842.

My dearest Mammy I came down here on Tuesday as I threatened, and if I dont keep my other promise of writing you an immense long letter: it is because I have written myself out in the last 4 days, so hard have I been at work—Near 25£ worth, that's a fact: but it's a sort of thing that one could not keep up: and its better economy to write oftener & less. It's the pleasantest greenest place in the world, pleasant woods close at hand, fields on the other side very quiet & happy to walk in, and Tunbridge Wells 3 miles off, which I examined with a queer sort of feelings. That lovely cottage we used to inhabit has gone to heaven, so has old Gramp the riding master, his son taking his place now the father is in another & better world. Cottages have grown upon the common: and as for the house at Penshurst wh. I thought rather a splendid affair, it is finer outside, but in the most woebegone condition within. I looked out for my old friend the dead man with the worms and was very near missing him strange to say: the fact is he has got up and changed his place from the gallery where he used to be to a front room: of course carrying all his worms with him. Penshurst is a royal country much more grand & picturesque than this—but even this look out of a green common with old oak trees, and a road with merry-looking gigs gingling up and down is better than Coram Street. O that bell at Coram Street, and that unhappy little room where I never can remain five minutes without some one rattling at the door, wh. I've vainly locked. Charles & Mary will think me very ungrateful—Amen. But all the same I admire him more than ever. I never saw such delightful humility, and carelessness of self. Mary's Doctor is not such a humbug as I first thought him, but has really I believe a strong admiration for that young lady.—I wonder [if it] makes me ill-pleased at these vulgar people admiring her?— Upon my word I don't think so but the style of thing is distasteful to me— Well, bating jealousy on her part, wh. you told me of, and of wh. I have seen some curious instances—she is a good fellow; she is as jealous of your love for me, and found a letter t'other day, wh. I read too—from her to you—in wh. she pointed out that *I* had formed other ties, but *she* was all your's she feels ashamed of it now, and spoke of it: I told her that she had to use a genteel phrase *pitched it too strong:*—she is of a passionate temper, and fancies those explosions of love in wh. she indulged formerly rather creditable and indicative of immense sensibility—it was all temperament. A person does not love you more because he hugs the breath out of your body. She is jealous of me & the G M.; says that I flatter her Bon dieu! and that *she* couldn't do what I do: and she has told me twice or thrice very kindly of the sums the old lady has given me: making tolerably long calculations in favor of G M's generosity. The fact is she is not pleased in her heart at having received G M's 100£: and is always making comparisons—measuring herself with this person & that; and fighting hard to maintain her own self-esteem. I don't think that *he*males have that sort of spirit generally.—or perhaps I'm trying to run her down myself because of the 500£. What's all this scandal?— the fact is, somehow, that she doesn't *agree* with me: and so be so good as to burn this if I don't burn it myself, wh. is just as likely. Ah! there was more nobleness and simplicity in that little woman that neither of you knew, than I've seen in most people in this world. God help her, and if ever he pleases to restore her to me mend both of us. It was pleasant walking about here in the fields on Thursday & thinking of Annie: my dear little girl, I hear her voice a dozen times a day, and when I write to her, it's a days work—blubbering just as I used to do when I left you to go to school—not from any excess of affection filial or paternal as I very well know; but from sentiment as they call it—the situation is pathetic. Look what a sentimental man Sterne was, ditto Coleridge who would have sent his children to the poor house—by Jove, they are a contemptible, impracticable selfish race, Titmarsh included and without any affectation: Depend upon it a good honest kindly man not cursed by a genius, that doesn't prate about his affections, and cries very little, & loves his home—is the real man to go through the world with. Look at   G P. and his steadiness of heart, with love for working-days as well as Sundays; how much superior that sort of enduring character and manliness is, to all our flashy touch-and-go theorizing about love—Shall I pay you some more compliments about him?—it seems indecent: only I know you like to have it told you, that I feel respect and attachment for him: and so there's an end on't.   It's a strange thing too that I should fill a page with abuse of Polly, and choke after three lines of praise of

G P: but it's awfully hard to say what you think in the complimentary way, whereas the scandal slips out quite naturally—It is I suppose the satirical propensity and be hanged to it: now Charles could write a folio of kind things about people, and never say a bad word.

Whether I go to London tomorrow or not depends upon the state of the bill here—my extras have been 1 pint cyder, 1 glass gin daily—no wine except one day a pint—and scribble scribble all day. The last thing in Fraser has made a sort of hit: and I've been writing for the F. Q. and a very low paper called Punch, but that's a secret—only its good pay, and a great opportunity for unrestrained laughing sneering kicking and gambadoing. Likewise I've done for Ainsworth 2 little articles for Fraser 3 long ones, so that I've not been idle since I've been away—wh. is a story by the way: but here there is so much stir, bustle and blood flowing, that the work is done in 1/2 the time. Fraser has paid my wife's last month, & has enough for the 2 next, and it will be a great pleasure to me if I can go to Ireland with my own earnings, and without touching Mary's money.

And now Madam having written a great deal more than I had any business to I shall respectfully wish you good night: and read Vols II & III of Anne of Geierstein—I got it at the old Library on the Pantiles (they're called Parade now) where when you & G P went to town I got the Italian. God bless all, and my dear little ones.

My dearest Mammy. This has been lying in the portfolio for some days and should have been properly burned: but until I am away again, I shall not have another chance to write you a long letter, so please you burn this and not me.

I am now pretty well fixed upon departure for Ireland, having collacuted with Chapman & Hall The other young people viz Charles & Mary talk of setting off on Tuesday next, but I hardly think she'll be strong enough—she looks pale, but well and handsome I think—Today Ive been paying visits and woe's me out of six found five at home. Old Turner composing a sermon, Mrs. Bitcherdear and others—she was was almost pleasant though, & Constantia a pretty girl. Your letter made me have that dismal sort of gladness wh. you know of. I wish I could see you all before I go, my dear old Mammy & children. Thank God for their all being so happy, as I intend to be directly I'm out of the tea-parties, visiting jobs, and endless racket of this place. Fare well.

W M T.

cottage we used to inhabit: during the summer of 1823.   *The last thing in Frazer:* "Fitz-Boodle's Confessions. Preface," which had appeared in the June 1842 issue of *Fraser's Magazine.*   *writing for the F. Q.:* "The German in England" and "The Last Fifteen Years of the Bourbons," both of which appeared in the July 1842 issue of *The Foreign Quarterly Review.*   *Punch:* Thackeray began contributing to *Punch* with "The Legend of Jawbrahim Heraudee," which appeared in the 18 June 1842 issue.   *Ainsworth 2 little articles:* "Sultan Stork" and "An Exhibition Gossip," which appeared in the February, May, and June 1842 issues of *Ainsworth's Magazine.*   *Fraser 3 long ones:* Thackeray's next three publications in *Fraser's Magazine* were "Professions of George FitzBoodle," "FitzBoodle's Confessions (No. II). Miss Löwe," and "Confessions of George FitzBoodle (No. III). Dorothea," which appeared in the July 1842, October 1842, and January 1843 issues, respectively.   *Anne of Geierstein:* a novel published by Sir Walter Scott in 1829.   *the Italian:* Ann Radcliffe's gothic novel of 1797.

61. TO EDWARD FITZGERALD
4 July 1842

Shelburne Hotel
Stephen Greed
Dublud.
July 4. 1842.

My dear old Yedward.   I am just come after a delightful tower to Chepstow, Bristol Hereford, Srowsbry, Chester, Liverpool, Llangollen, and Wales in general—I found your dismal letter waiting on arrival here—What the deuce are you in the dumps for? Dont flatter yourself but that I'll get on very well without you. Such a place as this hotel itself!—enough to make a chapter about—such filth, ruin and liberality—o my dear friend pray heaven on bended knee that tonight when I go to bed I find no (Turn over)   🐛 🐛 🐛 ▪   —Have

you remarked that the little ones of all sting worst?

I wanted to give you an idea of the splendor of the chambermaid at Chthlangothlen—The most sumptuous creature ever seen—yellow haired brown eyed dazzling fair with a neck like a marble pillar, and a busk o heavens!—

I wrote a poem in the Llangollen album as follows

> *a better glass nor a better Pipe*
> *I never had in all my life*
> *Saml. Rogers.*

Likewise a series of remarks by Thos Moore, beginning—'There is a little yellow bird frequenting the cataracts of the Tigris where it empties itself into the Tabreez lake &c.['] What nonsense is all this to write—well, but the fact is I am just disjointed after the [voyage] my legs rocking about like a tipthy bal frob the effeketh of the thteamer and I can't get to put down a sentence decently, and shan't be able for a couple of days or so.   But I just wanted to shake hands with somebody however far across the water.

Your Uncle's letter I've sent off (he has been very good naturedly to call & see if I had arrived) with my card pronounced here with that shuperfine elegance 'kyard'—Stuff there I go again,   well there I go again.—Its a queer state of mind to be sure.

Godblessyou.
W M T.

P S. I wish you could see the apotheosis of William IV represented on the cieling of the coffee-room such a picture! I shall get a most accurate copy of it fixing up easels telescopes &c—

Samuel Rogers: (1763-1855), poet.   *Uncle:* Peter Purcell, who lived in Halverstown.

62. TO MRS. HENRY CARMICHAEL-SMYTH
?-16 October 1842

My dearest Mammy I think the last letter was after having been at Halverstown put into the post on my way to FitzGerald's brother in the County Meath—the honestest best creature that ever was born. I stopped with him 3 days, on one going to see Trim wh. is near Laracor wh. is the place where Swift's living was: on another day to see Stane Castle a beautiful mansion belonging to my Lord Conyngham, and on another to see the Boyne water where as perhaps you have heard King William defeated King James. Fitz's benevolence would have done you good to witness: he thanked his coachman for driving us: his footman for bringing in the tea-urn: and seemed to be bubbling over with good humour and good will towards men. His wife a kind bigot of an Irishwoman who made me a present of Wiseman's lectures when I came away, hearing me say I would like to read them. Wiseman you must know is the great luminary of the R. C[atholic] church at present; and my conviction after reading 1/4 his book is that he is as [great a] hypocrite as ever lived.

From FitzGerald I went to Drogheda; where an hour was enough to show [the] filthy squalid crawling l---y town (see the blot is come for using that word it is the true word)—to show the dirty insecty town & suburbs, and the green old walls that Cromwell battered. He put all the garrison (except about 200 the garrison being 3000) to death here, and a great part of the inhabitants, bible in hand, praising God, and talking of this crowning mercy. His letter to the Speaker of the H of Commons is a wonder of fanaticism and brutal simplicity.

From Drogheda to Dundalk, where I went to old Thackeray, the most noble simple, humourous stupid delightful pious old fellow ever seen—Sir says he no person bearing the name of Thackeray must go through Dundalk without sleeping at my house: and though I represented that to remain at the Inn would be much more convenient, where I could smoke my cigar and write my page in quiet, there was nothing for it but to shift my quarters to his old dingy Vicarage: where he has a sick wife with rheumatism, and her sufferings made me think of my dear old Mother's, (it is true that allæopathy has been able to do nothing for her;)—and here the old gentleman ordered his curates to come and dine with me, and amused me all day taking me to Infant schools Hospitals and Institutions. Well, they were all delightful to see, especially the Infant Schools, God bless them, and the little ones singing in a way that makes the sternest ruffians cry—We went 1 day to Thackeray's living of Louth, the best in Ireland it was, worth 3000£ a year, but now only half. But 1500 or 3000 this man never has a shilling at the year's end, and has no expenses or extravagances of his own. He must live on 500 [and] the rest goes to Schools & hospitals and the poor, and curates. I am sure God [Almig]hty himself must be pleased to look down on honest Elias Thackeray, and [when I] hear of human depravity as applied to him and some others, can't believe [it for] the soul of me.

Have you remarked how stupid my letters are?. Solitude creates a muzziness and incoherency in me, and I must get back to the little ones that's clear—I am never thinking of what I am writing about, all the time I was writing of Thackeray there was something else in my thoughts & so on—so that I feel what dreadful dull things my letters must be. Well from Armagh I went to Newry where a Doctor of Divinity gave me good claret for dinner and showed me the saving's banks, the Poorhouse, and the town in general: from Newry to Armagh, where the service of the Cathedral is wonderfully performed, and I looked at the Primate with pleasure having heard of his noble generosity & bounty, and from Armagh by the railroad hither. I was to have been off this morning, but that at breakfast with a gentleman to whom I had an introduction, something came up about some monstrous intrigues of the Roman Catholic priesthood so awful that I thought they would make a good chapter for the book, and that I was bound to stop and get at the truth of the business; well, thank God I shall have no chapter on that subject, the story told me by a Reverend Gentleman, Moderator of the Synod of Alstor, turns out to be a rank & monstrous falsehood—a little truth that is with 90/100 parts of lies—like Mrs. Shawes about somebody you know—but they are all so in this country; all exaggerating in abuse of each other—Not but that the Priests are a disgusting body, and though I say thank God now as I ought if the truth must out, when I found the story against them was quite untrue, my first feeling was one of some mortification. This is the only town properly speaking I have seen in Ireland, bustling, prosperous, busy, unhumbugging[;] the people are like the Scotch, the physiognomies quite altered, the country hap[py] looking and thriving with neat houses and orchards and hedges—I [am glad I] have it for the end of my trip, and o I am glad the end of my trip is [near.] I have been heart-weary for months past that's the truth.

 Coleraine Sunday I intended to have addressed the remainder of this, just for the look of the thing from the 'Giants causeway'—but the place was so awful and lonely, that I was glad to run from it after a couple of hours visit—sea sickness in an infernal boat, tumbling and sprawling among rocks afterwards and a lonely dinner at a hotel situated over the cheerful spot—a huge place with not a sole in it the last company being a corpse wh. had just gone. I think the ghost was there still and got out of the place in a panic. It will make a capital chapter though, and that's something. The drive from Belfast along the coast is magnificent and I never enjoyed anything more in my life [bu]t I think I shall enjoy a ride to St. Germ[ain] still more. Meanwhile I dream of you [and G P] and the little ones every night, wh. to be sur[e is] not much comfort. I shall have done 5/6 of the book by the time I am with you, on the [1] November please God, and shall have easy [wo]rk with the rest. Does G. P recollect a [Col]onel Cairnes who was at Java?—Lever gave me a letter to him wh. I have just been to deliver 4 miles off at Port Rush—He is a great character by all accounts: what they call here a *dust* wh. phrase Miss Elizabeth Hamerton will be able to translate: but I think letters are rather a bore than otherwise—one can't work at the people's houses.

 And so—(dinner has come off since the above and the fire is just loaded with turf, and I'm going to try and set in for a night's scribing:

but first must say God bless my dearest old mother and all both little and tall at Saint Germains. A fortnight more please God, and I won't be far from them.[)]

If you have anything very pressing write to Dublin; the Shelburne; if not to London—I'll write once more too.

WMT

FitzGerald's brother: Peter FitzGerald (1807-75).   *Wiseman's Lectures: Lectures on the Principal Doctrines and Practices of the Catholic Church* (1836).   *His letter:* written on 17 September 1649.   *old Thackeray:* The Reverend Elias Thackeray (1771-1854), an uncle.   *the Primate:* Richard Whately (1787-1863), Archbishop of Dublin 1831-63.   *Lever:* Charles James Lever (1806-92), novelist, to whom Thackeray dedicated *The Irish Sketch Book*.   *a dust:* (slang) someone who causes a disturbance.

63. TO ANTONIO PANIZZI
December 1842

81 Champs Elysées Paris
Wednesday. December Something

My dear Panizzi

The bearer of this is my friend Mr. Venedey, a german gentleman following the ignoble trade of letters. He is redactor of the Leipzig Gazette and author of several works that ought by rights (if the Librarian took the slightest trouble) to be in the Britannic Museum.

The only thing I know against Mr. Venedey is that in early youth he caused himself to be banished from his native country of Cologne for conspiring somewhat, and for liberalism.

You however pourrez pardonner les égaremens de ce jeune cœur. Et si dans les occupations paisibles auxquelles il se livre maintenant, si dans les jouissances d'une littérature saine et abondante il peut oublier les temps orageux sa jeunesse bouillonnante, le philantrope ne doit que l'aider,—ses amis ne peuvent que s'en louer.

Sorté vous même (je frémis en y pensant!)—sorté dis je vous même du gouffre politique, donnez une main sécourable à un homme qui a souffert comme vous.

Il démande, dans un mot, un asyle parmi vos livres—qu'il s'instruise qu'il s'enrichisse de ses trésors! Le billet d'entrée que vous lui accorderez sera un billet (pour ainsi dire) tiré sur moi, j'y reponds par la reconnoissance éternelle.

With best respects to Mrs. Panizzi and your children
I am dear Sir
Your very faithful Servt.
Wilhelmina Thackeray.

P.S. I am just in a *delicate situation* expecting to lie in of twins on Ireland patrie de notre bon Dowling auquel j'écris aujourdui même.

Panizzi: Anthony (later Sir Anthony) Panizzi (1797-1879), who was made Keeper of Printed Books of the British Museum in 1837 and Principal Librarian in 1856. *Venedey:* Jacob Venedey (1805-71).   *the Librarian:* the Principal Librarian was Sir Henry Ellis (1779-1869).   *conspiring . . . for liberalism:* Panizzi, a conspirator of Liberal sympathies during his youth in Italy, was an exile from his homeland, like Venedey.   *pourrez . . . eternelle:* (Fr.) You, however, could pardon the bewilderment of this young heart. And if in the peaceful occupations to which he now gives himself, if in the enjoyments of a healthy and abundant literature, he is able to forget the stormy times of his impetuous youth, the philanthropist ought only to help him,— his friends can only be pleased with that. Extricate yourself (I tremble to think of it!), I say extricate yourself from the political whirlpool, give an assisting hand to a man who has suffered as you have. He asks in a word, an asylum among your books—so that he may instruct himself, that he may enrich himself with its treasures! The ticket of admission that you will give him will be a bill (so to say) drawn on me. I respond to it with eternal gratitude.   *Mrs. Panizzi . . . children:* Panizzi was a bachelor.   *lie in of twins:* the two volumes of *The Irish Sketch Book*.   *patrie . . . même* (Fr.) country of our dear Dowling to whom I am just writing today. (Dowling was an obscure Irish friend of Thackeray's.)

64. TO ANNE THACKERAY
1842?

I have nothing to send my dearest Anny but a little picture:— the picture is of some little girls I saw going to church, & one of them I thought was like Anny.

Well, this is all I have to say: for there is no time, because the person is waiting who is going to take this.

God bless the little girl to whom he is going to take it, & her little sister. Do you know their names and that their Papa loves them?

I . . . them?: Thackeray printed the letter. The picture is missing.

65. TO MRS. HENRY CARMICHAEL-SMYTH
March? 1843

My dearest Mammy. Your letter is just come in: and I thought it as well to write off to Dick straight, and tell him what the news were concerning the poor old lady. I am to dine with him tomorrow and went you may be sure to see Bess and get her news wh. and yours are good thank God: as for the 2 or 3 days per month it is nothing, it only shows how much better she is on other days.

Bess is magnificently lodged with a kind handsome exceedingly vulgar woman who drops her h's over one of the handsomest drawing rooms you ever saw: pillars, marble, stained glass hot & cold water all the way up the house, and luxuries and beauties innumerable. Squares upon Squares are springing up in the old quarter, and little Albion Street now lies shirking behind long rows of palaces, wh. have well nigh got to Bayswater. That day I looked out for Sir James in Oxford Terrace, but couldn't find him: however I suppose he will console himself at the delay.

The dinner-parties pour in rather too plentifully. I had 5 invitations for last Saturday; and a dinner every day in the week—the same this week; but the abuse of good dinners is wholesome in this respect that one grows used to the kind of life, and is not tempted to exceed. I've not had any soda-water this week: but my dear old Fitz and I have a cozy smoke at night over the fire, and the next day I get to work. It is curious that this racket agrees better with me than a quieter life and I have managed to write a good deal.

I've been making lots of drawings and the Punch people are beginning at last to find out that they are good. All the Irish blocks are spoiled: but no matter the public is too ignorant to know good from evil, and may possibly cry out that they are wonders.

As for Hickman I have intimated to him thro Black that I am not indisposed to compromise for 20£, and his letters after having been rampant are become quite mild & insinuating. I never answer any one of them: but shall gladly pay the 20£ to have the cust business over. I sent off a long letter yesterday to Hume and his Star: wh. is well spoken of here, and begins to make a stir: and have invented at least 4 schemes since I have been here for making immense sums of money—but let's wait till Spring before thinking of making my fortune.   Where shall I go live? I've been looking to day at a house in Brunswick Sqr. 100 a year not so big but cheerfuller than Coram Street, and with a wee bit of garden for the three children to play in— No 14 is just let for 90£ and not so good a house as mine—and the neighbouring houses are equally dear. Tomorrow I'm going to make an attack on the Brompton district

You'll let the Mrs. have the other half sheet. It's as usual just post hour; and may God bless you all and thank my dearest Nanny for her letter.   W. M. T.

Please send the note to Puzin.

Bess: Elizabeth Hamerton.   *Sir James:* Sir James Carmichael.   *Hickman:* a creditor of *The Constitutional,* for which Thackeray and Major Carmichael-Smyth were liable.   *Hume and his Star:* Hume, proprietor of *The Calcutta Star,* had assisted Thackeray on *The National Standard* in 1833.   *Puzin:* a doctor in Chaillot into whose care Thackeray had placed his wife.

66. TO GEORGE WILLIAM NICKISSON
8 April 1843

13 Gt. Coram St. April 8. 1843.

My dear Nickisson.

I was at no loss on reading the amusing 'Illustrations of Discount' in the Magazine to discover the name of the author. Mr. Deady Keane shook me by the hand only a fortnight since and at the very same time no doubt was writing the libel on me wh. appeared to my no small surprize in that very article.

I have advisedly let a week pass without deciding upon the course I ought to pursue. Few people (none that I have seen) know that the attack in question is levelled at myself, nor indeed have I any desire to make the public acquainted with that fact—But—as in a private house or an inn, if any person with no other provocation but that of drunkenness or natural malice, should take a fancy to call me by foul names, I should have a right to appeal to the host, and request him to have the individual so offending put out of doors—I may similarly complain to you that I have been grossly insulted in your Magazine.

Having written long in it: being known to you (please God) as an honest man and not an ungenerous one: I have a right to complain that a shameful and unprovoked attack has been made upon me in the Magazine, and as an act of justice to demand that the writer should no longer be permitted to contribute to Fraser.

If Mr. Deady Keane continues his contributions in any shape, mine must cease. I am one of the oldest and I believe one of the best of your contributors. A private individual I have been grossly abused in the Magazine, and must perforce withdraw from it unless I have your word that this act of justice shall be done me.

I make this demand not in the least as an act of retaliation against Mr. Keane, but as an act of justice wh. I owe to myself, and wh. is forced on me. At present at least it cannot be said that my anger is very revengeful or that his attack has rendered me particularly vindictive. It would be easy to fight him with the same weapons wh. he uses, could I condescend to employ them: but I feel myself, and I hope one day he will discover, that they are unworthy of an honest man. If he only take care to let it be publicly known that it is his intention to abuse in the public prints any private individuals, whose personal appearance or qualities may be disagreeable to him: it is surprising how popular he will become, how his society will be courted, and his interests in life advanced.

But I am sure you will no longer allow him to exercise his office of Satirist in your magazine: and hope (without the least wish to imply a threat) that for both our sakes, he will make no more attacks in print upon my person or my private character.

Faithfully yrs dear Nickisson
W M Thackeray.

I have no copy of this letter: but should you send it to Mr. Keane, will you please to make one[?].

'Illustrations of Discount' . . . *Keane:* David Deady Keane (1810?-70), whose article, which contained a hostile verbal caricature of Thackeray, was published in the April 1843 issue of *Fraser's Magazine.* It was Keane's only publication in the magazine.

67. TO MRS. WILLIAM MAKEPEACE THACKERAY
3? May 1843

My dearest little woman—I have a very bad excuse for not answering your kind letter, that I was waiting daily to say something about business, about the book, about the new house that I am going to take, and about some more matters. Well, all these things are as unsettled now as ever: and besides couldn't I have written even if they *were* unsettled? But you know how much business writing I have to do, & must be good-natured & pardon me.

Dear old Mrs. Sterling has gone to her long home: and poor John has likewise met with a calamity in the loss of his wife, who died suddenly after her confinement The poor fellow only got the news of his mother's death a few hours before his second loss. Old Sterling is very much affected: but you know his nature and that grief like his won't last very long.

I have at last finished the Irish book, wh. is to be out tomorrow, and has already been famously reviewed by Blanchard in Ainsworth's Magazine. I have written to the Times people who have promised me a kind review, and shall get plenty of puffing elsewhere. If the people will only buy the book as well as praise it my fortune is made. What else have I got to say?—I have been rather laid up with my old complaint but am better now, and very very soon please God hope to see my dear little people once more. They say the town is very gay; but I have almost left off going to Operas and Theatres, and come home early, when FitzGerald & I have a pipe together and so go quietly to bed. It is delightful to have him in the house but I'm afraid his Society makes me idle we sit and talk too much about books & pictures and smoke too many cigars. I don't think I have fallen in love with any body of late, except pretty Mrs. Brookfield. Mrs. Sartoris has given up her tea-parties conversazioni and tableaux vivans being of this figure. She is really as fat as Cottin and twice as ugly,

and if she is not to be confined till September, Heaven help us her babby will be a monster. Did I write to you about Mrs. Procter's grand ball, and how splendid Mrs. Dickens was in pink-satin and Mr. Dickens in a geranium & ringlets?. To night I am asked to no less than two balls, one to a publisher's lady; and one to an attorney's—and the probability is between ourselves that I shall go to neither. Every day I have been house-hunting with all my might & main, and have found nothing at all so large & cheap as poor old glum Coram Street: but I want a garden for you and the little ones and a good air and a thousand other good things wh. can't be had except for more money than I fear I can muster—I've not sent you the paper because I've not written in it of late—but I was an ass for my pains, and you shall have it more regularly for the future—that is to say not for a very long future, for I hope I shall see my dearest little woman before three weeks be over. And so God bless you my love, and write me a line ever so short; it will always be worth a guinea to me—Your afft W M T.

old Mrs. Sterling ... his wife: John Sterling's mother died on 16 April 1843, and his wife died two days later. *Blanchard in Ainsworth's Magazine:* Blanchard's review appeared in the May 1843 issue of *Ainsworth's Magazine.* *my old complaint:* his urethral stricture. *Mrs. Brookfield:* the former Jane Octavia

Elton (1821-96), wife of the Reverend William Henry Brookfield (1809-74), whose friendship with Thackeray had begun in Cambridge days.   *Cottin:* Elizabeth Cottin (d. 1866), sister-in-law of Dr. George Thackeray (1777-1850).

68. TO THE REV. WILLIAM HENRY BROOKFIELD
26 May 1843

If you like two or three
Of your cronies to see
There's a swarry
To-morry
At Mitre court B.

69. TO MRS. BRIAN WALLER PROCTER
August 1843

My dear Mrs. Procter. Although I have just lost my pocket-book containing 20£ (that is to say the pocket-book has been found again but the money has somehow dropped out of it) and although I am in a foreign land writing with a pencil, not speaking the language, & alone, yet I hope Procter will not consider it necessary & send off to his banker's, & pay my losses; & you too I trust will not fancy that the undersigned is more wretched than ordinary.—The fact of the pencil is that there is no ink in the room but such as blots up to the elbow, and as for the 20£, Procter can't send it unless he directs it Poste Restante Europe, in some part of wh. I shall pretty surely be (unless something happens of wh. no more at the present writing) but where I don't know.

But a friend of mine with whom I am come for a week's excursion, and who pays all the bills wh. makes matters tolerably easy, is gone out to see a fourth-rate company of Singers do a fourth rate opera (a sixteenth rate performance therefore) and the rain is dripping pitilessly into the canals, and the pattens are going clapping over the pavement in the dark, and I am left to my solitude with no

other companion but (upon my word & honor it is only small Bavarian beer and I have only had half of one of those queer little glasses as yet)—and a sort of circumstance to wh. I hardly dare allude occasioned the commencement of the present note.

Thinking about old friends & old times it suddenly occurred to me that this Bavarian bitter beer is exceedingly like (only not so strong as) the beer I used to drink occasionally in St. Johns Wood, & opposite the hatchment in Upper Harley St. and memory carried me back to those regions, and to a great number of pleasant days, the description of wh. is needless here as this is not a play, where the 2 characters begin by minutely describing things with wh. each is supposed to be perfectly acquainted,—and though the stream of my thoughts has its source in a glass of penny beer I hope it is not less limpid & clear for all that—Are you aware that the river Rhine springs out of a puddle, that the river Neva begins under some other river of wh. the name I think is Prtksxkcmpltskoi (it is mentioned in Custine's travels,) & that some rivers like the Nigoo, & the Nile though they have plenty of mouths have no earthly beginnings at all?—I have scratched out what was going to be the commencement of a moral to the above Similes, but it is best to leave out the apophthegm when in communication with persons above the age of 12

Poste Restante: (Fr.) General Delivery.   *a friend of mine:* Augustus Stevens. *Custine's travels:* an apparent invention of Thackeray's.

70. TO HIS FAMILY
17-18 December 1843

December 1[7].
27 Jermyn Street.

My dear ladies I have been looking out for the last 3 days for a letter from Paris being anxious to know how all there are faring. I write this from my bed a coach wheel having passed over my head and cut it off but a surgeon was luckily at hand who set it right again with sticking-plaster. This is the only personal news I have to give, I think, unless you would like to know what I have had for dinner every day since last week wh. would make a very long sum, or what I have been writing wh. I would not do over again for twice the money. I fear after all it will be New Year's day before I am back for my hands are very full of business, and I can't comfortably dispose of it until then—or indeed anyhow at all, for there is as much as would take 2 months to do. But it is a comfort to think that there is a decent income arranged for 1844 (please God my health hold good) and actually a prospect of saving money at the year's end. What a phœnix of a year 1845 will be if we see it!. These visions are so monstrous however, that I don't like to count upon them as realities, and so we will wait to realize them till '45 comes.

  I've nothing to say as usual for I don't leave this till 5 o'clock and take a little trudge as far as Pall-Mall or possibly the Garrick before dinner but the life I am sorry to say is a very jolly one—plenty of work that is and plenty of fun. My eyes oblige me to live moderately so that there are no excuses to do me harm. Here the letter stopped yesterday: and yours is just come to hand—What I admire in my dear Mammas correspondence is that igstreme ingenuity at finding out ills to wh. her darling is subject I have never been better in health than since I left home. I have had no headaches but in your poor old fancy—Now however and in spite of your injunctions to the contrary, and since the last page was written, I have got a swelled face—wh. will keep me to the house probably for a day or two, wh. I shall employ in working at a long article for the F. Q. R. Shouldn't you like to come off post to see it?—the worst is it wont wait for your coming, so you must make your mind as easy as suckinstances will permit.

  If you see Mrs. Hankey tell her with my compliments that I have done my very best with the lace, and placed it as I thought in much better hands than Miss Hamerton's. Ask her too with the same compliments where I shall leave what I can't sell of it?—If I had been caught smuggling it a young Embassy man told me the other day, I should have had an imprisonment and 300£ fine. The young fellow insinuated that I was a fool for my pains.—and upon my word I can't say I thinks he was very much in the wrong. But knowing this I decline taking it back again.

  As I could not go into the city with my swelled chop I have despatched G. P's letter to Lubbocks: and won't forget the other little commissions[.] I have begun with a story wh. is to last through the year in Fraser, and am to have my own way with the worthy Mr. Punch, whose pay is more than double of that I get anywhere else. Dickens has just published a charming Christmas book, wh. I won't forget to bring with me. I have made much friends with him and think your tirade against good dinners a monstrous piece of superstition. Why not be merry when one can? I was to have been merry tomorrow at the Harris'es at my own invite, b[ut] am held back by my jor. The Waddell and Mary Scott were at Kerwans t'other day—Mary looking none the better for her years—the Waddell magnificent in looks but as dull an idiot as I ever met—She sings popular songs in an extremely small pipe, and I don't think I got any credit with her by begging her to perform one of these ditties quicker.

God bless my dear Nanny I am glad to hear that she is good & Baby good too—Upon my word I am quite as tired of this town as you can be of my absence, and on New Years day please God I may see you all again. This is to be a letter for you and the little woman—I'm glad to hear G M is well again: and pray Heaven bless all.

W M T.

article for the F. Q. R.: "New Accounts of Paris," which appeared in the January 1844 issue of *The Foreign Quarterly Review.* *story . . . Fraser: Barry Lyndon.* *Dickens . . . Christmas book: A Christmas Carol,* which Thackeray reviewed in "A Box of Novels," in the February 1844 issue of *Fraser's Magazine.* *Kerwan:* Andrew Valentine Kirwan (1804–70), barrister and miscellaneous writer.

71. TO PETER PURCELL
25 December 1843

Xmas Day. 43

My dear P. P.

On this happy day I can't refrain from spending a penny to tender to you my respectful wishes. When (in my best clothes) I went to call on Mrs. Purcell in Portland Place and was informed by the futboy that you were gone to Ireland, I felt more ashamed of my self than I have done any time these three weeks—and thought 'Is [this] the Saxon return for Irish kindness and hospitality?' But you will please remember that I am a poor day-labourer in the winyard, and must work often when I would like to be taking my diversion—those last days of your's in London were just the busiest of all the month to me.

I have had on this sacred day ELEVEN invitations to dinner: wh. I can't help thinking of with a sort of pride: and in the overflowing of my busm, was anxious to write you a line by way of a shake-hands for Xmas & the ensuing new year—likewise to your lady your amiable family of daughters and Sons, Mr. Peter FitzGerald and his amiable partner, and Miss Kenny—also to his reverence and the rest of your party round the Halverstown turkey this day. As an agriculturist I would wish that the Humbug-crop should not be quite so plenteous in Ireland in 1844 as it has been in '43, and with this have the honor to subscribe myself my dear Mr. Purcell's affectionate Servant

Emily Jenkinson

Peter FitzGerald: (1807-75), a brother of Edward FitzGerald's.

72. TO MRS. HENRY CARMICHAEL-SMYTH
21-22 August 1844

Wednesday Evg. 21 August.

My dearest Mammy. I am going to write to you the great news: but my heart fails me as I send it, and I wish it weren't true. I have just (only yesterday) had an offer to go passage free by the Oriental Company to Lisbon, Cadiz, Gibraltar, Tangier, Athens Constantinople, Jericho, Smyrna Syria Jerusalem in 10 weeks and I thought the chance so great that Ive accepted—its very hard for I intended to come placidly across the water on Saturday to see my dear little people, and I'm sure I shall be miserable for the main part of this grand voyage. But it offers such a chance as I may never get again—a book of course is ordered and go I do, tomorrow—I shall be able to answer the Malta question from the place itself, but now coming from Egypt they tell me the Quarantine is as long as usual. Think of tossing in the Bay of Biscay, and the stewards and the basins! I hardly believe in it myself yet—The offer was made to me on Monday night only and accepted yesterday—I go with Mr. J. Emerson Tennant to the care of the British Consul Alexandria, we shall find there the mails of September and October by both of wh. please write putting my initials only at the outside of the letter —I don't a bit like it and am as uncomfortable as possible at this writing—perhaps because I have been up since 4 scribing as well as I could for Fraser. So farewell to Chaufontaine, wh. now I have lost it, I find the most beautiful place in the world and everything there the most delightful. If G. P will put my name to the 25£ bill he has hereby my authority (the practice is perfectly customary Bradbury & Evans the senders tell me), and it will serve to pay the expenses of the children back to Paris where please God I will meet them in November. I'm to write a book for 200£ for C & H. on the East first, or that Cockney part wh. I shall see—then to do Talleyrand. Lubbock will pay per Delenert Puzin's allowance for the poor wife in my absence—Charlotte Ritchie has just sent me an odd *hopeless* letter of her's. I'll keep the scrap for board ship to morrow. We leave London at 11. Southampton at 3 in the packet for the bay of Biscay O. Tennant is to introduce me to all the personages.

We are to see every thing & I'll send my dear mother the very last news from Palestine.

Southampton Thursday 22. On board the Lady Mary Wood—a fine ship, comfortable cabin—and quiet weather. God bless all behind, and give us a merry meeting at Xmas.

W M T.

a book: Notes of a Journey from Cornhill to Grand Cairo, published by Chapman and Hall in 1846.   *Tennant:* James (later Sir James) Emerson Tennent (1804-69), politician and miscellaneous writer.   *Bradbury & Evans:* William Bradbury (1800-69) and Frederick Mullett Evans (d. 1870), publishers.   *Talleyrand:* a biography of Talleyrand that remained unwritten.   *the bay of Biscay O:* from the song, "The Bay of Biscay," by Andrew Cherry (1762-1812) and John Davy.

73. TO MRS. WILLIAM MAKEPEACE THACKERAY
17 September 1844

Constantinople. 17 September.

My dearest little woman Who ever thought I should live to write you a letter from Constantinople!—here it is by all the Gods and I am sitting on a terrace under a tent at Pera, and looking out upon the actual gardens of the Seraglio across the blue Bosphorus yonder!

That is the Seraglio point—if you look well you will see a minaret—above among the cypresses is a great burying ground—Yonder mountains are the hills of Princess Islands, and beyond them Olympus—I believe Troy lies out there too—We passed the coast three days ago—a very ugly flat one no more picturesque than the entrance of the Thames.

Before that we passed the day at Smyrna—where I saw the most wonderful bazaars with the most astonishing Turks sitting and smoking in their dingy little shops—I saw the camels coming stalking along with their great splay feet and jangling bells—I saw the caravan just arrived from Persia—and smoked a cheboqeque—no a narghileh under the Cypress and acacia trees close by the Caravan bridge—A negro boy brought me sherbet, and sat down and played for us on a rebeck.

Before that I saw Athens, and the hill of the Acropolis, and the ruined temples of Jupiter and Theseus, they are magnificent & mouldy and of the colour of rotten Stilton cheese. Athens is filthy beggarly racketty lousy buggy full of dogs donkeys and other vermin—a beggarly place with the most noble hills round about it

Before Athens we saw Algiers rising up the hill, and before that Malta, where all the nations of the earth seem gathered together a royal stately old town. Palm trees grow there and prickly pears and the musquitoes bite like fury—before Malta we were at Gibraltar and from that I wrote my dearest little woman a little bit of a letter.

Yesterday I was in the bazaars at Constantinople and was thinking of buying you by way of a present a little black slave girl— they are to be had for 10£—but would you like a pair of papooshes better 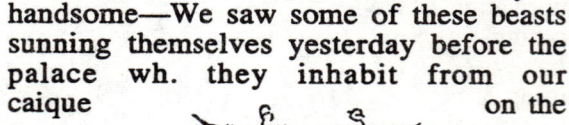 or a beautiful veil or yackmack such as the Turkish ladies wear?—You can only see their noses and eyes as they shuffle past in their yellow slippers, and I was warned off from a shop for looking at one too curiously She was a delectable creature —her eyelids painted and the tips of her fingers stained with dirty red—that fellow behind is one of the Eunuchs of the Sultan—only too handsome—We saw some of these beasts sunning themselves yesterday before the palace wh. they inhabit from our caique 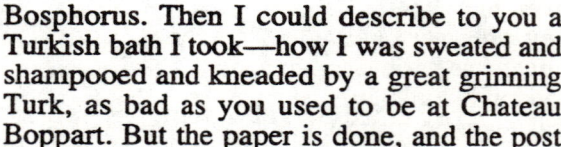 on the Bosphorus. Then I could describe to you a Turkish bath I took—how I was sweated and shampooed and kneaded by a great grinning Turk, as bad as you used to be at Chateau Boppart. But the paper is done, and the post is going away and I have to write to mother, and so only say God bless my dearest wife, and goodbye.

WMT.

cheboqeque: chiboque, a long-stemmed tobacco pipe, like the one that Thackeray is pictured smoking in Chapter 15 of *Notes of a Journey from Cornhill to Grand Cairo.*   *narghileh:* a tobacco water-pipe.   *rebeck:* a stringed musical instrument played with a bow.   *the Sultan:* Abdul Mechid, Sultan of Turkey 1839-61.   *shampooed:* lathered from head to foot.

74. TO CHAPMAN AND HALL
10 January 1845

Hotel d'Allemagne. Rome
January 10. 1845.

My dear Sirs

Although I looked 35 days running at the Post Office until I was sick and ashamed of applying the beasts would not give me your letters because they were supposed to be for Mr. *Jack*eray instead of Thackeray, and I have only just got the letters—the money was quite safe at Torlonia's, where the clerks had declined to have anything to do with my bills, and where as soon as they found their error they invited me to a ball—but I was too much enraged & disgusted to accept the invitation, and shan't be happy now until I am away from Rome.

I hope the Eastern Book will be successful—it is all but done—and seems to me to be—never mind what. I will go tooth and nail at Talleyrand directly I reach England, nay perhaps before at Paris where my family now are—they might have spared me much pain and uneasiness if they had known their own intention better, & not have determined me on this unlucky trip. For the last 3 weeks my annoyance has been so great at receiving no letters that I've done nothing—and it's only now the letters *are* come that I feel what a rage I have been in really. It seems such a shame to have kept a poor fellow pining & hoping, and I cant pardon them the bitterness of my feelings as I turned away day after day from the dd dd-dd-ddd-ddd post office. It is quite wonderful how I began cursing when your letters were given me, instead of being thankful for getting them at last—indeed they were very kind and I am much obliged to you for them. How I long to see the Strand again. It seems to me when I once get to London I shall never be a stranger & wanderer any more. Meanwhile I shake you both spirtually by the hand and am always sincerely yrs

W M T.

Dickens is to be here directly but I shant see him. Remembrances to all specially Forster whose mourning I deplore.

Torlonia: a bank on the Via Condotti, Rome.   *the Strand:* where Chapman and Hall had their office at Number 186.   *Forster . . . mourning:* for the death of his younger brother, Christopher, late in 1844.

75. TO RICHARD BEDINGFIELD
1 June 1845

88, St. James's Street.
Sunday, June 1.

My dear Bedingfield,—
    I was very sorry not to see you the other day when you called, but I wasn't in fit state to receive anybody, labouring under a violent attack of bilious sickness, for which the only fit company was a basin. Luckily, my illnesses don't last long nor come very often.
    I have read both your stories, and here you see they come back—that is cold encouragement to a man with a great deal of merit and imagination. I think they contain a great deal of good stuff, but I'm sure they are *not saleable*—that is the point. They are done in an old-fashioned manner, I think, and you could no more sell them than a tailor could a coat of 1830, or a milliner a bonnet which might have been quite the rage in the last reign.
    It's not the merits of the thing I fall foul of—though I should like to quarrel with a little *fine writing* here and there—but only the question of trade. It is not because a story is bad or an author a fool that either should not be popular nowadays, as you and I know, who see many donkeys crowned with laurels, while certain clever fellows of our acquaintance fight vainly for a maintenance or a reputation. I can suit the magazines (but I can't hit the public, be hanged to them), and, from my knowledge of the former, I should say you will *never* get a good sale for commodities like these. Quiet, sentimental novelets won't do nowadays, I'm sure. Think of the high-seasoned dishes the British public has been feeding on for the last 30 years, and you'll agree with me that they won't go back to such simple fare as you give them in "The Blind Lover." All I can say, my dear fellow, is Try again. In reality, your system may be the right one and mine the wrong, but I'm sure I'm right as to *the state of the market*.

Ever yours,
W. M. T.

Bedingfield: Richard Bedingfield, a cousin of Thackeray's, who published *The Blind Lover* in 1845.

76. TO MRS. HENRY CARMICHAEL-SMYTH
2 August 1845

    My dearest Mammy. I'm sure your advice is quite right—I'm not going to preach heterodoxy: I can't be hypocritical however, wh.

surely is a much greater sin against God. We don't know what orthodoxy is indeed. Your orthodoxy is not your neighbour's—Your opinion is personal to you as much as your eyes or your nose or the tone of your voice. Objects in nature make quite a different impression upon you to what they do upon any other individual. Why be unhappy then about the state of another's opinion?. It is to doubt of God to doubt of his mercy to another. It is awful presumption I think for any Bishop, Priest layman or laywoman to say I have the true Faith: I am right: Wo betide all who disagree with me. What right have you then to think of being unhappy about the state of my opinions? What right have you to say that I am without God because I can't believe that God ordered Abraham to kill Isaac or that he ordered the bears to eat the little children who laughed at Elisha for being bald. You don't believe it yourself. You fancy you do: you search out explanations to reconcile these awful things to your mind—the Belief is gone, directly the explanation is necessary. What did the Saviour mean by searching the Scriptures?—that a man was to read them to the best of his own reason or to take his neighbours? What did he do himself by the Old Testament—he repealed it. He said that it was not the Jews alone that the Almighty Father would bless: but that God was God of all the world: that you should *not* take an eye for an eye &c but that you should love one another—Wasn't that a truth that you should do as you would be done by before the Saviour said it, as well as afterwards? Was revenge an ordinance of God in the reign of Julius Caesar, and not in that of Augustus? And yet the Jews said that their law of revenge was from God. It couldn't have been. It was not right. It was solemnly repealed by the Saviour who said *It* has been said &c. but *I* say so & so. In saying so he himself denies that those words were as divine Authority—and the Jews murdered him for questioning their exclusive claims to divine favor: for propounding another law to that wh. they had been taught to believe came to them from Jehovah especially, for setting up himself against their God—Why do I love the Saviour? (I love and adore the Blessed Character so much that I don't like to speak of it, and know myself to be such a rascal that I don't dare)—Because He is all Goodness Truth Purity—I dislike the Old Testament because it is the very contrary: because it contains no Gentleness no Humility no forgiveness—nothing but exclusiveness and pride curses and arrogance—Fancy Lot, fancy Ezekiel remonstrating with God! Fancy the Divine name used as the slaughter of the Cannanites was going on—Using the very same name, acting on the very same law the descendants of Joshua murdered the Christ. How were they to know that he was the Messiah? by his miracles?—numberless people according to the Hebrew books performed miracles: by his doctrines? It was the very contrary of that wh. they had been taught to consider as Divine—and how could God

change?—his very appearance was contrary to their belief,—that is to their interpretation of Scripture. You can't be the Messiah, they might say—The prophets tell us expressly that he is to be a King, and that Judah is to be exalted by him over all the earth—they literally interpreted the Bible, and crucified the Blessed Speaker of Truth and Love and Humility.   I can't help applying as I read—I can't help seeing that two and two make an inevitable consequence of four—why is my dear old Mother to weep and be unhappy because my conclusions & her's don't tally? If you had been born a Catholic—you know what a good one you would have been: and then you would have been wretched if I had any doubts about the martyrdom of Polycarp or the Invention of the Holy Cross—and there are thousands of anxious mothers so deploring the errors of their sceptical children—But the Great Intelligence shines far far above all mothers and all sons—the Truth Absolute is God—And it seems to me hence almost blasphemous: that any blind prejudiced sinful mortal being should dare to be unhappy about the belief of another; should dare to say Lo I am right and my brothers must go to damnation—I Know God and my brother doesn't. And now I'll stop scolding my dearest old Mother about that favorite propensity of hers to be miserable. God bless all.
W M T.

preach heterodoxy: in his chapter on Jerusalem, in *Notes of a Journey from Cornhill to Grand Cairo.*   *martyrdom of Polycarp:* probably Polycarp (d. 155?), Bishop of Smyrna, who was reportedly burned to death.

77. TO MRS. HENRY CARMICHAEL-SMYTH
28 November 1845

My dearest Mammy. I have been so awfully busy for the last 4 days that Ive never had a quarter of an hour before post time to send you a certificate of health. I thrive with the work thank God: and plunge about from one thing to another with an activity surprising in one of my age size and corpulence. The Chronicle Articles are very well liked—they relieve the dullness of the estimable paper. We are all agog about the adhesion of Lord John and Lord Morpeth to the Corn Laws—Peel is to go out they say, and Whigs resume sway—What a lickspittle of a country it is, where a couple of Lords who have held aloof from the Corn-law battle calmly step in at the end of it, head the party and take all the prize-money. What a fine fellow Cobden is—His speech in to days paper is a model of oratory I think. So manly clear and upright.   Shall I be able to come and see you at Christmas?. I hope *not:* for if I dont come it will be for a very good reason, and to put some money in my purse. This is the place to earn it. Ah what would I give to— but never mind talking.   Heres a note for Anny—it took me about two hours: during the whole of wh. time I was blubbering—But they are best with you: nothing could replace you—no lady the best to be had for money.

Your letter is just come in—It is a story of a Cock as well as a Bull I'm sure. The thing is impossible. I have sent the letter to Jeames White: who will look to it. The little woman is wonderfully well, and I am very glad you gave me the caution. What a fool to say I gave presents! But Mrs. Bakewell is to all seeming an excellent worthy woman. The difference in the poor little woman's appearance is remarkable now that she has some one to look after her and keep her clean. She has been on a visit to Mrs. Nasmyth and indulges herself in excursions in a fly—My visits please her exceedingly. God bless her so I go almost every other day. My railroad matters are very bad: but I have bought the shares and am holding in hopes of better times. Atkinson Mary's friend was the unlucky fellow who let me in to the loss:—it was against all calculation: and more knowing hands than I have suffered desperately: I shall soon please God be able to clear my little losings. But the till has been swept quite clean. Dont however fancy I am pressed I can get as much as I want any day—My credit is wonderful among the booksellers and I have only to ask and have God bless all.

W M T.

Chronicle Articles: The Morning Chronicle, to which Thackeray contributed 35 articles 1844-48.   *Lord John* ... *Morpeth:* Lord John Russell (1792-1878) had just announced his decision to abandon protectionism and to support free trade. George Howard (1802-64), styled Lord Morpeth, later seventh Earl of Carlisle, allied himself with Russell.   *Cobden:* Richard Cobden (1804-65) was well known for his advocacy of free trade.   *put some money in my purse:* a variation on Iago's advice in *Othello*, I, iii.   *White:* the Reverend James White (1803-62).   *Mrs. Bakewell:* an inhabitant of Camberwell to whom Thackeray had recently entrusted the care of his wife after bringing her to England in October 1845.   *railroad matters:* Thackeray was a victim of the "railway mania" of 1845-46, losing his investment, like most of the other speculators.

78. TO ALEXANDER WILLIAM KINGLAKE
24 February 1846

24 Feb. 1846.

My dear Kinglake my dear friend   I have sent a letter to Tower wh. I implore you to take into your attention. Consider the nature of the testimony: the solemn terms of FitzGerald's denial: that the person on whose statements you are relying has deceived you both: and above all the frightful consequences of the quarrel to the friends of every party engaged in it *The cause of the meeting must come out.* Two innocent families will suffer the severest affliction. FitzGeralds admirable wife and children receive the stain thrown upon him. Your own mother whom you love so warmly is wounded for life by the exposure—And for what my God?

Upon my honor & conscience I believe in the sincerity of FitzGeralds protestations of innocence: I am sure that were the affair submit[t]ed to five hundred gentlemen they would say to a man that you were bound to receive them: and by every thing that is most sacred I adjure you to do so. Think what a price you pay to gratify your revenge: the wreck of your own fortunes in life: the wretchedness of the innocent wife & family of the man whom you want to force into hostilities: the possibility (a certainty with me) that you are lifting your hand to murder an innocent man: the irretrievable misery of those you love best and for whom you would make every sacrifice Make this one, my dear Kinglake, in the name of honor, family, reason—in the name of God Almighty and your own welfare.

Faithfully your friend
W M Thackeray.

Kinglake . . . Tower . . . FitzGerald: Alexander William Kinglake (1809-91), who had graduated from Trinity College, Cambridge, was a traveller and writer. Because Edward Marlborough FitzGerald (b. 1802) had introduced his mistress to Kinglake under the pretense that she was respectable, Kinglake challenged him to a duel, naming Tower as his second. Although the two principals and their seconds went to Calais for the purpose, FitzGerald then beat a retreat.   *mother:* Mrs. William Kinglake, the former Mary Woodforde.

79. TO MRS. HENRY CARMICHAEL-SMYTH
6 March 1846

Friday.

My dearest Mammy. I have had a letter begun these 4 days and carried about in my pocket till it grew crumpled and past sending. It said nothing however. There are never any news. One day's hurry and turmoil resembles the next, and with a great pother I do wonderfully little—The consideration of these subjects always makes me glum: that's why my letters to you are so dismal. And it doesn't make me much happier to get your's, wh. give me fits of homesickness. The Mrs. is very well indeed and lively and tolerably sensible: one of her letters to Anny begins very well indeed but it rambles off at the end to the Queen of Spain and the King of Hanover in unintelligible inanity—Aunt Becher sent me your letter; and a request for Titmarsh wh. I sent her: and now comes an offer to pay from the good old soul. Also I have had a packet from Luc—all the correspondence—with an appeal to my sense of justice and a request from Mary that I should read it. I don't think I shall, and have not yet read one line of it or answered her—I don't see what good I could do, or how it is possible to make friends now. The chronicle & I must part or I must cut down half the salary. They are most provokingly friendly all the time, and insist that I should neither resign nor disgorge—but how can one but act honorably by people who are so good-natured? Heighho I wish and I wish and I wish every day that you were here and I had a home wh. I should neglect when I had it. It is the nature of the beau to be dissatisfied.   My gaieties have had a considerable lull. I don't like or trust the new acquaintances, and shabby fashionable people. The women are abominably free and easy, and inspire one with involuntary doubts, that it is not all talk with them. Mrs. Brookfield is my beau-ideal. I have been in love with her these four years—not so as to endanger peace or appetite but she always seems to me to speak and do and think as a woman should. You should have seen the three Camberwell ladies the other day, my wife Mrs. Gloyne and Mrs. Bakewell—one mending the right hand breeches pocket another the left the third a hole in my coat-tail! Such a Paris among these three Venuses. Nothing though can be more kind honest and goodnatured, and the Bakewell especially is a treasure I rather dread the husband though: and don't know how our evenings will pass in his company.

Did you read Sir Henry Hardinge's letter about the battle of Ferozeshah and he and 'dear little Arthur' standing in front of their line to prevent the men from firing? It is the prettiest story in the world of chivalry: and little Arthur's mother must be the happiest & proudest woman in England. I saw Lord Fitzroy Somerset walking in St. James's Park—with 2 girls in black, and absolutely crying. He had just quarreled with his son about a marriage before receiving the news of the poor fellow's death, in that tremendous carnage. It is quite curious to see how many *new suits* of black clothes there appear to be about Harley St. and in the Indian district. I am going to day to dine with the Prinseps and all the Pattle girls.—By Jove I feel a hundred years old.

My dearest little Nanny's letter was capital. God bless both of them. By hook or by crook they must and shall come here soon: and all of you my dearest old Mother. My free mornings are past in house-hunting. I must light upon one before long.

Tell Mrs. Colmache with my best regards that her article will in all probability appear next month: but Ainsworth (with whom I made it a personal matter) is very full and though he would like occasional articles, can't take a regular series—indeed he has no space for them & does not even write himself How I wish we had money to stock the 6 acre farm G P to manage & the girls to run about in it!   God bless all. G. M must come to England & get well

a request for Titmarsh: Thackeray's new publication, *Notes of a Journey from Cornhill to Grand Cairo.   Luc:* Luc-sur-Mer in Calvados.   *Hardinge...* 'dear little Arthur': Sir Henry Hardinge (1785-1856), later first Viscount Hardinge of Lahore, who was Governor-General of India 1844-48. He placed himself and his sixteen-year-old son, Arthur, about thirty yards in front of his men as they advanced upon the Sikh encampment.   *little Arthur's mother:* the former Lady Emily Jane Stewart.   Lord FitzRoy Somerset: (1788-1855), later first Baron Raglan, who had quarrelled with his son, Major Arthur Somerset (1816-45), over the latter's marriage in July 1845. The son died from a wound suffered at the battle of Ferozeshah in December 1845.   *the Prinseps:* Henry Thoby Prinsep (1793-1878), a Director of the East India Company, and his wife, the former Sarah Pattle. *Mrs. Colmache:* Mme. Édouard Colmache, a miscellaneous writer. Her article, "The Last Ball at the Tuileries," appeared in the April 1846 issue of *The New Monthly Magazine,* which was edited by William Harrison Ainsworth.

80. TO MRS. HENRY CARMICHAEL-SMYTH
March 1846

My dearest Mammy. You get on these rare occasions when I write at all, the fag-end of my day, when I am quite weary of the sight of a pen and my hand aches with scribbling. That is why the letters have such a dismal tone I think. Its near 5 o'clock and it has been all day work work, & yesterday & 2 days before & tomorrow & so on. What a martyr I am to be sure!. I shouldn't have written to day but for the money. I believe it is your money too that I send: for in the last 3 months I have been paying off old advances from publishers to enable me to meet that abominable Railroad Smash: and don't like to appear too greedy or needy with them. 'The Novel without a hero' begins to come out on the first of May. I have done nothing to it since I came back, being pestered with innumerable small jobs and—not forced to it—that is the fact. I can't do anything now without force, and feel quite capable of carrying three or four packs more on my back. I spend my spare hours still house-hunting I have not the least fear of not myself getting on well—only of not being a good father of a family without a wife. I wouldn't break your heart and my children's for the sake of seeing them an hour a day. Unless I liked a Governess I couldn't live with her and if I did—O fie. The flesh is very weak, le coeur sent toujours le besoin d'aimer. What a mercy it is that I've kept clear hitherto—The dear little woman is extremely well at times. We have been to the play in a private box and she enjoys herself in her little way. I dine there when I can tomorrow and Thursday last. Only after a day's work it is poor holiday making

Was it poor Barwell's death the 3d. you speak of?. That of Macleod the Captain of the Great Liverpool shocked me a great deal: and that awful principle of mistaken honor. Who are Christians in the world? Priests and Aristocracy have killed the spirit of Christianity I think: the one by inventing curses, the other honor. What a moral sentiment! I get painfully moral every day and find myself talking so much and practising so little that I'm very very much afraid my dearest Mammy that your dearly beloved Son is only a —— I'm quite sure it is wrong of you to be so awfully proud of certain people as you evidently are. Who is humble? My dear old G P is a humble man I think. I wish you were all seated at my humble board: eating humble pie for I'm very hungry & tired. I have been poring over the life of David Hume all day: the most amiable & honest of heathens: his life is excellently selfish and good-humoured & correct and he went out of the world quite unconcerned and with a grin on his face, entering into Eternity as if he were stepping into a Court ball. I have written a little article about the book wh. is a very heavy one: and it is remaining *undigested* upon me—a great nuisance—And tomorrow I must go plunge into something else. Now I must go and dress and take a little walk and then—O the beefsteaks won't I punish them. It is a pleasure to dine alone as I shall do, and think of you and my dear dear little women

W M T.

'The Novel without a hero' . . . *May:* the publication of the first serial installment of *Vanity Fair* was delayed until the end of December 1846.   *le coeur . . . d'aimer:* (Fr.) the heart always feels the need to love.   *Macleod . . . mistaken honor:* after the *Great Liverpool*, commanded by Captain Macleod, was wrecked, with the loss of three lives, in spite of having been acquitted of blame he committed suicide.   *article:* Thackeray's review of John Burton's *The Life and Correspondence of David Hume* appeared in *The Morning Chronicle* of 23 March 1846.

81. TO MRS. BRYAN WALLER PROCTER
26 April 1846

88 St. James's St. Sunday. April 26. 1846

Mr. William Thackeray will have very much pleasure in dining with Mr and Mrs. Procter on Friday the 8 of May. He hopes to hear that Mrs. Procters indisposition has ceased and that she is restored to that drawing room of which woman is ever the most elegant ornament in the opinion of Mr. William Thackeray.

But Mr. William Thackeray had much rather not go to the Dentist's, as his tooth is a favorite still, although it has given him such pain. And how often (Mr William Thackeray remarks) are we loth to part from those whom long attachment has bound to us, although their conduct is only a source of affliction to us, and we know them to be rotten at the core!

That Mrs. Procter has often experienced the truth of this observation Mr. William Thackeray is quite sure: and o! how earnestly Mr. William Thackeray prays that a lady so amiable as Mrs. Procter may never be called upon by fate, by toothache, by the conduct of friends, or the ingratitude of her numerous children, to say 'Alas! Mr. William Thackerays remark was only (as usual) too correct![']

82. TO RICHARD MONCKTON MILNES
29 May 1846

Friday 29 May.

My dear Milnes

I will take charge of the money. It is very kind and good-natured of you indeed to send it. You benefit more persons than you are aware of, First Morton, nex the young woman and 3d. me, for I should have had to disburse had not Heaven sent such a good fellow to help all of us.

Morton's expression *'Milnes owes me 10£ for a sketch wh. I haven't done'* is beyond measure felicitous.

I'm not Editor of Punch a bit—and only write one article a week.

Yours dear Milnes sincerely
W M Thackeray.

83. TO HENRY VIZETELLY
13 September 1846

Dear Sir,—I return the drawings after making a few alterations in them. Present Mr. Titmarsh's compliments to your talented young man, and say M. A. T. would take it as a favour if he would kindly confine his improvements to the Mulligans' and Mrs. Perkins's other guests' extremities. In your young gentleman's otherwise praiseworthy corrections of my vile drawing, a certain *je ne sais quoi*, which I flatter myself exists in the original sketches, seems to have given him the slip, and I have tried in vain to recapture it. Somehow I prefer my own Nuremburg dolls to Mr. Thwaits's superfine wax models.—Yours,

W. M. T.

Sept. 13.

Vizetelly: Henry Vizetelly (1820-94), proprietor of a wood-engraving firm that prepared illustrations for several of Thackeray's publications. *Mrs. Perkins:* Thackeray's Christmas book for 1846, *Mrs. Perkins's Ball.* *je ne sais quoi:* (Fr.) an indefinable quality.

84. TO MRS. HENRY CARMICHAEL-SMYTH
4 December 1846

Friday. Decr. 4. 1846.

My dearest Mammy. I have been meditating a line to you day after day: but there are points we don't like to talk about though we think of them always: You know how it pains me to think of my dearest mother being unhappy. Anny read me your letter the other day: it brought back all sorts of early early times, and induced an irresistible burst of tears on my part, at wh. the child looked astonished. Her eyes were quite dry. They don't care: not even for you. They'll have to complain some day of the same indifference in your Grandgrandchildren. Now they are with me I am getting so fond of them that I can understand the pangs of the dear old mother who loses them: and who by instinct is 100 times fonder of them than ever a man could be. But it is best that they should be away from you:—at least that they should be away either from you or me. There can't be two first principles in a house. We should secretly be jealous of one another: or I should resign the parental place altogether to you, and be a bachelor still. Whereas now God Almighty grant I may be a father to my children. Continual thoughts of them chase I don't know how many wickednesses out of my mind: Their society makes many of my old amusements seem trivial & shameful. What bounties are there of Providence in the very instincts wh. God gives us—To talk about such things though is wrong I think and engenders pride. But think about them and be humble.

Only I write so far to give my dearest old Mother a consolation in her bereavement. Remember the children are in their natural place: with their nearest friend working their natural influence: getting and giving the good let us hope, wh. the Divine Benevolence appointed to result from the union between parents & children. May I hold fast by it I pray to God our Father.—

And how thankful this makes me to you & my dear old G P, who have kept the children for me and watched them so nobly & tenderly—Kind and affectionate hearts, dear & steadfast friends, for this I thank and bless you as the father of my children.

Good bye dearest old Mother—Venables is coming to dine here on Tuesday—my old schoolfellow you know who spoiled my profile. Should you like to come?

W M T.

Now they are with me: Thackeray had moved into a house at 13 Young Street, Kensington, in June 1846. His children came from Paris to live with him in September. *Venables:* George Stovin Venables (1810-88), who broke Thackeray's nose during a fistfight while they were attending Charterhouse.

85. TO BRADBURY AND EVANS
December 1846

My dear Sirs

My feelings about the title page you will see with this—but I dont care wh. is used. only I should like some mention to be made of the novel without a hero—

I have corrected the last corrections: and say now Amen & good luck to Vanity Fair—May the public relish it may the publishers profit may the author be always honest & kind-hearted.

I wish you all the luck of the season

Yours ever sincerely
W M Thackeray—

86. TO MRS. BRYAN WALLER PROCTER
1846?

13 Young St. Kensington
Wednesday.

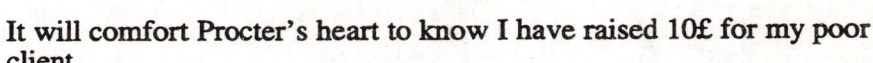

Madam. You heap coals of fire on my head. I can't come. But ah! it was kind of you to ask me.

May I come after dinner?. Will I ever say an unkyind word of Harley St again?. If I do I am a villain as well as

Your most faithful

S—B

It will comfort Procter's heart to know I have raised 10£ for my poor client.

heap coals of fire on my head: Proverbs 25: 22.

87. TO MRS. BRYAN WALLER PROCTER
January 1847

The little girls are glad and free to wait upon the Misses P. You ask my children as I see to come to dinner and to tea but why the deuce you dont ask me that is a point I cannot see.

88. TO THE REV. WILLIAM HENRY BROOKFIELD
3 February 1847

Under the confessional seal in the railway

My dear old Reverence.
I think from some words you let drop about 30 miles off, about my insanity yesterday, explanations is necessary on my part.

Without the æther I never shd. have broken out as I did about a certain personage (we are just come to a station) but in the æthereal or natural state my opinion is the same. I think the personage you know what. Her innocence, looks, angelical sweetness & kindness charm and ravish me to the highest degree: and every now & then in contemplating them I burst out into uncouth raptures. They are not the least dangerous—it is a sort of artistical delight (a spiritual sensuality so to speak)—other beautiful objects in Nature so affect me, children, landscapes, harmonies of colour, music, &c—Little Minny & the Person most of all. By my soul I think my love for the one is as pure as my love for the other—and believe I never had a bad thought for either. If I had, could I shake you by the hand or have for you a sincere & generous regard?—My dear old fellow, you & God Almighty may know all my thoughts about your wife;—Im not ashamed of one of them—since the days of the dear old two penny tart dinner till now.

The misfortune is incautious speaking about her. Such a person ought not to be praised in public and in my fits of enthusiasm I can not refrain. I shall try & correct this, & beg your pardon for it. Indeed I didn't intend that the Joseph the carpenter simile should go to her ears; and write you now under the seal of confession. My breast is so clean: that you will have no difficulty I think in giving me absolution.

Evins! Here is Wimbledon Station! Well, I have opened my bowels to you. Indeed there has not been much secret before: and I've always admired the generous spirit in wh. you have witnessed my queer raptures. If I had envy, or what you call passion, or a wicked thought (Tickets Gentlemen if you please) I should have cut you long ago: & could never have the rascality to say as I do now that I'm yours sincerely & affectionately

W M T.

This meditation wh. brought me exactly up to 9 Elms, took a great deal of thinking. I've been home since; the young ones charming well, and quite ready for a visitor when the time shall come.

certain personage: Mrs. Brookfield.   *dear old two penny tart dinner:* Thackeray first met Mrs. Brookfield in early 1842, when her husband unexpectedly brought him home to dinner, causing Mrs. Brookfield to supplement the meal by sending out for some tarts, which were served amid mutual amusement.

89. TO HENRY REEVE
23 February 1847

13 Young Street Kensington Tuesday 23 Feb

My dear Reeve

One note written yesterday to the public man Reeve lies before me. 'Tis addressed to the Privy Council and as the Stamp is already on the document I care not to alter its destination.

I can't come on the 4th.—that is I have got an hydraulic disorganization, wh. compels me to give up going out for a little—& can only dine at home at Clubs or where refuge is at hand with the instantaneous p-t de Ch-mbre.   By this post 4 invitations are respectfully declined.

But why not come and dine here *in boy* as the French say—It wd. be a charity to me and you know I could &c whenever I had a mind. You can have your claret & my mutton. Do you know my Persicos odi the very point alluded to by you.

Michael Angelo to his Cook

Dear Lucy you know what my wish is	Persicos odi
I hate all your Frenchified fuss.	Puer apparatus
Your silly entrées and made dishes	Displicent nexæ
Were never intended for us.	Philyra coronæ
No footman in lace & in ruffles	Mitte sectari
Need dangle behind my arm-chair	Rosa quo locorum
And never mind seeking for truffles	Sera moretur
Although they be ever so rare	

But a plain leg of mutton my Lucy	Simplici MYRTo
I prythee get ready at three	Nihil adlabores
Have it tender & smoking & juicy	Sedulus curo
And what better meat can there be?.	Neque te ministrum
And when it has feasted the master	Dedecet myrtus
'Twill amply provide for the maid	Neque me sub arctâ
Meanwhile I will smoke my Canaster	Vite bibentem
And tipple my ale in the shade.	

in boy: (Fr. *en garçon*) in male company.   *Persicos odi:* Horace, *Odes,* I, xxxviii.

90. TO MARK LEMON
24 February 1847

Feb. 24. 1847. Kensington.

My dear Lemon

That concluding benedictory paragraph in the Snobs I hope wont be construed in any unpleasant way by any other laborer on the paper. I mean of course I hope Jerrold won't fancy that I reflect on him now as he did in the Parson-Snob Controversy. I think his opinions are wrong on many points, but I'm sure he believes them honestly: and I don't think that he or any man *has* hit a foul blow in Punch.

What I mean applies to my own case, & that of all of us—who set up as Satirical-Moralists—and having such a vast multitude of readers whom we not only amuse but teach. And indeed—a solemn prayer to God Almighty was in my thoughts that we may never forget truth & justice and kindness as the great ends of our profession. Theres something of the same strain in Vanity Fair.   A few years ago I should have sneered at the idea of setting up as a teacher at all, and perhaps at this pompous and pious way of talking about a few papers of jokes in Punch—but I have got to believe in the business, and in many other things since then. And our profession seems to me to be as serious as the Parson's own.   Please God we'll be honest & kind was what I meant and all I meant. I swear nothing more.

                               Yours dear Lemon faithfully
                                          W M T.

Lemon: Mark Lemon (1809-70), who edited *Punch.*   *Snobs:* Thackeray's *The Book of Snobs,* which was to conclude its serial appearance in *Punch* on 27 February 1847.   *Jerrold . . . Parson-Snob Contoversy:* Douglas Jerrold (1803-57), a fellow Punch contributor, whose anti-clerical views caused him to react with hostility to Thackeray's "On Clerical Snobs" (16 May 1846), which had offered praise of some clergymen.

91. TO GEORGE WILLIAM NICKISSON
1 March 1847

13 Young St Kensington Sqr. March 1. 1847.

My dear Nickisson

I was attracted to the CharterHouse Article in the Magazine, and amazed by a certain paragraph—from Wesley to Titmarsh is a great break in the School-annuals, and the latter was a very bad scholar, who bitterly regrets his place of education. But it was very kind & well-meant of Cunningham I suppose to say such handsome things. I wonder whether they are true. Please God I'll be honest & not puffed up by this sort of laudation. Such compliments make me awfully grave, instead of being elated & joyful;—only they deserve acknowledgment of course wh. please hereby to receive.

I think the chief good I got out of Charterhouse was to learn to hate bullying & tyranny and to love kind hearted simple children. And I hope my own get the benefit of that sad experience I had there, and so escape rough words & brutal treatment—It's lucky the paper is no bigger, or you might be served with a homily. Thank you for the good-will, and believe me dear Nickisson

Yours Sincerely
W M Thackeray.

the CharterHouse Article: "Chronicles of Charter House" had appeared in the March 1847 issue of *Fraser's Magazine.* Its author was Peter Cunningham (1816-69), antiquarian, editor, and art critic of *The Pictorial Times. a certain paragraph:* one in which Cunningham had praised John Wesley and Thackeray.

92. TO MRS. HENRY CARMICHAEL-SMYTH
15 April 1847

My dearest Mammy I have lost stolen or mislaid a little note for you wh. ought to have gone 2 days ago to tell you not to be looking out quite so soon for what must happen before very many months or years though. The old lady is pretty cheerful orders the dinners: seems very fond of me: bullies Anny: and I think is as happy with us as may be—Quin told me of course that she was breaking up wh. was not much news, but did not say anything about Cancer—I am in a state of distraction with No V—I lost a whole week last week with our domestic perplexities, doubts about G M, comings & goings of Mrs. Gloyne &c—and must fly the house I see to get quiet. Mrs. Gloyne is gone—and the old lady quite resigned to her departure—I am therefore content—for Mrs. G was a very awkward customer in my house—being neither a servant nor a lady. Poor woman. I fear I have treated her with haughtiness and repent of that unchristianism. Arthur Shawe is gone back to his wife at last—Poor Langslow so poor as to be obliged to borrow money for the expenses of his wife's illness & funeral—My little women are delightful. The governess just the thing—and I feel easy in my mind that I shan't fall in love with her—I cant write—I'm thinking of V.

God bless you
W M T.

The old lady: Mrs. Butler, who was staying with Thackeray.   *Quin:* Dr. Frederick Quin (1799-1878), a homeopathic physician.

93. TO EDWARD CHAPMAN
29 May 1847

May 29. 1847.

My dear Sir

Coming home last night I found a lawyers letter from an Irish Railroad of wh. I've the good luck to be a registered proprietor, and of wh. the shares wh. I sold for some twopenny premium have been thrown back on my hands. I have to pay 150£ between today & Monday—

Can I realize on the 2nd Edition of Mrs. Perkins? I am horribly pressed or I should not think of dunning you; but please to consider the necessity of the case, & see what can be done for me.

Yours
W M Thackeray.

Edward Chapman: (1804-50), publisher.

94. TO MRS. HENRY CARMICHAEL-SMYTH
2 July 1847

My dearest Mammy. I have had 4 copies of L'Illustration sent to me by friends indignant at the owdacious piracy. It won't do me any harm, and besides I believe there is no remedy, were it ever so injurious. And this isn't the only evil out of the book—O'Gorman Mahon swears he is the particular Mulligan and that he will kill & eat me whenever we meet. There are 4 other Mulligans in London though not so warlike: but I am sorry about O'Gorman whose salt I have eaten, and whom I didn't know when I invented Mulligan first. So Bess has gone away more indignant than ever the Crowes tell me, and though every body gives it against me, I vow I can't see that I have done her any earthly wrong. There are no end of quarrels in this wicked Vanity Fair, and my feet are perpetually in hot water.

Jerrold hates me, Ainsworth hates me, Dickens mistrusts me, Forster says I am false as hell, and Bulwer curses me—he is the only one who has any reason—yes the others have a good one too as times go. I was the most popular man in the craft until within abt. 12 months—and behold I've begun to succeed. It makes me very sad at heart though, this envy and meanness—in the great sages & teachers of the world. Am I envious and mean too I wonder? These fellows think so I know. Amen. God knows only. I scarcely understand any motive for any action of my own or anybody else's—

Of course you are quite right about Vanity Fair and Amelia being selfish—it is mentioned in this very number. My object is not to make a perfect character or anything like it. Dont you see how odious all the people are in the book (with exception of Dobbin)—behind whom all there lies a dark moral I hope. What I want is to make a set of people living without God in the world (only that is a cant phrase) greedy pompous mean perfectly self-satisfied for the most part and at ease about their superior virtue. Dobbin & poor Briggs are the only 2 people with real humility as yet. Amelia's is to come, when her scoundrel of a husband is well dead with a ball in his odious bowels; when she has had sufferings, a child, and a religion—But she has at present a quality above most people whizz: LOVE—by wh. she shall be saved. Save me, save me too O my God and Father, cleanse my heart and teach me my duty. I wasn't going to write in this way when I began. But these thoughts pursue me plentifully. Will they ever come to a good end? I should doubt God who gave them if I doubted that.

Why I dont write to you more is partly because I am ashamed. What good to tell you what I have for dinner? it's always the same. The people talk the same things, I guttle down a great quantity of Champagne & Claret and laugh a great deal. But I haven't the face to put down the transactions on paper. They make one blush to think of them. I tell G M of the Lords I meet—it delights the old lady hugely. I have never met above 3 men who were not sneaks G P is one, I am not I am sorry to say: though I am sure I don't show it in my behaviour, except in little trivial instances to be remarked by psychologists. The other day poor old Mr. FitzGerald came out & fainted on the stairs at a party from heat and age and exhaustion—You should have seen what care we took of him getting him off to his carriage &c. But if he was cared for, how much more was Mrs. Fitz looked after?. She was quite unconscious in the great room listening to Alboni, & covered all over with diamonds & rouge—the attention every body paid her was something quite curious—The way in wh. we spared her feelings, and got her into somebody else's carriage was the best Vanity Fair benevolence I have seen since ever so long—since the night before almost. It's always going on. I pick up bits here and there, and keep my eyes pretty open, and am just as great a humbug as my neighbours—God help us. Who is conscious? Is poor Mary conscious? She fancies herself endowed with every virtue. I sicken as I see her hand-writing—That sacrament is awful. Why couldn't she go & fetch it?. She must order God to come to her. Follies so tremendous performed under the Eyes of the Divine Wisdom, I think only elevate (so to speak) one's notion of the latter—as one feels after looking into a microscope, how infinite littleness even is.

  I am glad you have got Mrs. Huyshe to comfort your old heart. I saw Wentworths tomb-stone over the boys' gallery at Harrow the other day: and took a walk with him on Tallaton Common—as the parson preached the foolishest sermon—It's a long time back—A great gap of sinful wasted life lies between—But it has been followed all through by the love of my dearest old Mother.

  As soon as the 3 Punch men who are gone to Paris for a holiday return, I will try & run over to Boulogne and take a house for wh. I shan't mind paying, as the old lady won't. But all she saves will be for you, and I am rather glad that some dear relations of mine should have their minds at ease, and know that I am not making any very serious drain on the purse of the poor old soul.

  Miss Drury continues to be a very jolly honest young lady I think and the children are still tolerable. Towards the end of the month I get so nervous that I don't speak to anybody scarcely, and once actually got up in the middle of the night and came down & wrote in my night-shimee: but that don't happen often, and I own I had had a nap after dinner that day. The publishers are quite contented—and now I must get to work. God bless my dearest old Mammy and G P: and send us a good meeting at Boulogne.

W M T.

piracy: apparently of *Mrs. Perkins's Ball.*   *O'Gorman Mahon:* Charles Mahon (1800-91), a fire-eating Irishman known as "the O'Gorman Mahon."   *this very number:* Number 7 for July 1847.   *without God in the world:* quoted from Ephesians 2: 12.   *Mr. FitzGerald:* John Purcell FitzGerald (d. 1852), who was married to the former Mary Francis.   *Alboni:* Marietta Alboni (1826-94), contralto. *Mrs. Huyshe:* wife of the Reverend Francis Huyshe (b. 1768). *Wentworth:* Wentworth Huyshe (1812-29), the only son of the Reverend Huyshe and his wife. *Miss Drury:* the governess.

95. TO WILLIAM SMITH WILLIAMS
23 October 1847

13 Young St. Kensington. October 23.

My dear Sir

I wish you had not sent me Jane Eyre. It interested me so much that I have lost (or won if you like) a whole day in reading it at the busiest period, with the printers I know waiting for copy. Who the author can be I can't guess—if a woman she knows her language better than most ladies do, or has had a 'classical' education. It is a fine book though—the man & woman capital—the style very generous and upright so to speak. I thought it was Kinglake for some time. The plot of the story is one with wh. I am familiar. Some of the love passages made me cry—to the astonishment of John who came in with the coals—St. John the Missionary is a failure I think but a good failure there are parts excellent I dont know why I tell you this but that I have been exceedingly moved & pleased by Jane Eyre. It is a womans writing, but whose? Give my respects and thanks to the author—whose novel is the first English one (& the French are only romances now) that I've been able to read for many a day.

Very truly yours my dear Sir

W M Thackeray—

Williams: William Smith Williams (1800-75), adviser of the firm of Smith, Elder, and Company, who had published Charlotte Brontë's *Jane Eyre*.

96. TO LEIGH HUNT
3 January 1848

13 Young St.
January 3. 184[8].

My dear Hunt

I have not only not had time to thank you for the Jar of Honey: but I have not even tasted any of it; nor of Tennyson's Medley—having been so consumedly occupied with business, and with Jollification subsequently in these latter days We have had supper parties singing parties dinner-parties headaches rather in the morning

&c—but the week must not pass over without saying Hail to Leigh Hunt.

Last week we were to have met at the Procters but I forgot & you were ill—Can we meet any where this week[?]. For instance tomorrow at 5 there will be 2 woodcocks presented by M. J. O'Connell: and you shall have a bit or not as you like: and with or without an answer.

My dear Hunt I wish you an H. N. Y.

Yours ever
W M Thackeray.

Jar of Honey . . . Tennyson's Medley: Hunt's *A Jar of Honey from Mount Hybla* and Tennyson's *The Princess. A Medley* had just been published. *O'Connell:* Morgan John O'Connell (1811-75), nephew of Daniel O'Connell (1775-1847).

97. TO WILLIAM SMITH WILLIAMS
January 1848

13 Young St. Kensington.

My dear Mr. Williams
I am quite vexed that by some blundering of mine I shd. have delayed answering Currer-Bell's enormous compliment so long. I didn't know what to say in reply: it quite flustered and upset me—Is it true I wonder? &c—but a truce to egotisms—thank you for your kindness in sending me the volumes, and (indirectly) for the greatest compliment I have ever recd. in my life

faithfully yours
W M Thackeray

enormous compliment: the second edition of *Jane Eyre* (1848) contained a powerful dedication to Thackeray.

98. TO MRS. EDWARD MARLBOROUGH FITZGERALD
31 January 1848

13 Young St.
Kensington.
Monday Jan 31.

My dear Mrs. FitzGerald
I know what you have been thinking the past week—but indeed it is not so—At the end of the month I always have a life-&-

death struggle to get out my Number of Vanity Fair—I am always engaged for a week before hand My life is passed in dining and pennyalining I have only 1 free day this week and that I must give to the children. Pray dont think I am neglectful—and let me come to see an old kind friend one day next week.

Ever faithfully yours
W M Thackeray.

99. TO MRS. JOHN RITCHIE
5 February 1848

Kensington. Feb 5. 1848.

My dear Aunt

You have very good right to complain of some nephews and nieces of your's who might put a pen to paper occasionally, and gratify an old aunt who sits in the country by her fireside lonely and without news—that is you may scold all except your nephew Titmarsh whose pen is so occupied in providing for the butcher the baker the candlestick-maker that he has very little time for his friends and relatives. Do you know I have not written to my mother for 3 weeks till yesterday, and then I was obliged to send her a scolding My dear old Mother is always tormenting herself about the children, and their illnesses You must know they have had the chicken pox—Anny rather badly: also she had a sore toe wh. has troubled her: and her poor Granny is so alarmed about these things that she writes me over the most dismal letters, telling me what to do, entreating me to employ her doctor, not mine &c—I am obliged to say no to these prayers: and also to be compelled to give annoyance to such a gentle and loving creature. Now both these young ladies are quite well and seated in my room in my arm chairs reading—

Their Governess has gone to pass the day with her family it being her sisters birthday, and we three are presently going out for a days holiday likewise—they to pass the day with some friends and I to take 4 little boys to the play. I like taking children to the play—their laughing makes me laugh if the play does not.

So Constantia has found a nice young man, has she? Amen. She is a nice young lass and I hope she will be happy. I should like a wife myself very much: but keep myself occupied by falling in love with twenty women at a time. You must know I am become quite a Lion now, and live with all sorts of great people: but their flattery has not turned my head as yet, please God, and my reign as a fashionable literary man will very soon be over: and somebody else will be favorite in my stead.

The Bedingfields have got the snuggest little cottage in the world every thing neat trim spick & span and apple pie. It wd. do your heart good to see. So Charles sent you some wine—do you want any thing else my dear Aunt? do tell me if you do: for indeed I would have no greater pleasure in life than in contributing in any way to your comfort. God bless you.

100. TO GEORGE HENRY LEWES
6 March 1848

13 Young St. Kensington.
6 March. 1848

My dear Sir
I have just read your notice in the Chronicle (I conclude it is a friend who has penned it) and am much affected by the friendliness of the sympathy, and by the kindness of the reproof of the critic.

That passage wh. you quote bears very hardly upon the poor alderman certainly: but I don't mean that the man deprived of turtle would as a consequence steal bread: only that he in the possession of luxuries and riding through life respectably in a gig, should be very chary of despising poor Lazarus on foot, & look very humbly and leniently upon the faults of his less fortunate brethren—If Becky had had 5000 a year I have no doubt in my mind that she would have been respectable; increased her fortune advanced her family in the world: laid up treasures for herself in the shape of 3 per cents, social position, reputation &c—like Louis Philippe let us say, or like many a person highly & comfortably placed in the world not guilty of many wrongs of commission, satisfied with himself, never doubting of his merit, and decorously angry at the errors of less lucky men—What satire is so awful as Lead us not into temptation? What is the Gospel and life of our Lord (excuse me for mentioning it) but a tremendous Protest against pride and self-righteousness? God forgive us all, I pray, and deliver us from evil.

I am quite aware of the dismal roguery wh. goes all through the Vanity Fair story—and God forbid that the world should be like it altogether: though I fear it is more like it than we like to own. But my object is to make every body engaged, engaged in the pursuit of Vanity and I must carry my story through in this dreary minor key, with only occasional hints here & there of better things—of better things wh. it does not become me to preach—

I never scarcely write letters to critics and beg you to excuse me for sending you this. It is only because I have just laid down the paper, and am much moved by the sincere good will of my critic.
Very faithfully yours
W M Thackeray.

Lewes: George Henry Lewes (1817-78), miscellaneous writer, who later lived with George Eliot.   *notice in the Chronicle:* in the issue of 6 March 1848.   *Lead us not into temptation:* Matthew 6: 13; Luke 11: 4.

101. TO EDWARD FITZGERALD
March-May 1848

My dear old Yedward It is not true what Gurlyle has written to you about my having become a tremenjuous lion &c—too grand to &c—but what is true is that a feller who is writing all day for money gets sick of pens and paper when his work is over, and I go on dawdling and thinking of writing and months pass away. All that about being a Lion is nonsense. I cant eat more dinners than I used last year and dine at home with my dear little women three times a week: but 2 or 3 great people ask me to their houses: and Vanity Fair does everything but pay. I am glad if you like it. I don't care a dem if some other people do or dont: and always try to keep that damper against flattery. 'What does it matter whether this man who is an ass likes your book or not' I have had the Edinburgh Review about me and upon my word haven't read it or so much as opened my copy. I looked at it at the Club but not through and—this modesty is furiously egotistical.

This was wrote I dont know how long ago: but my mind was unequal to the gigantic effort of filling a whole 1/2 sheet and I think another No. of V. F has been written since 'I penned the above lines'—as the Novelists say.

I caught a glimpse of the old Frau Mutter riding alone in the Park a few weeks ago: and looking very melancholy I've not had the courage to call, but I have seen both Ainsworth and Albert Smith. The latter is a good kind creature, though Heaven has written Snob undisguisedly on his mean keen good-natured intelligent face. As for Ainsworth he is more hairy than ever. He begins to sprout at his  under lip now and curls all over really its not unlike him. He was at dinner where I was yesterday, and made an observation about Harvey sauce o with such emphasis and solemnity. I burst out laughing but Jack Shepherd didn't know at what.

A letter from the young Madrileno of the Calle de las Caritas arrived yesterday he says 'Not a word from Fitz.[']

Your namesake they say has been stabbed in the *bas ventre* at Civita Vecchia. I am afraid he is recovering. The world does not contain a greater villain.

Gurlyle is immensely grand and savage now. He has a Cromwellian letter against the Irish in this weeks Examiner I declare it seems like insanity almost his contempt for all mankind, and the way in wh. he shirks from the argument when called upon to *préciser* his own remedies for the state of things. Last Sunday I saw Jeames Spending walking in the Park with some children and a lady from the country I am one of the swells there. I have got a Cob wh. is the admiration of all—strong handsome goodnatured fast and never tired. You shall have a ride behind me if you come to London. Why dont you?. I am going to give a party on the 9th. May. Mrs. Dickens & Miss Hogarth made me give it. And I am in a great funk. I have not got a shilling. Isn't it wonderful? I make a great deal of money and it goes pouring and pouring out in a frightful volubility.

My little women are delightful. They are drawing at my work table at this minute: and they act upon me after the world like soda water. God bless em. I have a governess for them an excellent woman but a great ass. Leech drew a caricature the other day of a little boy & Guardsman, under wh. was a dialogue with 'Little boy *loq*.['] Isn't Boyloq a French author? asked the governess—But I dont like to part with her she is so kind and thoroughly good.

I have got a black niece staying with me: daughter of a natural sister of mine. She was never in Europe before & wrote to my mother the other day as her 'dear Grandmamma' Fancy the astonishment of that dear majestic old woman!

This letter has been delayed and delayed until I fancied it would never go—Nevertheless I am always yours, and like you almost as much as I did 20 years ago—God bless you my dear old fellow

                                                                     W M T.

Edinburgh Review: the January 1848 issue had contained Abraham Hayward's article, "Thackeray's Writings."   *Albert Smith:* (1816-60), novelist, miscellaneous writer, and lecturer.   *Madrileno:* Saville Morton, who was Madrid correspondent for an unidentified London journal.   *namesake:* Edward Marlborough FitzGerald.   *bas ventre:* (Fr.) lower abdomen or private parts. *Cromwellian letter . . . Examiner:* Carlyle's "Repeal of the Union," which had appeared in *The Examiner* of 29 April 1848.   *préciser:* (Fr.) specify. *Spending:* James Spedding (1808-81), whom Thackeray had met at Trinity College, Cambridge, and who became a notable Bacon scholar.   *loq.:* (Lat.) speaks.   *natural sister:* Mrs. Blechynden.

102. TO JOHN FORSTER
14 April 1848

                                            Good Friday. Kensington.
My dear Forster,
      I would not write to thank you for Goldsmith, until I had finished reading him and although I wanted to write a life of him myself (after Fielding which has long been a favourite biographical project of mine)—what can I say, but that your book is delightful? I have read it with the greatest interest and pleasure, got a capital notion of Goldsmith out of it, and quite sympathise with your love for the dear simple kindly creature. I was in his chambers in Brick Court the other day. Davidson has them now, they were Sergt. Murphy's—the bedroom is a closet without any light in it. It quite pains me to think of the kind old fellow dying off there. There is some good carved work in the room: and one can fancy him with General Oglethorpe and the other Topham Beauclerc, wasn't it? and the fellow coming in with the screw of tea and sugar. What a fine picture Leslie would make of it. That crowd of hangers on and lazy good humour, how thoroughly Irish it is. Maginn used always to have a half dozen of tipsy fellows in his train, to whom he gave money and clothes, (by credit at the tailors) which they used to pawn. How prettily Horneck comes in, and lights up the story with a little smile of sentiment. I think both of them must have been in love with him.

"And as the hare whom hounds and horns pursue,
Pants to the place from which at first she flew."

What an exquisite simile it is! What language! What is it that brings tears to one's eyes in reading the lines? I passed two rainy days at Glengariff in Ireland, reading the Animated Nature with delight and surprize. What a charming simplicity and sweetness: what a dear old humourist! I have just come to his death the fact is—and I give you my word, I am quite affected by it. He is our personal friend. I'm sure I have a perfect notion of his individuality—his eyes, the quiver of his mouth, and his voice and brogue. I'm certain he had a *plaintive* look, not the heroic one which Reynolds tried to give him. How delightful is the love they all bore him and what pleasant courteous stately figures they are in the picture.

You see this is an interjectional commentary. I am delighted in a word with the book (except the first book which I don't think is full enough of the subject, and has too didactic and auctorial an air) and write off in a hurry to say how very much obliged to you I am for your gift.

Yours my dear Forster, most sincerely
W. M. Thackeray.

Goldsmith: Forster's *The Life and Adventures of Oliver Goldsmith*, which had just been published.   *Davidson:* Henry (later Sir Henry) Davison (1805?-60), barrister, to whom Thackeray later dedicated *The Virginians*.   *Murphy:* Francis Stack Murphy (1810?-60), barrister and M. P. for Cork.   *Oglethorpe:* General James Edward Oglethorpe (1696-1785).   *Topham Beauclerc:* (1739-80), best known as a friend of Dr. Johnson's.   *Leslie:* Charles Robert Leslie (1794-1859), genre and literary painter.   *both of them:* Mary Horneck ("the Jessamy Bride") and her sister Catherine.   *"And . . . flew":* taken from Goldsmith's *The Deserted Village* (1770), ll. 93-94.   *Animated Nature:* Goldsmith's *An History of the Earth and Animated Nature* (1774).   *heroic one . . . give him:* in Reynolds' portrait (National Gallery, London).

103. TO THE DUKE OF DEVONSHIRE
1 May 1848

Kensington. May 1. 1848.
My lord Duke
Mrs. Rawdon Crawley whom I saw last week and whom I informed of Your Grace's desire to have her portrait, was good

enough to permit me to copy a little drawing made of her 'in happier days', she said with a sigh by Smee the Royal Academician.

Mrs. Crawley now lives in a small but very pretty little house in Belgravia: and is conspicuous for her numerous charities wh. always get into the newspaper, and her unaffected piety. Many of the most exalted and spotless of her own sex visit her, and are of opinion that she is a *most injured woman.* There is no *sort of truth* in the stories regarding Mrs. Crawley & the late Lord Steyne. The licentious character of that nobleman alone gave rise to reports from wh. alas! the most spotless life and reputation cannot always defend themselves—

The present Sir Rawdon Crawley (who succeeded his late uncle Sir Pitt 1832, Sir Pitt died on the passing of the Reform Bill) does not see his mother: and his undutifulness is a cause of deepest grief, to that admirable lady. 'If it were not for *higher things,'* she says, how could she have borne up against the worlds calumny, a wicked husbands cruelty and falseness, and the thanklessness (sharper than a serpent's tooth) of an adored child? But she has been preserved mercifully preserved to bear all these griefs and awaits her reward *elsewhere.* The italics are Mrs. Crawley's own.

She took the style and title of Lady Crawley for some time after Sir Pitts death in 1832, but it turned out that Colonel Crawley Governor of Coventry Island had died of fever three months before his brother, whereupon Mrs. Rawdon was obliged to lay down the title wh. she had prematurely assumed.

The late Jos. Sedley, Esqre. of the Bengal Civil Service left her two lakhs of rupees, on the interest of wh. the widow lives in the practices of piety and benevolence before mentioned. She has lost what little good looks she once possessed, and wears false hair and teeth (the latter give her rather a ghastly look when she smiles) and—for a pious woman—is the best crinolined lady in Knightsbridge district.

Colonel and Mrs. W. Dobbin live in Hampshire near Sir R. Crawley: Lady Jane was godmother to their little girl: and the ladies are exceedingly attached to each other. The Colonel's 'History of the Punjaub' is looked for with much anxiety in some circles.

Captain & Lt. Colonel G. Sedley-Osborne (he wishes he says to be distinguished from some other branches of the Osborne family and is descended by the mothers side from Sir Charles Sedley) is I need not say well, for I saw him in a most richly embroidered cambric pink shirt with diamond studds) bowing to your Grace at the last party at Devonshire House. He is in Parliament: but the property left him by his Grandfather has, I hear, been a good deal overrated.

He was very sweet upon Miss Crawley Sir Pitt's daughter who married her cousin the present Baronet, and a good deal cut up when he was refused. He is not however a man to be permanently cast down by sentimental disappointments. His chief cause of annoyance at the present moment is that he is growing bald, but his whiskers are still without a gray hair, and the finest in London.

I think these are the latest particulars relating to a number of persons about whom Your Grace was good enough to express some interest. I am very glad to be enabled to give this information and am
Your Graces very much obliged Svnt
W. M. Thackeray.

P.S. Lady O'Dowd is at O'Dowdstown *arming*. She has just sent in a letter of adhesion to the Lord Lieutenant, wh. has been acknowledged by his Excellency's private secretary Mr. Corry Connellan. Miss Glorvina O'Dowd is thinking of coming up to the Castle to marry the last-named gentleman.

P.S. 2. The India mail just arrived announces the utter ruin of the Union Bank of Calcutta in wh. all Mrs. Crawleys money was. Will Fate never cease to persecute that suffering Saint?.

Duke: William George Spencer Cavendish (1790-1858), sixth Duke of Devonshire. *Crawley:* an accompanying drawing shows Becky reclining on a couch, reading *Altina*. On the floor lies an open copy of Choderlos de Laclos' *Les Liaisons Dangereuses.*   *serpent's tooth:* King Lear, II, 311-12: "How sharper than a serpent's tooth it is / To have a thankless child!"   *Sir Charles Sedley:* (1639?-1701), dramatist known for his wit and profligacy.

104. TO MRS. WILLIAM HENRY BROOKFIELD
June 1848

Dear Mrs. Brookfield Count Dorsay came to dinner on Friday, splendid in a large blue coat and an immense flower in his button gracious and good natured beyond measure. Jacob Omnium Morris of the Times, and K Macaulay with my little French friend formed the party—The little Frenchman remarked how the 2 latter were incessantly watching the great Dorsay during dinner. He drank wine with both of them, and pronounced Morris to be one of the handsomest men he had ever seen. So he is, beautiful, with an expression of melancholy tenderness in his large brown eyes, and a tone of voice that's quite heart-breaking—A little German governess said about him the other day—Il n'est pas permis d'avoir d'aussi beaux yeux que ça. *es ist polizey-verboten*—Dorsay charmed the young fellow with kindness.

He speaks the queerest English in the world and the most singular French. He doesn't speak French any more that is but a splendid jargon. He pleases I think by his unbounded good humour and generous sympathy with every body. It was a comfort to see him eat roast-beef such a quantity of it! He likes it just as well as the best of great dinners. He says it is the best and what is better.

He read us out a letter from a spirituel friend at Paris describing the scene—very brilliant lively and sparkling and false. By some strange coincidence the Times correspondent of yesterday had a passage in his contribution word for word the same as that wh. Dorsay read us. So these great folks are in relation with the Times are they? Lady Blessington read me a letter from the same place, from Madame Guiccioli now Madame de Boissy—The compliments wd. have staggered any weak person. They were stunning tremendous— Do women write often to each other in this way? I wonder.

Dorsay: Count Alfred d'Orsay (1801-52), wit and dandy.   *Jacob Omnium:* the pseudonym of Matthew James Higgins (1810-68), miscellaneous writer. Thackeray later dedicated *Philip* to him.   *Morris:* Mowbray Morris (1819-74), manager of *The Times.*   *K Macaulay:* Kenneth Macaulay (1815-67), barrister.   *Il n'est . . . que ça:* (Fr.) It is not permitted to have such beautiful eyes as that.   *es ist polizey-verboten:* (Ger.) it is prohibited by the police.   *spirituel:* (Fr.) witty.   *Lady Blessington:* the former Marguerite Power (1789-1849), Countess of Blessington, who lived with Count d'Orsay at Gore House, Kensington, where she was a prominent hostess.   *Madame Guiccioli now Madame de Boissy:* the former Teresa Gamba (d. 1873), who had been Byron's mistress when she was Countess Guiccioli, had recently married Hilaire Rouillé, Marquis de Boissy (1798-1866).

105. TO MRS. HENRY CARMICHAEL-SMYTH
29 June 1848

2[9] June.

My dearest old Mammy. Vanity Fair is this instant done and I have been worked so hard that I can hardly hold a pen and say God bless my dearest old Mother. I had not time even to listen to the awful cannonading in your town: Thank God you are going to leave it. Here are the children come in a fly to fetch me, we are going to have a little holiday and see the Rivals to night. The bore is that the Governess must come too, and instead of being with them, I must endure her. I am very much pleased to have done—very melancholy and beat; and humble in mind I hope praying to—not to feel elation &c for I get so much praise that I want keeping down— And I want to send one line just to kiss my dearest old Mother, and G P.

cannonading: an insurrection in Paris from 23 to 26 June 1848.   *the Rivals:* Richard Brinsley Sheridan's comedy (1775).

106. TO MRS. BRYAN WALLER PROCTER
29 June 1848

My dear Mrs. Procter. Engaged on Sunday: have been for past 10 days in such a state of work & excitement as have put me in a fever—Dont you see I am so nervous I can hardly write. Just come away from printing office, and waiting for little girls to go a pleasuring somewhere, then to see the Rivals this evening—if that Governess wd but have taken the broad hint I gave her & have gone home for the night but not she: and instead of having the childrens company in private box must sit back and see this stoopid young lady Is Procter here? there is a bachelor dinner knocked up yesterday at my house tomorrow at 7 1/2. Roast beef &c   R. S. V. P. Heres the slip of the dedi[ca]tion; just put in my hands you see it is very simple. I shd. have liked to put down you too but suppose mustnt say of a lady that I am affectionately yours

W M T.

the dedi[ca]tion: Vanity Fair is dedicated affectionately to B. W. Procter.

107. TO MRS. WILLIAM HENRY BROOKFIELD
10 July 1848

My dear Madam

On calling on our mutual friend Mrs. Procter yesterday she was polite enough to offer me a seat in her box at Drury Lane Theatre this evening, when *Her Majesty* honors the play-house with a visit for the benefit of Mr. Macready. Shakspeare is always amusing and I am told the aspect of the Beefeaters at the Royal box is very *imposing*.

I mentioned to Mrs. Procter that I had myself witnessed many entertainments of this nature and did not very much desire to be present: but intimated to her that I had a friend who I believed was most anxious to witness Mr. Macready's performance in the *august presence* of the Sovereign.

I mentioned the name of your husband, and found that *she had already* with her usual politeness despatched a card to that gentleman. Whom I shall therefore have the happiness of meeting this evening.

But, perhaps you are aware, that *a chosen few* are admitted *behind the scenes* of the Theatre, where when the Curtain rises, they appear *behind the performers,* and with loyal hearts join in the National Anthem at the very feet of their Queen. My reverend friend has an elegant voice—perhaps he would like to lift it up in a chorus, wh. though performed in the *Temple of Thespis,* I cannot but consider to be in the nature of a *hymn.* I send therefore a ticket of wh. I beg his polite acceptance, and am dear Madam
        With the utmost respect
           Your very faithful Servt
             W M Thackeray.

I was a little late for the magnificent entertainment of my *titled friends* Sir William & Lady Molesworth on Saturday, and indeed the first course had been removed when I made my appearance.

The banquet was sumptuous in the extreme, & the company of the most select order—I had the happiness of sitting next to Clarence Bulbul Esqe. M. P. and opposite was the Most Noble the Marquess of Steyne—Fancy my happiness in the company of persons so *distinguished.*

A delightful concert followed the dinner and the whole concluded with a Sumptuous supper: nor did the party separate until a late hour.

benefit of Mr. Macready: before leaving for America Macready gave a farewell performance on 10 July 1848, appearing in *Henry VIII.* *Molesworth:* Sir William Molesworth (1810-55), eighth Baronet, and his wife, the former Andalusia Carstairs (d. 1888). *Clarence Bulbul:* a character created by Thackeray in *Our Street,* who reappears in *Pendennis.*

108. TO MR. AND MRS. EDWARD JOHN SARTORIS
July 1848

Mr. Thackeray requests the pleasure of Mr. & Mrs. Sartoris's company to a little drum on Tuesday July 18.

drum: an evening gathering, which took place on Thackeray's thirty-seventh birthday.

109. TO ROBERT BELL
3 September 1848

Sunday Sepr. 3.

My dear Bell
    Although I have made a rule to myself never to thank critics yet I like to break it continually, and especially in the present instance for what I hope is the excellent article in Fraser. It seems to me very just in most points as regards the author: some he questions as usual— If I had put in more fresh air as you call it my object wd. have been defeated—It is to indicate, in cheerful terms, that we are for the most part an abominably foolish and selfish people 'desperately wicked' and all eager after vanities. Everybody you see is in that book—for instance if I had made Amelia a higher order of woman there would have been no vanity in Dobbins falling in love with her, whereas the impression at present is that he is a fool for his pains that he has married a silly little thing and in fact has found out his error rather a sweet & tender one however, *quia multum amavit.* I want to leave every body dissatisfied and unhappy at the end of the story—we ought

all to be with [our] own and all other stories. Good God dont I see (in that may-be cracked & warped looking glass in wh. I am always looking) my own weaknesses wickednesses lusts follies shortcomings?—in company let us hope with better qualities about wh. we will pretermit discourse. We must lift up our voices about these and howl to a congregation of fools: so much at least has been my endeavour. You have all of you taken my misanthropy to task—I wish I could myself: but take the world by a certain standard [*drawing of a large cross*] (you know what I mean) and who dares talk of having any virtue at all?. For instance Forster says [']After a scene with Blifil, the air is cleared by a laugh of Tom Jones'—why Tom Jones in my holding is as big a rogue as Blifil. Before God he is—I mean the man is selfish according to his nature as Blifil according to his. In fact I've a strong impression that we are most of us not fit for————never mind

Pathos I hold should be very occasional indeed in humourous works and indicated rather than expressed or expressed very rarely. In the passage where Amelia is represented as trying to separate her self from the boy—She goes up stairs and leaves him with his aunt 'as that poor Lady Jane Grey tried the axe wh. was to separate her slender life' I say that is a fine image whoever wrote it (& I came on it quite by surprize in a review the other day) that is greatly pathetic I think: it leaves you to make your own sad picture—We shouldn't do much more than that I think in comic books—In a story written in the pathetic key it would be different & then the comedy perhaps should be occasional. Some day—but a truce to egotistical twaddle. It seems to me such a time ago that V F was written that one may talk of it as of somebody else's performance. My dear Bell I am very thankful for your friendliness and pleased to have your good opinion.

           Faithfully yours
            W M Thackeray.

Bell . . . article: Robert Bell (1800-67), miscellaneous writer, had favorably reviewed *Vanity Fair* in the September 1848 issue of *Fraser's Magazine*. *'desperately wicked':* "The heart is deceitful above all things, and desperately wicked: who can know it?" (Jeremiah 17: 9).   *quia multum amavit:* (Lat.) because he loved much.   *Forster says:* in a review of *Vanity Fair* published in the 22 July 1848 issue of *The Examiner*.   *'as that poor Lady Jane Grey . . . life':* in Chapter 50.

110. TO MRS. WILLIAM HENRY BROOKFIELD
5 September 1848

New York. September 5. 1848.

Dear Madam

It seems to me a long time since I had the honour of seeing you. I should be glad to have some account of your health. We made a beautiful voyage of 13 & 1/2 days, and reached this fine city yesterday—the entrance of the bay is beautiful, the magnificent woods of the Susquehannah stretch down to the shore, & from Hoboken Lighthouse to Vancouvers Island the bay presents one brilliant blaze of natural & commercial loveliness—Hearing that Titmarsh was on board the steamer the Lord Mayor and Aldermen of New York came down to receive us, and the batteries on Long Island fired a salute. General Jackson called at my hotel (the Astor house) I found him a kind old man though he has a wooden leg and takes a great deal of snuff. Broadway has certainly disappointed me—it is nothing to be compared to our own dear Holborn Hill. But the beautiful range of the Alleyghanny mountains wh. I see from my windows, and the roar of the Niagara Cataract wh. empties itself out of the Mississippi into the Oregon Territory, have an effect, wh. your fine eye for the picturesque and keen sense of the Beautiful & the Natural would I am sure lead you to appreciate—The oysters here are much larger than ours: and the canvass-backed ducks are reckoned, and indeed are, a delicacy—The house where Washington is born is still shown, but the General I am informed is dead much regretted. The clergy here is both numerous and respected and the Archbishop of New York is a most venerable and delightful prelate, whose sermons are however a little long. The ladies are without exception the—but here the first gong sounds for dinner and the black Slave who waits on me comes up & says 'Massa! Hab only five minutes for dinnah! Make haste, git no pumpkin-pie else,' so unwillingly I am obliged to break off my note and to subscribe myself

My dear Madam
Your very faithful Servt
W M Thackeray

What I really mean is that I should like very much to come on Friday or Saturday evening if W is at home—

New York: not having seen Thackeray for a time, Mrs. Brookfield thought for a moment that he really might have gone to New York.

111. TO MRS. BRYAN WALLER PROCTER
13 September 1848

Kensington 13 Sepr.

My dear Mrs. Procter   I know what your opinion has been for some days past: but I am obliged to bear up against the unkind unjust cruel sentiments of many of my fellow creatures: and bow down gently to my persecutors. How do you know, I shd. like to know, whether I have not had my portmanteau packed and ready to start for Dover twice and what circumstances have intervened to prevent me? Once I went to Brighton for 2 days and departed swearing to go back again but it is always the same difficulty—A sea side lodging in the present state of my finances is impossible. I have got a pile of bills before me now that by heavens are perfectly ludicrous I have paid heaps since I came back. I have a leg of mutton and live at the rate of a coach and six. I dont know how it is—the old story wh. I am always grumbling to you about but the sea side trip is finished that is quite clear: and I cant think of transporting this extravagant household out of the parish. My mother is coming soon thank Heaven to take the command over me, and I shall be solvent some day let us hope. I think it is impossible for literary men to write natural letters any more: I was just going to say something, but thinks I in future ages when this letter comes to be &c—they will say 'he was in embarrassed circumstances he was reckless and laughed at his prodigality he was &c.[']

I have before me besides the bills 4 notes requesting advances of money. Ha Ha! isn't it enough to make one wild?

Two nights ago good-natured Forster asked the children to dinner and took us to the play: where I bored myself and slept a great deal. Brookfield and the other children were however perfectly happy with Paul Pry and the Wreck ashore, in wh. my beloved Miss Woolgar did not look her best I thought. No body does look so any more. At Brighton Virginia was on the sofa lovely, interesting and unwell—I did not care twopence. Here is somebody else on the sofa here looking uncommonly pretty too and with eyes just as bright as those wh. have rolled round me for the last 6 years—well—it's all over. I wish I could get into the Coach this minute and come and talk to you about it. But it *is* all done for. She never cared 2d 1/2 for me—and my heart is a vacuum. But I go and see her and have a kind tender fraternal or paternal regard & that sort of thing—but the rest is all gone. Why, we used to admire the Scottish Chiefs once and cry over Thaddeus of Warsaw—Fond follies of youth!   Tomorrow it will be eight years since my poor dear little wife jumped into the great calm sunshiny sea off the Isle of Wight: and she has been dead or worse ever since. Good God what a year of pain and hope the first one was and bitter bitter tears—that's all over too. Love, hope, infernal pain & disappointment. All I remember is that some people were very kind to me. You among the first my dear good friends.

Among the 4 letters is one from a man who used to give me very good dinners 12 years ago and whom Fate has pursued since— He recals the old times, & then fires off a salvo of compliments, introduces his own mishaps, and proposes a little loan of *deux ou trois livres sterlings* he doesn't say 2 or 3£ but puts it in French: and concludes with *Scusatemi* (in a clerk like Lombard Street hand) and 'Sincerely and devotedly yours' So & so. Isn't it pitiful?. I will shut up this note and go and have a walk with the little people.

Always afftly yours
W M T.

Paul Pry and the Wreck ashore: Paul Pry (1825) by John Poole (1786-1872) and *The Wreck Ashore* (1830) by John Baldwin Buckstone (1802-79).   *Miss Woolgar:* Sarah Jane Woolgar (1824-1909), who made her London debut in October 1843 at the Adelphi Theater.   *Virginia:* Virginia Pattle, later Lady Somers.   *eyes... 6 years:* those of Mrs. Brookfield.   *the Scottish Chiefs . . . Thaddeus of Warsaw:* novels by Jane Porter (1776-1850), published in 1803 and 1810 respectively.   *deux ou trois livres sterlings:* (Fr.) two or three pounds sterling. *Scusatemi:* (Ital.) Excuse me.

112. TO LADY CULLUM
4 October 1848

Dear Lady Cullum
    There is no fighting against fate, and I am obliged with a great deal of regret to give up the pleasure wh. I had promised myself of a visit to Hardwick. We were stopped up by a conglomeration of waggons in Smithfield, and arrived at the E. C. terminus at 1 minute past 11, so that my chance of coming was over until 3/30: and I picture to myself your carriage in waiting and your kindness exerted for me in vain.   I intended to come off at 3 1/2 but having 4 hours to wait about London, ill-advisedly went to see my publishers who told me what I knew very well that I had no business to leave my work & go pleasuring, that I must & ought to see my new ship launched before I took recreation of any kind—finally they worked upon my feelings so that (having taken leave already of my family) I am going I don't know actually whither, but to some solitary place for a week where I can work undisturbed—

If ever you will ask me again after so many refusals, or if you will pardon me I dont know but indeed it is a combat between duty & pleasure (as you will see on the frontispiece to the please God forthcoming story of Pendennis) and I am yielding to the former with the worst possible grace.

Most faithfully yours dear Lady Cullum
W M Thackeray.

Lady Cullum: the wife of The Reverend Sir Thomas Cullum (1777-1855), eighth Baronet, who lived at Hardwick, Bury St. Edmonds.

113. TO MRS. WILLIAM HENRY BROOKFIELD
7-9 October 1848

Brighton. Saturday—Monday.

Thank you for your letter dear Mrs. Brookfield it made this gay place look twice as gay yesterday when I got it—Last night when I had come home to work, 2 men spied a light in my room & came in and began smoking—they talked about racing and the odds all the time, one of them I am happy to say is a Lord, & the other a Brighton buck—when they were gone (& indeed I listened to them with a great deal of pleasure for I like to hear people of all sorts) at midnight & in the quiet I read your letter over again, and one from Miss Anny and from my dear old Mother who is to come on the 12th. and whose heart is yearning for her children—I must be at home to receive her and some days ten or so at least to make her comfortable, so, with many thanks for Mrs. Elton's invitation I must decline it for the present if you please. You may be sure I went the very first thing to Virginia and her sisters, who were very kind to me and I think are very fond of me, and their talk and V's beauty consoled me for my heart was very sore: and I was ill and out of spirits. A change, a fine air, a wonderful sunshine and moonlight, and a great spectacle of happy people perpetually rolling by has done me all the good in the world and then one of the Miss Smiths told me a story wh. is the very thing for the beginning of Pendennis wh. is actually begun and in progress—This is a comical beginning rather; the other, wh. I did not like, was sentimental; and will yet come in very well after the startling comical business has been played off.—See how beautifully I have put stops to the last sentence; and crossed the t's & dotted the i's! It was written 4 hours ago before dinner; before Jullien's concert, before a walk by the sea shore—I have been thinking what a number of ladies, and gentlemen too, live like you just now—in a smart papered room with rats gnawing behind the Wainscot. Be hanged to the rats! but they are a sort of company. You must have a poker ready, and if the rats come out, bang, beat them on the head. This is an allegory. Why, it would work up into a little moral poem, if you chose to write it. Jullien was splendid in his white waistcoat, and played famous easy music, wh. anybody may comprehend & like. There was a delightful cornet-à-piston (mark the ` on the a)—the fact is I am thinking about something else all the while, and very tired & weary—But I thought I would like to say good night to you: and what news shall I give you just for the last? Well then, Miss Virginia is gone away: not to come back while I am here. Good night, Mam if you please.

Madam I did not think about you one bit all yesterday, being entirely occupied with my 2 new friends Mrs. Pendennis & her son Mr. Arthur Pendennis. I got up very early again this morning and was with them for more than two hours before breakfast—He is a very good natured generous young fellow and I begin to like him considerably. I wonder whether he is interesting to me from selfish reasons and because I fancy we resemble each other in many points, & whether I can get the public to like him too? We had the most magnificent Sunshiny Sunday: and I passed the evening very rationally with Mr. Fonblanque, and Mr. Sheil—a great orator of whom perhaps you have heard, at present lying here afflicted with gout and with such an Irish wife. Never was a truer saying than that those people are foreigners—They have neither English notions, manners, nor morals—I mean what is right & natural to them is absurd, & unreasonable to us. It was as good as Mrs. O'Dowd to hear Mrs. Sheil interrupt her Richard, and give her opinions on the state of Ireland to those 2 great hard-headed keen accomplished men of the world. Richard listened to her foolishness with admirable forbearance & good-humour—I'm afraid I dont respect your sex enough though.—Yes I do when they are occupied with loving & sentiment rather than with other business of life.

I had a mind to send you a Weekly Paper, containing contemptuous remarks regarding an author of your acquaintance. I don't know who this critic is but he always has a shot at me once a month, & I bet a guinea he is an Irishman.

So we have got the Cholera. Are you looking out for a visit? Did you try the Stethoscope? and after listening at your chest did it say that your lungs were sore?—A gentleman here, Mr. Morier, told me on Saturday about Packman, that Packman had attended Mrs. Morier for many months pronounced her attacked with some complaint, did her no good, and has been succeeded by Rigby who says she has some other complaint and is curing her pretty quickly. This will make you comfortable against you come to town and tend to remove your faith in your Doctor—Trust not in men nor the (male) children of men—What can be said of a man who says one day Lie flat on the peril of your life, & the next Get up walk run drink porter at midday and quinine all the afternoon. They know nothing; they grope about in the darkness and hit or miss—Every body does—

I suppose you wont come to London for several weeks. It is all very well saying that you go for only 3: but we know better. I go back tomorrow morning—and on Thursday I expect o joy a letter from you?—no that was not [what] I meant or would venture to say—but my Pa & Ma. Dear old soul—She is going to be or to try and be happy for the first time this many a long year. My heart melts as I think of her constant constant affection. Other people I suppose have not mothers made of this sort. I look at her character, and go down on my knees as it were with wonder and pity. It is Mater Dolorosa, with a heart bleeding with love. Is not that a pretty phrase? I wrote it yesterday in a book, whilst I was thinking about her—and have no shame somehow now in writing thus sentimentally to all the public; though there are very few people in the world to whom I would have the face to talk in this way tête-a-tête—To you I can because you are made of the same soft stuff: and that is why—why you see that is why &c.   God bless you dear lady and I know you believe me to be faithfully & affectionately yours

W M T.

P.S. Did you ever hear me mention a young lady whom I admired rather, a Miss Pattle? She is gone to London, and leaves it tomorrow to pass the winter in France.

Mrs. Elton: the former Rhoda Susan Willis (d. 1873), wife of Arthur Hallam Elton (1818-83), later seventh Baronet, who lived at Clevedon Court, near Bristol. *one of the Miss Smiths:* Eliza Smith, a daughter of the author, Horace Smith (1779-1849).   *Jullien:* the conductor, Louis Jullien (1812-60).   *cornet-à-piston:* (Fr.) cornet.   *Fonblanque:* the journalist, Albany Fonblanque (1793-1872).   *Sheil . . . Irish wife:* the dramatist and politician, Richard Lalor Sheil (1791-1851), husband of the former Mrs. Anastasia Power.   *Morier:* James Justinian Morier (d. 1849), author of *Hajji Baba* (1824).   *Packman:* Dr. F. W. S. Packman.   *Rigby:* Dr. Edward Rigby.   *Mater Dolorosa . . . in a book: Pendennis*, ch. 2.

114. TO MRS. WILLIAM HENRY BROOKFIELD
1 November 1848

Dear Mrs. Brookfield. I was at Oxford by the time your dinner was over, and found eight or nine jovial gentlemen in black feasting in the common-room, and drinking Port wine solemnly. I found there my friend whom I mistook for the man of the train and they are indeed very much alike, and I emused the society by telling them of the event wh. had just occurred—We had a great sitting of Port wine, and I daresay the evening was pleasant enough I was thinking of the last 4 or 5 days—I think I've never known any happier ones: and intend to love that dear old Clevedon for all the days of my life—They gave me a bed in college, such a bed, I could not sleep: I hope you did well after that long journey and all those blunders and delays and agitations—Yesterday (for this is 7 1/2 o'clock in the morning would you believe it?) a party of us drove in an Oxford cart  to Blenheim: where we saw some noble pictures—a portrait by Raphael—one of the great Raphaels of the world (look this is College paper with beautiful lines already made) a series of magnificent Rubens,—one of wh. representing himself walking in a garden with Mrs. Rubens and the Babby, did one good to look at and remember, and some very questionable Titians indeed (I mean on the score of authenticity not of morals though the subjects are taken from the loves of those extraordinary Gods & Goddesses mentioned in Lempriere's Dictionary) and we walked in the Park with much profit surveying the great copper-coloured trees, and the glum old bridge and pillar and Rosamonds Well, and the queer grand ugly but magnificent house—a piece of splendid barbarism, yet grand and imposing somehow, like a chief raddled over with war-paint and attired with careful hideousness—well I cant make out the simile on paper though it is in my own mind pretty clear. What you would have liked best was the Chapel dedicated to God & the Duke of Marlborough—the monument to the latter occupies the whole place almost so that the Former is quite secondary. O what comes!—It was the Scout who brought me your letter, and I am very much obliged to you for it, and very sorry indeed to hear that you have been ill and in pain. Shall I set off this instant and come to Portman St.? —it is only about 2 1/2 hours off. No—you wouldn't let me in. I will come on Friday. I was afraid the journey would agitate you. That was what I was thinking of as I was lying in the Oxford man's bed awake.

 After Blenheim I went to Magdalen Chapel to a High Mass there—O cherubim and Seraphim, how you would like it! The Chapel is the most sumptuous edifice carved & frittered all over with the richest stone work like the lace of a lady's boudoir—the windows are filled with pictures of the Saints painted in a grey colour real Catholic Saints male & female I mean so that I wondered how

they got there: and this makes a sort of rich twilight in the Church, wh. is lighted up by a multitude of wax candles in gold sconces: and you say your prayers in carved stalls wadded with velvet cushions. They have a full chorus of boys some two dozen I should think; who sing quite ravishingly. It is a sort of perfection of sensuous gratification: childrens voices charm me so that they set all my sensibilities into a quiver—do they you? I am sure they do. These pretty brats with sweet innocent faces and white robes sang quite celestially, no not celestially—for I don't believe it is devotion at all: but a high delight out of wh. one comes not impurified I hope: but with a thankful pleased gentle frame of mind. I suppose I have a great faculty of enjoyment—At Clevedon I had gratification in looking at trees landscapes effects of shine and shadow &c—wh. made that dear old inspector who walked with me wonder—well, there can be no harm in these I'm sure—What a shame it is to go on bragging about what is after all sheer roaring good health for the most part—o my dear lady that you could be well—And now I'm going to breakfast. Gby I have been lionizing the town ever since, and am come home quite tired I have breakfasted here lunched at Xt Church seen Merton and all Souls with Norman Macdonald where there is a beautiful library and a boar's head in the kitchen over wh. it was good to see Normans eyes gloating: and it being all Saints day am going to Chapel here: where they have also a very good music I am told. Are you better Mam? I hope you are. On Friday I hope to have the pleasure to see you: and am till then and even till Saturday yours

W M T.

Lempriere: John Lemprière (d. 1824), author of the *Classical Dictionary* (1788ff.). *Rosamond's Well:* a spring named for Rosamond Clifford (d. 1176?), mistress of Henry II. *Macdonald:* Norman Hilton Macdonald (1807?-57), Fellow of All Souls College.

115. TO EDWARD CHAPMAN
22 November 1848

Novr. 22.

Dear Chapman
    The Elias Howle affair will make a good author's misery for Punch—It didn't annoy me a bit: farther than to think that a man who was once very kind to me and I believe fond of me, should have committed himself so far. To make remarks about my person, the honesty or dishonesty of my appearance can't injure me—I have

pushed the caricaturing of myself almost to affectation—but it wont profit Lever to gibbet a rival in that way. 'Snooks in the Holy land' is quite fair that is to say my sort of writing carried to the absurd—that is what I was trying to do in those parodies in Punch one of wh. I suppose has got me the Howle rejoinder—

> And so let us give his old sowl
> A howl
> For twas he got the noggin to rowl.

I suppose that's the meaning—and thought already in another Number of Roland Cashel I detected a shot against myself.

I cant make it a condition of my liking for a man that I should like his books or praise them not liking them. I never could bring myself to consider Lever seriously as an author, but thought him one of the most charming and agreeable men I ever met in my life. I know for my part that a man may like my writing or not, and I don't care a straw, at least I think not.

Out of those Punch parodies I left his bad French wh is one of the great points a caricaturist would not fail to seize—in fact it was with the gloves I was sparring I am very sorry he has taken them off. If caricaturing with the pencil is, as I hold it, quite fair, why not that with the pen? Lever has a right to by far the greater part of his attack on me—all but the sheer personality of wh. I am sorry and annoyed to hear a man use, as one would be if a gentleman in public suddenly used bad language. It is not the person assailed but the assailant one feels for. Somebody should tell him that such behaviour will hurt him without in the least injuring me.

If he has had his fire and is content—I wonder whether he will be able to understand that it is not out of fear of future castigation that I am ready to shake hands with him? Fancy a literary war in wh. a man descends to describing odious personal peculiarities in his rival!

What I think you might do is to warn him at least to stop— Why, he doesnt write English let alone French and German—and you as my publisher my friend and a gentleman are not called upon to have your house made the office for publishing this dreary personality. Make fun of my books, my style, my public works—but of me a gentleman—o for shame.

Ever yours dear Chapman
W M T.

Elias Howle affair: in number Seven for November 1848 of his novel *Roland Cashel*, Charles Lever caricatured Thackeray as "Elias Howle." *author's misery:* as an "Author's Misery" piece, Thackeray drew "Mr. Tims and a Good-natured Friend," which appeared in the 2 December 1848 issue of *Punch*. *those parodies:*

Thackeray's series "*Punch*'s Prize Novelists," one of which parodied Lever's military novels—"Phil Fogarty. A Tale of the Fighting Onety-Oneth," which appeared in the 7, 14, and 21 August 1847 issues of *Punch*.

116. TO ARTHUR HUGH CLOUGH
26 November 1848

13 Young St. Kensington
26 Novr.

My dear Mr. Clough. I have been reading the Bothy all the morning and am charmed with it. I have never been there but I think it must be like Scotland—Scotland hexametrically laid out that is (Ive only got this sheet of paper & you see have been making exercises on it) and it seems to me to give one the proper Idyllic feeling wh. is 1/2 sensual & 1/2 spiritual I take it—serene beauty awakening pleasant meditation—what is it?—Your description of the Sky & the landscape—and that figure of the young fellow bathing shapely with shining limbs and the blue blue sky for a background—are delightful to me—I can imagine to myself the Goddess of bathing in a sort of shimmer under the water—Was it as clear as Rosamond's Well?—I have been going over some of the same ground (of youth) in this present number of Pendennis: wh. I fear will be considered rather warm by the puritans: but I think you'll understand it—that is if you care for such trivialities, or take the trouble to look under the stream of the story.

I must tell you that I was very much pleased indeed by your sending me the book, and dont mind owning that I took a great liking to you. When you come to London I hope you will come and see me. Mrs. Pendennis is living with me (She is my mother) and I have a couple of little girls whom you shall hear read if you like.

I owe Neate a letter about his Dialogues but the fact is—that I have only last night finished my work and lazing in bed this morning Your poem arrived in wh. I read as far as the Goddess of Bathing, and thought I would write off at once at a heat.

Faithfully yours
W M Thackeray.

Clough: Arthur Hugh Clough (1819-61), a former Fellow of Oriel College, Oxford.   *the Bothy:* Clough's recently-published poem, best known under its revised title, *The Bothie of Tober-Na-Vuolich*.   *as clear as Rosamond's Well:* see Letter 114. Sir Walter Scott's *Woodstock* (1826), ch. 18, had characterized it as especially pure.   *Neate ... his Dialogues:* Charles Neate (1806-79), Fellow of

Oriel College, whom Thackeray had visited at Oxford several weeks previously. Neate had recently published *Dialogues des Morts: Guizot et Louis Blanc*.

117. TO MRS. WILLIAM HENRY BROOKFIELD
29 November 1848

My dear lady   I am very much pained and shocked at the news brought at dinner to day that poor dear Charles Buller is gone. Good God think about the poor mother surviving and what an anguish that must be! If I were to die I can't bear to think of my mother living beyond me, as I daresay she will: but isn't it an awful awful sudden summons? There go wit fame friendship ambition high repute. Ah aimons nous bien, it seems to me that is the only thing we can carry away. When we go let us have some who love us wherever we are. I send you this little line as I tell you & Wm. most things. Good night.

Charles Buller is gone: Buller had died on 29 November 1848.   *aimons nous bien:* (Fr.) let us love one another well.

118. TO MRS. WILLIAM HENRY BROOKFIELD
December 1848?

As I am waiting to see Mrs. Buller I find an old review, with an advertisement in it containing a great part of an article I wrote about Fielding in 1840, in the Times. Perhaps Madam will like to see it and Mr. Williams.
    My wife was just sickening at that moment. I wrote it at Margate where I had taken her and used to walk out 3 miles to a little bowling green and write there in an arbour—coming home and wondering what was the melancholy oppressing the poor little woman.   The Times gave me 5 guineas for the article. I recollect I thought it rather shabby pay. And 12 days after it appeared in the paper, my poor little wife's malady showed itself by an attempt at suicide.
    How queer it is to be carried back all of a sudden to that time, and all that belonged to it—and read this article over. Doesn't the apology for Fielding read like an apology for somebody else too? God help us. What a deal of cares and pleasures and struggles and happiness I have had since that day in the little Sunshiny arbour where with scarcely any money in my pocket, & a crazy wife, and 2 little children (Minny was a baby 2 months old) I was writing this notice

about Fielding. Grief, Love, Fame if you like—I have had no little of all since then—(I dont mean to take the Fame for more than it's worth, or brag about it with any peculiar elation) [. . .]

article . . . Fielding: Thackeray's essay, "Fielding's Works," which appeared in the 2 September 1840 issue of *The Times.*   *Mr. Williams:* one of Thackeray's names for the Reverend Brookfield.   [. . .]: the rest of the letter is missing.

119. TO EDWARD FITZGERALD
19 December 1848

Brighton Old Club. Tuesday.
My dear old Cupid. I did not come to see thee for I was working day & night to finish that Xmas affair—and the few spare hours I had went—R! never mind where. As soon as the book & Punch & the plates for Pendennis were done and the very day when somebody left town I came down to this Mirean Eboad—And am directly very much better, I slept well, I have laughed already twice this morning: I have begun Pendennis III: and have leisure to think of my friend & wish he was here. Come, Eros! Come, Boy-god of the twanging bow! Is not Venus thy mother here?—thou shalt ride in her chariot and by thy side shall be if not Mars at least Titmars.

How these men of letters dash off these things! C'est étonnant ma parole d'honneur, c'est étonnant.

that Xmas affair: Thackeray's Christmas book for 1848, *Dr. Birch and His Young Friends.*   *C'est . . . étonnant:* (Fr.) it is astonishing, upon my word of honor, it is astonishing.

120. TO LADY BLESSINGTON
1848

Kensington. The morning after.
Dear Lady Blessington.
I whish to igsplain what I meant last night with regard to a certain antipathy to a certain great author. I have no sort of personal dislike (not that it matters much whether I have or not) to Sir E L B L on the contrary the only time I met him, at the immortal Ainsworth's years ago, I thought him very pleasant: and I know, from his conduct to my dear little Blanchard, that he can be a most generous and delicate minded friend. BUT there are sentiments in his writing wh. always

anger me, big words wh. make me furious, and a premeditated fine writing against wh. I cant help rebelling. My antipathy don't go any farther than this: and it is accompanied by a great deal of admiration.

I felt ashamed of myself when I came home and thought how needlessly I had spoken of this. What does it matter one way or the other, and what cause had I to select Sir H Bulwer of all men in the world for these odious confidences?. It was very rude. I am always making rude speeches and apologizing for them, like a nuisance to society.

And now I remember how Sir B. Lytton spoke in a very different manner to a mutual friend about

Your very humble Servt
W M Thackeray

Sir H Bulwer: Sir William Henry Lytton Earle Bulwer (1801-72), later first Baron Dalling and Bulwer, brother of Sir Edward Lytton Bulwer-Lytton.

121. TO MRS. EYRE EVANS CROWE
1848?

Madam. On the death of Mr. Thackeray, the accompanying singular note was found among the papers of the eccentric and unfortunate gentleman. Playful to the last he appears to have invited you to a dinner of wh. he subsequently repented, and wh. of course sinc[e] his untimely end in the water-butt is adjourned sine die.

My dear Mrs. Crowe

Cant ye come on Chewsday? Sure the Waddells have pramised me, and we'll be eble to see if Miss Eloiza or Miss Eugania is the ogliest. We doine at 6 a'clack and Oive a Frinch Ortist steeing with me, whom ye regealed once at Saint Cloud.

Canstantly yours
The Mulligan.

sine die: (Lat.) indefinitely. *Eloiza:* Thackeray mentions the beautiful Miss Waddell several times in his correspondence, but she remains otherwise unidentified. *Eugania:* Eugènie Crowe (b. 1829), later Mrs. Robert Wynne. *Frinch Ortist:* presumably Louis Marvy, who stayed with Thackeray for a year, beginning in 1848. *Mulligan:* Thackeray borrows the name of an Irishman whom he had created in his December 1846 Christmas book, *Mrs. Perkins's Ball.*

122. TO MRS. WILLIAM HENRY BROOKFIELD
4-5 February 1849

My dear lady, I have been to see a great character to day and another still greater yesterday. To days was Jules Janin, whose books you never read nor do I suppose you could very well. He is the critic of the Journal des Debats and has made his weekly feuilleton famous throughout Europe. He does not know a word of English but he translated Sterne and I think Clarissa Harlowe: one week having no theatres to describe in his feuilleton or no other subject handy, he described his own marriage wh. took place in fact that week and absolutely made a present of his sensations to all the European public—He has the most wonderful verve, humour, oddity, honesty, bonhommie: he was ill with the gout or recovering perhaps but bounced about the room gesticulating joking gasconading quoting Latin—pulling out his books wh. are very handsome, and tossing about his curling brown hair—a magnificent jolly intelligent face such as would suit Pan I should think a flood of humourous rich jovial talk—and now I have described this how are you to have the least idea of him? I daresay it's not a bit like him. He recommended me to read Diderot wh. I have been reading in at his recommendation; and that is a remarkable Sentimental Cynic too in his ways of thinking and sudden humours not unlike—not unlike Mr. Bows of the Chatteris Theatre. I can fancy Harry Pendennis and him seated on the bridge and talking of their mutual mishap—no Arthur Pendennis the boy's name is—I shall be forgetting my own next. But mind you my similes don't go any farther: and I hope you don't go for to fancy that you know anybody like Miss Fotheringay You dont suppose that I think *you* have no heart do you? but theres many a woman who has none and about whom men go crazy—such was the other character I saw yesterday. We had a long talk: in wh. she showed me her interior and I inspected it and left it in a state of wonderment wh. I can't describe—This woman six years ago was my sister and we were generously fond of each other up to about 10 years since. She is kind frank open-handed not very refined: with a warm outpouring of language—and thinks herself the most feeling creature in the world. The way in wh. she fascinates some people is quite extraordinary. She affected me by telling me of an old friend of our's in the country Dr. Portman's daughter indeed who was a parson in our parts—who died of consumption the other day, after leading the purest and saintliest life and who after she had recd. the sacrament read over her friends letter and actually died with it on the bed. Her husband adores her—He is an old Cavalry Colonel of 60 and the poor fellow away now in India and yearning after her writes her yards & yards of the most tender submissive frantic letters—Five or six other men are crazy about her.

She trotted them all out one after another before me last night—not humourously I mean or making fun of them, but complacently describing their adoration for her and acquiescing in their opinion of herself—Friends lovers husband she coaxes them all and no more cares for them than worthy Miss Fotheringay did. O Becky is a trifle to her: and I am sure I might draw her picture and she never wd. know in the least that it was herself. I suppose I did not fall in love with her myself because we were brought up together—She was a very simple generous creature then—

Tuesday—Friends came in as I was writing last night—perhaps in time to stop my chattering But I am encore tout émerveillé de [ma cousine]. By all the Gods I never had the opportunity of inspecting such a naturalness and coquetry.—Not that I suppose there are not many such women. But I have only myself known one or two women intimately: and I daresay the novelty would wear off if I knew more— I had the Revue des 2 Mondes & the Journal des Debats to dinner, and what do you think by way of a delicate attention the chef served us up? mock-turtle soup again: and uncommonly good it was too. After dinner I went to a ball at the Prefecture of Police—the most splendid apartments I ever saw in my life, such lights pillars marble hangings carving and gilding. I'm sure King Belshazzar could not have been more magnificently lodged. There must have been fifteen hundred people: of whom I did not know one single soul. I am surprized that the people did not faint in the saloons wh. were like burning fiery furnaces, but there they were dancing and tripping away—ogling & flirting and I suppose not finding the place a bit inconveniently warm. The women were very queer looking bodies for the most part I thought, but the men dandies every one fierce and trim with curling little mustachios: I felt dimly that I was 3 inches taller than any body in the room, but I hope nobody took notice of me. There was a rush for ices at a footman who brought those refreshments wh. was perfectly terrific—They were scattered melting over the heads of the crowd as I ran out of it in a panic. There was an old British dowager with two daughters seated up against a wall, very dowdy & sad. Poor old body I wonder what she wanted there? and whether that was what she called pleasure?

I went to see Wms. old friend and mine Bowes—He has 40000 a year and palaces in the country, and here he is a manager of the Theatre of Varieties—and his talk was about actors and coulisses all the time of our interview. I wish it could be the last: but he has made me promise to dine with him and go I must to be killed by his melancholy gentlemanlikeness. I think that's all I did yesterday. Dear lady I am pained at your having been unwell—I thought you must have been when Saturday came without any letter. There won't be one to day I bet twopence. I am going to a lecture at the Institute—a lecture on Burns by M. Chasles who is Professor of English literature. What a course of lionizing isn't it? But it must stop for isn't the month the shortest of months?

I went to see my old haunts when I came to Paris thirteen years ago and made believe to be a painter—just after I was ruined and before I fell in love and took to marriage & writing. It was a very jolly time. I was as poor as Job: and sketched away most abominably but pretty contented: and we used to meet in each others little rooms and talk about Art and smoke pipes and drink bad brandy & water. That awful habit still remains; but where is Art that dear Mistress whom I loved though in a very indolent capricious manner but with a real sincerity? I see her far, very far off. I jilted her, I know it very well: but you see it was Fate ordained that marriage never should take place: and forced me to take on with another lady, two other ladies, three other ladies. I mean the Muse, and my wife, and &c—Well, you are very good to listen to all this egotistic prattle, chère sœur si douce et si bonne—I have no reason to be ashamed of my loves seeing that all three are quite lawful. Did you go to see my people yesterday?—Some day when his Reverence is away will you have the children? and not if you please be so vain as to fancy that you cant amuse them or that they will be bored in your house. They must & shall be fond of you if you please— Alfred's open mouth as he looked at the broken bottle and spilt wine must have been a grand picture of agony.

I couldn't find the Lecture Room at the Institute so I went to the Louvre instead, and took a feast with the statues and pictures. The Venus of Milo is the grandest figure of figures. The wave of the lines of the figure wherever seen fills my senses with pleasure. What is it that so charms and satisfies one in certain lines? O the man who atchieved that statue was a beautiful genius—I have been sitting thinking of it these 10 minutes in a delightful sensuous rumination. The colours of the Titian pictures comfort one's eyes similarly and after these feasts wh. wouldn't please my lady very much I daresay, being I should think too earthy for you, I went and looked at a picture I usedn't to care much for in old days, an Angel saluting a Virgin & Child by Pietro of Cortona—a sweet smiling angel with a lily in her hand looking so tender and gentle—I wished that instant to make a copy of it and do it beautifully wh. I can't, and present it to somebody on Lady day.—There now; just fancy it is done, and presented in a neat compliment and hung up in your room—a pretty piece dainty and devotional—I drove about with [my cousin] and wondered at her more and more—She is come to my dearest William now: though she doesn't care a phig for me: she told me astonishing thing[s] showed me a letter in wh. every word was true and wh. was a fib from beginning to end—a miracle of deception—flattered fondled coaxed— O she was worth coming to Paris for. [And my mother bred this woman that is] the wonder. Pray God to keep us simple. I have never looked at anything in my life wh. has so amazed me—Why this is as good almost as if I had you to talk to. Let us go out and have another walk.

Jules Janin: (1804-74), French critic and miscellaneous writer. *feuilleton:* (Fr.) newspaper article. *Clarissa Harlowe:* novel (1747-48) by Samuel Richardson (1689-1761). *bonhommie:* (Fr.: *bonhomie*) good-naturedness. *encore tout émerveillé de [ma cousine]:* (Fr.) again completely amazed by my cousin. (Here and below—[my cousin], [And . . . that is]—the words within brackets are conjectural because of heavy overscoring—apparently by Mrs. Brookfield.) *Belshazzar:* son of Nebuchadnezzar and last King of Babylonia, noted for giving a splendid feast at which his doom was prophesied (Daniel 5). *Bowes:* John Bowes Bowes. *coulisses:* (Fr.) wings of the stage. *the Institute:* the Institut de France, a learned society. *Chasles:* Philarète Chasles (1798-1873), critic and man of letters. He was on the editorial staff of the *Journal des Débats* and a Professor at the Collège de France. *chère sœur si douce et si bonne:* (Fr.) dear sister, so sweet and so good. *Lady day:* 25 March, the Feast of the Annunciation, Mrs. Brookfield's birthday.

123. TO MRS. CHARLES ARTHUR GORE
March 1849?

Anecdote & Impromptu.

The ingenious Mrs. Gore whose novels though disfigured by some *Gallicisms* are amongst the most lively & witty of the (alas immoral!) productions of the XIX century, appears to have been a person given to much hospitality. On one of the many occasions when she asked the eccentric Thackeray to dinner, that wayward *child of the Muses*, sat down & wrote the following absurd

Impromptu.

A man is but a slave to fate—I yield me to its dark decree
I may not come to dine at eight but I should like to come to tea.

The laughter with wh. this sally was received in the *gilded salons* of the lady novelist (who assembled round about her the *wits & statesmen* of the day and whose daughter is said to have possessed no ordinary mental and personal attractions) may be imagined by the gentle reader—Titmarshs partiality for muffins is well known, and he

died of a surfeit occasioned by partaking too freely of that delicious condiment in the month of March 1849.
>From Wiggins (of Massachusetts) Historical Anecdotes
of the Light Literature of Old England.
Boston. 1950.

whose novels: in "*Punch*'s Prize Novelists" (1847), Mrs. Gore's novels had been the subject of Thackeray's parody, "Lords and Liveries," but they had remained friends.   *daughter:* Cecilia Gore, who later married Lord Edward Thynne.

124. TO ADELAIDE ANN PROCTER
April 1849

My dear Miss Procter
   My parents have just arrived from Paris and have presented their child with a new gold pen, I try it on this sheet Yours is the first name I have written with it and the first use I make of it is to declare with its aid that I am the most faithful of your servants

After reading over Captain Higginsons passionate appeal Emily sate for some moments in deep meditation. She did not love him & yet she thought she ought to reward so much constancy. Her aunt Mrs. Heavyside observed her in silence.

Don't you think that you ought to have some return for that beautiful pair of slippers? If you were to work a pair for me, and were to ask for a lock of my hair I'm sure I would give it you with your Mammas permission.

125. TO LADY BLESSINGTON
6 May 1849

Kensington. May 6.

Dear Lady Blessington
    On the day I was starting into the country last month (and upon an errand wh. didn't admit of any delay) I got Miss Power's note

saying that you were going to Paris and kindly wanted to say Goodbye. I hate saying Goodbye to people who have been kind to me. Isn't it much better to say How do you do my lady? Are you well? are you merry at Paris and snugly settled in the dear old place?— I've been once at Gore House since. *C'etoit nâvrant*—I won't talk to you about it—But I'm glad I went There was nobody there I knew but the maitre-d'hotel looking very sad—I should have liked to shake hands with him: so I gave him a suvering instead—I don't say this for a brag about my generosity only I liked it. As for the house, I beg to say Madam that it wasn't the beautiful ornaments and furnitures that made the house but the kind people in it—its nothing now you are gone; and I vow and declare my belief that you can talk just as pleasantly from a mahogany chair, as from one whereof the legs were covered with the most precious goold.

Well, because there are no rents from Ireland, shall there be no more Œufs à l'Espartéro? When did we ever have a better dinner than on that day at Burnham beeches when the Herr Graf cooked the potatoes and I came from Brighton with the game pie containing 2 grouse 2 partridges 3 ostriches 2 cassowaries &c—only I forgot it. Cannot a contented mind be happy with potatoes and a giggot? I bet 2d. that in 6 months you will be more gay in Paris than at Kensington, & as for those young ladies, how nice it will be to make them wait upon us old folks (there's a galanterie)—and then they shall sit down afterwards to cold potatoes.

Every day I get more ashamed of my yellow cover & former misanthropical turn. The world is a great deal better than some satirists have painted it—and I am forced to say so when folks speak about you. What is there nobody going to say an unkind word about Lady Blessington? says I to myself—and indeed I've not heard one— Nothing but esteem for your kindness, nothing but sympathy and regard, and of course a little natural selfish regret that we shd. have lost a house where so many people were made so happy. The way in wh. people speak about you does credit to the world as well as you— isn't it worth while almost to have a touch of mishap if it brings you as indeed it has brought you, such a deal of friendly sympathy?

I began a letter the day I had finished my number—but tore it up because it contained too much about myself—indeed I suppose we have all got our own bitter griefs—I have for my part and have been for the last month the glummest & most melancholy author who ever cracked a joke with a sad heart. My work shows my dullness I think—but on the other hand there is a fellow by the name of Dickens who is bringing out a rival publication and who has written beautifully. Bravo Dickens! Davy Copperfield has beautiful things in it—those sweet little inimitable bits wh. make one so fond of him. And let me tell your Ladyship that I think he has been reading a certain yellow-covered book and with advantage too: for he has simplified his style: kept out of the fine words and in fact is doing his best. I am glad of it. I hope it will put somebody on his mettle—somebody who has been careless of everything of late—but I wont go into the dolefuls—Ah, my lady who hasn't his share?

I believe the world goes on being very gay. I reel from dinner party to dinner-party—I wallow in turtle and swim in claret and Shampang—I would like a cozy dinner with you very much better if you please. Won't we go & dine at Restaurants and have a matelotte at Bercy, when I come to Paris? Bedad we will ladies: and I hope I'll come soon. But a railroad in your native country wh. Evn confound I mean the railroad has swept down violently upon me and almost carried me off my legs—I'm as poor as Job: but it's not that wh. makes me unhappy—It's—never mind what I say. One person has about as many crosses as another I suppose.

Good bye dear Lady Blessington. Present my most respectful homages to the young ladies, and inform Monsieur D'Orsay that I should like to have one of his great shakes of the hand. And believe me, ever faithfully yours

W M Thackeray

at Gore House since: since financial difficulties had forced Lady Blessington to sell Gore House and its contents, and move to France. *C'etoit nâvrant:* (Fr.) it was heart-rending. *maitre-d'hotel:* (Fr.) major-domo. *Oeufs à l'Espartéro:* (Fr.) eggs in the Espartero style, named for the Spanish general, Baldomero Espartero (1792-1879). *Herr Graf:* (Ger.) the Count—i. e. Count d'Orsay. *cassowaries:* ostrich-like birds. *giggot:* (Fr. *gigot*) leg of mutton. *those young ladies:* Lady Blessington's nieces, Ellen and Marguerite Power (1815-67). *galanterie:* (Fr.) pretty speech to a lady. *matelotte:* (Fr. *matelote*) fish-stew. *your native country:* Ireland.

126. TO MRS. WILLIAM HENRY BROOKFIELD
17-19 May 1849

My dear Turpin.

After the fatal night of the Literary Fund disaster, when I came home to bed (breaking out into exglimations in the cab and letting off madly parts of the speech wh. wouldn't explode at the proper time) I found the house lighted up, and the poor old mother waiting to hear the result of the day—so I told her that I was utterly beaten & had made a fool of myself, upon wh. with a sort of cry she says 'No you didn't old man'—and it appears that she had been behind a pillar in the gallery all the time and heard the speeches—and as for mine she thinks it was beautiful.—So you see if theres no pleasing everybody, yet some people are easily enough satisfied—The children came down in the morning and told me about my beautiful speech wh. Granny had heard. She got up early and told them the story about it you may be sure: *her* story, wh. is not the true one but like what womens stories are.

I have a faint glimmering notion of Sir Charles Hedges having made his appearance somewhere in the middle of the speech, but of what was said I haven't the smallest idea. The discomfiture will make a good chapter for Pen. It is thus we make flêche de tout bois and I suppose every single circumstance wh. occurs to pain or please me henceforth, will go into print somehow or the other so take care if you please to be very well behaved and kind to me, or else you may come in for a savage chapter in the very next number.

As soon as I rallied from the abominable headache wh. the Free Masons tavern always gives, I went out to see some ladies who are quite like sisters to me, they are so kind lively and cheerful. Old Lady Morley was there and we had a jolly lunch, and afterwards one of these ladies told me by whom she sate at Lansdowne House, and what they talked about and how pleased she my friend was. She is a kind generous soul and I love her sincerely.

After the luncheon (this is wrote on Saturday, for all yesterday I was so busy from nine till five when my hoss was brought & I took a ride and it was too late for the post) I went to see Matthew that friend of my youth whom I used to think 20 years ago the most fascinating accomplished witty and delightful of men—I found an old man in a room smelling of brandy & water at 5 o'clock at Islington, quite the same man that I remember, only grown coarser and stale somehow, like a piece of goods that has been hanging up in a shop window. He has had 15 years of a vulgar wife, much solitude, very much brandy & water I should think, and a depressing profession: for what can be more depressing than a long course of hypocrisy to a man of no small sense of humour? It was a painful meeting We tried to talk unreservedly, and as I looked at his face I remembered the fellow I was so fond of—he asked me if I still consorted with any Cambridge men, and so I mentioned Kinglake and one Brookfield of whom I saw a good deal. He was surprized at this as he heard Brookfield was so violent a Puseyite as to be just on the point of going to Rome. He cant walk, having paralysis in his legs, but he preaches every Sunday he says, being hoisted into his pulpit before service, and waiting there whilst his curate reads down below. I think he has very likely repented: he spoke of his preaching seriously and without affectation: perhaps he has got to be sincere at last after a long dark lonely life. He showed me his daughter of 15, a prettyish girl with a shrewish face, and bad manners—the wife did not show—He must have been glad too when I went away and I daresay is more scornful about me than I about him—Fa, I used to worship him for about 6 months: and now he points a moral and adorns a tale such as it is in Pendennis. He lives in the D of Bedfords Park at Woburn, and wanted me to come down and see him, and go to the Abbey he said where the Duke wd. be so glad to have me—but I declined this treat—o fie for shame. How proud we get! Poor old Harry Matthew, and this battered vulgar man was my idol of youth! My dear old FitzGerald is always right about men: and said from the first that this was a bad one and a sham. You see, some folks have a knack of setting up for themselves idols to worship—Dont be flying off in one of your fits of passion, I don't mean you.

Then I went to dine at Alfred Montgomerys where were his wife and sister. I dont think so much of the wife tho she is pretty and clever—but Beckyfied somehow and too much of a petite maitresse I suppose a deal of flattery has been poured into her ears, and numberless men have dangled round that pretty light little creature. The sister with her bright eyes was very nice though, and I passed an evening in great delectation till midnight drawing nonsense pictures for these ladies who have both plenty of relish for nonsense. I wish to the deuce I had somebody who liked it at home. Yesterday after working all day, & then going to the London Library to audit accounts doesn't that sound grand? and taking a ride, I came home to dinner, fell asleep as usual afterwards slep for 12 hours, and am now going to attack Monsieur Pendennis.

Here is the journal. Now Mum how have you been emused? Is Kings very fine, is Trinity better? did you have a nice T at Mrs. Maine's? When are you coming back? Lord & Lady Castlereagh came here yesterday and I want you to come back so that I may give them an entertainment—for I told my lady that I wanted to show her that other lady mentioned in the Punch article as mending her husband's chest of drawers—but I said waistcoat.　　Sir Bulwer Lytton called yesterday—To night I am going to the bar dinner, and shall probbbly make another speech—I dont mind about failing there so I shall do pretty well. I rode by Portman Street on Thursday—Please to write and let me know whether you'll dine on the 28th. or the 30th. or can give me both those days to choose from. And so God bless both on you.

Turpin: the name of Mrs. Brookfield's maid.　　*the Literary Fund disaster:* Thackeray's incoherent address at the dinner of the Royal Literary Fund on 16 May 1849.　*Sir Charles Hedges:* (d. 1714), Secretary of State when Addison was appointed Under-Secretary in 1706. *flêche de tout bois:* (Fr.) use of every means to attain an end. *ladies who are quite like sisters to me:* Mrs. Thomas Frederick Elliot (d. 1861), the former Jane Perry, wife of an official (1808-80) in the Colonial Office, and her sister, Kate Perry. *Old Lady Morley:* the Dowager Lady Morley (d. 1857), the former Frances Talbot, widow of the first Earl. *Matthew:* Henry Matthew, who had become Rector of Eversholt in Bedfordshire. *points a moral and adorns a tale:* Johnson, "The Vanity of Human Wishes," 1. 220.   *D of Bedford:* Francis Russell (1788-1861), seventh Duke of Bedford. *Alfred Montgomery:* civil servant and man about town.   *petite maitresse:* (Fr.) someone who behaves affectedly.   *Mrs. Maine:* Mrs. Henry Sumner Maine, the former Jane Maine. Her husband (1822-88) was Regius Professor of Civil Law at Cambridge 1847-54.   *Castlereagh:* Frederick William Robert Stewart (1805-72), styled Viscount Castlereagh, later fourth Marquess of Londonderry. He was married to the former Lady Frances Jocelyn (1813-84).   *article:* "Some More Words About the Ladies," which had appeared in the 14 April 1849 issue of *Punch*. *Portman Street:* where the Brookfields lived at Number 15.

127. TO MRS. GRANTHAM MUNTON YORKE
1 June 1849

13 Young St Kensington Sqre June 1. 1849.

Dear Mrs. Yorke

In the matter of the curacy I pen the following lines, and address them to you because of the softness of your sex, and in order to try and interest you unduly for a gentleman who is in want of just such a cure as Mr Yorke seems to have vacant

Mr. Thomas one of the Curates of St. Jamess, of High Church Principles, wants very much to be married. He has been engaged this ever so many years in the most romantic manner. He could be made every way happy by such an addition to his means. He can be perfectly recommended I don't know whether he is not going to write to Mr. Yorke.   Mentioning the latters need the other day to my friend Mr. School inspector Brookfield, his wife overheard the conversation, and you must know it is she who is Mr. Thomas's patron or matron in the matter; and who interests herself in promoting not only the cause of the church wh. she has very much at heart but a pretty little love affair, wh. I think all good-natured persons like to forward.   And as for me, I wish prosperity to both with all my heart. Always dear Mrs. Yorke yours very sincerely

W M Thackeray

Mrs. Yorke: the former Marian Emily Montgomery (d. 1895), wife of the Reverend Grantham Yorke (1809-79).

128. TO MRS. THOMAS FREDERICK ELLIOT AND KATE PERRY
29 June 1849

29 June. Friday.

Private. Confidential & to be put into the

My dear ladies

I have only this minute done my work and have leisure to ask how you are—It is a week since one of you was taken unwell. Is she better now. Shall I come to Richmond to see her—to breakfast any day next week? I am free now for a little, as much as that miserable villain can be said to be free who is flogged night & day by a cruel tyrant who shall be nameless—and at my age too—to be whapped so by a boy!—

But enough of this. I am always yours

WMT.

129. TO ADELAIDE ANN PROCTER
5? August 1849

Kensington. Sunday evg.

My dear Adelaide   Where is the letter I, nearly, wrote you the day before yesterday on receipt of the beautiful purse? It was finished all but ever such a little bit on Friday when I had to go & wish somebody good bye who was going out of town—Since then writing for love has been impossible I was ill all yesterday with a headache,+ have been writing till this minute to day (at 5 o'clock.) But I do not like the splendid purse the less for that, nor am I less thankful to the giver. I shall keep it and value it sincerely, and hope that the donor for whom I had a regard ever since the time when my head was black and she wore a pinafore, and the owner of the purse will be good friends until we stop altogether. Your parents have been of the best friends I have ever had—Twelve years ago when I was a poor struggling fellow they were just as good to me as now when—when I'm a poor struggling man still: with a little additional stock of reputation and a vast deal more care and doubt. How much one has gone through since one knew them to be sure!—I cant help tracing over the ground from that distant landmark—nearly the third part and all the busiest part of my life lies within it. I've made in that time about 100000 acquaintances, and 2 sets of intimate friends besides those in your house—I suppose one wont make any more now—I feel so good-naturedly indifferent to new people, that I cant expect them to have any more than indifference for me & don't care if they do or don't thats the truth: or 2d. for reputation except for the substantial part of it, or for any except a very very few people—If it had been a new acquaintance who as I thought hesitated about   I shouldn't have & been

hurt in the least or made a bluster. Thank God I was wrong.

 I wonder whether it is the conclusion of the Season, & everybodys being out of town, or the Lord Mayors dinner yesterday (where I drank wine & water, think of that!) or the remnants of yesterday's headache or the lassitude produced by writing all day against the will that makes me so profoundly egotistic & melancholy? But I can't delay writing any longer to thank you for the splendid present: and if I am happy or otherwise (or out of humour wh. if you please Miss is very rare indeed) I must show it. So you get me at an unlucky minute with a black-edged border round me, and a dismal news within. Excuse my lugubriousness—I can't grin when I'm melancholy: and Tom Fool at home is known to have occasional fits of depression—By the way I had to send for my neighbour Mr. Merryman—I declare he comes in quite pat to make the joke.

But tomorrow I'll perfectly astonish every body with the liveliness of my rattle. Forster shant be anything to me in his lightest moods. And now farewell and believe me my dear Adelaide
Yours till death

+ a headache brought on by going to Vauxhall I believe and sitting up very late: not by any excess of either feasting or grief.

Lord Mayor: Sir James Duke (1792-1873), first Baronet. *Merryman:* Dr. John Jones Merriman (1800-81).

130. TO MRS. WILLIAM HENRY BROOKFIELD
18 September 1849

My dear Lady. I was in such hagnies at dinner that though they got me a slipper (by wh. I had the advantage of showing a neat stocking to Lady Rodd) I was obliged to go home and send for a doctor. He put me to bed, where I am to stop today & perhaps tomorrow working at Pendennis: wh. was just beginning when your note arrived—Merci Madame. I suppose it is full of blunders the biography I mean—I was reading in Anny's French grammar this morning about the participles wh. disquieted me, and I find as follows.

—Well I can't find the passage now after looking for 10 minutes during wh. the enormous Higgins is chattering at my bedside.

My leg is to be amputated tomorrow, but I shall be well on Thursday. D V. and shall come to see you with my leg in my hand.

I suppose one only gets to simplicity à force d'artifice—and gradually casts off the skin of fine-writing—Is it honesty or only consummate roguery? both I think—honesty & policy. I pray God to keep me honest in my dealings and thoughts and affections for my children & for you my dear friends.

G. b. y.

put me to bed: after Thackeray was put to bed, his condition worsened significantly. He was seriously ill for a month with bilious fever accompanied by inflammation of various organs, and he had a slow recovery thereafter. Publication of *Pendennis* was halted until the end of December 1849. *à force d'artifice:* (Fr.) by means of artifice.

131. TO MRS. BRYAN WALLER PROCTER
17 October 1849

Wednesday. October 17.

My dear Mrs. Procter

I hope you are very well. I am pretty well. I have been ill in bed for 4 weeks, and had to take a great deal of med-i-cine, but as the Doctor said it was good for me, I took it like a good boy and am now better

When I was ill a kind lady came and brought me some nice grapes, I ate and liked them very much. Then she went to her Cook and said [']Cook make some jelly for a little boy who is ill.' I ate all the jelly, and O it was very good. Then she sent me some turtle soup wh. I would like to eat too, but the Doctor will not let me, and though I am very sorry I do not cry. Is not that being good?—Well you see though I am not well enough to sit up much yet, I am well enough to begin to be a tomfool, and that is a great point gained. All the rest will follow in due season, and I hope to be quite strong & frisky before long. What a kind world it is, what kind folks in it, what a number of kind friends some people have!—I like to write a line to one of the kindest of all and to say dear Mrs. Procter how sincerely & affectionately I am yours

W M T.

the Doctor: Dr. John Elliotson (1791-1868).

132. TO TOM TAYLOR
29-30 December 1849

Saturday Night.

My dear T. T.

Before going to sleep I think I can't do better than tell you how much I liked Diogenes and how glad I am (you know I said the contrary before I saw it) that you wrote it: not for the wit though it's plenty, or the dialogue which is uncommonly neat and pretty, but for the healthy animus and tender truth-loving moral. I think it must do good to people to see it, and that it is written by a good man. I admired the last verses and that fine tableau at the end: both brought tears into my eyes somehow, and gave me a wholesome glow: making me say to myself 'Please God I will try and tell the truth too and love my neighbour.' Isn't that what you wanted to make people feel? Here is one man at any rate who for a night or an hour or two at least fancies himself a little the better for listening to you. Amen, I hope the good impression may last; and so I thank you for it before I put out the light and begin snoring—Good night: and thank you

W. M. T.

And besides I must tell you that the piece drove some selfish and painful thoughts out of my mind, and made me feel ashamed of my selfishness, and think there were better things to do, than to be indulging in sentimental egotism.

Here I put out the candle last night—finding I was going to indulge in that very egotism which I deprecated.

T. T.: Tom Taylor (1817-80), dramatist and journalist, a *Punch* colleague. *Diogenes:* Taylor's burlesque, *Diogenes and his Lantern; or, A Hue and Cry after Honesty,* which opened at the Strand Theatre on 26 December 1849.

133. TO LADY CASTLEREAGH
3 January 1850

Kensington. Jan 3. 1850.

Dear Lady Castlereagh

I am very sorry to hear that you are still a prisoner and should have liked very much to have been allowed to visit your place of captivity on New Years Day, and wish you better health for 1850, and, (extending my arms over your couch with my fine eyes lifted towards the cieling) to have given you an old man's blessing. Pray accept the same at this writing: it is a benediction, like the homœopathic remedies, that mayn't do any good, but at least it can't do any harm.

How artful of you to say you *were just going to read* Rebecca & Rowena! Ah Madam, do you suppose that I am not acquainted with that stratagem? When we get a book from the author and suspect, from his known character and from the common chances of life, that the book is stupid, we are always *going to read* it. But why should I complain at being served as I serve my neighbours?

I have very bad news about the trip to Paris. No money. All gone to pay bills. No Paris: no fun this month—Life is made up of disappointments and behold here is one. But there are compensations too, and there's Monday still to look forward too I shall come with my usual fine appetite and alacrity and am till Monday, and for all the rest of the year

Yours very faithfully dear Lady Castlereagh
W M Thackeray

Rebecca & Rowena: published in December 1849.

134. TO JAMES SPEDDING
5 January 1850

Kensington Jan 5. 1850.

My dear Spedding
    Although I didn't do that wh. I ought to have done, you know we don't in the prayer-book, and I was very glad to hear from you and that you were pleased to remember me. Well, another reason why I did not answer was that the other day Fitz came grumbling & growling into my room, and said you were expected instantly in London: and I thought that &c &c—there's no use in going on with excuses: wh. are seldom good for any thing unless they are lies, and these I never employ for common use.   I have got back nearly to my former flesh and strength, and rattle about London pretty much in the old way—out 4 times a week like a gay young dog. I had a severe bout of it and was very nearly transmitted to the next world: but behold there is a reprieve, and I am left to blunder on yet a little longer. I'm not satisfied with what I do either as a man or a littary man—I will not bother you with forebodings though. I have been now 3 days trying to write an article for Punch and not canning. The fun goes out of a man at 40: where are the jokes that came in such plenty? Ah me as Tom Carlyle says he was here the other day and very kind. I wish you could have heard him though, in a different mood, at Procter's. He fell foul of Reeve, who had a stiff white neckcloth, wh. probably offended the Seer. He tossed Reeve and gored yea as a bull he chased him and horned him: for an hour or more he pitched him about ripping open his bowels and plunging his muzzle into Reeves smoking entrails. Reeve had to appear perfectly good-humoured all the time of the operation, and indeed bore it with wonderful face & patience. I dont think I know of any thing else. I am going to breakfast with Macaulay. Rogers is all but extinct and flickers so feebly that you would fancy that old lamp must go out with a piff. The Sterling Club

is called the Tuesday Club: but as there are no lords I don't go. Alfred has taken rooms in Forster's house. The Queen Dowager is dead much lamented. My shaving water is getting cold. The Elliots are well and kind. My dear Inspectress of Schools beautiful as ever, is about very soon to become a Mamma. A comic poet once singing of an Irishwoman said 'Children if she bear blest will be their daddy'. And indeed I can conceive few positions more agreeable than his who is called upon to perform the part of husband to so sweet a creature.

Good bye my dear Spedding I wish you a happy Year: and am ever truly yours

W M Thackeray

I didn't do that ... prayer-book: from the General Confession, *Book of Common Prayer.* *Rogers ... extinct:* Samuel Rogers lived until 1855. *Sterling Club:* founded in 1838 by John Sterling. *Queen Dowager:* Queen Adelaide, widow of William IV, had died on 2 December 1849. *Inspectress:* Mrs. Brookfield, whose husband was Inspector of Schools. *A comic poet once singing:* Thackeray in "Peg of Limavaddy."

135. TO ABRAHAM HAYWARD
1 February 1850

Kensington. Feb 1. 1850.

My dear Hayward.

Thank you for your kind note. I was quite prepared for the issue of the kind effort made at the Athenæum in my behalf: indeed as a satirical writer, I rather wonder that I have not made more enemies than I have—I don't mean enemies in a bad sense, but men conscientiously opposed to my style, art, opinions, impertinences & so forth. There must be thousands of men to whom the practice of ridicule must be very offensive: doesn't one see such in society or in one's own family?—persons whom Nature has not gifted with a sense of humour? Such a man would be wrong not to give me a blackball or whatever it is called—a negatory nod of his honest respectable stupid old head. And I submit to his verdict without the slightest feeling of animosity against my judge. Why, Doctor Johnson would certainly have blackballed Fielding, whom he pronounced 'a dull fellow Sir a dull fellow'—& why shouldn't my friend at the Athenæum? About getting in I do not care 2d.: but indeed I am very much pleased to have had 2 such sureties as Hallam & Milman; and to know that the gentlemen whom you mention were so generous in their efforts to serve me. What does the rest matter? If you should ever know the old gentleman (for old I am sure he is, steady and respectable) who

objects to me, give him my best compliments, and say I think he was quite right to exercise his judgment honestly, and to act according to that reason with wh. Heaven has mercifully endowed him. But that he would be slow, I wouldn't in the least object to meet him: and he in his turn would think me flippant &c—enough of these egotisms. Didn't I tell you once before that I feel frightened almost at the kindness of people regarding me? May we all be honest fellows and keep our heads from too much vanity. Your case was a very different one, your's was a stab with the sharp point; and the wound I know must have been a most severe one—So much the better in you to have borne it as you did. I never heard in the least that your honor suffered by the injury done you, or that you lost the esteem (how should you?) of any single friend, because an enemy dealt you a savage blow. The opponent in your case exercised a right to do a wrong: whereas in the other, my Athenæum friend has done no earthly harm to any mortal, but has established his own character, & got a great number of kind testimonials to mine.
    Always dear Hayward yours very truly
        W M Thackeray

Hayward: Abraham Hayward (1801-84), barrister and miscellaneous writer, had unsuccessfully sought committee approval of Thackeray's proposed membership in the Athenæum Club. Thackeray was admitted in 1851. *'a dull . . . fellow':* Johnson actually pronounced Fielding "a blockhead," "a barren rascal" (Boswell, *The Life of Johnson,* ed. George Birkbeck Hill and L. F. Powell, 6 vols. [1934-40], 2: 173-74). *Hallam:* Henry Hallam (1777-1859), historian. *Milman:* Henry Hart Milman (1791-1868), Dean of St. Paul's.

136. TO MAGDALENE BROOKFIELD
26 February 1850

        13 Young St. Kensington.
        Feb 26. 1850.

My dear Miss Brookfield
  I send you my very best love and compliments upon your appearance in this world, where I hope you will long remain, so as to make your Mamma & Papa happy. Sometimes they will talk to you perhaps, about a gentleman who was a great friend of theirs once. He was a writer of books wh. were popular in their day, but by the time you are able to read this they will be quite forgotten—Therefore the author himself did not much care about them: and he does not in the least wish you to read them. But what he would like you to remember is that he was very fond of your dear mother, and that he

and your Papa were very good friends to one another, helping each other as occasion served in life.

And this gentleman who has 2 daughters of his own and likes them very much, was at your house a quarter of an hour before you were born to day; and he drank your health in a glass of Burgundy wine at night; and he prays heartily to God Almighty for the welfare of yourself and your dear mother and your father.   And so good bye my dear little girl, and believe me to be your affectionate friend

W M Thackeray

137. TO MRS. CHARLES S. FANSHAWE
March? 1850

Anecdote.

Poor Thackeray in his life time had a great regard (indeed he was rather a general admirer of the sex) for the wife of an esteemed clergyman the Revd. C. Fanshawe afterwards Bishop of Bundlecund: Before his elevation to the episcopate Mr. F lived in humble though genteel apartments near P-rtm-n Square—and the Author of Vanity Fair calling one day and finding Mrs. F. too unwell to receive his visit, asked for pen ink & paper & dashed off the following

Impromptu.

Ive come for the twentieth time I think to ask to know how be you, and consider it very hard indeed that Im not allowed to see you— And as I cant I should like to sit on the stair case landing near you, and vith my vicked jokes and vit to enliven you and cheer you—But then as you have lost your woice you know I couldnt hear you—And as you and Totty have your night caps on, to see you would distress you: and to enter into a lady's bed-room! Good lor I mustn't press you! So I send you my love, my kind little F, and heartily pray God bless you.

There is nothing in the lines to give any indication of the talent wh. this to us overrated writer was said to possess: but they at least show that in the midst of all his irregularities eccentricities, nay crimes his heart was not altogether devoid of kind feeling at this period of his career.

Its melancholy end is well known. Who would have thought in 1850 that this man whom the great world received and who had many friends and well-wishers should perish a Convict in Norfolk Islands?

Hogson's Anecdotes of the Press, & the Literary
Men of the 19th. Century.

Fanshawe: Mrs. Charles S. Fanshawe was a friend of Mrs. Brookfield's. Her husband, the Reverend Fanshawe, was Perpetual Curate of Holy Trinity Church, Southampton. *Totty:* Mrs. Fanshawe's daughter, Rosa.

138. TO JOHN FORSTER
3 April 1850

Kensington April 3. 1850

My dear Monsieur I shall come with great pleasure but like an Ass I burned the note and forgot the hour.

Yours ever
W M Thackeray

P.S You can't write as small as this. I can write much smaller.

P.S. 2 I come though I think it will be a bore: but the old fellow was uncommonly kind to me when I was a boy and I like him very much. And I think it is exceedingly good and kind-hearted of you to ask him and that you ought to be supported and that you get more benevolent every day, and that it was very kind of your mother to wait for a day before she gave you buth. And I wish you many happy returns of your buth day, Dickens of his marriage-day, & both of you of the day previous.

as small as this: the note is written in a minute hand, which Thackeray jokingly used on occasion. *wait for a day . . . the day previous:* 2 April was Forster's birthday and Dickens' wedding day.

139. TO THE REV. WILLIAM HENRY BROOKFIELD
April? 1850

My dear Vew

I wish you would go & call on Lady Ashburton. Twice Ashburton has told me that she wants to make your acquaintance and twice remarked that it wd. be but an act of politeness in you to call on a lady in distress who wants your services. Both times I have said you were uncommonly proud & shy and last night told him he'd best call on you: wh. he said he should hasten to do. But surely you might stretch a leg over the barrier when theres a lady actually beckoning to you to come over & such an uncommonly good dinner laid on the other side. There was just a vacant place yesterday as you might ave ad: and such a company of jolly dogs! Con: St. Davids Harry Hallam (Sr), & ever so many more of our set. Do go if you can, and believe me to be Yours

A. Pendennis. Major H. P.

Vew: (Fr. *vieux*) old man. *Lady Ashburton:* the former Lady Harriet Montagu (1805-57), first wife of William Bingham Baring (1799-1864), second Baron Ashburton. Thackeray dedicated *Henry Esmond* to him. *Con: St. Davids*: Connop Thirlwall (1797-1875), Bishop of St. Davids. *H. P.:* half pay.

140. TO ELIOT WARBURTON
13 April 1850

13 Young St. Kensington. April 13. 1850.

My dear Warburton

You will think there is no common gratitude or decency left in me that I delay answering so long your kind letter. It is very hard to answer, you see, that sort of praise—What can one say about it, or do but blush and look outwardly modest and shy, and be inwardly pleased & elated out of measure? Laudari a laudato &c you know has been considered from old times to be the pleasantest of all manners of compliments—and—here I come to the hesitating and stammering point again—indeed I am very glad to have your good opinion—I like it, although I may sometimes get a little elsewhere, but not enough—how can one ever have enough of that or of money? My bankers book shows a meagre balance that is always almost trembling on the unfavorable side—I spend as much money as I get having had many losses and drawbacks however of wh. I am beginning to see an alleviation if not an ending and I suppose I shall never make more than I do now. I was very near dying the other day, when the hat would have gone round as it has for so many many a man of my unlucky trade. You have your acres—be they ever so encumbered happy you. The Irish are all mad against me just now and firing into me about an unlucky slip of memory I made, in speaking about Catherine Hayes in conjunction with Barnwell & Bluebeard: meaning the English Murderess and quite forgetting the Irish Singer of that name who is a perfectly nice well conducted lady. O Murther! How they have abused me: such names as they've called me! Sir it is the friends of Costigan and Mulligan who are assassinating me under the Hayes pretext: and they outmulliganize Mull: in the way in wh. they conduct the argument against me. Why the deuce is it that I can't make a good person?—its because I'm a bad man myself I'm afraid. In a better frame of mind one wd. contemplate higher and purer characters—

loftier conditions of one's own mind that is: for no man knows anything about any body else, except a few mere surface points. Perhaps you of the ideal and imaginative school are righter than we of the real and denying. Sometimes I fancy one could come to a great conversion, deny all the past; ask pardon barefooted; strive and yearn after Sublimer truth—Is there any Sublimer Truth? is praying the height of the intellect and are you nearer on your knees to the Truth, than upright with your hat on, regarding the devellopment of nature round about you? We gauge the Truth with clumsy and inefficient mortal instruments. Let us be allowed to see it with spiritual eyes, and who knows how prodigious the change of our ideas will be? St Augustin may not be much better than chawbacon: Sceptic laughing & sneering may be testifying to the Divinity as much as Stephen—I mean the ways and works of one and the other when measured by the Infinite standard shall seem so puny, as that you shall hardly choose between the first-class (mortal) intelligence and the last class, between Milton writing Paradise Lost and Mungo scratching himself under a palm-tree.

Who knows when he begins a note whither it will lead him; or when he sets out in the morning what tile may drop on him? I meant to say briefly that though I never thanked you for Rupert and the kind note wh. accompanied it, it was because you went abroad very soon after and I delayed writing until I had time to read well in the book. I read it with great interest and pleasure admired its ability and eloquence and, (hush, shall I whisper?) doubted about its accuracy of portraiture, and read it rather as a brilliant apology and eulogy than as a real downright black and white description such as I would like, wherein pokers are pokers and nothing else—But who does see or write or comprehend the truth?—I leave off in a panic Is it Glocester or Worcester you're living at? I'm away from home and couldn't find your letter were I there no doubt—I hope some day I shall have the pleasure of making Mrs. Warburtons acquaintance and am yours very truly dear Warburton

W M Thackeray.

Warburton: Eliot Warburton (1810-52), who had graduated from Trinity College, Cambridge, was an Irish traveller and writer.   *Laudari . . . &c:* quoted from Cicero, *Epistolae ad Familiares*, V, xii, 7: "*laudari . . . a laudato viro*" (to be praised by one who has himself been praised).   *Catherine Hayes . . . Barnwell & Bluebeard:* a comment in Number 15 of Pendennis for April 1850 that provoked rabid, ignorant Irish verbal attacks upon Thackeray. The murderous Catherine Hayes, executed in 1726 for killing her husband and dismembering his body, was the mock-heroine of Thackeray's *Catherine* (1839-40). Barnwell was the murderous title-figure of George Lillo's (1693-1739) drama, *The History of George Barnwell* (1731).   *the Irish Singer:* Catherine Hayes (1825-61).   *Rupert:* Warburton's

Memoirs of Prince Rupert (1849).   *wherein pokers are pokers:* see also Letter 151.

141. TO ANNE AND HARRIET THACKERAY
26 May 1850

My dearest Fattyminny   As I have not written a single word this day I think I may have a five minutes' talk to your ladyships. You went to St Mary's church I suppose. I recollect it in the year 1817 when I was a miserable little beggar, at school at the Polygon under an odious little blackguard who used to starve and cane us. Times are changed since then and you young women have not had much starving or scolding in the course of your easy lives. Whilst you have been at Church I have at least been doing no manner of work: for I have been at Richmond all day dawdling in the sun under a tree, or making sketches for the Miss Berrys with my goold pen. The ease and tranquillity were very refreshing after the hard work of the past 4 or 5 days. I looked about to see if there were tempting looking lodgings any where about, But the prices are very heavy for good rooms, and if Miss Trulock is going away what the deuce are we to do?—A plague upon such misadventures.   As I think over matters just now, I shant be able to go to the I of Wight with you, and I dont see why you shouldn't travel back as safely as you went. So you must please to write and say by what train you'll come away on Thursday, and the carriage and your Papa, or else James his Vice[r]e[g]ent upon earth, shall be at Waterloo Station to meet you.   I am going out of town tomorrow evening to stay over Wednesday, & to return on Thursday—Shall I get a new Governess or shall I send you to school after the midsummer holy days. I do believe the latter would be the best plan—and then you'd learn something As it is—ballottées from one Governess to another now at London & next at Aix la Chapelle, your young days pass away without any larning—and in fine I'm in a great puzzle concerning you. That is all I have to say I think. It isn't very amusing or very wise is it?   Give my love to your Aunt Fanshawe and a kiss to Totty: and remember young ladies that I'm always your affectionate father.

W M T.

blackguard: a Mr. Arthur, who kept a school at Southampton.   *the Miss Berrys:* Agnes (1764-1852) and Mary Berry (1763-1852), best known for their friendship with Horace Walpole (1717-97) and for their literary salon.   *Miss Trulock:* Alice Jane Trulock, the current governess.   *ballottées:* (Fr.) beings who are tossed.

142. TO MRS. WILLIAM HENRY BROOKFIELD
21 August 1850

From the old Shop. 21.

Is it pouring with rain at Park Lodge, and the most dismal wretched cat and dog day ever seen! O its so gloomy at 13 Young Street: but I have been laboring all day drawing that is and doing my plates, until my &s are ready to drop off for weariness. But they mustn't stop for yet a little while, and until I have said how do you do to my dear lady, and the young folks at Southampton.—I hardly had time to know I was gone and that happy fortnight was over until this morning. At the train whom do you think I found Miss [Gore] who says she is Blanche Amory, and I think she is Blanche Amory, amiable (at times) amusing, clever and depraved. We talked and persifflated all the way to London; and the idea of her will help me to a good chapter, in wh. I will make Pen and Blanche play at being in love—such a wicked false humbugging London love as two blasés London people might act and half deceive themselves that they were in earnest. That will complete the cycle of Mr. Pens worldly experiences, and then we will make a try & make a good man of him. O me we are wicked worldlings most of us; may God better us and cleanse us.

I wonder whether ever again I shall have such a happy peaceful fortnight as that last? How sunshiny the landscape remains in my mind, I hope for always, and the smiles of dear children and the aspect of the kindest and tenderest face in the world to me. God bless you God bless you my sister. I know what you'll do when you read this—Well, so am I. I can hardly see as I write for the eye-water. But its not with grief; but for the natural pathos of the thing. How happy your dear regard makes me! How it takes off the solitude and eases it. May it continue pray God till your head is as white as mine, and our children have children of their own. O Love and Duty—I hope you'll never leave us quite. Instead of being unhappy because that delightful holyday is over or all but over; I intend that the thoughts of it should serve to make me only the more cheerful: and help me, please God, to do my duty better. Ah such pleasures ought to brace and strengthen one against work-days—and lo here they are!. I hope you'll be immensely punctual at breakfast and dinner, and do all your businesses of life with cheerfulness and briskness, after the example of Holy Philip Neri whom you wot of. Thats your duty Madam: and mine is to pursue my h. c. and so I go back to it with a full grateful heart and say God bless all—If it hadn't poured a rain so I think I should have gone off to his Reverence at Brighton, I send him my very best regards: and a whole boxfull of kisses to the children.

Farewell. it'll soon be Sunday & then & then & then. wont we be appy if you please?

Park Lodge: Mrs. Brookfield's address in Southampton. *Neri:* St. Philip Neri (1515-95), Italian priest, founder (1564) of the Institute of the Oratory, was known for his humility, piety, and cheerfulness.

143. TO MRS. WILLIAM HENRY BROOKFIELD
23 December 1850

White Lion. Bristol.
Monday.

My dear Lady. With the gold pen there's no knowing how and what I write—the handwriting is quite different and it seems as if one was speaking with a different voice. Fancy a man stepping up to speak to you in stilts & trying to make a bow, or paying you compliments through a Punch's whistle—Not that I ever did pay you a compliment you know: but I cant, or I shan't be able for a line or two to approach you naturally, and must skate along over this shiny paper—   I went to Clevedon & saw the last rites performed for poor dear Harry. I went from here and waited at Candy's till the time of the funeral in such cold weather! Candy's shop was full of ceaseless customers all the time—there never was a little boy buying candles or an old woman with the toothache (only [loo]k (the last word is look) at this paper) all the time I was there—at last the moment drew nigh, and Tinling in a scarf & hatband driving himself down from the Court passed the shop & I went down to the Church. It looked very tranquil and well ordained, and I had half an hour there before the procession came in view—Those ceremonies over a corpse the immortal soul of a man being in the keeping of G .., and beyond the reach of all Undertakers always appear to me shocking rather than solemn, and the horses and the plumes gave me pain—The awful moment was when the dear old father the coffin being lowered into the vault where so much of his affection and tenderest love lies buried went down into the cave, and gave the coffin a last kiss. There was no standing that last most affecting touch of Nature.

Then we went back to Clevedon Court where every body was very kind, and where Aggy & Beatrice and I had a great talk and play. It's odd how one can make fun & dance with other folks children and not with one's own—I cant be jocular with them somehow. Mr. Hallam who had been up stairs came down after an hour or two, and I was so sorry that I had decided on coming back to Bristol when he asked whether I wasn't going to stay? Why didn't I? I had written & proposed myself to Dean Elliot in the morning personally, & I find he is out of town on returning here, in the coldest night to the most discomfortable inn, writing paper, gold pen.

There was a great fog and in the walks and terrace one could scarcely see anything. Arthur your uncle the Captain & your father and Parr and T-nd-l how do you spell his name? and Wm. who was very much affected and F. Lushington made the funeral party—Mrs. Elton was very kind and hospitable and I like her always though she *didnt* ask me to Clevedon with the children, but I suppose there is no room for me, and it will be better that I should go to Paris with A & M whilst you are in your old home quarters—My dear Sister what matters a week or 2 more or less? Duty Duty is the word: and I hope & pray you will do it *cheerfully* Now it is to comfort & help the weak hearted: & so may your comforter & helper raise you up when you fall.   I wonder whether what I said to you yesterday was true? I know what I think about the famous chapter of St. Paul that we heard to day—one glory of the Sun & another of the moon, and one flesh of birds & one of fishes and so forth—premature definitions—yearnings and strivings of a great heart after the truth—Ah me—When shall we reach the truth? How can we with imperfect organs? but we can get nearer & nearer or at least eliminate falsehood.

Tomorrow then for Sir Joncamobbus. Write to me there dear Sister I know you will. And tell me you are cheerful: and that your baby is well and that you love your affectionate old brother.   When will you see the children? Tomorrow I hope: and now I will go (I'm obliged to write with fierce desperation on this dreadful paper) I will go to bed & pray as best I can for you and yours and for your nieces and your faithful old Makepeace

It writes here but on the other side
it wont mark without agonies
G B Y.

poor dear Harry: Henry Hallam's son, Henry Fitzmaurice Hallam, who had died on 24 October 1850 in Siena, was buried at Clevedon on 23 December.   *Tinling:* the Reverend Edward Tinling (d. 1897), husband of Mrs. Brookfield's sister, the former Katherine Maria Elton (d. 1876).   *Aggy & Beatrice:* Mary Agnes and Laura Beatrice Elton, daughters of Mrs. Brookfield's brother, Arthur Hallam Elton (1818-83).   *Dean Elliot:* the Very Reverend Gilbert Elliot (1800-91), D. D., Dean of Bristol, brother of Thomas Frederick Elliot.   *your uncle:* Henry Hallam. *the Captain:* Captain George Robbins, husband of Mrs. Brookfield's sister, the former Maria Katherine Elton (d. 1899).   *your father:* Sir Charles Elton (1778-1853), sixth Baronet.   *Parr:* Thomas Clements Parr (1804?-63), barrister, husband of Mrs. Brookfield's sister, the former Julia Elizabeth Elton (d. 1881). *T-nd-l:* Thomas Tyndall (d. 1869), husband of Mrs. Brookfield's sister, the former Caroline Lucy Elton.   *Lushington:* Franklin Lushington, a friend of Henry Fitzmaurice Hallam's from Trinity College, Cambridge days.   *the famous chapter . . . to day:* 1 Corinthians 15, 39, and 41, which is part of The Order for the Burial of the Dead in *The Book of Common Prayer*.   *Sir Joncamobbus:* Sir John Cam Hobhouse (1786-1869), later first Baron Broughton, statesman, writer, and friend of Byron. Thackeray was his guest at Erle Stoke, Westbury, Wiltshire.

144. TO ANNE THACKERAY
24 December 1850

My dearest Fat.   This will be one more of those disappointments wh. are blighting always your miserable existence: I dont know Mrs. Lewes's address—and have wrote the enclosed for her apropos of that handsome article in the Leader. If you have not sent it to Granny yet: I should like you to show it to the Brookfields: and that you and Minny should go there tomorrow taking this with you if you like to Mrs. B; and wishing our love and a happy Xmas to all of them. I wrote her a note yesterday, & will again from Erlstoke— You might go to Wilton Crescent just before you went to Aunt Mary. Look out Sir J. Hobhouse's address in the Court Guide: and forward letters to me.

Yesterday passed away pretty well: it was very affecting to see Mr. Hallam go down into the vault, to have one last look at the grave of his dear Son. But the ceremonial and the scarfs, and feathers and hatbands of the Funeral annoyed me—One wished it could have been done without all that old-world mummery. When I am buried, you will have the goodness to remember that there are no hatbands scarfs or feathers—and that unless black coaches have come down in price by that time, the people go in cabs.

I intended to have passed the evening with Dr. Elliot but he was away, so I went to bed early to one of my big sleeps—

God bless my dear women: and all who love us and give us all a happy Xmas—

W M T.

Mrs. Lewes . . . the Leader: Mrs. George Henry Lewes (1822-1902), the former Agnes Jervis. Her husband's very favorable review of *Pendennis* had appeared in the 21 December 1850 issue of *The Leader*.   *Wilton Crescent:* the home of Henry Hallam, with whom the Brookfields were staying.

145. TO ROBERT SMITH SURTEES
29 December 1850

Kensington. Sunday 29 Decr.

My dear Surtees

I send on your note to Leech reproaching myself as I see your hand-writing with benefits not forgot but unacknowledged. I ought, of course I ought, to have thanked you for your presents of books: and to have written to you—but there came a journey in the autumn, and then such hard work afterwards that writing for anything but money was out of the question I mean that the sight of a pen becomes odious to a man after some periods of labour and he can't take it up except in compulsion. Can you? felix ter et amplius you who can afford to jaunt & jollify when you like only, and never miss a days sport but when you choose it. Sir, when I came back from the country to the bosom of my family last night there was the printers devil waiting in the Hall. He's always there, always waiting—I'm surprized we get any letters written at all.

As you only read books in a lump, I'll send you Pendennis with my very best regards and hope it may serve to set you to sleep these winter evenings. I dont know whether it is stupid as a whole. I am sure the binders are stupid who have put the dedication and preface into the second volume, but please when it comes accept it faults and all, and may you live a many score merry Xmases prays

Yours very truly
W M Thackeray

Surtees: Robert Smith Surtees (1803-64), author of humorous sporting novels, including *Jorrocks' Jaunts and Jollities* (1838).   *felix ter et amplius:* (Lat.) thrice happy and more (Horace, *Odes*, I, xiii, 17).

146. TO LADY EASTLAKE
7 January 1851

Kensington. Jan 7. 1851.

Dear Lady Eastlake.

Will you give the President a copy of Pendennis from his friend and brother Carthusian. And I should have liked to send a Xmas book too to take a day or two's place on your table but the wood cuts were spoiled and the writing not first rate: and, Madam, I dont like to try *you* with second rate articles. The public has been delighted

However a rogue in the Times has found me out and assaulted me: hence has arisen a controversy wh. is very pretty controversy for any body who likes mischief Do they like mischief FitzroySquareabouts? If so

I am very faithfully yours
W M Thackeray

Lady Eastlake: the former Elizabeth Rigby (1809-93), wife of Sir Charles Lock Eastlake, who had become President of the Royal Academy in November 1850. *a Xmas book:* The Kickleburys on the Rhine.   *a rogue in the Times:* Charles Kenney on 3 January 1851.   *a controversy:* Thackeray responded to Kenney's attack with a preface to the second edition of the *Kickleburys*: "An Essay on Thunder and Small Beer."   *FitzroySquareabouts:* Sir Charles and Lady Eastlake resided at 7 Fitzroy Square.

147. TO THE REV. WILLIAM HENRY BROOKFIELD
18 March 1851

March 18. Kensington.
My dear Wm.   I have just received your kind message and melancholy news. Thank you for thinking that I'm interested in what concerns you, and sympathize in what gives you pleasure or grief. Well, I don't think there is much more than this to say: but I recal what you have said in our many talks of your father, and remember the affection and respect with wh. you always regarded and spoke of him. Who would wish for more than honor love obedience and a tranquil end to old age? And so that generation wh. engendered us passes away & their place knows them not: and our turn comes when we're to say good bye to our joys, struggles, pains, affections—and our young ones will grieve and be consoled for us—and so on. We've lived as much in 40 as your good old father in his fourscore years, don't you think so—and how awfully tired and lonely we are? I picture to myself the placid face of the kind old father with all that trouble & doubt over—his life expiring with supreme blessings for you all—for you & Jane and unconcious little Magdalene prattling and laughing, at Life's threshhold: and know that you will be tenderly cheered & consoled by the good man's blessing for the three of you; while yet, but a minute, but yesterday, but all eternity ago, he was here loving and suffering.—I go on with the paper before me—I

know there's nothing to say—but I assure you of my sympathy, and that I am yours my dear old friend afftly.

W M Thackeray

melancholy news: the death of Brookfield's father on 17 March 1851.   *honor love obedience:* Macbeth, V, iii, 25.   *their place knows them not:* Job 7: 10.

148. TO THOMAS JOHN MAZZINGHI
April? 1851

My dear Mazzinghi,—I only find your letter here to-day and am very much grieved at its contents. If I can help you, I will. That is all I can say at present, for it requires time and chance and occasion to find work for a man. Perhaps there comes no chance, no occasion; that is the worst of it. In the meanwhile, is a little (a very little you understand, for I am always as poor as a church-mouse) present help wanted? My dear fellow in that case pray command me in this case and think that it is I who am thankful if I can aid you. Always truly yours, dear Mazzinghi,

W. M. Thackeray.

Mazzinghi: Thomas John Mazzinghi (1811-93), barrister, whom Thackeray had known at Charterhouse and at Trinity College, Cambridge.

149. TO MRS. WILLIAM HENRY BROOKFIELD
29 April 1851

April 29.

Madam and dear lady, Will you have a little letter to day or a long letter tomorrow for theres only half an hour to post time—a little letter today?—I dont wonder at poets being selfish, such as Wordsworth and Alfred—I've been for 5 days a poet, and have thought or remembered nothing else but my self and my rhymes and my measure—If somebody had come to me and said Mrs. Brookfield has just had her arm cut off I should have gone on with Queen of innumerable isles tidumtidytidumtidy and not stirred from the chair— the children and nobody haven't seen me except at night—and now though the work is just done (I'm just returned from taking it to the Times office) I hardly see the paper before me, so utterly beat, nervous, bilious & overcome I feel. So you see you chose a very bad day Mum for a letter from yours very sincerely—if you were at

Cadogan Place I would walk in I dar[e]say, say God bless you, and then ask leave to go to sleep—   Now you must be thinking of coming back to Pumlico soon for the lectures are to begin on the 15th. I tried the great room at Willis's yesterday, and recited a part of the multiplication table to a waiter at the opposite end so as to try the woice. He said he could hear perfectly: and I dare say he could but the thoughts somehow swell and amplify with that high-pitched voice and elaborate distinctness—as I perceive how poets become selfish I see how orators become humbugs and selfish in their way too: absorbed in that selfish pursuit and turning of periods—It is curious to take those dips into a life new to me as yet, and try it and come out and say how I like it isn't it?—Ah me —Idleness [is] best that is quiet and repose of mind, and somebody to love and be fond of, and nil admirari in fine. The gentlemen of the G tell me, and another auditor from the Macready dinner, that my style of horatory was conspicuous for consummate ease and impudence, I all the while feeling in so terrible a panic that I scarcely knew at the time what I was uttering, & didn't know at all when I sat down—This is all I have to tell you about self and ten days wh. have passed away like a fever—Why if we were to let the poetic cock turn & run there's no end of it I think. Would you like me now to become a great—fiddlededydee—no more egotisms Mr. Makepeace if you please.   I should have liked to see your master on Sunday but how could I & Lord I had such a headache and Dicky Doyle came and we went to Soyers Symposium and the Christial Palace together where the great calm leviathan steam-engines and machines lying alongside like [a] great line of battle ships did wonderfully move me, and I think the English Compartment do beat the rest entirely and that (let alone our Ingynes wh. be incomparable) our painters artificers makers of busts and statuas do deserve to compare with the best foreign,—

—This I am sure will interest and please Miss Brookfield very much. God bless that dear little lady. I would give 2d. to hear her say more tea—O—by the way—Can I have that young woman of whom Rossiter spoke? Mary goes away at the end of the week, and a cook is coming and I want a maid but have had no leisure to think of one, till now when my natural affairs and affections are beginning to return to my mind and when I am my dear ladys friend and servant, (and G B her)

W M T.

the work: Thackeray's "May Day Ode," which appeared in the 30 April 1851 issue of *The Times.*   *Cadogan Place:* the Brookfields lived at Number 64.   *nil admirari:* (Lat.) to admire nothing (Horace, *Epistles,* I, vi, 1).   *the G:* the Garrick Club.   *Lord I had . . . foreign,—:* a parody of Samuel Pepys (1633-1703), in the style of Thackeray's *Punch* colleague, Percival Leigh (1813-89), author of *Mr. Pips his Diary*, which was appended to a series of drawings in *Punch, Ye Manners and Customs of Ye Englyshe* (1849), by Richard Doyle (1824-83). *Christial Palace*: the Crystal Palace, site of the Great Exhibition of 1851.

150. TO MRS. WILLIAM HENRY BROOKFIELD
1 May 1851

Amie—I write you a little word after that Exhibition from home, & why do you think I came home? for a letter from somebody that I longed for: and was going away quite disconsolate at not finding it when Anny to whom I'd been talking mentioned that she had got & forgot one. But why havent you written all this time? What is the matter? Is Wm. really unwell at Southton?. It was I ordered Jane Elliot to write to you like a good dear soul as she is; the Ode has had a great success What do you mean by an Ode as she calls, vive dieu Madame 'tis either an ode or nix. (the German for nothing)—and as for the Exhibition wh. dont interest me at all so much, it was a noble awful great love inspiring goose flesh bringing sight. I got a good place by good luck, and saw the whole affair of wh. no particular item is wonderful but the general effect the multitude the riches the peace the splendour the security the sunshine great to see—much grander than a coronation—the vastest & sublimest popular festival that the world has ever witnessed—What can one say about it but commonplaces?— There was a Chinese with a face like a

pantomime mask and shoes who went up and

kissed the Duke of Wellington much to the old boys surprize, and the Queen looked not uninteresting and Prince Albert grave handsome & princely, and the Prince of W & the Princess Royal are nice children— very eager to talk and observe they seemed—and while the Archbishop was saying his prayer beginning with Paternoster (wh. sounded in that wonderful throng inexpressibly sweet and awful) 3 Romish priests were staring about with opera glasses: wh. made me feel as angry as the Jews who stoned Stephen—

I think this is all I have to say: I'm very tired & the day not over for I have promised the children to take them to the play in recompense for their disappointment in not getting to the Exhibition wh. they had hopes of seeing through my friend Cole. God bless you—and you'll come back on the seventh will you? God keep you that & all days my sister my lady.

W M T.

vive dieu: (Fr.) glory be!   *Prince of W:* Albert Edward (1841-1910), Prince of Wales, later Edward VII.   *Princess Royal:* Princess Victoria (1840-1901).   *the Jews who stoned Stephen:* Acts 7: 59.   *Cole:* Henry (later Sir Henry) Cole (1808-82), a member of the executive committee of the Great Exhibition of 1851.

151. TO DAVID MASSON
6? May 1851

Kensington. Tuesday Mg.

My dear Sir

I received the N B Review and am very glad to know the name of the critic who has spoken so kindly in my favor. Did I not once before see your handwriting, in a note wh. pointed out to me a friendly notice of Vanity Fair—then not very well known or much cared for, and struggling to get a place in the world? If you were the author of the article to wh. I allude, let me thank you for that too; I remember it as gratefully, as a boy remembers his 'tips' at school, when sovereigns were rare & precious to him. I don't know what to say respecting your present paper, comparisons being difficult, & no two minds in the least alike. I think Mr. Dickens has in many things quite a divine genius so to speak, and certain notes in his song are so delightful and admirable, that I should never think of trying to imitate him, only hold my tongue and admire him I quarrel with his Art in many respects: wh. I don't think represents nature duly; for instance Micawber appears to me an exaggeration of a man, as his name is of a name. It is delightful and makes me laugh: but it is no more a real man than my friend Punch is; and in so far I protest against him—and against the doctrine quoted by my Reviewer from Goethe too— holding that the Art of Novels *is* to represent nature: to convey as strongly as possible the sentiment of reality—In a tragedy or a poem or a lofty drama you aim at producing different emotions; the figures moving, and their words sounding, heroically: but in a drawing room drama a coat is a coat and a poker a poker; and must be nothing else according to my ethics, not an embroidered tunic, nor a great red-hot instrument like the Pantomime weapon. But let what defects you (or rather I) will, be in Dickenss theory—there is no doubt according to my notion that his writing has one admirable quality—it is *charming*— that answer's everything another may write the most perfect English have the greatest fund of wit learning & so forth—but I doubt if any novel-writer has that quality, that wonderful sweetness & freshness

wh. belongs to Dickens—and now I have carried my note out of all bounds and remain dear Sir
Yours very faithfully
W M Thackeray

Masson: David Masson (1822-1907), who had published *"Pendennis and Copperfield:* Thackeray and Dickens" in *The North British Review* for May 1851. *a friendly notice of Vanity Fair:* Masson's "Popular Serial Literature" in *The North British Review* for May 1847. *the doctrine quoted ... from Goethe:* "Art is called Art, says Goethe, precisely because it is *not* Nature."

152. TO MR. AND MRS. THOMAS CARLYLE
23? May 1851

My dear Mrs. Carlyle my dear Carlyle you are both very kind to me: and always have been my kind old friends and I am yours in return very gratefully & sincerely indeed
W M Thackeray
Equilibrist and Tightrope dance[r] in ordinary to the nobility & the Literati

I think it was very kind of Mazzini to ask. T. O.

Equilibrist . . . Literati: Thackeray had begun his lectures on the English humorists of the eighteenth century on 22 May 1851, with Carlyle and apparently

Mrs. Carlyle in the audience.   *Mazzini:* Giuseppi Mazzini (1805-72), Italian revolutionary living in exile in England.   *T. O.:* [i. e. turn over] nothing is written on the verso.

153. TO LEIGH HUNT
29-30 May 1851

Thursday

My dear Hunt   I only knew for certain on Tuesday who was the writer of the Spectator article: and you understand I can't speak about it. My mother and children may thank you but I can't: only I ought to be very thankful and humble before God Almighty if it's true. Is it I wonder? I swear I don't know. I fancy part of it may be so sometimes—but that's a cause rather of fear than elation. Forster told me at his own table last night flatly that I should see this fashion die out: and that my lecture didnt contain one single word of wit or humour—The Examiner is perhaps as far from the mark as the Spectator here—and a man must take a steady count of both these opinions to keep his own balance right. The thing wh. touches me most at heart is your last word that I'm honest—to this pray God amen—It's an awful word somehow and the Truth a great presence to stand in. Good bye and thank you—I know Ive nothing to say in reply to your words: how can I?

Always, faithfully yours
W M Thackeray

Friday. I forgot to enclose this letter yesterday before I went out and saw you[r] friendly little trio afar off.

the Spectator article: Hunt's warm review of Thackeray's opening lecture on Swift had appeared in *The Spectator* on 24 May 1851, the same day as Forster's unsympathetic review in *The Examiner.*

154. TO JOHN FORSTER
June 1851

My dear Forster

You didnt say anything unsatisfactory to me at all. What did I say that should bear such an interpretation? When I speak I'm so frightened that I dont know what happens, and sit down unconscious of what is done in the struggle. But my object was to tell Dickens and you his familiar friends, that I'm not his enemy: and I think the world is large enough for fifty such coaches as he and I drive. And I was thankful to Talfourd for giving me the opportunity of coming to the dinner and allowing me loyally to shake hands with you all. As for you and me, I'm sure that each has a sincere regard for the other. You showed it when I was ill. Do you suppose I can ever forget that? But I dont pretend to tell you that I think you are fair towards me as a critic. My success such as it is angers you some how. Was ever such a charge made against a man, as that wh. you my benefactor of a few months before, made against me of wishing 'to curry favor with the non-literary class by abusing my own profession'—It was my honour that you attacked, & when I rebutted the charge as absurd (not touching on it's unkindness) you dont publish my answer, but say I have lost my temper, and end with a sneer at a man who dines with lords—to hint at these things is like sneering at the chastity of a woman in print. What do I care, being honest in my own heart, that you think and print me a sneak? I have had great services from you. I believe in your inward kindness for me. I forgive you—I try to be friends with you and your friends, I always hold out my hand and mean it too. I go & dine with you (expecting something, confound it,) and what do I get at your table? A speech that 'I lecture on wit & humour & *there's not a word of wit or humour* in my lecture.'— Those are your words, my host's words were they hospitable, or necessary, are they true? psha. I swear I feel no anger: and am kindly & affectionately disposed towards you. You are to me: but—but we're on different sides of the house. Well, God bless you my dear old fellow, whatever colours you wear; I don't believe in the Guild of Literature I dont believe in the Theatrical scheme; I think *that* is against the dignity of our profession,—but you are honest and clever men and free to your opinion (thank you for nothing say you) well, believe that mine's loyally entertained too. Try and get out of your head that I am a sneak and a schemer: & to think that I have a little heart. I know I have, & that there's a great deal of kindness in it for you my dear old Forster.

W M T.

Talfourd: Thomas (later Sir Thomas) Noon Talfourd (1795-1854), politician and miscellaneous writer.   *the dinner:* Talfourd gave a dinner on 11 June 1851 to commemorate *David Copperfield.*   *when I was ill:* Forster had brought Dr. John Elliotson to Thackeray's bedside in September 1849.   *'to curry favor . . . profession':* Thackeray is paraphrasing Forster's language in *The Examiner* on 5 January 1850, where Forster charged that Thackeray was frequently willing "to pay court to the non-literary class by disparaging his fellow-labourers."   *'I . . . my lecture':* Forster's comments at a dinner he gave, apparently on 28 May 1851. *Guild of Literature . . . Theatrical scheme . . . dignity of our profession:* in

January 1851 Dickens had proposed establishing a Guild of Literature and Art, which was to be funded by performances of Bulwer's *Not So Bad As We Seem* (1851), conducted by amateur actors like himself for the benefit of members of the literary profession. Thackeray was dubious about the project and its assumptions about the undignified status of literary writers. See Letter 196.

155. TO KATE PERRY
September 1851

[. . .] I dont see how any woman should not love a man who had loved her as I did J.: I don't see how any man shd. not love a woman so beautiful so unhappy so tender: I dont see how any husband however he might have treated his treasure should be indifferent at the idea of losing it: But that I knew I was safe (I mean that any wrong was out of the question on our children's account) I suppose I should have broken away myself. I'm sure that one & the other on their side were wrong in not dismissing me: but a part of poor Brookfields pride of possession was that we should envy him and admire her; and of all this weakness goodness love generosity vanity, *playing with edged tools*, we are all paying the penalty. I dont see how it can be averted for any of us.

I see nothing but time to heal this wound of amputation wh. it is: we must all suffer and limp for the rest of our lives. How can apologies soothe?—nobody can make any. How can I help or regret having loved her? Whenever I could say a word for him I did, as the other day when I carried that humiliating message to him. I grieve that we are all wretched I wish that I had never loved her. *I* have been played with by a woman, and flung over at a beck from the lord & master—that's what I feel—I treat her tenderly and like a gentleman: I will fetch, carry, write, stop, what she pleases—but I leave her. I mean I will do what she wishes in decency and moderation—It's death I tell you between us. I was packing away yesterday the letters of years—*these* didn't make me cry. They made me laugh, as I knew they would. It was for this that I gave my heart away. It is 'When are you coming dear Mr. Thackeray,' and 'William will be so happy' and 'I thought after you had gone away how I had forgot to &c'—and at a word from Brookfield afterwards it is—'I reverence & admire him and love him with not merely a dutiful but a genuine love'—Amen The thought that I have been made a fool of, is the bitterest of all perhaps—and a lucky thing for all it is perhaps that it should be so. As for me, I cant make any advances more than I have. I have offered to see him, but he refused. Dear Friends as before we can't be, that is we are: but there is separation between us inevitable. We must part in peace. I have loved his wife too much, to be able to bear to see her belong even to her husband any more—thats the truth. There's a decency after the past wh. says 'Go you must stay here no more.' Good bye. I wish it was my novel Id been writing on all these pages

Your affte
W M T.

[. . .]: the first two leaves are missing; the text begins on a leaf numbered "3." *loved her:* Mrs. Brookfield.   *amputation:* a quarrel between Thackeray and Brookfield over the former's love for Mrs. Brookfield and the latter's treatment of her had caused a break in the relations between Thackeray and the Brookfields that proved to be permanent.   *my novel:* Thackeray had recently begun *Esmond.*

156. TO MRS. THOMAS FREDERICK ELLIOT AND KATE PERRY
26 September 1851

Chatsworth if you please.
Friday.

Ladies you will see into what quarters I am got, and I daresay you think I write merely that I may have the pleasure of dating as above, but that is not the reason. I came down to Matlock—made a sketch at Haddon Hall and a very bad sketch too, wrote read worked hard but it wouldn't do to drive dull care away, and yesterday I moved off intending for Bakewell, but seeing the Chatsworth omnibus, suddenly mounted on it; came to a famous Inn here wrote and read, and ah the devil was with me still: and this morning wrote to Mr. Paxton saying how I was in the country, didnt know the Duke was here; didnt like to come & didnt like to go away and the answer was Paxton in a carriage to fetch me and my trunks and a gracious reception from the Duke Its been pouring with rain all day. I've been round the house and seen the interior splendors—pictures, and state-rooms, and manuscripts in the library & so forth and oh but the Devil is with me still gnawing away and making me miserable. As we were going about from room to room & gallery to gallery, I had a great mind to say 'Show me the Bluebeard Closet where the dead wives and the murdered secrets are: you must have a Bluebeard closet—every body has one. Let me go & sit in that—it's that I like best.' And I write because I'm unhappy—If I write my book in this frame of mind it will be diabolical—I wrote a bit yesterday that was quite Satanic, and raged about with a dreadful gaiety.   Can you do any thing to soothe and ease that poor lady? Mrs. Fanshawe sent me a letter of hers about me and *at* me—and what do you think I did? I wrote back to Mrs. F to inform her principal that even these roundabout correspondences oughtn't to be: that her husband acting at this moment nobly & gently must be nobly and gently used—and that until he authorized a correspondence none such must be. And now, and now if she's in torment take her a drop of water will you from another soul in purgatory? I know it will soothe her to think that I'm unhappy—or rather that she wd. be more unhappy if she thought I didn't feel at parting with her. O me—the only thing is Duty Duty Duty. Her husband *is* a good fellow and does love her: and I think of his constant fondness for me & kindness and how cruelly I've stabbed him and outraged him with my words—Well, I'd do it again—though I wish that it could have been any other dagger than mine to strike the blow—The sword must have fallen someday or the other. I am glad that she did her duty and threw me over for him—and though in my moments of pique & rage I dont forgive her, I do at better times & say God bless her. But we must bear our fates. We shant and cant and musnt meet again as heretofore—it was for that I stabbed the husband expres[s] to put her up as high as I could and to make the zusammenkunft impossible. Poor old boy, I forget that he has ever been cruel, and think of 500 jolly meetings and kind greetings I have had from him. Who would have divined that all that friendship, that such a good fellow, should end in treason?—for a treason it is say what I will.

Paxton: Joseph (later Sir Joseph) Paxton (1803-65), superintendent of the Duke of Devonshire's gardens at Chatsworth, and designer of the building that housed the Great Exhibition of 1851.   *poor lady:* Mrs. Brookfield.   *zusammenkunft:* (Ger.) reunion.

157. TO LADY EDWARD JOHN STANLEY OF ALDERLEY
28? October 1851

Kensington. Tuesday night.

My dear Lady Stanley.
    I have often had that young lady in my mind who has been married a month or more, and for whom I have got a little twopenny memento from a very sincere friend of hers. I had a nice copy of Vanity Fair, the Tauchnitz Edition much prettier than the English, and sent it to a man to bind who gave me the most solemn promises that it should be ready by the 25 ult—but it was never ready for a week after and then came back such a homely ugly book that I couldn't think of

sending it to a Countess as a present on such a festive occasion: and so got another book wh. has had to be bound and is now just come home. Tell me please how I shall send to Airlie Castle N. B. and if the lady there is well; and if you of Cheshire are happy too and not angry with me. I was within 25 miles of you for a day or two, & intended to come on but was too ill (parole d'honneur) to be in any body's house but my own. I am writing a book of cutthroat melancholy suitable to my state, and have no news of myself or any body to give you that shouldn't be written on black-edged paper and sealed with a hatchment. I would have written had it been otherwise; and asked to come to you but for the above dismal reasons. I am going to the Grange for 2 or 3 days at the end of the week, & then to Oxford & Cambridge barking about with my lecture thence to the modern Awthens. How far is Airlie Castle from Awthens? I'll take Vanity Fair to Edinburgh at any rate and send it if I can—the only cheerful face I have seen is Milnes's just come back and looking as if he quite liked being married: he told us to night (this Madam is written in the loneliness of midnight) that Mrs. Milnes insists on his going to the Bloomer ball tomorrow. Do you know what Bloomers are in Cheshire?—It is a new kind of bonnet wh. the ladies wear. If I go to the ball and dance there I will write you about it, when the letter may be more cheerful than this one from yours very faithfully indeed
W M Thackeray
Carlyle's Life of Sterling is delightful have you read it?

Lady Stanley: the former Lady Henrietta Maria Dillon-Lee (1808-96), wife of Edward John Stanley (1802-69), second Baron.   *that young lady:* Lady Stanley's daughter, Henrietta Blanche (1829-1821), who had married David Graham Ogilvy (1826-81), seventh Earl of Airlie on 23 September 1851.   *you of Cheshire:* Lord and Lady Stanley lived at Alderley Park, Cheshire.   *parole d'honneur:* (Fr.) word of honor.   *the Grange:* residence of Lord and Lady Ashburton in Alresford, Hampshire.   *Milnes ... married:* Milnes had married Annabella Hungerford (1814-74) on 31 July 1851.   *Bloomer ball:* a Bloomer ball was apparently held in late October 1851 at the Hanover Square Rooms.

158. TO MRS. HENRY CARMICHAEL-SMYTH
10 November 1851

Monday.
My dearest Mammy Before I go off on my circuiteering I must send you that letter that has been so often begun & burned in this month past: during wh. I have not been the happiest mad wag in all England but in a very bearable condition of mind nevertheless and an

easy frame of body. The Brookfield party is finally off for Madeira and we met at the Grange and parted not friends, but not enemies—and so there's an end of it. And now the Oxford & Cambridge business begins, at Oxford Monday & Tuesday: at Cambridge Friday & Saturday, at home between days except next week when I go to old Sir Thomas Cullum who has asked me so often that I cant refuse any more.—Then in December for 3 weeks to Scotland. Then in January at the Portman Square Rooms London, where they make me an offer of 150£ wh. is pretty well, for 6 hours I think, and by the end of January my novel please God will be finished and I can go to America. I was thinking of sending the young ones to their Granny in December when I went Northwards: but it will be very dismal & lonely to be a month in London without them when I come back, so that they will hardly be with you before February, when they will spend I suppose a good half year in your nest.   If all things go well I shall have made a pretty little start in the world by that time, and have saved enough money to keep them at least from starving. I dont see why not. God speed the campaign, wh. opens to night. Old Stoddart is my host at Oxford and I dont know how matters will go there: of Cambridge I am surer expecting a great auditory there. It is curious isn't it to be arrived actually at the day when some money will be put by for the young ones?—they will probably be worth 30£ apiece to night.

Crowe dined with me yesterday and Lord Stanley whom I asked to meet him—I tremble about him. Joe has lost his place at the Daily News and Crowe has thrown up his—Good God what are they to do? I see 50£ out of somebodys pocket before long. He is not to go yet: but his departure is decided; and then? its awful to think of the sword coming down—of the precipices we all walk on. I am on my knees to Stanley and Palmerston to get something for Crowe, who has been the best servant Lord P has ever had—but one stands aghast before the fate of these poor people, and cowardly self-love cries out Save Save Save—or you may starve too. So please God we will and do that work resolutely for the next year—I am very well in health I think, having staved off my old complaint, and the only thing that alarms me sometimes is the absurd fancy that now the money making is actually at hand some disaster may drop down and topple me over. But thats a fancy only.

Fonblanque dined here yesterday too and has *re*taken me into a great affection: but with poor Jack Forster it is well not to try to be friends again—it's best not to pick up some acquaintances when they are dropped.

The novel is getting on pretty well & gaily I mean—What I wrote a month ago is frightfully glum. And I shall write it better now that the fierceness of a certain pain is over. The truth is I've had an awful time of it: and don't know how miserable I was until I look back at such & such days. But I'm easy now. I wish the other folks were as happy: but they are both wretched I fear. Perhaps I'm rather ashamed of myself for taking things so easily. God bless you my dearest old Mother and G P: and now let's call a cab & go to Oxford.

W M T.

In Kensington. The lady of S James Esq. of a son.

circuiteering: Thackeray's travels in England and Scotland delivering his lectures on the English humorists of the eighteenth century.   *Old Stoddart:* William Wellwood Stoddart (1809-56) of St. John's College, Oxford, whom Thackeray had known since boyhood.   *Joe:* Joseph (later Sir Joseph) Crowe (1825-96), son of Eyre Evans Crowe.   *my old complaint:* his urethral stricture.   *S. James:* Thackeray's man-servant, Samuel James.

159. TO GEORGE SMITH
26 December 1851

Decr. 26. 1851.
Kensington.

My dear Smith.

I have so far bad news to give you that I have not advanced 5 pages whilst I was in Edinburgh It was impossible to write. And if it doesn't interfere with your plans much I am glad of the delay—Every month is of importance towards effecting a cure of a complaint wh. would have made the book dismal & a failure. And I'm immensely better & have brought back a hat full of money and all over Edinburgh laurels.

Take the Dutchman's 25 with thankfulness on behalf of Yours very truly

W M Thackeray

I shall be at home about the 6th. and am to be heard of till the 1st. at Lord Ashburton's The Grange Alresford afterwd at Lord Broughton's. Erlestoke. Westbury.

Smith: George Smith (1827-1901), publisher, who had contracted with Thackeray for *Henry Esmond.*

160. TO MRS. JOHN BROWN
5 January 1852

Erlestoke. Westbury. Jan 5, 1852.

My dear Mrs. Brown.

The children write me from afar off that you have written them a kind letter: and though I think it is 20 years ago since I left Edinburgh, I have not forgotten you and write a stupid line to say how do you and the Doctor and Jock and Helen—Since I came away I have been out a visiting and write this on this grand thick official paper from a grand house, where I am treated very hospitably (as usual) and propose to pass 2 or 3 days or more. Then back to London: & thence to Brighton very possibly to try and work a little—All this pleasuring has unfitted me for it and I begin to fancy I am a gentleman of 5000£ a year. They spoiled the youngest of my girls at Lord Ashburton's: I should have done better to bring them to Scotland, and show them simple kind people—not that these are not too: but—but it's different: and I doubt whether yours isn't the best. I have no earthly news to send you—only the most stupid good-wishes but I wish instead of waiting up in my room here for dinner and 3 courses and silver and champaign, I was looking forward to 23, and that dear old Small-beer. And then we would have a cab and go to the Music Hall to hear Mrs. Kemble. I sometimes fancy that having been at Edinburgh is a dream—only there are the daguerreotypes and a box of that horrid short-bread still—and the hatfull of money to be sure. It wasn't at all cold coming to London—and the town of Berwick on Tweed looked beautiful: and I think my fellow passenger must have wondered to see how cleverly I slept. He was a young Cambridge man, and knew your humble servant perfectly well. It was in the railroad I got the great news of Palmerstons going out. It didn't frighten you in Rutland Street much I daresay, but in the houses where I go we still talk about it and I amongst the number as gravely as if I was a Minister myself. Why do we? What does it matter to me who's Minister?—Depend on it 23 Rutland St. is the best and good dear kind friends, and quiet talk and honest beer.

You see by the absurd foregoing paragraphs that I've nothing in the world to say: but I want to shake you and the Doctor by the hand and say

Thank you and God bless you.
W M Thackeray

Mrs. Brown: wife (d. 1864) of Dr. John Brown (1810-82), Scottish physician and miscellaneous writer.   *Jock and Helen:* Dr. and Mrs. Brown's two children. *Mrs. Kemble:* the actress, Fanny Kemble. *Palmerstons going out:* Lord John Russell dismissed Palmerston as Foreign Minister on 19 December 1851.

161. TO MRS. THOMAS FREDERICK ELLIOT AND KATE PERRY
7? January 1852

What an awful thing this is! You may suppose I knew nothing of it yesterday when I sent off joking letters to your house. I think that it might have been my chance, and of my dear young ones at home sitting fatherless, and my heart quite melts about poor Warburton's—God help them. There must be a pension for the widow—I know you'll agitate that directly. I write to you as I've just done to Kinglake who was always his fast and affectionate friend, more for writing's and speaking's sake, than because of any good I can do: and my first feeling was to order a carriage and come away and sit with you and have a talk—but the owner of the house insists so upon my staying till Saturday that I couldn't without rudeness refuse him—Ah mon Dieu, and so it's ended—the harmless life of that kindly gentle soul. Don't you see his sad face, and melancholy foreboding (now we know & can interpret those signs) written on it? I think of those people I love in these moments—and see your kind face and another's coming to my bedside when I was all but gone—I'll come and see you all on Sunday I daresay—meanwhile you know that I'm yours always
W M T.

poor Warburton: Eliot Warburton had died in a fire that swept the steamer *Amazon* on 4 January 1852.   *owner of the house:* Sir John Cam Hobhouse, first Baron Broughton.   *another's:* Mrs. Brookfield's.

162. TO LADY POLLOCK
January 1852

Friday.

My dear Lady Pollock,
    It gave me very great pleasure the other night to see your two friendly faces in the audience, and I was going to write to tell you that I was grateful for your countenance, and thought it very kind of the Chief Baron to quit his fireside after a day's work and come and sit in

hard benches, to listen to me talking. Now I am doubly pleased to think you are pleased with the lecture—and though the scheme has not yielded a fortune as yet, it has brought me the first £500 I have ever saved, and I think there are a score more of hundred pounds in the country to be had for the asking then I shall go to America and rob the Yankees—Then I will come home rich, and marry the Vizier's daughter, &c. You remember Alnaschar and the girl who counted the produce of her eggs. Well, it seems very good luck and I know that my friends rejoice in it. I was thinking whether I should write to you from Edinburgh when I saw in the papers the misfortune that had befallen you but I have had the same grief myself to endure and remember; and know there's no comfort that another can give: and in presence of these calamities take off my hat and pass on in silence generally. It is always the lost one of the flock we miss the most: Be sure that I feel sincerely for the grief of such good friends as you and my kind Chief Baron have ever shown yourselves to

Yours always most sincerely,
W. M. Thackeray

Lady Pollock: the former Sarah Langslow, wife of Sir Jonathan Frederick Pollock (1783-1870), Lord Chief Baron of the Court of Exchequer.   *misfortune:* the death of her infant son, Gerald.   *grief:* the death of his infant daughter, Jane, in 1839.

163. TO MRS. HENRY CARMICHAEL-SMYTH
15 March 1852

March 15.

My dearest Mammy I was going to write on this very little sheet of paper when your letter came in—M de Wailly is the very man of all France I would like to translate me but is it possible he can give as much as 4000 francs to me?—there must be some mistake I fear. Nevertheless I empower you to act, and get what you can for me. I have given up & only had for a day or two the notion of the book in numbers. Its much too grave & sad for that & the incident not sufficient. You will dislike it very much It was written at a period of grief and pain so severe that I dont like to think of it, and am ashamed now to be well and rid so soon of my melancholy—The house in the Square has been long since given up. It is delightfully comfortable but would cost 500£ and I should be no better off—About Sloane St. must be my mark when I move. I dont see or suffer by the vulgarity of the great folks I find a great deal of kindness for me and mine. My dearest Nan is very popular and Minny too of course: & as they must have some friends, when they go into the world why not good ones? How much kindness haven't I had from people eager to serve me? It's we who make the haughtiness of the grandees—not they. They're never thinking of it at least my experience goes so far: and coming to know people whom I have thought insolent & air-giving, such as Lord & Lady John for instance, I find 2 as simple folks as you & G P—and no more gêne at their tea-table than your's. What can I do but speak of the world as I find it?

    I am very much pained indeed to hear of Morton, and you may say that I say so. He is *shocking* about women. Directly I hear of his being fond of one, I feel sorry for her. He lusts after her and leaves her. You may read this to him if you like. No there's no use nor in speaking to Mrs. S. Women think about *reclaiming* a libertine & then, & then all the fat is in the fire. Did the children tell you about little Streatfield? I wrote to Dr. Saunders begging him to let the boy come to me, stayed at home waiting for him;—no boy, no answer to my note: and I didn't like to write again for a little and haven't had a free Saturday since: but I shall get one soon I hope. I thought his mother charming; and recollect his father's pretty round face as a boy. I went & sate with poor old Miss Berry last night and amused her with a comic story wh. I was quite astonished as I told myself as I don't generally perform the wag or talk much. Eyre Crowe is not Elliot's secretary, but mine for the nonce & Professor of drawing to the young ladies, I can quite utilize him, and like dictating to him: and Miss Holmes has arrived and been here 3 days & goes to day—There's something very natural and good in her—She seems to me to play very soberly and finely: she says Minny takes to learning the theory of music surprizingly, and that they both may play very well, and have been taught very well by Miss Trulock too—who is mortified at the new professor, but bears her mortification very kindly. She's a good woman Poor Miss Holmes is not a lovely object to look upon with red hair and nose, the lady of Babylon is scarcely more scarlet. I have told her that she must come & give her lesson and be off without much talking else she will be theologizing but I shall be glad if the gals can be taught music by an *artist* who has the brains and heart as well as the fingers of her art. And so my little page is full, and I am my dearest old Mothers & G P's affte

W M T.

    When Wm. Grey goes to Paris you'll have the use of the bag again.

Wailly: Armand François Léon de Wailly (1804-63), French writer who published a translation of *Esmond* in 1856.   *Lord & Lady John:* Lord John Russell and his wife, the former Lady Frances Elliot.   *gêne:* (Fr.) constraint.   *Saunders:* Dr. Augustus Page Saunders (1801-78), Headmaster of Charterhouse 1832-53.

mother . . . father: Mrs. Streatfeild, wife of Major Sidney Robert Streatfeild (b. 1808), whom Thackeray had known at Charterhouse, which their son, Sidney Richard (b. 1841), was presently attending.   *poor old Miss Berry:* Mary Berry, whose sister Agnes had died in January 1852.   *Eyre Crowe:* (b. 1824), painter. *Miss Holmes:* Mary Holmes, who gave music lessons to Thackeray's daughters. *lady of Babylon . . . scarlet:* Revelation 17: 4-5.   *Grey:* William George Grey (1819-65), diplomatist.

164. TO ANNE AND HARRIET THACKERAY
22 April 1852

Glasgow Thursday.

My dearest women. Whenever you don't have a letter for days together you may be sure either that your Papa has a dreadful illness and has tumbled down a well or had his head knocked off by a cannon-ball, or else that he is very busy quill-driving—That's what is going on at present, and I've nothing to say except that the book is getting on and occupying me almost all day, and at nights I go out a lecturing or a dining and so the day passes quickly off. I finish here on Tuesday, but Monday & Wednesday I go to Grenock and perform a couple of lectures there. I have had no answer from Manchester as yet and don't know when or whether that business will come off. I may take it on my way to London, and Liverpool and Birmingham too and arrange matters for the future, but I think the odds are that I'll come home by the first of May, and see the chimney sweeps and my dear gals. Granny has got a letter by this time: and I have found as usual a score of kind people here who are ready with kindness and hospitality—professors of the College here, soldier-officers merchants and all sorts. And as usual I get too many good dinners and don't take exercise enough. It's my lot *ici bas:* and eating & drinking a part of your poor dear Fathers business in this world. I may go to Edinburgh on Saturday, Sunday—no steamers are allowed to run, no railroads to carry passengers on Sunday: and 400000 people that might have fresh air are kept from it, because the Parsons say that travelling or amusement on Sunday are contrary to the word of God—And if they think so, why shouldn't they say so, and stay at home? Is one of the cards from the Royal Academy? But send everything as Postage is not much, and answers may be required—I've got one or two more little sketches but haven't time for many and so Anny kiss Minny & Minny kiss Anny for

Papa.

chimney sweeps: sweeps wore finery on 1 May.   *ici bas:* (Fr.) on this earth.

165. TO ANNE AND HARRIET THACKERAY
18-20 June 1852

Augsburg Friday.
Munich Sunday.

My dearest Nan. The first line I write though it is but a stupid one must be for my daughters and I beg you to kiss each other 6 times for Papa, and I will pay you when we come together again. I set off from Frankfurt that dismal Monday night, so melancholy that I had almost turned back and gone after you to Heidelberg, and was one of six in a carriage travelling all night to Wurtzbourg was it? Well I think it was to Wurtzbourg. There we arrived at 8 in the morning and it must be said that your melancholy father slept uncommonly well on the journey: but not enough not to be stupid all day at Wurtzbourg wh. I saw as in a sort of dream, a great old-fashioned city with nobody in it—vast Churches where there used to be Prince Bishops in old times who have gone the way of the deuce with all their court, and enormous palaces and convents now of no use to anybody—Well I hate writing 'descriptions' except for money and if ever I do anything with this business it will be for money only. After being stupified all day at Wurzbourg, I found towards nightfall that there was no way of getting out of the place except at midnight or midday or that very evening, so I set off and had another evenings ride one of six in a tight carriage with a cursed rheumatism in the waking time, and found myself coming through Bamberg at 4 in the morning and at Nuremberg at about 7.

The first aspect of Nuremberg was 'Well, this is as fine as Venice' and I wished for some company I had had at Venice last year. But the stupor of 2 nights in the Diligence I suppose followed me about all day (though I had a warm bath a nap, and every luxury) I have brought away little recollection of the place except as through a dream, and it appears to me now a long long while ago since I was there. I made a drawing in my little metallic book, and almost forget the place now. The fact is I daresay I was thinking of other things all the time and hence didn't see the place properly.

But yesterday morning after a great big sleep I woke up as fresh as a daisy and came on to Augsbourg wh. is but an ugly place not old enough to be interesting and yet I like it for the Inn is very comfortable, and I read Grannys & G P's name in the book in 1841 with numbers more of my friends last night. In the bed there were animals I think called bugs—I look ruefully at it hard by being just about to have another spell at it, having returned from a trip to Blenheim wh. I wanted to see—an hour by the railroad and 2 hours by a coach farther—What I was pleased with was to find that Blenheim was just exactly the place I had figured to myself except that the village is larger, but I fancy I had actually been there—so like the aspect of it was to what I looked for—and who knows perhaps one *does* go to places in the spirit—I saw the brook wh. H. Esmond crossed, and almost the spot where he fell wounded and walked down to the Danube and mused mighty thoughts over it. It seems grand to walk down to the Danube: but the Thames at Putney is twice as big and handsome as the river is here—and then I came back to a late dinner here and now I am come to bed and to say God bless my dearest girls and their Granny and G P—

My dearest Min. This morning came a little letter, wh. they might as well have given to me yesterday (You see I give you my *other* hand—as when we walk together I give one hand to Anny and one to you.)—They might I say have given me the letter when I went to the post for it yesterday, for there it has been lying these 3 days.

Yesterday when I arrived it was all rain and melancholy here: and to day, Sunday, it's all Sunshine and pleasure—the great streets thronged with people—such ugly women in such caps! and bands of brass-music blowing beautifully all about the town. It's full of the most extraordinary churches pictures statues and gimcracks of every sort. I went into many churches yesterday—one something like the splendid S. Ambrogio at Milan you remember; but spick and span new and most byooootifully gilt painted and decorated with tableaux representing his life and miracles in wh. latter anybody may believe who chooses. In one of the confessionals of another church another most byoooooootifle sham-antique church, where I was at dusk I heard whisswhisswhisspiring in the confessional, and then hummummumbrum the Priest talking, and all this excited my awe and curiosity and I thought to myself perhaps there is some lovely creature on her knees to a venerable friar confessing some most tremenjuous crime: But presently hopped out of the confessional a little old speckled hunched back frog of a creature in a green shawl, and plopped down on its knees and said some prayers—wh. it was quite right no doubt to say—but all the romance was gone at the sight of the queer little trot of a woman, who I am sure could have only had the most trumpery little Sins to chatter about and so I came out of the church not a bit better Catholic than I went in. Dont you see if she had been a lovely Countess who had just killed her Grandmother or smothered her babby, I might have gone on being interested and awe stricken? but Polly the Cook maid who owns to having given a piece of pie to the Policeman, or melted the fat into the grease-pot I can't go for to waste my compassion and wonder upon her. And heres the mistake about these fine churches pictures music and splendid and gracious sights and sounds with wh. the Catholics entrap many people   Their senses are delighted and they fancy they are growing religious: it's a romantic wonder not a religious one. We must set to work to learn the Truth with all our hearts and Soul and Strength and take care not to be juggled by romanticalities and sentimentalities. This church of St. Louis is ornamented with the most beautiful dolls you ever saw the size of life and painted and tickled up in the most charming way with pink cheeks fresh gilt glories white eyes wooden lilies and everything that's nice. And the people kneel before them in crowds and worship Madonna and her Sacred Infant and the beautiful Saint Louis of Gonzaga and the beautiful Saint Francis of the Indies—that is to say charming figures representing these holy persons, and acting them in wood. But do I believe that the Souls of the blest go about with gilt cart-wheels round their heads? Fiddledee. These are but childish symbols and play—and theres the dinner bell—and as I love my children on earth I know the Father of us all loves us.

    P. S. I send my love to G P. and my dear old Mother.

I saw the brook . . . fell wounded: Esmond, Book II, chapter 9.   *other hand*: Thackeray changed at this point from his slanting handwriting to his upright.

166. TO MRS. THOMAS FREDERICK ELLIOT AND KATE PERRY
21 June 1852

Munich. Monday. 21. June

Mes bonnes amies I will try and write you a letter this morning before breakfast though the fountain of ink is dry or my old pen so tired that it hardly has the courage to go and dip in it. Why should I trouble friends with my blue devils and ennui? Only what were friends made for specially such kind soles as you 2, but to come to when one is in trouble and hipped—I have begun 2 or 3 notes in this gloomy strain to you and left off—We've been away a fortnight now, and I am travelling a solitary bachelor: having sent away the children and the elders to Switzerland Zürich from Frankfurt on Monday and coming away with a very sad heart from my dear girls. But being with 'em was like traversing the cart and fitting the halter an endless leave taking: so suddenly I jumped off at Frankfurt and left them to their good old Granny: who will never own that she was delighted to have them without their Papa, and will now command her little kingdom entirely in her own way. It will be a year nearly before we shall be together again. I don't know whether I shall have the heart to have more leave takings: and so Fate orders and unites and separates and next year it will be the poor mother's turn of sorrow and parting pangs. I have had a charming letter from the children: but writing to them plays the deuce with my lacrymal ducts.

This isn't very good fun, is it? I knew you must go through this glum preface before you could get at any thing decently cheerful—And, now the preface is over, what shall we say in the book? Thats not outrageously laughable either—I came from Frankfurt by night, one of 6 miserable Jonases in the stomach of a grumbling diligence, and reached Wurtzbourg in due season, where I passed a day not unpleasantly in rambling about the queer old abdicated place, and sate down gravely and made a hideous drawing of some buildings there. I wonder why we do 'em when we do them so badly? This drawing makes me laugh its so bad. Here's a wonderful church ancient and beautiful without, but converted within into a sort of periwig-paradise enormous stucco ornaments sprawling everywhere and hiding the delicate proportions and pure lines of the old building—This will be coming into the professional business if I don't mind. Halte la, mon Garcon! on n'écrit pas de ces sottises à ses bonnes amies—on les garde pour ce bon public—It is only acting, our business We are but quacks and mountebanks more or less painted and gay and solemn. Even Philip Van—Hush again, be quiet Sir! The worst of Wurzbourg was that I was obliged to have another night in the belly of the Whale in order to leave it: and so got to Bamberg at early dawn and thence to Nürnberg by railroad—royally in the first class. I like the first class, for one is alone—I did not want a bit to speak to the two dirty women and the commercial gents with whom I had made the journey overnight—So I arrived finely stupefied after a couple of nights coaching to enjoy Nurnberg—wh. is indeed a beautiful old sight and the quaintest Rücksicht into the past world—I think its as pretty as Venice almost: and here I made a pooty little sketch in my pocket book; and was very decently happy in a kind of moody contentment among the great churches and tall gabled houses and quaint fountains and up in that charming old world castle wh. I daresay you have been there. I would have stopped on but that the Inn was so noisy that sleep was impossible after 4 o'clock in the morning. Shall I go back again? I don't know in the least where I am going. Why not? One place is pretty much like another to the most blased of men.   Then I went to Augsburg to that famous Trei Mohren where I saw in a pretty little handwriting Mr. & Mrs. Frederick Elliot and Miss Perry, and shook hands with you there my dear kind friends—and I thought what a capital bit of professional business might be done out of that Album des Voyageurs and its contrasts and history. There was Mr. & Mrs. Temple West and presently afterwards Sir Wm. Molesworth Bart travelling there in 1815. Viscount Dillon his Vi[s]countess and the Hon Miss Henrietta Maria Dillon &c—There was Earl of Roden

Countess of Roden Lady Elizabeth Jocelyn leur fille, and with them travelling the Viscount Powerscourt—There was General the Honbl. Chas Stuart avec famille et 5 domestiques allant au Congres de Vienne and so forth—And I think the foreign book is even more amusing than the other—With Napoleon and poor Josephine and Marie Louise presently and their Highnesses the swaggering French Marshals, and the deputations from Paris and Italy to compliment the Emperor & King on his Austrian campaign—and then the Austrians, and the Russians and the English going to Vienna or Verona—In fine it was a good and queer and amusing book to read in—I went from Augsbourg to Blenheim dutifully and was pleased to find how extraordinary well I had conceived the place in my own mind, and felt quite as if I had been there before. Perhaps I have. Who knows where we travel in the spirit? I saw the place where Lieutenant Henry Esmond was wounded before Blenheim on our left you know, where poor Wade was shot down at the pallisades and where our attack failed as Eugene's did entirely on the right—and there was the little Nebel dividing our 2 armies running peacefully through the great meadow, wh. I remember swarming with our men and the French before the battle began—Hey Fiddledee! begone absurd images of the fancy. Between you and me it is a confounded lie—I wasn't at the battle of Blenheim at all—I am old enough but I wasn't there, and was safe in London the whole time.

 Then on Saturday I came on to Munich: and lo here I am. I liked Sunday very much on account of the sunshine and the great kindness and happiness of the honest Bavarians; and the brass bands of music blowing about the Streets everywhere—and I walked in the pretty Park and so to a garden outside the town where there was more Blechmusik; and sate there for an hour not unhappily close by a pretty emblematic tree in the garden. On the emblematic tree there were hanging a parasol & a sabre and a jolly soldier and a kind prettyish girl were sitting underneath the tree; as happy as might be, and drinking beer out of the same mug. I drink my beer alone God help me. What right have I to envy another man's liquor? Kiss your jolly soldier my pretty lass—Well now haven't I filled the paper? and all before breakfast too!—If you wrote to me at Ems I ordered the letter to Stuttgart and I haven't been to Stuttgart and mayn't go—I dont know nor yet I don't care where I'm a going. God bless you my dear kind friends—and the Reverend Frederic Elliot I send him my best regards and glad or sorry you know that I'm always affectionately yours.
W. M. T.

 Say a very kind word. to Miss Berry & Tom Phillips for me. You know how suddenly I left London and how sorry I was not to see them.

Mes bonnes amies: (Fr.) My good friends. *traversing the cart and fitting the halter:* from Matthew Prior (1664-1721), "The Thief and the Cordelier": "Now fitted the halter, now traversed the cart, / And often took leave, but seem'd loth to depart!" *Halte ... public:* (Fr.) Stop there, my boy! one does not write this foolishness to his good lady friends—one saves it for the good public. *Philip Van:* Henry (later Sir Henry) Taylor (1800-86), author of *Philip van Artevelde* (1834). *Rücksicht:* (Ger.) retrospect. *Trei Mohren:* (Ger.) the Three Moors. *Dillon:* Henry Augustus Dillon-Lee (1777-1832), thirteenth Viscount Dillon, his wife, the former Henrietta Browne (d. 1862), and their daughter, Henrietta, who became Lady Stanley of Alderley. *Roden ... Powerscourt:* Robert Jocelyn (1756-1820), second Earl of Roden, his second wife, the former Juliana Orde (d. 1856), and their daughter, Frances, who married Richard Wingfield (1790-1823), fifth Viscount Powerscourt, in 1815. *Stuart:* Charles Stuart (1779-1845), later first Baron Stuart de Rothesay, and his wife, the former Lady Elizabeth Yorke (d. 1867). *avec ... Vienne:* (Fr.) with his family and 5 servants travelling to the Congress of Vienna. *poor Josephine:* (1763-1814), the former Empress of the French, who had been divorced by Napoleon in 1809, and replaced by his second wife, Marie Louise (1791-1847). *Blechmusik:* (Ger.) brass music.

167. TO WILLIAM ALLINGHAM
6 August 1852

Kensington,
Friday.

My dear Allingham,—Were you ever thanked for the salmon which you sent more than two moons ago? Did I write? I think I didn't. The fish came on the very day I was going abroad with my children, and,—and was in that state in which George I. liked fish, and into which men and fish and nations inevitably fall. But the kindness smells sweet still and I am quite as much obliged to you now as if I had eaten the salmon unto satiety, and thank you for thinking of me.

I reached home yesterday after a journey to Vienna, Tyrol, Munich, &c; and if I had not fifty letters on other people's affairs to write, I think I would like to send you some manuscript: but I must do the other letters and shake you by the hand, and am yours very truly, dear Allingham,

W. M. Thackeray.

Allingham: William Allingham (1824-89), poet.

168. TO MARY HOLMES
10 August 1852

10 August. Kensington.

My dear Miss Holmes

I am come back without the children and am going to work hard upon some lectures for the Americans whom I shall visit in 2 months or so probably.

I musn't wear your medal. You see what is religion with your principles, wd. be irreligion, under mine. I profess to be quite willing to go or to stay (indeed I cannot help myself for the matter of that) and as one must die sometime or the other, why provide one's self with a fetish at all?

I met Lady Georgina Fullerton going to Spa, and talked to her about you—and Herbert yesterday at the Club. I'm pained to think that you are without a place as yet. I shall see a Catholic lady at Richmond and met a clergyman of your's there on Sunday, a pleasant gentleman. We talked about Achilli—a rascal hypocrite no doubt; but; as the law is, the verdict was right—though I think the Judge's behaviour a[t] the trial was most unfair and unworthy. The ladies of Norwood got justice, you see, in that trumpery charge against them—We mean justly enough in England—I'm sure.

I have been to Vienna Berlin Munich Hanover—proposing to write a book. But l'homme propose. I found I had nothing worthy to say, and that the book was best left alone.

I think Miss Bronte is unhappy and that makes her unjust. Novel writers should not be in a passion with their characters as I imagine, but describe them, good or bad, with a like calm—

If you are in town I hope I shall come & see you soon. Meanwhile I am always

Yours very sincerely
W M Thackeray.

Lady Georgi[a]na Fullerton: (1812-85), novelist. She was a Catholic, like Miss Holmes. *Herbert:* John Rogers Herbert (1810-90), painter, who was also a Catholic. *Achilli . . . the verdict:* Giovanni Achilli (b. 1803), an apostate Dominican, whose attacks on the Catholic Church had caused John Henry Newman, in *Lectures on the Present Position of Catholics in England* (1851), to reveal some of Achilli's sexual exploits while still a monk. Achilli brought suit for libel and won his case, as a result of which Newman was fined £100 and costs, and received a lecture from the judge. *Norwood:* site of a Catholic nunnery. *l'homme propose:* from Thomas À Kempis (1380-1471), *The Imitation of Christ:* "Man proposes but God disposes."

169. TO DR. JOHN BROWN
6 October 1852

85 Renshaw St. Liverpool.
Wednesday 6.

My dear Brown. Your constant kindness deserves not mere good will on my part for that you have but better marks of friendship than my laziness is inclined to show. My time is drawing near for the ingens æquor: I have taken places for self and Crowe Jr. by the Canada wh. departs on the 30th. of this month: a Saturday and all you who pray for travellers by land & water (if you do pray in your Scotch church) are entreated to offer up supplications for me. I don't like going at all: have dismal presentiments sometimes but the right thing is to go: & the pleasant one will be to come back again with a little money for those young ladies. I hope to send you Esmond before I sail: if not it will follow me as a legacy I doubt whether it will be popular although it has cost me so much trouble: but it has been written as you know with a weight of griefs and cares on my back, wh. diminish daily however, and now are all but cured. That's to say the wound's healed but the weakness is not over quite—a little change of air and scene will end that and who knows when I come back I may tell you I'm in love with somebody else; and have begun Act I of another tragedy or farce wh. is it?

That poor Morton killed at Paris was a most intimate friend of mine and I've a gloomy pleasure in thinking that knowing of the intrigue in wh. he was engaged I did my very utmost with him and her to break it off. The husband who murdered Morton used his wife horribly lived with and on a strumpet in London (Morton told me) neglected and insulted his wife in every way and avenged his honor by stabbing her seducer. There was no excuse for Morton. He did not care for the woman—at least she was one of a dozen that the poor headlong fellow pursued. I always thought & said he would come to a violent end: and now it's not he but his poor mother & sisters who are to be deplored. Luckily the latter are Plymouth sisters and have their devotion to draw themselves with. A little wickedness more or less in one of the reprobate can make little difference to them—all the family were crazy, and my poor Savile the maddest wildest & gentlest of creatures—scarce answerable for his actions or his passions.

I wish this place were like Edinburgh: but I get only a small audience say 300 in a hall capable of holding 3000 at least and all the papers will cry out at the smallness of the attendance—At Manchester the audience isn't greater but looks greater for the room is small—And though pecuniarily the affair is a failure it is not so really—I air my reputation and the people who do come seem to like what they hear hugely.

Have I written to you since I came from abroad? It was a dreary lonely journey. My mother wanted the children so much that I gave them up nor was it possible that we could travel together, and the girls have two powers over them. So I had a dismal holyday alone in place of a pleasant one with them: and I think the poor old mother though she had them wasn't half satisfied She would have had me too—and she would like to do for us all and that we shd. read the Washerwoman of Finchley Common together at her old knees—Ah me what a deal of misery and division that (so called) religion has caused in the world! Carlyle is away in Germany looking after Frederick the Great—I don't know what Literature is about. I heard Jas Martineau (the Unitarian) on Sunday and was struck with his lofty devotional spirit, and afterwards an old schoolfellow on the Evangelical dodge. Ah what rubbish!

And so is this wh. I'm writing. I think its partly owing to an uncomfortable pen but with bad pen or good I am always yours and your wifes sincerely

W M T.

Let me have another line here: if you have time the last was but a lazy scrap.

ingens æquor: Horace, *Odes,* I, vii, 32: *cras ingens iterabimus aequor* (tomorrow we will again take our course over the mighty sea). *Crowe Jr.:* Eyre Crowe, who served as Thackeray's secretary in America. *travellers by land & water:* The Litany, *Book of Common Prayer:* "That it may please Thee to preserve all that travel by land or water." *Morton . . . husband:* Saville Morton, who was killed on 1 October 1852 by the journalist, Elliott Bower, upon discovering that his wife had been Morton's mistress. *the Washerwoman of Finchley Common:* an Evangelical religious tract written by Thackeray's Lady Emily Sheepshanks; see *Vanity Fair,* ch. 33. *Martineau:* James Martineau (1805-1900), a Liverpool pastor.

170. TO ANNE THACKERAY
October 1852

My dearest Nannykin. I must and will go to America not because I like it, but because it is right I should secure some money against my death for your poor mother and you 2 girls—And I think if I have luck I may secure nearly a third of the sum that I think I ought to have behind me by a six month's tour in the States. And you children during that time must consider yourselves as at College; and work work with all your heart. You'll never have such another opportunity; when I come back please God your studies will be interrupted as I shall want a secretary—So now please to learn French very well and to play the piano if you can. It will be a comfort to me in future days: when we shall be in some quieter place and manner of life than here in London and I shall like my women to make music for me—

I should read all the books that Granny wishes, if I were you: and you must come to your own deductions about them as every honest man and woman must and does. When I was of your age I was accustomed to hear and read a great deal of the Evangelical (so called) doctrine and got an extreme distaste for that sort of composition—for Newton, for Scott, for the preachers I heard & the prayer-meetings I attended. I have not looked into a half dozen books of the French modern reformed churchmen: but those I have seen are odious to me. Daubigné I believe is the best man of the modern French Reformers: and a worse guide to historical truth (for one who has a reputation) I dont know—if M. Gossaint argues that because Our Lord quoted the Hebrew Scriptures therefore the Scriptures are of direct divine composition: you may make yourself quite easy; and the works of a reasoner who would maintain an argument so monstrous need not I should think occupy a great portion of your time. Our Lord not only quoted the Hebrew writings (drawing illustrations from everything familiar to the people among whom He taught, from their books poetic and historic, from the landscape round about, from the flowers the children the beautiful works of God) but he contradicted the Old Scriptures flatly; told the people that he brought them a new commandment—and that new commandment was not a complement but a contradiction of the Old—a repeal of a bad unjust law on their Statute books wh. he would suffer to remain there no more. It has been said an eye for an eye &c But *I* say to you no such thing *Love* your enemies &c—It could not have been right to hate your enemies on Tuesday and to love them on Wednesday. What is right must always have been right: before it was practised as well as after. And if such and such a Commandment delivered by Moses was wrong—depend on it, it was not delivered by God: and the whole question of complete inspiration goes at once.

And the misfortune of dogmatic belief is that the first principle granted that the Book called the Bible is written under the direct dictation of God for instance—that the Catholic Church is under the direct dictation of God and solely communicates with him—that Quashimaboo is the direct appointed priest of God & so forth—pain, cruelty, persecution, separation of dear relatives, follow as a matter of course. What person possessing the secret of Divine Truth by wh. she or he is assured of Heaven and wh. idea she or he worships as if it was God, but must pass nights of tears and days of grief and lamentation if persons naturally dear cannot be got to see this necessary truth? Smith's truth being established in Smiths mind as the Divine one, persecution follows as a matter of course—Martyrs have roasted all over Europe—all over Gods world—upon this dogma— Granted that you possess the real truth; it is just that you extirpate heretics, and lies that might poison the minds of yet unborn generations: and you have as good a right to hang a man for breaking the law and doubting the 39 Articles—the Romish religion—the Turkish or any you like, as you have to destroy him for any other public treason. A man who steals my purse steals trash; but a man who takes away from my children their Koran, their jewel, their trust in Mahomet the Prophet takes what is infinitely more precious, their faith and their chances of Paradise hereafter—away with him—impale him Allah il Ullah and Mahomet is the Prophet of God—Did you hear the Chapter of the Sunday before last about Jehu murdering the Priests of Baal? The Lord says Cut away Jehu, the Lord says Murder them Jehu Smite smash run them through the body Kill 'em old and young Do you believe the Lord directly gave any such orders: or that a chief of an Eastern race, devout, alone, worshipping one God, and finding his people perverted by idolators his neighbours determined to make an end of his enemy by slaughtering the priests who led them. The Lord ordered Robespierre to set the guillotine up a Jehu Napoleon to slaughter the people before St Roch just in the same way—And you may read the Hebrew scriptures rationally or literally as you like. To my mind Scripture only means a writing and Bible means a Book. It contains Divine Truths: and the history of a Divine Character: but imperfect but not containing a thousandth part of Him—and it would be an Untruth before God were I to hide my feelings from my dearest children: as it would be a sin, if having other opinions and believing literally in the Mosaic writings, in the 6 days cosmogony, in the serpent and apple and consequent damnation of the human race, I should hide them; and not try to make those I loved best adopt opinions of such immense importance to them. And so God bless my darlings and teach us the Truth. Every one of us in every fact, book, circumstance of life sees a different meaning & moral and so it must be about religion: But we can all love each other and say Our Father.

Newton . . . Scott: John Newton (1725-1807) and Thomas Scott (1747-1821), Evangelical ministers. *Daubigné:* Jean d'Aubigné (1794-1872), French Protestant minister. *an eye for an eye . . . Love your enemies:* Exodus 21: 24. The words of Jesus occur frequently in the New Testament. *A man . . . trash:* Othello, III, iii, 157. *Jehu . . . Baal:* 2 Kings, 11: 17-20, and 2 Chronicles, 23: 16-21.

171. TO EDWARD FITZGERALD
27 October 1852

October 27.

My dearest old friend
  I mustn't go away without shaking your hand and saying Farewell and God bless you—If any thing happens to me you by these presents must get ready the Book of Ballads wh. you like and wh. I had not time to prepare before embarking on this voyage. And I should like my daughters to remember that you are the best and oldest friend their Father ever had; and that you would act as such: as my literary executor and so forth—My books would yield a something as copy right—and should any thing occur I have commissioned friends in good place to get a pension for my poor little wife—I should have insured my life but for my complaint (a stricture) wh. I am told increases the annual payment so much that it is not worth the prœmium. Does not this read gloomily—Well, who knows what Fate is in store; and I feel not at all downcast but very grave and solemn just on the brink of a great voyage—
  I shall send you a copy of Esmond tomorrow or so wh. you shall yawn over when you are inclined—But the great comfort I have in thinking about my dear old boy is that recollection of our youth when we loved each other as I do now while I write Farewell.
  Laurence has done a capital head of me ordered by Smith the Publisher and I have ordered a copy & Lord Ashburton another—If Smith gives me this one: I shall send the copy to you—I care for you as you know and always like to think that I am fondly & affectionately yours

                 W M T.
  I sail from Lpool on Saturday Mg. by the Canada for Boston.

Laurence: Samuel Laurence (1812-84), portrait painter.

172. TO MRS. BRYAN WALLER PROCTER
29 October 1852

[Octo]ber 29. 1852
Liverpool.

My dear Friend
  I should have called on you last night; but after 2 or 3 farewell visits I had not the heart to say more goodbyes and went and dined alone at a Club and sate an hour with people for whom I did not care at parting. You know that could never be with you; and though I

mightn't see you, I never could cease to regard you; and remember affectionately old times and intercourse. When I come back from America how very gladly I come to shake your hand! I wish the time was come—I feel very solemn at parting and think about my friends with a God bless them—kiss Adelaide for me, and give my love to my dear old friend your husband, and drink my health tomorrow please and all on board the Canada. Of course I think of poor Warburton going. Amen. We are in God's hands on sea or shore: and I can't be wrong in trying to earn a little money for my children. I haven't seen them I hate parting, and on such occasions behave like a baby very often.

I've written your name in a copy of Esmond, wh. you will get tomorrow and won't like much I doubt. It's awfully melancholy—I could not be otherwise for this past year. How much some people were wrong who fancied I was always hunting after great folks—I took what came to me and cared but for one or two. Ah, we must try and lose as few Friends as we can. God bless you, my dear Mrs. Procter and believe that I am always affectionately yours

W M Thackeray

173. TO ANNE AND HARRIET THACKERAY
4-11 November 1852

Thursday. 6 November. I try and write a little with a pencil to my dearest women—now the troubles of sea sickness are over, the appetite come back, the sky bright overhead, the sea of a wonderful purple except in the wake of the ship where there quivers a long line of emerald six sea gulls still following after the ship, twelve hundred miles think of that; when they are tired they ride & sleep like Barry Cornwall in the Sea the Sea. Lord how sick he would have been! and how absurd it is to write about the Ocean in Upper Harley Street, and say you would 'ever be' there. Nobody really likes it. They go through with it with a brave heart but the Captain & all like the fireside & home 1000 times better . . . I find the wessel pitches so I can't write, and my sentences lurch about and grasp hold of anything to support themselves—So I'll stop; but you see I thought I would like to kiss my darlings this morning and say God bless my children—In that horrid little cabin below where we are tumbling & rolling and bumping and creaking in the roaring black midnight you may be sure I'm often thinking of you. I know you look at the sky, & G P at the glass, (I don't mean the looking glass)—& speculate how the Canada makes way. Well, we have had the wind dead against us, and got on well in spite of it and are now some 1100 miles out at sea. Lat 50.32 Lon

27.36 I was trying as I lay awake last night to see if I could at last understand the difference between latitude & longitude and now I really think I do. Poor Eyre has been very puky he is the worst Secretary and the best creature in—where are we now?—

Sunday 7. Lon 44.37. Lat 48.18—For Thursday was the 4th. & not the 6th. as I wrote comme un donkey—We have got a good wind at last, and are slapping along at 13 miles an hour, and tomorrow night shall see land Cape Race and are all almost on our legs again: Even the Presbyterian Doctor Revd. Dr. Cooke of Quebec who preached a jolly sermon to us just now; and has since partaken of his first comfortable meal and a pint of champagne. We have all been brought round by pints of Champagne, though nobody is really well thats my belief, and as for writing letters thats out of all question—But as I've been saying my prayers and I know some as has too, I thought I would say good day to two young ladies: who are no doubt in their best bonnets walking in the Shomdeleesy: for, Law bless you, its 4 o'clock where you are and its only 1 where I am. It's wonderful what knowledge of geography one picks up a travelling! the postman brought me a letter from you 2 days ago: that is I did not like to read it till then—Well, I shall be glad to be back and see the lady who brought me the swimming belt: and I hope I never shall have to swim in it: and what a smell it du make in the cabin to be sure! The rest of this valuable sheet I shall keep to send from Halifax, and here is just room for God bless my dearest children, Granny, G P.

Wednesday 11. Lat 44.55 Lon. 60.56. [Is it real]ly 6 days since I began to write and 11 since we left England? It seems years— Its awfully stupid the life aboard—I'm weary of guttling and gorging and bumping in bed all night and being 1/2 sick all day:—not quite— I've not been ill since the 2 first days—but o it will be comfortable to be in a bed that doesnt jolt, and on a floor that doesn't give way under you—We are to be at Halifax tonight; we had a gale of wind on Sunday & Monday just after I wrote, and if all goes well at Boston on Friday. We have had a tolerable bad passage wind against us all the way: even against that except in the very bad weather running 10 miles an hour—Isn't it wonderful? Instead of going over yonder thundering wave why don't we go right down and disappear?—Looking at the little life-belt and then at the ocean makes one laugh—The waves are immense: about 4 of them go to the horizon—but I'm disappointed in the grandeur of the prospect. It looks small somehow—not near so extensive as 1000 landscapes we have seen. Ah where shall we pass next November? Shall we go to Rome? Shall I make a good bit of money for you in America and write a book about it?—I think not. It seems impudent to write a book; and mere sketches now are somehow below my rank in the world—I mean a grave old gentleman, father of young ladies, mustn't be comic and grinning too much

I wonder are the critics praising or abusing Esmond? I have forgotten all about him and he seems like everything else to have happened 100 years ago—And now I shan't write any more: but give a kiss and a blessing to my darling children and to the dear G P and Granny who are so kind to them as they were and are to W M T.

Barry Cornwall . . . the Sea: "The Sea!," by B. W. Procter ("Barry Cornwall"), in *English Songs* (1832, 1844, 1851). *Cooke:* The Reverend John Cook (1805-92). *the lady . . . swimming belt:* Mrs. Carmichael-Smyth.

174. TO GEORGE SMITH
26 November 1852

New-York. Clarendon-Hotel.
Novr 26th. '52.

My dear Smith

Messrs. Harper through your friend Mr. Low have communicated with me & to-night after the Lecture made me a offer of 1,000,$ for the publication of my Lectures, simultaneously with the re-issue in England; I shall thankfully accept the same & keep this little sum for myself this time. There has been no attempt as yet to do more than give a synopsis of the Lectures; and this the only city in wh. piracy is, I think, most to be feared. All the papers are extremely civil & kind to me with the exception of the Herald wh. calls me names, & abuses me with much acrimony. Besides the Harpers the Appletons give me money for other reprints one or perhaps two hundred pounds more. I am going to repeat the Lectures here; & affairs really look more prosperous for me than they have ever before done these twenty years.

My friends sent me out the Spectator, Leader, & Athenæum; & the first did for me, what no review has ever done before, brought tears into my eyes. I trust in God that what the critic says is true; & then though the book we have published together, may not be very greatly popular, it will be a credit to both of us. I hope it will be successful enough to enable me to publish the American continuation some-day.

Writing, thinking, & quiet, are however, here impossible, though money-making proceeds at a brilliant rate.

Should no pirate carry my prize off, I shall even be able to give my Lectures over again on my return to London, before publishing them. At any rate there is no hurry about it. If you have any news for me, a letter will be sure to be welcome please write to me, care of Messrs. Ticknor & Fields at Boston where I shall be about

Christmas & believe me always, my dear Smith, yours, (though another holds the pen for me, (but I know you treat me in the same way) [. . .] [)]

Low: Sampson Low (1797-1886), whose publishing firm, Sampson Low and Sons, was the London agent for Harper and Brothers.   *Appleton:* by the time of Thackeray's arrival in New York Appleton had already published (without permission) five volumes of his miscellaneous shorter works. After reaching an agreement with him they published five additional volumes.   *Spectator, Leader, & Athenæum:* in *The Spectator* of 6 November, George Brimley had called *Esmond* a "delightful book," that "has the great charm of reality" and is written in a style "manly, clear, terse, and vigorous, reflecting every mood—pathetic, grave, or sarcastic—of the writer." Thackeray appears to have been especially moved by Brimley's comments about him personally: "The moral antithesis of actual and ideal is the root from which springs the peculiar charm of Mr. Thackeray's writings"—"the contradictory consciousness of man as a being with senses and passions and limited knowledge, yet with a conscience and a reason speaking to him of eternal laws and a moral order of the universe. It is this that makes Mr. Thackeray a profound moralist. . . . He could not have painted Vanity Fair as he has, unless Eden had been shining brightly in his inner eyes." George Henry Lewes in *The Leader* of the same date called it "a beautiful book," "representing a new phase in Thackeray's growth," "a landmark on his career," a work that touches and delights the reader causing him to love "the book and its author." *The Athenæum's* reviewer, D. Owen Maddyn, also writing on 6 November, was less enthusiastic, however, calling *Esmond* a "highly-wrought work," but finding it "improbable," sketchy in its recreation of historical characters, lacking in "vital heat," and repeating Thackeray's former work rather than achieving "a new triumph for the author."   *[. . .]:* The signature and part of a postscript have been cut away.

175. TO MRS. THOMAS FREDERICK ELLIOT AND KATE PERRY
7 December 1852

Decr. 7. New York.
I send but a line and a God bless you: and a scrap of a paper wh. I think my dear Somebody will like to read—It's nothing here but dollars & flattery: but I dont think it turns my head as I keep in constant view that the people are always exaggerating: and that I am not half such a swell in my own country as they make me out here— And my own country is the best ladies—for us that is—and O I wish I was back with a little money in my pocket!.

As Lord John heard my Goldsmith lecture I should like him to see the end of it as delivered here. Don't laugh but I should: and dont say anything but keep my counsel as I know you will. When we bring back a back bone, and a graver reputation & &c, who knows what a man may look to?—to sit in parliament and marry the Vizier's daughter perhaps. But something may be done I sometimes fancy: never having had any ambition until the time came when it was useful and right to be ambitious—And now that Bulwer is a Tory, and Disraeli has been found picking Thiers pocket at the Duke's funeral, who knows what may not be possible on our side? I have not had a line from home, through my cleverness in not leaving directions when I came out but I know and feel you are all well—The alibi is the thing as Fred says: and a wounded heart you know of heals in this climate and with all these excitements—I don't intend definitively to make a book—No No. The goose is much too good a goosey to be killed—In fact I'm looking ahead, & my dear friends must help me.

Ive been here and there in the 'Upper Ten' world but not much. It's the most curious Varnish of Civilization The girls are dressed like the most stunning French actresses—the houses furnished like the most splendid gambling houses. Its all gold and yellow brocade & the little dandies are like little French shop boys—and the houses are all so new that the walls are not even papered and on the walls in the midst of the hangings of brocade and the enormous goold frames and mirrors you see little twopenny pictures and coloured prints—There was a dreadful daub in one house wh. the lady told me was a view of Harwich—it was poor old Drachenfels and Nonnenwerth—How I wish I could see 'em again!

The jolly manner answers here very well, wh. I have from Nature or art possibly—and the Press & I, with the exception of the Herald wh. abuses me like anythink, are the best friends—You should have heard how Bancroft flattered them all at a Press Dinner the other day! There were 30 present, and they made as many speeches in every one of wh. they fired a great thundering compliment point blank at me—I didn't flatter a word in reply actually, nor do the cordial business like Dickens—but adopted a certain—in fine all men before the public must humbug more or less—but we wont humbug at home, will we? nor will dear kind friends whom we love. God bless you my d k f—and kiss a dear sweet lady for me—How mad poor Tomkins must be at the Press selecting those particular passages—He will treat her better ever after though—God keep her & bless her—

You should have seen J. Kelly Esqr. rise and make his speech in the church! I thought at first it was some fellow going to attack me about Swift—The Irishmen are furious, and their press has been flinging hot potatoes at me—Love to Fred, & Kinglake & Horace & Hig & goodbye

PS. I think of Erskine wishing his pamphlet to go to the big-wigs.

Somebody: Mrs. Brookfield.   *Lord John:* Lord John Russell.   *Bulwer*...
Tory: Bulwer joined the Conservatives and was elected M. P. for Hertfordshire in
1852.   *Disraeli*...*funeral:* in a eulogy for the Duke of Wellington delivered
on 15 November 1852, Disraeli had plagiarized from a eulogy by Thiers (1797-
1877) on Marshal St. Cyr that had appeared in English translation during 1848 in
The Morning Chronicle. Drachenfels and Nonnenwerth: Drachenfels is a
mountain on the east bank of the Rhine, just below Bonn; Nonnenwerth is an
island in the river, at its foot.   *Bancroft:* George Bancroft (1800-91), the
American historian.   *a dear sweet lady*...*poor Tomkins:* Mrs. Brookfield and
her husband.   *J. Kelly*...*church:* actually Robert Kelly, President of the Board
of Education, who offered three resolutions thanking Thackeray for his lectures.
Thackeray lectured in the First Unitarian Church of New York.   *Horace*...*Hig:*
Horace Mayhew (1818-72), a fellow *Punch* contributor, and Matthew James
Higgins.   *Erskine:* Sir Thomas Erskine Perry (1806-82), brother of Mrs. Elliot
and Kate Perry.

176. TO SARAH BAXTER
22 December 1852

[Boston.] Wednesday.

I have put the two letters in the fire wh. I wrote yesterday—
two very fine long fond sentimental letters—They were too long and
sentimental and fond. A pen that's so practised as mine is runs on
talking and talking: I fancy the people I speak to are sitting with me;
and pour out the sense and nonsense jokes and the contrary,
egotisms—whatever comes upper most. And you know what was
uppermost yesterday. My heart was longing and yearning after you
full of love and gratitude for your welcome of me—but the words
grew a little too warm. You wouldn't like me to write letters in that
strain You might tell me to write no more: and if you did I should
burst out into a misanthropical rage again—Please to let me write on:
and make my frank claim to have a little place in Beatrix's heart. I told
my children what a place she had got in mine—I would not hide from
them or from you those honest generous feelings. When the destined
man comes, with a good head and a good heart fit to win such a girl,
and love and guide her; then old Mr. Thackeray will make his bow and
say God bless her; as the fair creature steps away from church on the
bridegroom's arm: and when she's old and I am under the daisies,
she'll think of me as the Jessamy Bride of poor Noll Goldsmith—(I
looked at those beaux yeux as I was telling the story the other night—
that last night of the lecture don't you remember about 10 years ago

when I was at New York?) or the lady to whom the French poet wrote the noble verses I told her

> Quand vous serez bien vieille, le soir à la chandelle
> Assise auprès du feu dévisant et filant,
> Direz, chantant mes vers en vous esmerveillant,
> Ronsard m'a célèbré au temps que j'étais belle.
>   Lors il n'y a personne oyant telle nouvelle &c.

I forget the rest: but the one song has been sung ever since the world began—I'm sure when those pretty eyelids are all wrinkled, and the bright eyes look sadder than now they
    Enter Dr. O. W. Holmes half an hour—a dear little fellow a true poet I told him how much I liked his verses and what do you think he did? *His* eyes began to water. Well, it's a comfort to have given pleasure to that kind soul.
    After him come Judge Warren and Mr. Davis—Mr. Davis is an old old Fogey 80 years old. Judge Warren is descended from William de Warenne who came with the Conqueror.
    And now Interruption no 3—actually as I wrote the last r in Conqueror and that is 1, 2, 3 letters from home that have been lying here ever so long—What a pity I didn't get them this morning before I sent off mine by the Steamer.   I send you one of Anny's—Isn't it a fine letter Miss Sara? Isn't she a noble soul?   My mother says she is grown so fat she looks 20—Thats a pretty picture of the grand old mother and her old husband, such a fine gentleman & lady—So handsome—I've never seen any one so handsome Mademoiselle no NEVER. Little Min writes. 'We are to go to M. Monod, and he is to preach us a sermon every week, and we are to copy it and I daresay I will make a hash of it.'   I suppose you know that the two handwritings are by the same hand: and hope you dont think it is Mr. Crowe the Secretary writing.
    I wonder whether if any body were to say Come Friend & pass Christmas Day with us—you can be here to dinner—You can pass Sunday here and a part of Monday—I wonder whether I would come? New Years day is not so pleasant. There are visitors all that time and all those visitors would be saying theres that old Mr. Thackeray here again—May I come? You kind dear Mrs. Baxter Your first impression will be yes. Your second very likely no. Think over for half an hour wh. way it shall be: and whether you will have me gladden my eyes by seeing your faces again Why its only a few hours from here to the Second Avenue: and I whisk off the car at 27th. Street and leave my bag at the Clarendon and am down 18th. St. in no time. Say 'if you approve and honour the proposal.'

[. . .]

Sarah Baxter: (1833-61), daughter of George (1801-80) and Anna Baxter (1798-85) of New York. Thackeray became very fond of the family, notably of its female members: Mrs. Baxter, her daughter Lucy (1836-1922), and Sarah, especially the latter.   *Beatrix:* Sarah Baxter, who Thackeray thought resembled Beatrix Esmond.   *beaux yeux:* (Fr.) beautiful eyes.   *the lady . . . French poet:* Hélène de Surgères, for whom Ronsard (1524-85) wrote the following poem (from *Sonnets pour Hélène* [1578]).   *Quand . . . nouvelle:* "When you are quite old, at evening by candlelight, seated by the fire chatting and spinning, chant my verses and, marvelling, say: 'Ronsard sang my praises when I was beautiful.' Then no one hearing it . . . " [partly misquoted]. Thackeray had published a free adaptation, "Ronsard to His Mistress," in the January 1846 issue of *Fraser's Magazine*.   *Monod:* Adolphe Frédéric Théodore Monod (1802-56), Pastor of the Reformed Church of Paris.   *two handwritings:* Thackeray began the letter using his slanted handwriting, changed to upright with the quotation from Ronsard, and shifted back to slanted at the beginning of this sentence.   *Clarendon:* the Clarendon Hotel.   *'if . . . proposal':* quoted in Thackeray's lecture, "Sterne and Goldsmith," from Sterne's letter of March 1767 to Eliza Draper.   *[. . .]:* the final portion has been cut away.

177. TO MRS. BRYAN WALLER PROCTER
22 December 1852

Decr. 22. Wednesday
Boston

My dear Friend
    I should like to send you a longer letter than can be written in a quarter of an hour when the mails close for that ship wh. is on the slips to start for dear old home but a word I know will please you to tell you how happy I am what many many friends I have found (I have found Beatrix Esmond and lost my heart to her) and what a fortunate venture this is likely to prove to me. Last night was the first lecture here to 1200 people I should think—and I left behind me near a thousand pounds at New York wh. Baring's house will invest for me, so that my girls will be very considerably the better for this journey and grim Death if ever he come to me will find that I have the £. S. D. There's a parody! I find I'm constantly talking of dying somehow—but hope to wait time enough to see the poor wife and children provided. It would have been worth my while even for my books to come out here: the publishers are liberal enough and will be still more so with any future thing I may do. As for writing about this Country, about Goshen, about Canaan flowing with milk and honey, about the

friends I have found here and who are helping me to procure independence for my children if I cut jokes against them may I choke on the instant—If I can say anything to show that my name is really Makepeace and to increase the sense of Love between the two countries then please God I will—The laugh dies out as we get old you see—but the Love and the Truth don't praised be God and I begin to think of the responsibilities of this here pen now writing to you with a feeling of no small awe. The first name I heard in the railroad going hence to New York was my own by a pretty child selling books, and I was touched somehow by his fresh voice and kind face, and should have liked to take him by the hand—So—here it is after 15 years thinks I here's the fame they talk about—my impression though was one of awe and humility rather than exultation and to pray God I might keep honest and tell truth always.

This is about nothing but ego but I know you like that—I was very very glad to get your letter: God bless you and all your's and my dear old Dickey Doyle when you see him. The success of Esmond has quite surprized me for I only looked for a few to like it and wrote above the public I thought. I didn't even read poor Forsters review—I know my good fortune makes him and his people angry and bear him nothing but good will. Farewell Farewell the 1/4 hour is over.

Write again to Appleton. N. York please to

Yours affectionately
W M T.

Baring's house: Baring Brothers, bankers.   *grim Death:* quoted from *Paradise Lost*, II, 804.   *Canaan . . . honey:* Exodus 3: 8.   *poor Forster's review:* Forster's negative review of *Esmond* in *The Examiner* of 13 November 1852.

178. TO MRS. GEORGE BAXTER
2 January 1853

[Boston]

My dear Mrs. Baxter.
Thank you for your kind friendly wishes and for the welcome you have given me—God bless you. How very very kind you have been to me—I think the young girls write dear pretty letters: and as for the eldest it is just possible you found out what I thought of her. Isn't it all written before in the Chronicle of Esmond the Son of Esmond? That weak and elderly gentleman saw a number of faults in a certain bright & beautiful Mistress Beatrix, who nevertheless played the mischief with his heart: and I don't [think] he was ever more glum than I at this present sitting alone and looking at the bleak and sulky

snow coming down on my prospect at the commencement of this happy New Year. Do *all* the victims I wonder come and pour out their griefs to you? Poor Bingham! I feel like him rather, as if I had been just on the point of going down; & escaped only in my clothes, leaving I dont know how much of the most valuable of my heart's luggage behind me—

I wish I hadn't sent away my aide de camp. Its dreadfully lonely and dismal here—awfully slippery in the Streets. How can people go out to lectures in such weather? I was quite angry with the audience for being so foolish last night—I went to the Ticknors last night and our talk fell on the Mildmays Humphrey and Bingham: and I mentioned how the latter had introduced me to a family at New York—a family of the name of Baxter and the girls began such a laughter! They were on the other side of Lake George it appears last year and he used to go over and pour out his Soul to them about Miss Baxter. The report was that he was going to be married to her. Is he? says I. Confound him, then I hope he'll never come back again— Then I owned myself that I was far gone about that young lady dilated on her good qualities: run up her flag, and owned I sailed under it. 'And they heard me as I talked an hour of thee Eliza' with &c &c—

I shall see you all once again before I go after the dollars and who knows? the Mississippi Snags—We will try and be jolly a little next week, won't we? and then I shall go on my way like an old Mountebank, (I get more ashamed and disgusted of my nostrums daily) and send round the hat through this republic.

Isn't this a merry letter for a new year? Well the writer isn't very merry: but he is very Sincerely and afftly Yours all

W M T

young girls: Lucy Baxter and her cousin, "Libby" Strong (b. 1836). *the eldest:* Sarah Baxter. *Bingham:* Henry Bingham Mildmay (1828-1905), an Englishman related to Lady Ashburton, and one of Sarah Baxter's unsuccessful suitors. *Ticknors:* George Ticknor (1791-1871), historian, and his wife, the former Anna Eliot. *Humphrey:* Humphrey Mildmay (1825-66), older brother of Bingham Mildmay. *'And ... Eliza':* paraphrased from a letter of Sterne's to Mrs. Draper of March? 1767, cited in Thackeray's lecture on Sterne and Goldsmith.

179. TO HENRY MARIE BRACKENRIDGE
19 February 1853

Washington. Feb 19. 1853.

Dear Sir

Your kind letter could not but be welcome to me: and I am glad you like the book best wh. has cost me the most pains, and wh. I wrote more for credit's sake than popularity's though I am pleased to think it has acquired some of this too. Several of the London Critics deal very hardly with it; and when those who know the times of wh. I write & the noble language I wished to reproduce, better than some of the above-named literary gentlemen, praise my labor; you may be sure their good words are welcome. I thank you for your's; and, if ever I come into your country, hope to drink a glass of the good wine sub arctâ vite with the friendly grower. Believe me

Your obliged & faithful Servant
W M Thackeray

Brackenridge: Henry Marie Brackenridge (1786-1871) a former lawyer, judge, and Pennsylvania congressman who had retired to an estate near Pittsburgh to devote himself to authorship.   *sub arctâ vite:* Horace, *Odes,* I, xxxviii, 7-8: *sub arta / vite bibentem* (drinking beneath the thick-leaved vine).

180. TO ALBANY FONBLANQUE
4 March 1853

Richmond. Virginia. March 4. 1853.

My dear Fonblanque.   I hope you have kept carefully all those 'Letters of a traveller in America' wh. will form the basis of my future work in 6 volumes—the drawings are not the least valuable part dont you think so? *entre nous* young Crowe touched them up and—enough of this small joking wh. may reach you about the First of April and wh. please to put down to the compliments of that waggish season. I've not written a word thats the truth. I've seen and remarked nothing: in the great cities I had hardly leisure to write to my family and those one or two kind female correspondentesses to whom a man writes not about the country he is travelling in but about himself—and all I have to say about this great country thats worth saying might be put down on the remainder of this side of paper.   What could Dickens mean by writing that book of American Notes? No man should write about the country under 5 years of experience, and as many of previous reading. A visit to the Tombs to Laura Bridgman & the Blind Asylum, a description of Broadway—O Lord is that describing America? It's a mole or a pimple on the great Republican body or a hair of his awful beard and no more. I have hardly seen as much as that; and gave up sight-seeing at once as impossible to a man in my position here. Your room is besieged all day by visitors, you go about from dinner to tea-party and ball, and the people dont talk to you but try & make you talk. Well Sir How do you like our Country Sir? that's the formula and as you are answering this query, the host comes up and says allow me Sir to introduce you to Mr. Jones of Alabama Sir—shake hands with Jones of Alabama query as before; it is not answered when you are presented to Mr. Smith of Tennessee. We know you very well Sir says S of T. Your works are extensively read among us allow me to present you to my lady Sir who is a great admirer of &c—Mrs. Smith of Tennessee then commences How do you like our &c Sir—and by Heaven evening after evening passes off in this way. I know 100 people more every day; and walk the street in terror lest every man & lady I meet should be my acquaintance of the night before. It makes one half crazy the constant representation—and what must it have been in Dickens's time when deputations met him daily and his life was watched by myriads of admirers? I have refused to be a personage with all my might, nor indeed has there been much of that sort of honour thrust upon me; & though I have had plenty of praise from the newspapers I have had plenty of assaults too wh. were quite refreshing. Ah Mosieur! if one might but hit again, here & on t'other side of the water, how invigorating & pleasant it would be! There are 2 dear friends I know of in my beloved country—O for the day when Makepeace might just cease to be Makepeace and 'go in'!

A great good wh. an English man who has seen men & cities gets by coming hither, is that he rubs a deal of Cockney arrogance off, and finds men and women above all as good as our own. You learn to sympathize with a great hearty nation of 26 millions of English-speakers not quite ourselves but so like the difference is not worth our scorn certainly; nay I'm not sure I dont think the people are our superiors. There's a rush and activity of life quite astounding a splendid recklessness about money wh. has in it something admirable too. Dam the money says every man. He's as good as the richest for that day. If he wants champagne he has champagne, Mr. Astor can't do more. You get an equality wh. may shock ever so little at first, but has something hearty & generous in it. I like the citizenship and general freedom—And in the struggles wh. every man with whom you talk is pretty sure to have had, the ups and downs of his life, the trades or professions he has been in begets a rough & tumble education wh. gives a certain piquancy to his talk and company— When they are talking their best and doing English with us they are quite affected and ojous—they are worth 10 times as much on their native heath—and at home with their children jumping about their knees. There's beautiful affection in this country immense tenderness, romantic personal enthusiasm, and a general kindliness and serviceableness and good nature, wh. is very pleasant & curious to witness for us folks at home who are mostly ashamed of our best emotions; and turn on our heel with a laugh sometimes when we are most pleased & touched. If a man falls into a difficulty a score of men are ready to help—The Editor of a newspaper in this little city with 12000 whites and as many negroes was shot in a duel—the city subscribed 200£ a year for his orphans—Meagher told me yesterday (a fine fellow Meagher, manly, modest brave, funny, handsome, immensely in earnest, & at war with the priests) that there came a girl to Washington from N. York bound to Louisiana. She asked leave to sleep on board the boat at Washington the Captain took her to his own house, gave her in charge to the conductor of the Railway at Acquia Creek, who saw her through the journey to Richmond and ran off instantly thence to get her a carriage & see her luggage safely packed and herself forwarded to the Southern Station. And the Queen being abused by an Englishman at New York, who should be her champion but this Meagher the rebel—(this is par parenthèse). Three as fine Irishmen as ever I met were he & Dillon & O'Gorman refugees and flourishing lawyers at N. York now. I tell you its grand country entirely. The young blood beating in its pulses warms one, like the company of young men in England I don't know what I wouldn't do if I were 10 years younger—if I were 10 years younger I might sneer to be sure and satirize Jordan because it wasn't like Abanah & Pharphar rivers of Damascus—As a refuge for men who cant make their way at home, it's a great place. What a country where a laboring-man begins with earning a dollar a day. An Irishman dictating a letter home to his friends in Ireland out of Maryland, bade his master write 'My dear Phil, me masther is the best of masthers, and I ayt mayt three toimes a week'—'Three times a week['] says the Master—[']you eat it 3 times a day you rogue and 6 times if you like!' [']Hush Master!['] says Paddy—[']Sure they wouldn't believe me if I said more than 3 times a week' Think of country-laborers in England and 10 children and 10/ a week!—and to be sure let us set to and bemoan the blacks afterwards, and sign the Sutherland House Womanifesto!

The happiness of these niggers is quite a curiosity to witness. The little niggers are trotting and grinning about the streets, the women are fat & in good case, I wish you could see that waiter at our hotel with 5 gold medals in his shirt 2 gold chains & a gold ring. The African Church on a Sunday I am told is a perfect blaze of pea-green, crimson, earrings lace collars satin & velvet wh. the poor darkies wear. I dont mean to say that Slavery is right but that if you want to move your bowels with compassion for human unhappiness, that sort of aperient is to be found in such plenty at home, that it's a  wonder people wont seek it there. I dont think its of long duration though—unless perhaps in the cotton-growing countries where the whites can't live and the negroes can—Every person I have talked to here about it deplores it and owns that it's the most costly domestic machinery ever devised. In a house where 4 servants would do with us (servants whom we can send about their business too when they get ill & past work like true philanthropists as we are)—there must be a dozen blacks here and the work not well done—The hire of a house slave from his owner is 120$ 25£ besides of course his keep clothing &c. When he is old he must be kept well and kindly and is—the little niggers wait upon the old effete niggers. The slave-servants working in the tobacco manufactories can lay by 100$ a year. The rule is kindness, the exception no doubt may be cruelty—the great plenty in the country ensures every one enough to eat. And the people here entreat me to go on a plantation, to go about by myself ask questions where & how I like and see if the black people are happy or not. This to be sure leaves the great question untouched that Slavery is a wrong. But if you could decree the Abolition tomorrow by the Lord it would be the most awful curse & ruin to the black, wh. Fate ever yet sent him. Of course we feel the cruelty of flogging and enslaving a negro—of course they feel here the cruelty of starving an English laborer or of dooming an English child to a mine—Brother Brother we are &c.

  I am doing very well with the lectures—the 2 Presidents came at Washington—I've saved some money 2000£ in this country & shall probably make half as much more: but o how sick I am of the business! I bid you a shake of the hand & am yours always dear Fonblanque

W M Thackeray.

entre nous: (Fr.) confidentially.   *Tombs . . . Broadway:* allusions to the descriptions in Dickens' *American Notes for General Circulation* (1842), chs. 3 and 6. The Tombs was a New York City prison. Laura Bridgman (1829-89), who lived at the Perkins Institution in Boston, was the first blind, deaf mute to be systematically educated.   *seen men & cities:* a reminiscence of Horace's rendering, in *The Art of Poetry*, of Homer's characterization of Odysseus: *virum . . . qui mores hominum multorum videt et urbes* (the man . . . who saw the manners and cities of many men).   *Astor:* William Backhouse Astor (1792-1875), American multi-millionaire.   *Meagher:* Thomas Francis Meagher (1823-67), Irish political figure involved with the Young Ireland rebellion of 1848.   *Acquia Creek:* Aquia Creek joins the Potomac River ca. 30 miles south of Washington, D. C.   *par parenthèse:* (Fr.) parenthetically.   *Dillon & O'Gorman:* John Blake Dillon (1814-66) and Richard O'Gorman (1820-95), also Young Ireland refugees.   *Jordan . . . Pharpar:* an allusion to the statement of Naaman: "Are not Abana and Pharpar, rivers of Damascus, better than all the waters of Israel?" (2 Kings 5: 12). *Sutherland House Womanifesto:* a document inspired by *Uncle Tom's Cabin* that protested against slavery and was signed by various English ladies, including the Duchess of Sutherland (d. 1868). Thackeray felt it was self-righteous and ineffectual.   *in good case:* in good physical condition.   *2 Presidents:* Millard Fillmore (1800-74), thirteenth President of the United States, and Franklin Pierce (1804-69), President-Elect.

181. TO LUCY BAXTER
April 1853

With Flowers for a young lady's birthday.

      Seventeen rose-buds in a ring,
      Thick with sister-flowers beset,
      In a fragrant coronet,
      Lucy's servants this day bring.
      Be it the birthday wreath she wears
      Fresh and bright, and symbolling
      The young number of her years,
      The fresh roses of her Spring.

Types of Youth and Love & Hope,
Friendly hearts your Mistress greet:
Be you ever pure and sweet,
And grow lovelier as you ope!
Gentle blossom, fenced about
By fond care, and cherished so
Scarce you've heard of storms without
Thorns that bite or winds that blow!

Kindly has your life begun
And we pray that Heaven may send
This fair flowret a warm sun
A bright summer, a sweet end.
And where'er shall be your place
Here or in a husband's home
Live expanding into bloom
And developing in grace.

W M Thackeray.
New York. April. 1853.

182. TO MRS. HENRY CARMICHAEL-SMYTH
19 April 1853

My dearest Mammy. I wonder how many more letters I shall write from this republic? But for one or two buts I would be off tomorrow by the Europa; the weather is as fine as Spring can be: I am home-sick and longing to see my women. I think I shall lecture no more My conscience revolts against reading these old sermons over and over: and I have given up St. Louis & the West, and declined Montreal.

183. TO MRS. GEORGE TICKNOR
20 April 1853

From the Europa. April 20.
The pilot going off

Good bye dear Mrs. Ticknor whom I thought to have seen in a day or two—It seems cowardly running away without bidding friends good bye—but parting is the dreariest of lifes occupations. I should have come to Boston only to be perfectly odious & miserable, and I prefer to come back happy and eager next fall to see Canada and the West wh. I've not seen; & the friends whom I want to see again. I greet you all at Boston, and am

Yours always sincerely
W M Thackeray

184. TO MRS. GEORGE BAXTER
May? 1853

[...]—I have torn off a page here, and burned another that was written about a certain young lady; who complains that I went away suddenly, and would have liked a week of preparation and farewell. Some day, please God, I will walk in as suddenly as I ran away: and Lucy will give me the kiss she owes me and couldn't give me for crying. How is Bleecker? I think very kindly of Bleecker—of any body who is fond of Lucy.

As I sit here thinking and tearing up page after page England fades away and I am yonder again. Ghosts of past days, fond longings, bitter disappointments & scorns rise up, that I thought were laid in the Atlantic. But I have taken a resolution to laugh at them since ever so long: and no ghosts can stand ridicule. I defy them and my poor Sarah's bright eyes—I wonder what it was I said that made her cry? The other day I saw *l'autre's* husband, who was guarded kind and most polite. I fell to joking instantly and perfectly scared him with laughter and scorn and good, or should I say evil? spirits. Where do they come from those jokes? I used to throttle scores of them when I was sitting with you all in the Second Avenue. When the good Angel of Love is driven away, then the Devils come, the mischievous amusing denying Devils. It's not so when I think about l'autre—a halo of goodness & beauty surrounds her, and I adore her memory.— Hullo!—I *will* go on—well I can't tear up any more—but this bit Lady Castlewood will please leave out when she hands over the letter to the young folks

l'autre: (Fr.) the other—i. e. Mrs. Brookfield, Thackeray's "other" love.

185. TO THE GEORGE BAXTERS
18-19 May 1853

19 Rue d'Angoulême St. Honoré. Paris. 18, 19 May.
It is not a month ago, and New York seems to me years off. Is it possible there were people there quite sad when I came away, and that I was half ready to cry at leaving them? We don't use any more pocket-handkerchiefs now—we think very quietly about dear friends across the Atlantic—Since I've been here especially I have been in such a whirl and jangle that solitude is out of the question, and even quiet thought: my room is opposite a braziers who begins at day-break with a thousand clinking hammers: I cant hear myself speak to you across the water. An hour before breakfast, (this is 2 hours before breakfast) the girls begin whirring away on the piano. They have made immense progress: they will really play very well and all for love not of music but of their father.—they know what tunes I like— solemn old fashioned airs of Haydn and Mozart and intend to treat me to these. Anny is grown a complete young woman—not pretty a bit— but with a healthy fair complexion and proportions of the Miss Berryman order and hands & feet wh. wd. frighten folks at New York. Minny is no beauty neither but quite pretty enough for me: and I would not change them for girls 10 times as handsome—Don't I thank God as I think of them that they are so fond of me?—I am puzzled what to do next though—The excellent governess whom they have had here is much too young & pretty to come to a single man's house, and too proud to bear the subordinate position these ladies must take in London: where people slight them dont invite them &c &c Here her daily lessons over she goes into the world with her mother and is anybody's equal. It's a funny little world my old folks live in—quite unlike the great one to wh. I'm accustomed and I walk round my mother's little circle a stranger and a heavy old Swell annoyed at the airs wh. I can't help fancying I give myself. My portrait the original of the print as large as life swaggers in the little drawing-room so and looks so pompous from every corner that I can't help looking at it. I've not been well since I have been here. That has given the kind old step-father an opportunity to administer globules—He is 72 and the brave old soldier who mounted breaches and led storming parties is quite a quiet old man lean & slippered. My mother is as handsome and as good as ever: and all her little society worships her—You see I am falling into the regular small-town small talk. I have not been into the world at all: and have been here a week and it seems an age. From a twaddling society what can you have but twaddling? Its hard that there should be something narrowing about narrow circumstances. The misdeeds of maids-of-all-work form no small part of the little conversations I hear: and yesterday morning I caught Miss Minny in

the kitchen with a rueful face taking leave of Louise our ex-maid, who was going away and who had been kind to my girls. I did not like to give her more than 10 francs: but am glad I arrived time enough to console her parting hour with that gratuity. Now what am I to do without a governess and ought I to take the girls away from one who teaches them so capitally and shall I begin a novel in 20 numbers or shall I get ready to come back to New York?—here are a set of questions and I've nothing but these egotistical queries to write.

The advance of this place in material splendour is wonderful: they are pulling down and building up as eagerly as in New York; and the Rue de Rivoli is going to be the grandest street in the World—all the houses as tall as the St. Nicholas—and the palaces and the gardens looking so ancient and noble. The place swarms with Americans I'm told: and I'm quite angry to see how like Broadway beaux are to the Boulevard dandies. Borrowing their coats from Frenchmen—for shame! Silly monkies why don't they have tails of their own—I mean coat-tails—and not ape these little creatures?—I wish I had not forgotten the name of your relative here—her who writes to Sarah about the fashions—I would like to go & talk to some one who knows you. Bingham Mildmay bounced in on me just as I was closing my last letter; and it was all for the sake of you that we shook hands so cordially

Thursday. Having just assumed one of Lucy's garments, I did to it what I always do at dewy morn when I fall in with her neat little handywork; (I think of the ship state-room, and myself rolling about in the queer operation of kissing the collar of a shirt.) Yesterday I spent by myself for the most part: refused all invitations went to see the pictures, went to dine at the Trois Frères, went to the play by myself—and enjoyed the amusement not a little and the solitude still more. Met 2 fellow passengers out of the Europa; one a Philadelphia Quaker in an imbroydered waistcoat and yellow gloves walking the streets at 5 o'clock—going to dine with 18 Americans at Véry's he said. I think I should like to have been one—that twang sounds very friendly indeed to me: and in fact I feel just as much at home on your side as on our's. So Sarah and Mildmay had a many walks and rides, had they? Lucky dog! And I that used to come for weeks and weeks & could never get a chance—there was the milliner or the French mistress or something—Poor old fellow!—Will they never bring the breakfast? If the old folks had been but a little earlier, I should not have written that last sentence and got through the letter without jibes & scorn. But these grow milder as time passes: and when I think of your kindness and constant welcome I promise you there is no scorn in my mind then. God bless you all. Write to Kensington toujours please: and as many as will to Yours ever

W M T.

lean & slippered: As You Like It, II, vii, 158.

186. TO SIR EDWARD BULWER-LYTTON
21 June 1853

June 21.

Dear Sir Edward Lytton.
  Looking over some American reprints of my books, I find one containing a preface written by me when I was in New York in wh. are the following words—
  ["]The careless papers written at an early period and never seen since the printer's boy carried them away, are brought back and laid at the father's door, and he cannot, if he would forget or disown his own children.
  Why were some of these little brats brought out of their obscurity? I own to a feeling of anything but pleasure in reviewing some of these juvenile misshapen creatures, wh. the publisher has disinterred and resuscitated. There are two performances especially (among the critical & biographical works of the erudite Mr. Yellowplush) wh. I am very sorry to see reproduced: and I ask pardon of the author of the Caxtons for a lampoon wh. I know he himself has forgiven, and wh. I wish I could recal. I had never seen that eminent writer but once in public when this satire was penned, and wonder at the recklessness of the young man who could fancy such satire was harmless jocularity, and never calculate that it might give pain." K. T. L.
  I dont know whether you ever were made aware of this cry of peccavi: but with the book in wh. it appears just fresh before me, I think it fair to write a line to acquaint you with the existence of such an apology; and to assure you of the author's repentance for the past: and this present sincere good will with wh. he is

Yours most faithfully
W. M. Thackeray.

preface: the Appleton edition of *Mr. Brown's Letters to a Young Man About Town*, Thackeray's preface to which was written in December 1852. The Yellowplush reprints had been published before Thackeray's arrival in America and without his permission.   *K. T. L.:* (Gk.) *kai ta loipa* (et cetera).   *peccavi:* (Lat.) I have sinned.

187. TO SARAH BAXTER
4-5 July 1853

4 of July. Hip Hip Hurra
In the last 10 days the undersigned has been so undecided ('undersigned' 'undecided'—not good language—and then that blot oughtn't I to begin a new sheet[)]—well I think I have at last determined that we set off on Wednesday to Hombourg wh. will be our first halt and where I shall try and do some of my new book. It won't be a good one—not a step forwards as some ambitious young American folks would have it; but a retreat rather—however if I can get 3000£ for my darters I mean 3000 *to put away* besides living. I will go backwards or forwards or any way. It torments me incessantly, and I wander about with it in my interior, lonely & gloomy as if a secret remorse was haunting me. I saw a pretty American girl in a carriage in the Rue Vivienne to day She was like you She had your colour &c—a great gush of feelings came tumbling out of this bussam at the sight. I wanted to run after the carriage: to stop it and speak to her and say 'Do you know any thing of one S B of New York?' The carriage whisked away leaving me alone with my feelings—O ye old ghosts! I declare I saw nothing of the crowded city for a minute or two so completely did the *revenans* hem me in— Nothing is forgotten. We bury 'em but they pop out of their graves now and again and say Here we are Master. Do you think we are dead? No No, only asleep We wake up sometimes we come to you we shall come to you when you are ever so old; we shall always be as fresh and mischievous as we are now We shall say [']Do you remember S S B do you remember her eyes? Do you think she had 2 dimples in her cheeks and don't you recollect this was the note of her laugh, that used to be quite affected at times but you know the music of it you poor old rogue.' Yes the laugh and the looks flash out of the past every now and then, and whisk by me just like that carriage in the Rue Vivienne—A novel thought! Suppose I make the hero of the new book in love with some one? and then suppose I make him jilted? He won't break his heart: I dont think he'll have much of a heart: and besides breaking it in the very first numbers would be preposterous— (Another blot on the next page this ink is very liquid). I wrote your mother about sleeping in Sterne's room at Calais: wasn't it queer? I wonder whether all literary men are humbugs and have no hearts. I know one who has none. Why you may marry any body you please &

I don't care: I dare say there is some young fellow at Newport or Saratoga at this very minute—and I'm amused I give you my honour I'm amused. *L'autre* and her lord & master are reconciled and I'm not in the least annoyed: and one of my loves being here the other day with two babies I nursed the youngest with a graceful affection that the father himself couldn't have equalled.—Its my lot—I fall in love. I moan & sigh, & I end by nursing other people's babies. Isn't the dinner coming? What a pocket full of news I am giving you!

July 5. Chawles Pearman my new servant arrived from London last night, and brought me no letter from you. Do you know Mademoiselle that this is most igstordinary and unpleasant? How can you tell that he didn't come from London solely in order that I might have that letter? and now—rien—nothing—nix! We all march tomorrow-morning, Shall I have time to fill this sheet ere we go. Ingrate! I *should* have had time but I have nothing to reply to. A friend of many people here an Irish Doctor has just been to be knighted in England; and so they are going to give him a dinner; and so I am to be in the chair and make the speeches; that is my last appearance at Paris, & tomorrow o for fun & freedom & fresh air!

What letters haven't I been answering all day!—No more small hand-writing Miss Sarah, no more cramped hand no time for that. But I *will* send this away from Paris, and before I get farther from you: although I know there's nothing in it but that I'm yours &c &c &c.

One of the letters was from Mrs. Gore—Tell Mrs. Dearing this, please;—Miss Cecy yesterday was married to the Lord Edward Thynne—a widower Lord Baths Son & Uncle—a sad scape-grace I'm afraid ruined long ago How can such a couple get on? How could I write a congratulatory letter to Mamma? I tried & it was as glum as a funeral. All I could say by way of consolation was Marriages that seem to augur very well often turn out very unhappy—therefore this that looks so bad may turn out quite the reverse—It was pleasant to get a heap of fine invitations from London and think one was free of them—Did I tell you in page 1 or 2 that I think of passing a good bit of the winter here? My dear kind old Stepfather gets very old. His goodness to the children has been admirable. They are a little too much for him & even for my mother I think but they will be very unhappy without them so instead of going to Rome as I thought, why we will sit down here in a little tranquillity, and I'll try & do my duty filially as well as paternally. O how I wish you would all come here for the winter! What wouldn't I give to hear somebody laugh, and see somebody smile! I don't like to think of your dear kind Mother's illness; and the non-receipt of these letters somehow fills me with a queer disquiet about you.— I have been reading Nile Notes. Do you know its uncommonly clever? Or is it because of that criticism in Putnams that my grateful eyes are opened to Curtis's merits. The book is capital—awfully sensual and too luscious to read much of at a time; but I send the Author my regards and am glad to like what he has done so.

Now I will shut up this. Now I will send my love to you all: now I take Sarahs two hands the last you know and look in her face (don't smile in that saucy way Miss) then say Good bye dear Sarah always remember I'm your affectionate old friend

W M T.

my new book: The Newcomes, which began to appear with the serial installment for October 1852. *revenans:* (Fr.) ghosts. *Irish Doctor:* Sir Joseph Francis Olliffe (1808-69), physician to the British Embassy in Paris. *fresh air!:* at this point Thackeray changed from his small upright handwriting to his slanted handwriting. *Mrs. Dearing:* Mrs. Baxter's sister, Mrs. Nicoll Havens Dering (1796-1889), the former Sarah Huggins Strong. *Miss Cecy . . . Thynne:* on 4 July 1853 Cecilia Gore (d. 1879) married Lord Edward Thynne (1807-84), sixth son of the second Marquess of Bath. *Nile Notes: Nile Notes of a Howadji* (1851) by George William Curtis (1824-92). *criticism in Putnams:* "Thackeray in America," in the June 1853 issue of *Putnam's Monthly Magazine,* by Curtis.

188. TO MRS. THOMAS FREDERICK ELLIOT AND KATE PERRY
13-15 July 1853

Baden Baden. Wednesday July 13.
Whilst those lazy children are dressing and their father is waiting for breakfast, I think I may begin a little letter to mes bonnes sœurs, and ask the healths of all of them this fine July morning. Our journey hitherto has been a great success—Indeed it was only from Paris last Wednesday to Nancy and thence to Mannheim and this place: but the happiness of the girls, and their artless goodness and affection works upon me with I don't know what happiness: I dont remember the day these 10 years when I have felt so much at ease. And this helps me to write too. Three days ago I broke ground with the new book, and have done 2 day's work ever since upon it—The girls read French and German for 2 hours in the day, & this is all their occupation: they often talk about your children: and when we are having a very pleasant drive or are sitting over a very pleasant prospect or see an empty corner in the rail-way carriage I know who I wish was with us. God Almighty bless her and make her happy, dearest fondest & truest of women.

Lord Lord how much better this is than being in London! We have a little wickedness here too I have already lost 5 napoleons at roulette. The lovely Ribblesdale is the belle des eaux I'm told: the Normanbys are here my lord with a paralyzed arm and side—wonderful Julia Errington in a broad Spanish hat and a sash that would make a dress for any moderate person and 3 little girls in three little broad Spanish hats & 3 little large blue sashes. Glenelk also—it is not true that he lost a heavy stake at R et N last Sunday evening

We shant stay many more days though but go on to Switzerland taking matters very easily and so as always to have work in view. It's a great comfort to want no books & nothing but fresh ink and a good pen & paper. My new Servant is a mighty convenience a meek and intelligent lad striving with my daughters the other 2 slaves to make me comfortable. I have been reading Don Quixote and Tacitus in French & part of the latter in Latin—the deuce is in it if my style does not improve from the study of these great authors.

It's a very long time that the girls are keeping me waiting for breakfast though. Yesterday Anny went to take a walk before breakfast and of course was late—It was good to see Minny lingering when I said I would have my brfast; and declaring she saw Anny on the hill; and hinting that I had best wait till she came. Isn't this a funny thing & a great piece of news to tell you? So your brother made a very good fight at Liverpool. It's almost as good as getting in, losing with such a great minority. *Are* you coming to breakfast, young people?

(Enter Miss Thackeray with a face shining like a full moon)

This is Friday morning, and by all the powers I am waiting for breakfast again. Haven't I got a sweet temper? mustn't the girls be very insubordinate?—Well, they & I get up when we wake. A deal of sleep seems to suit the family; and of all God's gifts I doubt whether that isn't one of the best. I think I've nothing to say except a repetition of morning greetings and good wills. In the day time I can't write 'cause I am tired of the pen after four or five hours romancing. It goes pretty well: like the other yellow books—not so high-toned or so carefully finished as Esmond but that you see was a failure besides being immoral. We must take pains and write careful books when we have made the 10000 for the young ladies

Yesterday we had no work but a fine drive over the hills we saw the Rhine winding through an immense plain and Mountains all round about it the Vosges mountains & the Hardt mountains and the mountains of the Brisgau and right in the centre of the plain stood up Strasburg Cathedral tall and grey. How perfectly the scene is described in these few words: isn't it? Fiddlestick: but I suppose an author seeing the vanity of his own attempts at description, and how the words he uses wd. apply to 10000 other scenes besides that wh.

he is a writing about shouldn't therefore eschew descriptive writing—If incorrect or unsatisfactory nevertheless it begets in the reader's mind pictures & landscapes to suit him, and so—Fiddlestick again—There is in fact nothing to say but twaddling; but that we're waiting for breakfast; but that on Wednesday night I won my 5 naps back and 5 more: but that yesterday we had a party to dine at the old Schloss—very merry and plenty of champagne and talk and a nice woman by my side Lady Augustus Loftus; and by nine o'clock I was at home with my daughters who had been starved poor young wretches in my absence, having had for dinner beefsteak pour un avec pommes de terre & nothing more—a most miserable repast Lady Georgina Fullarton passed through who is always a very great favorite of mine, and I told her how the day before I had heard Anny telling Grantley Manor to her Sister. Then Anny told me how there was a lady in England who used to tell them the stories of books forgetting nothing, only making them much better & more amusing often than the books were: and behold I conjured up the image of such a person with children near her and (in my phansy Mesdames) heard the sweetest voice and saw the sweetest eyes that ever I shall look at or listen to in this wicked world. I dont know a bit where to tell you to write: but the children send their love to yours and their Pa says God bless you all.

W M T.

mes bonnes sœurs: (Fr.) my good sisters.   *bless her:* Mrs. Brookfield.   *Ribblesdale:* the former Emma Mure (1833-1911), who in May of 1853 had married Thomas Lister (1828-76), third Baron Ribblesdale.   *belle des eaux:* (Fr.) belle of the waters.   *Normanbys:* Constantine Henry Phipps (1797-1863), first Marquess of Normanby, former British Ambassador at Paris, and his wife (d. 1882), the former Maria Liddell.   *Julia Errington:* the wife of John Errington (1806-62), railway engineer.   *Glenelk:* Charles Grant Glenelg (1778-1866), first Baron Glenelg.   *R et N:* rouge et noir.   *your brother:* Sir Thomas Erskine Perry came in third place after the two winning Conservative candidates in an election held at Liverpool on 7 July 1853.   *Schloss:* (Ger.) castle.   *Loftus:* the former Emma Greville (d. 1902), who in 1845 had married Augustus Loftus (1817-1904), fourth son of the second Marquess of Ely.   *pour un avec pommes de terre:* (Fr.) for one person, with potatoes.   *Grantley Manor:* Lady Georgiana Fullerton's novel, *Grantley Manor,* had been published in 1847.

189. TO SARAH BAXTER
26 July - 7 August 1853

Vevey. July 26.

The fourth of July landed a little letter wh. has been 3 weeks on its way since, before it found the person to whom it was addressed I got it at Lausanne the day before yesterday—a glum little letter, hinting reproaches and ennui and disquiet. What for do you reproach me? How can you say you are indifferent to me? Haven't I written you 3 letters for one? Except one person, and my own girls whom do I care for if not for you?—Sometimes I think not for any one, person and girls and you included. Not being allowed that wh. my heart would have, it seems as if it's dead or buried. These complaints aught not to be trusted to pen and ink however; as you formulize your sentimental griefs you increase them—And at my age they become ridiculous—I'm old enough to be a grandfather and am I to go on puling because I cant get ever a female partner of my loves & woes?

You stupid old fool, get to your books; give up your laziness, don't spend your great stupid time hankering after women. Leave that to young people. My dear Sarah though I shall never forgive you keeping me waiting those 3 times and writing me those little bits of letters when I went to the South, and so slaying the elderly Cupid within me—yet he was so absurd and untimely a little brute that Death was the best thing wh. could happen to him. He was ludicrous, being born at my time of life, as Jacob was no I mean Isaac, when your Biblical namesake laughed at the idea of his appearance in the world, Theres a time for all things: for brilliant young Sarah Baxters; bright eyes and coquetry and triumphs and passions and filial duties—for old folks like me; art and ambition and money-getting and parental cares. I think I should have liked to hear of that gallant young Charley Pomeroy being made happy—I like him because he's handsome and honest. And as for you I think you have got so much character resolution and good temper that you would make yourself (decently) happy in making other folks so—and would accommodate yourself to deficiencies in savoir vivre like a young philosopheress. Besides that young fellow as far as I could see is a thorough gentleman and why should not his belongings be so? I'd sooner hear of your being Mrs. Pomeroy than Mrs. Mild-april for example—Bingham is spoiled by the heartlessness of London—wh. is awful to think of—the most godless respectable thing—thing's not the word—but I can't get it—I mean that world is base and prosperous and content, not unkind—very well bred—very unaffected in manner not dissolute—clean in person and raiment and going to church every Sunday—but in the eyes of the great Judge of right & wrong what rank will those people have with all their fine manners and spotless characters and linen?

They never feel love, but directly it's born, they throttle it and fling it under the sewer as poor girls do their unlawful children—they make up money-marriages and are content—Then the father goes to the house of Commons or the Counting House, the mother to her balls and visits—the children lurk up stairs with their governess, and when their turn comes are bought and sold and respectable and heartless as their parents before them.

Hullo!—I say—Stop!—where is this tirade a going to and apropos of what?—Well—I was fancying my brave young Sarah (who has tried a little of the pomps & vanities of her world) transplanted to our's and a London woman of society—with a husband that she had taken as she threatens to take one sometimes just because he is a good parti. No—go and live in a clearing—marry a husband masticatory expectoratory, dubious of linen, but with a heart below that rumpled garment—let the children eat with their precious knives—help the help, and give a hand to the dinner yourself—yea, it is better than to be a woman of fashion in London, and sit down to a French dinner where no love is. Immense Moralist! I think I'll call in Anny now, and give her a turn at the new novel: I see a chapter out of the above sermon and you know I must have an i to the main chance—

(The same evening) I called in Miss Anny at the above moment of writing, and we had a good time till dinner-time the story advancing very pleasantly. I am not to be the Author of it. Mr. Pendennis is to be the writer of his friend's memoirs: and by the help of this little mask (wh. I borrowed from Pisistratus, Bulwer I suppose) I shall be able to talk more at ease than in my own person. I only thought of the plan last night and am immensely relieved by adopting it. Alexander Smith is a grand young fellow and has shot one or two bow shots immensely high but he is not up to the great Keats or the great Alfred yet and [I] doubt whether he ever can be—As for my Small beer: why talk about [it] in the same breath?—Well Small beer is good of its sort—some day you'll have my little barrel, and I hope you'll relish a glass or two.

There's such a magnificent landscape or lakescape at my windows as I write. The Sun just now has been departing westwards, *you*wards so splendidly! Theres such a crowd of Americans at this hotel—almost all the women pretty, some of the men so awfully vulgar. I read in the Strangers book.

Name	Country	Profession	Whence come	Whither going
Smith J Smith T.	USA.	Clergyman	Genêvre	over the whole lot

Fancy *Genêvre* and *'over the whole lot'*! There it is in the Stranger's book

August 7. Bon Dieu! It is 12 days since this little note was begun: It has been stopped because I had not calculated the steamers well, because I was busy writing, because we have been travelling—to Geneva to Lausanne to Vevey again and thence to Bulle, Freyburg, Berne—It has cost 80£ for one month for 3 people and a servant, travelling gently and living soberly. 400 dollars—so you see what you may do: but if you travel hard you must add other 100 dollars to this reckoning. At Vevey among the 100000 Americans I saw the name of BLEECKER can it be Lucy's young man?—and there was a lady, I think her name was Post, who I am sure must be Mrs. Charles Strong's sister like her in person and in voice especially—and I was going to speak to her but she had a nice little son whom she bullied so that I could not open my mouth. I pass whole days sometimes and scarce open it if the people are not to my liking I cant speak, and seem igh and aughty—I'm in low spirits about the Newcomes It's not good. It's stupid. It haunts me like a great stupid ghost. I think it says why do you go on writing this rubbish? You are old, you have no more invention &cc—Write sober books, books of history, leave novels to younger folks—You see half of my life is grumbling; and lecturing or novel writing or sentimentalizing I am never content. What a noble character my girl Anny is! how cheerful how honest how kind and artless! She makes friends wherever we go. They make friends. As for me I have hardly seen a person I could speak to & am rather pleased I think at being unpopular. Are there any more letters come from America for me? Yesterday we were walking up a hill from Freyburg, I come to a carriage, and a voice from within calls out How is Miss Baxter? Fancy a voice calling out How is Miss Baxter on the top of a Swiss hill! It was a friend of Mrs. Sturgis's—And the lonely cavities of my heart echoed how is Miss Baxter—Anny and I had been talking about you just before and she had been telling me how my step-father, when I was away and the girls had been out on a walk, would say to them on their return 'O I have had a visit from Miss Sally Baxter'.

This is Sunday. We go to church when we are abroad but yesterday we met the clergyman at the table d'hote and he was so awfully pompous grandiloquent and stupid that I couldn't go to hear him sermonize. We may go towards England tomorrow, or to Munich—I never know. I have no will of my own and don't care to have one when there is no call for it—I think about you constantly and very very very kindly—and of all of you. Why does every body else bore me the great world & all and why do I feel so at home always in that Brown House? God bless all there: and never for a moment go for to doubt that I am your affectionate old friend.

W M T.

Berne. August 7.

savoir vivre: (Fr.) knowing how to live.   *pomps & vanities:* The Catechism, Book of Common Prayer.   *parti:* (Fr.) marital catch.   *a French dinner where no love is:* a variation on Proverbs 15: 17—"Better is a dinner of herbs where love is, than a stalled ox and hatred therewith."   *Pisistratus, Bulwer:* Pisistratus Caxton, the hero of Bulwer's *The Caxtons* (1849), is the purported author of Bulwer's *My Novel* (1853).   *Alexander Smith:* (1830-67), the "spasmodic" poet, whose *Poems* had appeared in April 1853.   *Mrs. Charles Strong:* the former Jeannette Bradley (1795-1856), Mrs. Baxter's sister-in-law.   *that Brown House:* the Baxter's house at 286 Second Avenue, New York City.

190. TO BRYAN WALLER PROCTER
September 1853

Kensington. Monday.

My dear Procter.

I am so sorry to think that tother day when I was at Brighton I might have seen you and didn't. They only told me afterwards at your house how you were all away. I came back from Switzerland ailing and took my complaints to the Brighton club, where I often have left them before.

I shall value the books very much my dear old friend and the picture of the giver. Shall I come down and see you tomorrow or next day? I daresay I will. We are off again very soon for 2 or 3 months at Paris, and then for 4 or 5 at Rome—I can go where I like now there are no pictures to do, and there was more than one good reason for giving Doyle that job. But the chief reason was—well if you can serve your friend and yourself too, aren't you lucky?

I wonder whether that is true about Mr. Fielding I think he had brutified his life, and his intellect suffered by the bad-women's company he kept: but haven't we sometimes laughed at Macready for being jealous of the memory of Garrick? I read Don Quixote nearly through when I was away. What a vitality in those 2 characters! What gentlemen they both are! I wish Don Q. was not thrashed so very often. There are sweet pastoralities through the book; and that piping of shepherds and pretty sylvan ballet wh. dances always round the principal figures is delightfully pleasant to me—it would kill any book now to make it so long, and introduce all those long fantastic processions interludes & the like. Also I read in Tacitus leisurely with an uncommonly good French translation and began to read Monte Cristo at 6 one morning and never stopped till 11 at night!

   I hope I shall come tomorrow to Brighton and to tea at 7 1/2 or so at Bedford Square

Always yours
W M Thackeray

books: the two volumes of Procter's *Essays and Tales in Prose* (1852). *giving Doyle that job:* illustrating *The Newcomes*. *Mr. Fielding:* the novelist, Henry Fielding.

191. TO MRS. THOMAS FREDERICK ELLIOT AND KATE PERRY
October 1853

Maison Valin. Champs Élysées Paris
Thursday.

  Do not be very angry that I have passed through Boulogne without coming to see you. The fault was not mine, and I should have liked of all things to pass a day or two with you, and your sick nursery. But I did not dare. We have been delayed from day to day until my poor mother here grew so anxious that I knew, if I staid on the road, she would suffer from that complaint some women have chronically, fancy I didn't like to come to her—sought pretexts for delay—& so on—and so the good of the visit here would have been done away with and the pleasure too on both sides all embittered by— the German word is Eifersüchtigkeit. If I come, I must come back hence; and pass a day with my kind K P. What for do people make themselves so needlessly unhappy in the world? Let us, who have pretty good tempers, be thankful for that happy natural gift. I was absolutely about to stop my bag at the Railway hand over the girls to Mr. & Miss—what are their names?—the Italian conspirators who were always at the Berrys?—and have come back to you, but the thought of the dear old mothers disappointment prevailed and I am glad I came on & made her happy. We have a very nice roomy apartment in the Champs Élysées—Our presence is a comfort to the old folks. I dare say I will come & see you before the month is over or I shall be coming to London & we shall meet. Here's a letter from J E. dated 30 August I haven't opened it yet—all those posthumous letters are dismal to read. I daresay this one contains news of that other dear J. whom I have seen in London but always with the children or in the company of the poor Inspector, who tries his best to smother his hatred for me—only Jack in the box comes rushing out again. I fancy

I see him clapping down the lid. As for J O B—I remember a passage of a novel called Esmond wh. says when Mr. E thought of the splendor & purity of his dear mistress's love, the thought of it smote him on to his knees &c. I behold that beautiful constancy with wonder & thanks to God—with such a feeling as one looks at the Alps or the stars in Heaven. I admire human nature in thinking of her. I think I am nearer her, when away than when sitting by her, talking of things we don't feel—with poor Tomkins's restless eye ever & again trying *not* to look at us. I knew the time when she walked: but never went. It mustn't be: it mustn't be: and it's happier that we should love each other in the grave as it were, than that we should meet by shamchance, & that there should be secrets or deceit. When you see her preach this to her again & again. Many & many a time a friend of mine whispers me (he is represented in pictures with horns & a tail) My good friend *à quoi bon* all this longing & yearning & disappointment; yonder gnawing grief and daily nightly brooding? A couple of lies & the whole thing might be remedied. Do you suppose other folks are so particular? Behold there are 4 children put their innocent figures between the Devil and me: and the wretched old fiend shirks off with his tail between his hoofs. Go and wipe away her tears, you dear kind sisters of charity. My girls I suppose see all about it: but they love her all the same.   Have you had a letter from Kinglake? I had 2 lines to say his mother was dead: and when I was in England I went and reconciled my self with Mrs. Procter (only those pitchers when mended wont hold water any more) & with Higgins who had been offended too at my not going to him; and paid dutiful visits to all my step-father's relations & my own; & bought a pretty house 36 Onslow Square Brompton next door to Marochetti: & am to pay for it in 3 years £700 a year or thereabouts. Whether we go to Rome or not is now undetermined: most likely not. I had some talk with another publisher about doing another kind of work editing Walpole & writing a life of him. It rains money with me. I may make 5000£ in the next year think of that!—These are all my news for the present. I should like a letter very much. Give our love to your girls and my remembrances to their papa; and remember that I am always affectionately yours & J E's.

Eifersüchtigkeit: (Ger.) jealousy.   *the Berrys:* Agnes and Mary Berry.   *à quoi bon:* (Fr.) for what good.   *Marochetti:* the sculptor Carlo Marochetti (1805-67), who lived at 34 Onslow Square.

192. TO ELIZABETH STRONG AND LUCY BAXTER
17-18 October-3 November 1853

Somewhere in October & November.
Paris. 1853.

My dear little birds. There is no use in getting out of temper and scolding and rating me in that way. I know very well that I owe you a letter: and that you are going about saying to everybody Why doesn't Mr. Thackeray answer us? Weren't we very kind to him? Didn't we make him some brandy-peaches and pickled-walnuts (I just think how clever it would have been had I said pandy-breaches and wickled-palnuts ho ho ho! You will kill me with laughing if you go on in that way!) Didn't he kiss us both when he went away (*now* you are caught. I have put this in just in order that you mayn't show the letter. You daren't now. I defy you). And we write to him the prettiest little letters, and we always think kindly of him, and he owes us a letter this ever so long!—O you little absurd birds! (I wish I could hear you pronounce them 2 wuerds absuerd buerds in your New York tone! You are sitting on one perch and I will knock you both down with one little stone[)].

I think I have told you all the news in the preceding page and you may rely upon every word I have said as correct. I was so glad to hear from Mamma, I mean Mother I mean Aunt Anna, that you were both married and living in great comfort in Fifty Sixth Street—I don't like Libbie's marrying a pastry cook but que voulez vous? We have our prejudices in Europe: when my youngest girl was married to the black footman I was for a long time inconsolable but the little tawny graces of my infantile grandson have reconciled me to his mother's choice and the bandy legs and woolly head of his father.

Do you know what all this is about?. Well I will tell you. My daughters & I are going out to tea with their Granny. We went to dress together. I mean at the same time you know I am in that elegant coat & waistcoat que vous savez—the very garments—and I thought I would begin a letter to you, and write a little stuff-and-nonsense until they were ready. Here they are. Away we go to tea. Good night Mesdemoiselles L.L.

We have been here for a fortnight—[(]this is written the next morning you know)—And I don't know whether we shall make out our visit to Rome this winter. It is always a hard matter to get a family on the march—the botheration of moving—the tears of Grandmother &c. I wish the girls would let me go by myself for a month, & they wd. but they wouldn't forgive me afterwards. I don't know that Paris is very pleasant. I know 2, 3, 4 distinct sets of people, and between them all cant see anyone comfortably. The best way is to do as at New York, go to nobody, only to one house, say a brown one at the corner of a street, and neglect all the rest of the world. Did I tell you that I have bought a pretty little house at Brompton? looking into a very pretty square (Onslow Sqe.)—the girls are to have a floor to themselves and a little bath-room. I know where I got the hint of the bath-room: and we shall give up old Kensington and go and live there. But the house is not so roomy as Kensington. I can only make out at the most 2 spare bed rooms. I got your Mother's letter yesterday: and I went right away to see for Mrs. Bayley but she is gone. Two nights ago at the theatre I saw the fat face of an old acquaintance from Providence R. I. Creighton isn't his name? a podgy little dandy. I was glad to set eyes on him People from your country whom I knew there cant understand I daresay, how glad I am to see them. What makes me like it so?—the Brown House, and one or two more—but the B. H. most of all.

Yesterday (This is written weeks and weeks after the other part) me and the gals, went to Fountainebleau; and the wind blows fair for Rome now I think. I shall be glad to be on the move again, so as to be quiet. Do you know that when we were in that pleasant forest yesterday, and walking through those trim old gardens all carpeted with red leaves and admiring that quaint old palace, I often wished for some young ladies? Corbin gave us a grand dinner last Saturday. He had a Lord on each side of him and the whole feast was very splendid: and Bancroft Davis has just arrived and I see your compatriots flaunting about every where in grand barouches with splendid livery-menials and cockayds in their hats—& I wish I wish for you girls that's the truth—No one has such good tea—such good peaches—such good walnuts—Why isn't Second Avenue next door that I might leave my books and papers and step in where I know I should be welcome if it was only to talk nonsense like this

Good bye young ladies accept my respectful salutations Remember me to Aunt Snelling & to George & to Wyllie and so Good B.

                           W M T

Aunt Anna: Mrs. Baxter was Libby Strong's maternal aunt. *que voulez vous?:* (Fr.) what do you expect? *que vous savez:* (Fr.) that you know. *L.L.:* Libby and Lucy. *Aunt Snelling:* the former Eliza Templeton Strong (1804-69), Mrs. Baxter's sister, the wife of Andrew Symmes Snelling (b. 1797). *George . . . Wyllie:* Mrs. Baxter's sons, George Strong Baxter (1845-1928) and Wyllys Pomeroy Baxter (1839-72).

193. TO MRS. HENRY CARMICHAEL-SMYTH
5 December 1853

My dearest Mammy. This shall serve as envelope to the girls letter, wh. I see is full of raptures and pleasure: and that is something déja worth travelling for—One can't but be made happy by Anny's happiness and obstinate determination to be pleased with everything. Minny takes matters much more quietly: and req[uires a] great deal more to stir her than her Sister. Did a letter I left at Maison Valin for Miss Shawe go off, please? (Do y[ou see the conn]exion between the above 2 sentences?) Our journey has cost us, how much do you think? 1200 francs. I thought 1000 w[ould have done] it. We have very comfortable quarters at the Hotel where I lived before; and where the Landlord never sent me a bill for 3 months during wh. I got no letters: so I was bound to come back to him and m'en suis bien trouvé except for some animal that bit me furiously while I was asleep yesterday on the sofa. It cant be a bug of course—the chambermaid declares she has never seen such a thing, nor so much as a flea—So it must be a scorpion I suppose I am glad I brought a sarving-man. He has been useful in a score [of] ways, and is quite honest active and willing. We went to St. Peters yesterday and Miss Anny & I agreed Pisa is the best: the other is a huge Heathen parade: all the Statues represent lies almost: & the founder of the religion utterly disappears under the enormous pile of fiction and ceremony that has been built round him, I'm not quite sure that I think St. Peters handsome:—yes as handsome as one of those splendid strumpets I saw at the ball at Paris. The front is positively ugly that's certain: but nevertheless the city is glorious— we had a famous walk on the Pincio, and the sun set for us with a splendor quite imperial. I wasn't sorry when the journey from C[ivita Vec]chia was over, having eighty or ninety louis in my pocket, I should have been good meat for the brigands had they chosen to come. Every body I have met is more or less a thief or a beggar. If I had given the postillions 5 louis a piece they would have said it was too little. I gave the last fellow a double pour-boire and he remained half an hour in the hotel, bawling for more, and roaring because part of his money had been paid in copper. Every miserable official at every post house, customs, what not holds out his swindling hand and begs—and the earth swarms with myriads of priests and friars who neither toil nor spin, but live on the people and perform fetish and interpret the Will of the Gods. Quamdiu? I wonder when it will be over?—And I wonder when my daughters are coming to breakfast? I, you must know, went to bed at eight o'clock last night, and slept without a turn till past 6. And to day what shall we do? What governess shall we find? What friends? We saw none yesterday. God bless my dearest old Mother & G P.

W M T.

Hotel Franz. Via Condotti. Monday. Decr. 5. Address care of Messrs. Macbean, Bankers

déja: (Fr.) already.   *m'en suis bien trouvé:* (Fr.) I am all the better for it.
pour-boire: (Fr.) tip.   *neither toil nor spin:* Matthew 6: 28 and Luke 12: 27.
Quamdiu?: (Lat.) how long?

194. TO MRS. BRYAN WALLER PROCTER
January - 4 February 1854

Via della Croce 81. Rome.
(Care of Messrs. Macbean. Corso. Rome)

My dear Mrs. Procter. Your letter has been the only reminiscence I have had from England of any friends that I have there—not a single line from any mortal. Was there ever such ingratitude? But then on the other hand it must be owned that I write to no one not even to the nameless Lady of Lyons (It was Marseilles) who may have answered me and whose letter may be at the post, where they like to keep 'em, and give them in a heap just as one is going away. Ever since I have had this ruby pen I have taken to the old original handwriting the upright business does not work nearly so well with it. You are quite right that I might have done my work just as well at Brompton as at Rome. I haven't seen Rome, and don't know a single Roman except the housemaid, & my landlord who speaks English. But the girls are as happy as young women need be. If I am glum myself their good spirits give me pleasure, and if I can't leave them a fortune why we must try and leave them the memory of having had a good time with their papa. Isn't this sentimental? It is the grey of evening and I scarce see the melancholy lines as I write them on the paper.   Here comes Octavia with the lights. Perhaps I dont write because I am growing glummer and glummer every day: or lazier and lazier is it?—I am hard at work. Then out for a pretty long walk. Then comes dinner at home most days: and tea parties enough when I am inclined. I go and look at the pictures statues churches and so forth: but what has come to them or the eyes that behold them? I declare that Dying Gladiator is very well but it is no such wonder As for the Domenichino Sybil (it is at the Capitol, you know over the way)—Pish! it is a great clumsy woman affected ogling and in a great turban. Mrs. Butler had such a fine turban on the other night! I have almost learned to like her. She is kind exceedingly to the girls and to me: so is that good excellent Adelaide Sartoris, who is all good nature, and very happy now indeed she says; her Edward being everything that is good. There never was such a kind creature with such a scowling countenance. They give quite the pleasantest parties in Rome, & she sings as well as ever she did I think. Lockhart goes sometimes: and I see him once in a month. I thought we might have made company together but he is too unwell to care for any society at least for mine, so I cant tell you much about your favorite. The most interesting man I have met here is a convert, Mr. Pollen whom Doyle sent with a letter: and we have neutral ground on the Fine Arts, Books & so forth: and I try and understand from him what can be the Secret of the religion for wh. he has given up rank chances all good things of this life. I am as far off from believing it, as ever saving your presence: and I fear poor Pollen when he finds that I am only looking at it artistically as at Paganism Mahometanism or any other ism will withdraw from me in sorrow, and that our pleasant acquaintance won't come to much. The good Brownings I see pretty often and the Storys Americans very nice people indeed—and Miss Wynn once in a fortnight. She has been ill from the climate so has W M T twice: and I didn't begin to rally until some brisk cold weather came, and now I'm well, and presently who knows? perhaps shall be cheerful. You shall have a letter then—not a series of inarticulate moans like the present.

  The best thing at Rome is the Sunset over Saint Peters every evening. Gods what a flaming splendor it is! the worst thing [is] that one can't drink wine as in Weymouth Street—not though it's ever so good wh. it isn't No wine is so good as Weymouth Street wine. I aven't ad my ealth at all here that is the fact: but for the last month have been in constant work: and am now in the middle of No VIII I'm pleased to say. I think it is good never to hear about one's writings. Your's and my mothers have been the only criticisms that have come to me, and Pollen says Newman read the two first numbers and thought the style the right sort of thing. The Colonel is going to India the day after tomorrow. You'll be glad to hear that I know—He is a dear old boy but confess you think he is rather a twaddler?—When I read of Dickens's triumphs before the Hoperatives at Manchester my soul is full of envy; and I think of coming back and reading Yellowplush in costume at Islington. Is poor old Forster well again? Your winter must have been awful. Here we have had open windows every day & all day Lord I wish I was back again (in a whisper)—not at Brompton; I don't like the idea of Brompton at all; and—here dinner came and Mr. Pollen to partake of it; and we sat till 12 o'clock very pleasantly. I told him Jerrold's story about my conversion to Romanism, and I daresay the good fellow went home and asked his favorite saint to *convert* me—all but my nose and that is past praying for. And yesterday, at work on No VIII, crack, I broke my favorite ruby pen and am now obliged to return to an old gold one wh. will only write upright hand. We have had a dear little frost, & my health has braced up wonderfully with the cold weather. Lord! how the stars shine in the Evans!—those luminous objects said to be worlds by some—I dont think you see them in London. You only see coals and gas and fogs and mud & snow—but then Madeira and that bottle of Crockford wh. B C *will* bring out and a snug talk by the fire! We have had breakfast ever so long ago and yet it is only nine o'clock. I don't go to work; because presently I am going to see some friends of mine off: who will go to Paris and take a letter to my mother, and say they have seen me in the flesh the very last thing. If you see any body who cares to know, say too that I am well please. Anny wrote to Cadogan Place but there has come back never an answer nor have they written from Chesham Place—from no place. Miss Wynn & her Sister the Widow go to Naples anon. So would I, if I could let my beautiful lodgings, but I darenot otherwise be so expensive.

Saturday. Feb 4. It is a shame how long this letter has been in completion. I lost it and find it only now in the midst of a heap of No VIII, wh. has been completed thank the Stars: and now since 7 o'clock this morning am at work at No IX. Seven o'clock in the morning That is your true secret. Early to bed. Away with tea-parties Have the day to yourself from 12 o'clock till eleven at night and then go sleep.—But with this regimen the author may flourish but the friend perishes—the writing of letters becomes impossible and the sight of ink ojous. Tell Adelaide If you write to her and with my respectful remembrances that on Candlemas Day I met at breakfast The Abbot of St. Bernards (England) and his aide de Camp Father Ignatius in white Cistercian habits: Dr. Manning—he has just been Doctored by his Holiness Messrs. Vaughan & Wynn in minor orders; with hats like Don Basilio—we walked out afterwards—and had as pleasant a breakfast as ever I knew at Pollens Doyle's friend. And yesterday I met the Holy Father in the street and had a most comfortable bow from him: and to night I take T with Mrs. Kemble, not daring to refuse her. And so I send very kind regards to all who come near Weymouth Street, and am Yours my dear Mrs. Procter and my dear old B C's always

W M T

Lady of Lyons: heroine of Bulwer's play of that name (1838).   *the upright business:* these words are written in Thackeray's upright hand.   *Lockhart:* John Gibson Lockhart (1794-1854), Sir Walter Scott's son-in-law and biographer.   *Pollen:* John Hungerford Pollen, a fellow of Merton College, Oxford, until his conversion to Roman Catholicism in 1852.   *Doyle:* Richard Doyle, a fellow Catholic.   *the Storys:* William Wetmore Story (1819-95), the American sculptor, and his wife, the former Emelyn Eldredge.   *Miss Wynn:* Charlotte Williams-Wynn (1807-67).   *Weymouth Street:* in the spring of 1853 the Procters had moved to 32 Weymouth Street.   *Dickens's . . . Manchester:* a reading of *A Christmas Carol* on a working people's night during late December 1854 at Birmingham, not Manchester.   *Lord . . . again (in a whisper):* the words "Lord I wish I was back again" are written in tiny, upright characters.   *Jerrold's story:* Douglas Jerrold, Thackeray's *Punch* colleague, on hearing an unfounded rumor about Thackeray's proposed conversion to Roman Catholicism, said: "he'd better begin with his nose," Thackeray's nose having been disfigured during a schoolboy fight.   *bottle of Crockford:* probably an "own label" bottle of wine from the celebrated auction at Christie and Manson on 16 February 1852 of the holdings of Crockford's gambling club, 50 St. James's Street.   *some friends of mine:* Lord and Lady Airlie.   *Cadogan Place:* where the Brookfields lived.   *Chesham Place:* where the Elliots and Kate Perry lived.   *her Sister:* Mrs. John Lindsay.   *Dr. Manning:* Henry Edward (later Cardinal) Manning (1808-92).   *his Holiness:* Pius IX, Pope 1846-78.   *Don Basilio:* in Rossini's *The Barber of Seville.*

195. TO KATE PERRY
19? March 1854

[Naples]

My dear K E P.   I wrote a little note two days since but I am glad it was too late for the steamer, and my servant brought it back for it was but a little scrap, and now I can give a longer story. A dismal story it will be to be sure as all those I have written from Italy (there haven't been many letters to any one.) It has been the decree of Allah that the writer of this his slave should undergo many tribulations in this region. I had 2 severe attacks of illness at Rome and have been visited here with other two. Add to wh. the girls have had the scarlatina, and I leave you to fancy how pleasant our sojourn has been. We have no maid so Minny & I nursed Anny No 1: then Minny sickened and went to bed No 2: then your servant was toppled over with a severe private attack of his own. But o good Fortune! on the day of Min's seizure it chanced that a certain lady parted with her monthly nurse, who came to us—otherwise with the three of us all on our backs in three adjoining rooms facing the Mediterranean Sea, shunned by waiters for fear of the infection, and constantly requiring our little arrowroots lemonades and draughts not so agreeable what would have happened to us all? Well with all this it really has been a tolerably happy time. I do not like to say Thanks to a Gracious Providence wh. ordained every body's recovery: because say what one will thanks for recovery imply dissatisfaction at illness: and behold the true believer should receive ill and well with a like acquiescence and a benign gravity. All I can say without flying into quasi-raptures of gratitude—is that it's a comfort to find the good arising out of certain little hardships, wherewith the Dispenser of them mingles a deal of blessing and sweetness—there are the children helping one another:—there mayhap is the heavy Father disguising his private griefs and ailments, and scuffling away out of bed in his old slippers to look after the sick young ones: and the little suffering child, after a night of restless fever, calling out in the morning with her poor little weak voice to know how Papa is. And then, after a little, Health comes back to all. Laus Deo. Amen is the greatest of the names of Allah. Some day will assuredly come when we shall have the fever without the recovery. Shan't we say Amen for that too? Two days since, in the early early morning, looking out of the window on Capri yonder and the beautiful beautiful rosy-tinted (not indigo-tinted) nature;

I was thinking of the girls convalescing, and asleep close by: and of that day 15 years ago when their little sister died at sunrise. O you sweet and bitter thoughts! So we have all been ill, and are well again: & they talk of you women being more prolix in your letters than men are—you would be 10 times as ill, and nurse 100 children: & only say in half a line 'Poor Flora has been suffering, and I have not been quite well' and have done with it: whereas here is a whole letter nearly about nothing else but Doctor's stuff.

But then there's nothing else to write about. What goes on here I know no more than the folks who are buried at Pompeii. Nevertheless the Spring has just set in; and it's delightful to see the sea from the windows and drink the delicious blue atmosphere out of the sky overhead. The streets I see swarm with pictures, though I can't do them. The town is full of gaiety though I can't partake of it. Numbers of the British-Romans are arrived. They all come in a swarm: wait here for a fortnight; swarm to Pompeii, Baiæ, Museo Borbonico, and so forth, and swarm back to Rome for the Holy Week—for the sights of wh. I do not care a button. Did I tell you when we were at Rome how they had the Colosseum lighted up with pink and green fire?—the great gabies! as if the Sun wasn't good enough to light the place. All my private Art-business at Rome was an utter failure. It was no more possible than an intime conversation in Chesham Place with your girls and mine in the room: and as mine, on my little excursions were pretty nearly always with me, Art turned away her Countenance or I did not dare to interrogate her. But there is very little Art thats the fact—not that great blustering hulking Colosseum for instance; nor those simpering Canovas, sickly Guidos, swaggering Caracci—only little bits here and there. I went yesterday to see the Farnese Hercules made by Glykon the Athenian as he announces at the foot of the Statue and Glykon has been passed as you know as well as the Statue for a stunning fine fellow. O the great coarse bumptious old braggart! Playing a smart piece on the piano: or cutting a neat figure of 8 on the Serpentine, or writing a Review ar[ticle] is really as good as that thumping piece of Skill. There are avenues of worthless marble and canvass here and at Rome—There goes Miss Anny singing in the next room. Her grave cheerfulness her willingness to be pleased and to please, is delightful at the present juncture, when her Papa's jocularity is pretty well worn out.

Do you remember how I wrote to you from Charleston last year and a commission you executed for Lady Day? Will you do it this year please? I have bought some old English paper marked 1837, made when we were tolerably young people; and it's such a comfort to write on, with an old fashioned quill. But I ought to be writing No XI & XII of the Newcomes Miss—and though the first volume is rather slow, I promise you the second shall have plenty of interesting business in it.

I dont know where to bid friends write to me now or what our movements will be. I have just come from the library and seen an extract from Newcomes in a paper—a pretty extract but full of faults in the punctuation. It's a pity those pretty things should be spoiled for a few commas and colons. I am sure the quiet business is the right one in the end; spite of all the long faces the publishers pull.

I have just been called to see Miss Min in her frock for the first time—they make a regular quarantine of these complaints here, and never stir out before the 40 days are over after convalescence. Otherwise they say people swell up and die! The Hollands have been untiringly good-natured with good offices from the kitchen jellies and biscuits galore I wish I could like her but I cant—So are the Cravens & Lowthers as kind as possible and the little glimpse of Neapolitan Society I had at Mrs. Cravens was very pleasant indeed. And now the paper's full. And I send my love to all good people, and am always the grateful friend of kind J's & K's—

W M T.

Naples 16 March. We read here of troops departing—Salisbury & Derry dying—Poor old Down derry down! Good bye. Miss my girls send their love to yours.

Laus Deo: (Lat.) Praise God.   *Flora:* Flora Perry, daughter of Sir Erskine. *Museo Borbonico:* the present-day Museo Nazionale, established in Naples in 1837 by Carlo Borbone, heir of the Farnese family.   *commission . . . Lady Day:* On 3 March 1853 Thackeray had written from America asking the sisters to purchase a lily with two lilies on the stem for Mrs. Brookfield, who had given birth to her second child, Arthur, on 18 March 1853. Lady Day, the Feast of the Annunciation, coincided with Mrs. Brookfield's birthday.   *Hollands:* Henry Edward Fox (1802-59), fourth Baron Holland, and his wife, the former Lady Augusta-Mary Coventry.   *Cravens:* Augustus Craven (d. 1884) and his wife, the former Pauline de la Ferronays.   *Lowthers:* William Lowther (1821-1912), Secretary of the British Legation in Naples, and his wife.

196. TO PAUL ÉMILE DAURAND FORGUES
16 September 1854

36 Onslow Sqre. Brompton. London
September 16.

Dear Forgues.

I have just read the Article in the R. des D. Mondes and am glad to write a line of thanks and good-will to the author, with whom, as I think Pichot has already told you, I have been angry for 3 whole years. In 1851, apropos of my Lectures, you wrote in a French paper published here, that 'I had been praising Addison in order to curry favor with the English aristocracy' or words to that effect. My honour was wounded at the idea that a friend should make such a charge against me;—a critic may like or dislike my books and of course is welcome to his opinion: but he has no right to attribute to me mean motives, or at least I have a right to be angry if he does. The Examiner here and I had a feud upon a similar point—the Examiner saying that I abused the Literary class in order to curry favor with the non-literary public.

And now I will give you the history of my praise of Addison: whom I don't like personally but whose humour I admire with all my heart. More than his humour I admire his conduct through life—Rich or poor he was upright, dignified, honest, a gentleman, a worthy man of letters. He underwent bad fortune with admirable serenity I thought it was right to praise him *as one of our profession*, and leave the reader to make his own moral from what I said.

You see there has long been an absurd outcry made here about neglected men of genius; about the excuses to be made for literary men, they are to get drunk, to bilk their tradesmen, to leave their children without bread &c—poor men of genius! Society is so cruel to them!

Society psha! In our days they have been the authors of their own misfortunes; indulging in bad reckless habits and leading disreputable lives. I have been earning my own bread with my pen for near twenty years now: and sometimes very hardly too, but in the worst times please God, never lost my own respect or my tailor's. By the way that is an error about the Constitutional and our *Refugeedom*. We lost a considerable Sum of money, but we paid all we owed. There was no time when our own Country was ever shut to my family on account of debt: but, having incurred great pecuniary losses, it was pleasanter and more economical to live in Paris than in London: hence our voluntary exile.

The insisting upon the point that men of letters were well treated by English society was an opposition to the contrary Doctrine propounded by 'the Guild of Literature' set whom you notice: and who got up a theatrical entertainment to provide funds for decayed literary men. That project I thought and think unworthy and derogatory to our calling. I do not like to think of our *confrères* painting their faces and grinning in farces for the sake of their oppressed brethren.

If you look at the Dedications of Addison's time you will understand why I called Lord Ashburton 'Right Honorable'—th[ose] bows and ceremonies were a part of the costume: and I am indebted to Lord & Lady Ashburton for the very greatest kindness at a period of the deepest grief and calamity. They knew very well the meaning of that dedication. I have said somewhere it is the unwritten part of books that wd. be the most interesting. Also I knew very well that people would cry out O the sneak! he has dedicated his book to a grand seigneur. If that book ever should come to life again, and I think it may, I should like it to be known that I the writer have received the tenderest obligation from this Lord & Lady.   This is private and *entre nous deux*.

My dear good old Step-father lives at Paris still, and might be hurt at the passage in the Revue indicating that we were refugees for debt; I don't know whether it is worth while contradicting in the Revue.

Meanwhile and at an unconscionable length, I have said my say: and have told you how I was angry & am so no more but

Yours very faithfully dear Forgues
W M Thackeray.

Forgues: Paul Émile Daurand Forgues (1813-83), French writer and translator. *the Article:* "W. M. Thackeray et ses romans," in the 1 September 1854 issue of the *Revue des deux Mondes.*   *Pichot:* Amédée Pichot (1796-1877), French writer and translator.   *my tailor's:* an allusion to the dedicatee of *The Paris Sketch Book,* Thackeray's tailor, M. Aretz.   *confrères:* (Fr.) colleagues.   *called . . .*

'*Right Honorable*': in the dedication to *Esmond*. *indebted:* because Lord and Lady Ashburton helped to bring about a nominal reconciliation between Thackeray and Brookfield in 1852. *I have said somewhere: Pendennis,* ch. 41. *entre nous deux:* (Fr.) between the two of us.

197. TO DR. AND MRS. JOHN BROWN
31 December 1854

December 31. 1854.
Brighton.

My dear Dr. & Mrs. John
    I must send you a word of thanks Sir & Madam for your kind note and beautiful cake and plenty of good wishes and hopes that the next year may bring you more health & happiness than this one I fear has brought any of us.
    I have been constantly unwell myself and when not busy with my work (wh. has been wofully delayed by ill health) so glum & hypochondriacal that I have left off writing to my friends, or even trying to see them very often: for what is the use of spoiling other people's good humour or bothering them about my own ill ones? I can call to mind one or two letters begun to Dr. John, and put in the fire on account of the blue devils that would get on the page. This one will go between the bars too if I dont stop the inveterate habit of grumbling.
    My girls are away at Paris so that the cake wont be eaten before 3 weeks. We have a pretty little cheerful new house at Brompton. Newcomes goes pretty well in spite of the war. I think that is all my news. I am about 100 years older than when I saw you last: and through the mist of ages look back with affection and gratitude to that jolly time at Edinburgh—when don't you remember? I used to grumble too. At Spa I saw that cheery good-natured Mrs. Crowe whom I met at your house: and my first question to her was how is Dr. Scott?—meaning you. Then she told me you were dead, and I was in a dreadful panic; but you are alive & well please God—prosperous, riding about in that fine carriage, taking fees all day, for Jock and his sisters future behoof.
    Blackwood sent me his Magazine with an article wh. pleased me very much, and wh. I think uncommonly friendly and timely. I dont believe Bulwer is the first of that triumvirate the reviewer talks of: I think Dickens is (not that I have read him of late: but thinking back of him I think he is the greatest *genius* of the 3.) But, Sir & Madam, what after all does it matter who is first or third in such a twopenny race? Kindness matters and love and good will, and doing your duty if you can: and leaving a little store for Young Jocks & Ellens, or Annies

& Minnies. May all such be jolly and love their papas & mammas: and we oldsters have as happy a new year as God shall send us.

Farewell & believe me always sincerely and afftly yours

W M Thackeray.

the war: the Crimean War, 1854-56.   *Blackwood:* the publisher, John Blackwood (1818-79).   *an article:* "Mr. Thackeray and his Novels," which appeared in the January 1855 issue of *Blackwood's Edinburgh Magazine.*

198. TO THE REV. JOHN ALLEN
7 February 1855

36 Onslow Sqe. Brompton
Feb 7.

My dear Allen

Thank you for your kind letter, and what you tell me of old friends of old times. My eldest daughter (I have 2) remembers at least the name of May Allen quite well. She is nearly 18 now, the younger one near 15. I shall be very glad indeed if some day the young ones and we old people can meet.   I have just brought my girls back from Paris where they have been staying with my mother; and now they are just set to work with a German Governess & are going to be very industrious for some months I hope: add to wh. Anny is my secretary and about to appear as house-mistress here. The poor dear little wife whom you remember is very well and very cheerful thank God, though cut off for 15 years from husband & children. She does not miss them though: and the care of her serves to maintain a very worthy old couple who treat her with the utmost kindness and watchfulness— so that her illness serves for some good.

The waiter at the Athenæum did not give me your letter till Monday night: and I was full of business all yesterday so that I could not get down to Bedford Row.

You have see the death of Mrs. FitzGerald in the papers? That generation is pretty well died out & the turn of our rank is coming. Of the old cronies I saw Spedding the other day. He looks always the same: as old as 25 years ago: and our dear old E F G. is as good as he was then I think. It's dismal stretching our hands across the gulf of time, isn't it? My dear Allen I always remember you kindly, and am yours and your wife's [. . .]

death of Mrs. FitzGerald: on 30 January 1855.   *[. . .]:* the signature has been cut away.

199. TO GEORGE HENRY LEWES
28 April 1855

London, 28th April, 1855.

Dear Lewes,—I wish I had more to tell you regarding Weimar and Goethe. Five-and-twenty years ago, at least a score of young English lads used to live at Weimar for study, or sport, or society; all of which were to be had in the friendly little Saxon capital. The Grand Duke and Duchess received us with the kindliest hospitality. The Court was splendid, but yet most pleasant and homely. We were invited in our turns to dinners, balls and assemblies there. Such young men as had a right, appeared in uniforms, diplomatic and military. Some, I remember, invented gorgeous clothing: the kind old Hof Marschall of those days, M. de Spiegel (who had two of the most lovely daughters eyes ever looked on), being in nowise difficult as to the admission of these young Englanders. Of the winter nights we used to charter sedan chairs, in which we were carried through the snow to those pleasant Court entertainments. I for my part had the good luck to purchase Schiller's sword, which formed a part of my court costume, and still hangs in my study, and puts me in mind of days of youth the most kindly and delightful.

We knew the whole society of the little city, and but that the young ladies, one and all, spoke admirable English, we surely might have learned the very best German. The society met constantly. The ladies of the Court had their evenings. The theatre was open twice or thrice in the week, where we assembled, a large family party. Goethe had retired from the direction, but the great traditions remained still. The theatre was admirably conducted; and besides the excellent Weimar company, famous actors and singers from various parts of Germany performed *Gastrolle* through the winter. In that winter I remember we had Ludwig Devrient in Shylock, Hamlet, Falstaff, and the *Robbers;* and the beautiful Schröder in *Fidelio.*

After three-and-twenty years absence, I passed a couple of summer days in the well-remembered place, and was fortunate enough to find some of the friends of my youth. Madame de Goethe was there, and received me and my daughters with the kindness of old days. We drank tea in the open air at the famous cottage in the Park, which still belongs to the family, and had been so often inhabited by her illustrious father.

In 1831, though he had retired from the world, Goethe would nevertheless very kindly receive strangers. His daughter-in-law's tea-table was always spread for us. We passed hours after hours there, and night after night with the pleasantest talk and music. We read over endless novels and poems in French, English, and German. My delight in those days was to make caricatures for children. I was touched to find that they were remembered, and some even kept until the present time; and very proud to be told, as a lad, that the great Goethe had looked at some of them.

He remained in his private apartments, where only a very few privileged persons were admitted; but he liked to know all that was happening, and interested himself about all strangers. Whenever a countenance struck his fancy, there was an artist settled in Weimar who made a portrait of it. Goethe had quite a gallery of heads, in black and white, taken by this painter. His house was all over pictures, drawings, casts, statues and medals.

Of course I remember very well the perturbation of spirit with which, as a lad of nineteen, I received the long expected intimation that the Herr Geheimrath would see me on such a morning. This notable audience took place in a little ante-chamber of his private apartments, covered all round with antique casts and bas-reliefs. He was habited in a long grey or drab redingot, with a white neckcloth and a red ribbon in his buttonhole. He kept his hands behind his back, just as in Rauch's statuette. His complexion was very bright, clear and rosy. His eyes extraordinarily dark, piercing and brilliant. I felt quite afraid before them, and recollect comparing them to the eyes of the hero of a certain romance called *Melmoth the Wanderer,* which used to alarm us boys thirty years ago; eyes of an individual who had made a bargain with a Certain Person, and at an extreme old age retained these eyes in all their awful splendour. I fancied Goethe must have been still more handsome as an old man than even in the days of his youth. His voice was very rich and sweet. He asked me questions about myself, which I answered as best I could. I recollect I was at first astonished, and then somewhat relieved, when I found he spoke French with not a good accent.

Vidi tantum. I saw him but three times. Once walking in the garden of his house in the *Frauenplan;* once going to step into his chariot on a sunshiny day, wearing a cap and a cloak with a red collar. He was caressing at the time a beautiful little golden-haired granddaughter, over whose sweet fair face the earth has long since closed too.

Any of us who had books or magazines from England sent them to him, and he examined them eagerly. *Frazer's Magazine* had lately come out, and I remember he was interested in those admirable outline portraits which appeared for awhile in its pages. But there was one, a very ghastly caricature of Mr. Rogers, which, as Madame de Goethe told me, he shut up and put away from him angrily. "They would make me look like that", he said; though in truth I can fancy nothing more serene, majestic, and *healthy* looking than the grand old Goethe.

Though his sun was setting, the sky round about was calm and bright, and that little Weimar illumined by it. In every one of those kind salons the talk was still of Art and letters. The theatre, though possessing no very extraordinary actors, was still conducted with a noble intelligence and order. The actors read books, and were men of letters and gentlemen, holding a not unkindly relationship with the *Adel.* At Court the conversation was exceedingly friendly, simple and polished. The Grand Duchess (the present Grand Duchess Dowager), a lady of very remarkable endowments, would kindly borrow our books from us, lend us her own, and graciously talk to us young men about our literary tastes and pursuits. In the respect paid by this Court to the Patriarch of letters, there was something ennobling, I think, alike to the subject and sovereign. With a five-and-twenty years' experience since those happy days of which I write, and an acquaintance with an immense variety of human kind, I think I have never seen a society more simple, charitable, courteous, gentlemanlike than that of the dear little Saxon city, where the good Schiller and the great Goethe lived and lie buried.

Very sincerely yours,
W. M. Thackeray.

Duchess: Maria Paulowna (1796-1872). *Hof Marschall:* (Ger.) Lord Chamberlain. *daughters:* Melanie (later von Seckendorf) and Louise (later von Eglosstein). *Gastrolle:* (Ger.) guest roles. *Ludwig Devrient:* (1784-1832), German actor noted for his Shakespearean roles. *the Robbers:* Schiller's *Die Räuber* (1781). *the beautiful Schröder:* Wilhelmine Schröder-Devrient (1804-60), soprano. *Madame de Goethe:* Goethe's daughter-in-law, Frau August von Goethe (1786-1859), the former Ottilie von Pogwisch. *Herr Geheimrath:* (Ger.) Privy Counsellor. *redingot:* a double-breasted outer coat. *Rauch:* Christian Daniel Rauch (1777-1857), sculptor. *Melmoth the Wanderer:* (1820) by Charles Robert Maturin (1782-1824). *Vidi tantum:* (Lat.) I only just saw him—said of Vergil by Ovid in *Tristia*, IV, x, 51. *granddaughter:* Alma von Goethe (1827-44). *caricature of Mr. Rogers:* a caricature of Samuel Rogers by Daniel Maclise that had appeared in the September 1830 issue of *Fraser's Magazine.* *Adel:* (Ger.) nobility.

200. TO S. N. ROWLAND
2 May 1855

36 Onslow Sqre. Brompton.
May 2. 1855.

Dear Sir
    I myself represent a branch of the Webb family, and use their crest and arms (wh. are much prettier and more ancient than my own) by right of my paternal grandmother daughter & heiress of Colonel J. Richmond-Webb who lies in Westminster Abbey at this writing.

When I wrote Esmond I thought (for so the tradition was in our family) that I was a lineal descendant of the General—but since have had, & mislaid among my heaps of papers, a pedigree of the Webb's tracing them to Edward I. lineally—but I am sorry to say the General is not in *my* direct line. We branch from a common-ancestor in Charles II's time 2 generations off. This pedigree was compiled by my late uncle the Revd. Francis Thackeray Our Webbs were of Lydiard-Tregoze in Wiltshire. I suppose you know that the General's park at Luggershall was laid out with trees after the plan of Wynendael. He appears to have bragged a great deal about that atchievement wh. was in truth one of the most brilliant and timely actions ever fought by British men.

My memory is the worst in the world and only retains results not details. When I was writing Esmond I read the Marlborough battles very carefully,—a great deal more carefully than Alison who blunders in numerous details—Berwick's, Colbert's memoirs, and the remarkable French collections relative to the war of the Succession, printed in L. Philippes reign—and my impression distinctly was as stated in Esmond that Marlborough who was in treaty to receive a bribe of three millions of crowns for the raising of the siege of Lille— gave information to his nephew the Duke of Berwick of the departure of Webb with the convoy from Ostend, and intended to sacrifice him, wh. he would have done but for the unexpected issue of that brilliant little battle.   The verses about General Webbs personal beauty 'like Paris handsome & like Hector brave' were from a contemporary poem called the battle of Oudenarde, wh. my uncle had; but on wh. I have not been able to lay hands.   Of course you have read in Swifts Journal to Stella what there is about the General, and know the accounts of him in the elderly Biographical Dictionaries—Some writer abused me for my inaccuracy about Webbs regiment of Fusiliers but I took it out of Chamberlayne; and indeed had chapter & verse for every action and movement of the army wh. I narrated. Of course the latter part of the book about the Pretender's coming to England is fabulous, but there was a meeting at Kensington, and there was a famous general to be set up in opposition to Marlborough, and this one I think was most likely John Richmond Webb.

    We appear to have held greatly to this alliance in our family. My father was christian-named Richmond, and one of my uncle's Webb. Sir Richmond Shakespear of the Bengal Artillery my cousin is named after my father, and had I had a son he would have got the same baptismal name wh. is certainly prettier than that family one of
                  Your very faithful Servant
                            William Makepeace Thackeray.

I should be glad to see the General's miniature—My poor Uncle Francis had a so-called portrait of him but I doubt its authenticity.

my paternal grandmother: Amelia Webb (1757-1810), daughter of Colonel John Richmond Webb (1715-85).   *the General:* General John Richmond Webb (1667?-1724).   *Alison . . . Berwick . . . Colbert:* Sir Archibald Alison, *Military Life of John, Duke of Marlborough* (1847); Jacques Fitz-James, Duc de Berwick, *Mémoirs* (1778); Jean Baptiste Colbert, Marquis de Torcy, *Mémoires de M. de ***.*   *French collections:* François Eugène de Vault, ed., *Mémoires militaires relatifs à la Succession d'Èspagne sous Louis XIV,* 11 vols. (Paris, 1835-62).   *a contemporary poem:* an anonymous ballad entitled "The Battle of Audenard."   *Chamberlayne:* Edward Chamberlayne, *Angliæ Notitia, or The Present State of England* (1669).

201. TO WILLIAM RITCHIE
25 May 1855

36 Onslow Square. May 25.
My dear William.   1000 pardons. Your letter came when I was ill abed: then I got up and went to the Derby wh. made me ill again for yesterday—and when ill pen-writing makes me so much worser that I avoid all I can of it. The girls and I will make you and Augusta (to whom in this familiar manner I send my love) as comfortable as we can Your quarters will be awfully narrow, but with a contented mind, why should you not bear them for a brief space? There will be let offs not only on the 31 of May, but on the ensuing day—We find it cheaper to give double-barrelled dinner parties though deucedly unpleasant to give two or one—The house is turned upside down—Frantic knife-cleaning goes on—sham footmen prowl about the premises—My rest is destroyed: Anny has no more head than a

—I wish we might do it au hotel—My mind trembles with fear and fluster even now a week off!—and as soon as I have written this little note (and about 18 more[)] I am going to take a portmanteau into the country somewhere, and stay away for 3 or 4 days and recruit. I asked Wm. Stirling to meet you—but my dinners ain't good enough for him or he is going out of town. But you will see a few small lions, and I hope we shall get on.

At the Derby I was next carriage to Mowbray Morris who looked very languid and handsome drinking champagne and eating venison pie as he lay back in his barouche—I believe it was a very good race. I lost my money though—Sixpence to Sir Edwin Landseer who backed the favorite against the field. What frivolity is this I write! Sir I am not thinking of this but of those 18 other letters wh. I have to produce before I go countrywards. In London there's no affection no leisure no relationship no cordiality nothing but fierce business and then fierce pleasure, and then a spell of illness during wh. one has leisure to think a little. I declare I have quite enjoyed 2 or 3 days this past week wh. kept me in bed though with the most atrocious pains of the inner-man. (I am sure, you see, your wife will read this otherwise I should have used the plumper word.) Well, it will be pleasant to see a great colony of Ritchie's in the Sun shine by the sea-shore (What a row they are making under my windows!)—And O, how I wish those 2 dinner parties were over dont you?

I send my love to all and am always my dear old Wm's
Affectionate
W M T.

He proceeds with the next letter

Sir In reply to your proposal from the Hull Royal Literary Society I regret &c. &c.

Augusta: William Ritchie's wife, the former Augusta Trimmer (1817?-88). They and their two eldest children came on a visit from India in 1855. *Stirling:* William Stirling (1818-78), later Sir William Stirling-Maxwell, art historian.

202. TO MRS. THOMAS FREDERICK ELLIOT AND KATE PERRY
2 July 1855

36 Rue Godot de Mauroy. Paris
July 2.

Mes bonnes Sœurs.

I think it is time you should hear from your elderly relative and as J may be on her way to her holydays and Miss K. I know is in

England. I write my little line to Eaton Place West wishing my very best wishes to all Js & Ks.

We have had a pretty busy pleasant time here: except that as in London & everywhere else there has been a little too much feasting for me too much Burgundy too much Bordeaux. Isn't this hot weather feverish enough without these stirrers of the blood? I have cut off 2 dinners for to day & tomorrow. It is true they would have been very stupid: but it's at those stupid dinners the claret is most dangerous.

Last Thursday the 28th. at 7 o'clock in the evening I wrote the last line of the poor Old Newcomes with a very sad heart. And afterwards what do you think I did? Suppose I said my prayers and humbly prayed God Almighty to bless those I love & who love me, and to help me to see & speak the truth and to do my duty? You wouldn't wonder at that would you? That finis at the end of a book is a solemn word. One need not be Mr. Gibbon of Lausanne to write it. There go 2 years more of my life spent over those pages. I was quite sorry to part with a number of kind people with whom I had been living & talking these 20 months past, & to draw a line so ———— on a sheet of paper, beyond wh. their honest figures couldn't pass, and that melancholy leave taken I went out to dine by myself, and to see a Pantomime over wh. I fell into a sweet roseate slumber. The girls were gone to see the great Italian tragedian the Ristori who was acting Mary Stuart that night but I thought it would be pleasanter to see Clown jump through a window than a Queen have her wicked head chopped off. By the way she is not made wicked in the play. It is Schiller's and she is as pure as alablaster.

I have been twice or thrice to the Exposition des Bosarts. The English pictures show very well indeed I think. One night with Maclise the painter I went to the Chateau des Fleurs wh. inspired him with ravishment & me with mortal melancholy. Crowds were standing round Lais & Phryne dancing the cancan—all sorts of elderly fogies and respectable people. What was Bonneval doing in the Castle of Flowers I should like to know? Venoit il en cueillir le monstre— leaving his own languid lily at home? At Lady Ashburtons next day there was the Duchesse d'Istrie at dinner—beautiful splendid a thought aged & stale—she put me in mind of the handsome wicked chateau des Fleurs. Mérimée came in—its very odd, admiring his writing as I do, what an antipathy I have to him—I had a capital breakfast with honest Jules Janin, who lives up in his cinquieme quite poor & honest & merry—I went moreover to see the Demimonde—It put me in mind of myself rather—it's a comedy of Beckys & Madame de Cruchecassées & the like. It is wonderfully acted—there is a man—M. Dupuis the jeune premier who is quite a pleasure to behold—so easy quiet nonchalant & gentlemanlike is he. And these Mesdames I think have been all my doings—If any of our friends want to hear about them you can say please. God bless all friends. We grow old; we work & struggle on with our days burthens we groan and we laugh and we scheme for next year—and lo the end comes, doesn't it? This letter is not gay Eh! what will you? One is no longer gay at our age: one is content. The girls are very well. Anny is a perfect well-spring of happiness in herself. Thank God. The thought of parting with them for the American expedition disgusts me more & more. Fired with emulation by Dickens's capital speech I have been getting one up—another—but not so good as his though I wonder whether I shall come back to London by next Wednesday week to speak it? I dont know in the least what I'm going to do: but am

      Yours always my dear kind friends   W. M T.

Mr. Gibbon: Edward Gibbon, whose *Memoirs* contain the account of his completing *The Decline and Fall of the Roman Empire* at Lausanne on 27 June 1787.   *Ristori:* Adelaide Ristori (1822-1906), actress.   *Exposition des Bosarts:* (Angl. Fr.) Fine Arts Exhibition.   *Chateau des Fleurs:* (Fr.) Castle of Flowers, a public garden on the Champs Élysées.   *Laïs & Phryne:* famous courtesans in ancient Greece.   *Bonneval:* Count Lionel de Bonneval.   *Venoit il en cueillir le monstre:* (Fr.) Did he come to pluck a lot of flowers, the monster?   *lily at home:* the former Caroline Gallwey, wife of Count de Bonneval.   *Duchesse d'Istrie:* wife of Napoléon Bessières (b. 1802), Duc d'Istrie.   *Mérimée:* Prosper Mérimée (1803-70), French novelist.   *cinquieme:* (Fr.) fifth floor room—i. e. garret.   *Demimonde: Le Demi-Monde* (1855), a comedy by Alexandre Dumas *fils* (1824-95).   *Dupuis:* Adolphe Dupuis (1825-91), French actor.   *jeune premier:* (Fr.) young leading man.   *Dickens's capital speech:* given on 27 June 1855 at a meeting of the Administrative Reform Association.

203. TO HIS FAMILY
30-31 October 1855

Clarendon Hotel New York. Tuesday Wednesday 30.31.

  Only time for another scrap to my dearest old mother and daughters haven't had time to take even a walk in New York—been busy all day until late at night getting lectures ready—arrived at Boston on Thursday night, found the good Baxters there to welcome me—a score more friends very glad to see me, a sincere pleasure on my own part at seeing again these friendly people, a great growth of reputation, a chance that the ensuing lectures will be as profitable as the last—came to New York on Saturday night to the same rooms—have turned the sitting room into a bed room, dress in adjoining bed room, where

Charles sleeps within call and where he copies the lectures all the morning in the most beautiful hand-writing as dear as print. How glad I am I brought him.   If health holds out I shall repeat the lectures 4 times in and about New York before 1 December Go to Boston for a fortnight then—then to the West (I think its the West—Buffalo Chicago Cincinnati St. Louis doose knows where—the gentlemen here are to make out a plan of campaign for me—the various societies will take the business part in their hands, & D. V. will be a little richer. The compliments somebody gets on all hands would please some ladies—one touched me yesterday. Dr. Kane the tremendous Arctic traveller has just come back—and says that he saw one of his seamen in one of the eternal nights crouched over a book for hours and hours and behold it was Pendennis. Shant have any time for dining out after this week—so much the better—where I was yesterday with American fashionable folks (a pretty little heiress with nearly a million of money of her own)—I was disgusted with their confounded vulgarity My dear old Mrs. Baxter is a fine lady though— on the day I left New York I had certain brandy peaches out of a bottle of wh. I very much approved—On Sunday at dinner the good soul brings out the bottle with the rest of the peaches untouched Lucy is just as nice & pretty—Sally is not improved She has been awfully flattered since I went away and O Minny! What do you think Shes going to be—to be—mum mum—married!—wh. I don't envy the young man—who they say is a fine fellow.   And I think this is all my news—& I am waiting for Sam Ward who is to breakfast with me; and I feel as much at home here almost as at Brompton. At Boston saw the Stones and Mrs. Shawe who is coming on here. Why didn't I bring the daughters? says every body I'm sure they would have been most kindly entertained—but that passage is nasty sicky stinky—They would have to meet people I shouldnt want them to know. They are better in quiet with G P and Granny—And when the summer comes, o ye gracious powers what a good time we'll have! The sky here is as fine as the finest Eyetalian the City has grown immensely. All the seats for the lectures are taken—What the deuce do the people mean? What more news have I to send—only the sta[l]e news that I am my dearest old Mother's and G Ps and Annyminnyamylira's

W M T.

   Go on writing here till further horders please.
   Wednesday mg. early. Its such a bright sky, and sunrise I cant sleep here more than 6 or 7 hours—the air is wondrous keen & exhilarating. I write a parting kiss to send by the mail wh. goes to day. had a very pleasant dinner with S. Ward & a party at Delmonico's— came home late and o had an awful escape—tremble when I think of it. Took my key at the bar entered my apartment and began

straightway to pull off boots &c &c—when a sweet female voice from the room within igsclaimed 'Georgy!' I had gone into the second floor room instead of the third. I gathered my raiment about me and dashed out of the premises. The welcome and friendliness of this people is surprizing & touching—thats all I have to say this last of October morning to my dear ones across the ocean. I'm glad I came. I wish you all as well & as happy as I am—God bless you again old & young.

Charles: Charles Pearman, Thackeray's man-servant. *Dr. Kane:* Elisha Kane (1820-57). *the young man:* Frank Hampton (1829-63). *Sam Ward:* (1814-84), financier and lobbyist. *Amy:* Amy Crowe (1831-65), later Mrs. Edward Thackeray, a companion to Thackeray's daughters.

204. TO MRS. HENRY CARMICHAEL-SMYTH
16?-20 November 1855

In both visits to America I have found the effects of the air here the same. I have a difficulty in forming the letters as I write them down on this page—in answering questions, in finding the most simple words to form the answers. A gentleman asked me how long I had been in New York—I hesitated and then said a week—I had arrived the day before—I could not gather my thoughts together readily enough to be able to reply to him—hardly know what is said am thinking of something else nothing definite, with an irrepressible longing to be in motion. I sleep 3 hours less than in England, making up however with a heavy long sleep every 4th. night or so. Talking yesterday with a very clever man (T Appleton of Boston) he says the effect upon him on his return from Europe is the same—There is some electric influence in the air & sun here wh. we dont experience on our side of the globe. Under this Sun people cant sit still people can't ruminate over their dinners dawdle in their studies and be lazy and tranquil—they must keep moving, rush from one activity to another, jump out of sleep and to their business, have lean eager faces—I want to dash into the street now. At home after breakfast I want to read my paper leisurely and then get to my books and work. The men here read surprizingly—one tells me, a busy man keeping a great Store in the City, that he does all his reading in the railway-cars as he comes in & out from his country residence daily. Fancy an English City Grocer reading Tennyson & Browning on his way from Brighton to Bread Street every day! A look over the Times, a snooze for the rest of the journey wd. be enough for him. Yesterday as some rain began to fall, I felt a leaden cap taken off my brain pan and began to speak calmly and reasonably, & not wish to quit my place.

We were going a party of 4 to dine with Mr. Dening Duer banker—a most kind worthy man. We crossed at the Ferry whence the Liverpool steamers sail (I had my wishes as I saw one there in the dock)—the pavement is infernal—disgraceful to a great city: the steam ferry boat admirably commodious—every body has described the steam ferry boats. We drove through a part of Jersey City—a great raw comfortless city it is, and presently through the grounds of Mr. Kings country place, wh. are famous for their beauty. A fine thunderstorm darkened the place as we passed it and a hurricane blew for a minute—I could only see in the grounds very lean spindle shanked little trees with their naked branches shivering—About Mr. Duers house were the same scrubby melancholy bushes. I had been looking at sketches (by an excellent artist Kensett) all in the morning of New England wood & sea-shore scenery—and the character of them seemed to me scraggy wan melancholy like an American beauty at 35. I like the English style best from habit and education—a great buxom elm tree, a jolly green sward, a fair sonsy lady of what age shall we say?—better than these lean trees haggard landscapes and shrivelled matrons. That woman a beauty but a few years since! (I am thinking of one I saw lately with her children) the sight of her was a pitiable satire—a hundred thousand crows had left marks in her yellow face—they croaked in her voice. Her daughter a beautiful young creature of 17 had already begun to lose her bloom— Some pretty friends of mine and their parents have been more fortunate—I see no change in their kind faces since last I looked at them 3 years since.

I went to see Lawrence who is doing very well. It does me good says he to see an English coat—I understand the home feeling. An English servant maid opened the door at a friends house yesterday & spoke in her kind modest way—My man complains sadly that no one will speak a civil word to him—those polite accents wh. we remember in Ireland from the people, are changed here to a brusque sharp nasal defiant tone—not sweet to listen to. Looking for my companion the other day as we arrived from Boston through a line of several cars—the cars set off in motion down the Street, and I begged the driver to let me out he began through his nose a shrill blast of curses quite curious to hear—he was only squealing the steam off. Thar! now! Jomp farrerd says he not unkindly and I jumped and ran back to the Station.

Saturday 17. Dined with Mr. C. King—President of Columbia College—son of a minister to England—man of fortune once as some of his brothers still are. then unlucky—Editor of 'the American' newspaper—now College President lively amusing bright well-read English accent thorough gentleman of the old school—very few like him. Was at school at Harrow with Peel & Byron.—spoke still in admiration of Byrons pluck. Harrow challenged Eton to a match at cricket. Eton wh. had just been playing Westminster refused Harrow saying that 'Eton only played matches with schools of royal foundation'.—[']I am not good at cricket['] said Byron, alluding to his foot: [']but if you will get up an Eleven to fight an Eton eleven I should like to be one of our's. Peel a lazy boy not mingling in games at all was very good-natured. The boys would crowd round him before going into school begging Peel to do their verses—Greek Iambics or Latin Hexameters, nothing came amiss to him, and he wd. scribble off copy after copy of verses for the idle or dull ones. He was celebrated as a 'Shy'—his pleasure was to walk the fields solitary with a pocket-full of nice round stones; and, if he saw a bird on a bough, to fire at it; and his skill was such as to bring down one bird in three—he would bring home strings of little birds with him. Byron would have been good-looking but his complexion was tallowy and his black hair had a greasy look.

Novr. 20 N. Y.

This is not very good fun is it? I dont know that it's worth keeping a journal but I think I shall go on—got my dear old Mothers letter & am thankful all are so well & busy. No of course Anny wont go out without a friend except to very intimate homely people. Poor Amy's case I pity, & dont advise on. The lectures go better & better; the lecturer very well—God bless all at home he says and o but he longs to be there! Havent been able to write this mg for the visitors pouring in.

W M T.

Appleton: Thomas Gold Appleton (1812-84), wit and miscellaneous writer. *Duer:* William Denning Duer (b. 1812). *Kings country place:* Charles King (1789-1867), President of Columbia College 1849-64, had an estate in Elizabethtown, New Jersey. *Kensett:* John Frederick Kensett (1816-72), landscape painter and engraver. *sonsy:* buxom, comely, and pleasant. *Lawrence:* the English painter, Samuel Laurence. *minister to England:* Rufus King (1755-1827). *'the American':* The New York American, which King had edited 1823-45.

205. TO MRS. GEORGE BAXTER AND SARAH BAXTER
11 December 1855

Tremont. 11 Decr.

My dear Friend. I feel as if I was doing wrong though I am doing right. I lay awake for hours that night when Baxter said he wished me to come to N. Y. for tomorrow, & thought of your kindness & regard and that I ought & wd. do any thing to please you. But an engagement was made for me here for Wednesday evening—another on Thursday. Ought a man with a chill & fever on him to break a contract, travel 9 hours & 9 hours next day to see a pretty lass made happy? You would be more angry if I were ill than I should be myself: and I think the chances were against my well-ness if I had done those 2 journies—After four hours I am feverish anxious and obliged to lie down. No. My duty was to stay away. I heartily pray God bless Sarah and make her happy. I heard such a fine character of her husband from Mrs. Perkins yesterday. *She* Mrs. P. was so changed improved *happyfied* by her marriage that it did one good to see her. May your girl be so too. I know your heart & time are full & send only a shake of the hand & the kindest kindest wishes for you all from

                                        W M T.

    My dear Sarah. I must not come: but say with all my heart God bless you and your husband. I hope he will be my friend & that I always may be

                            affectionately yours
                              W M Thackeray.

made happy: Sarah Baxter was married to Frank Hampton on 12 December 1855.

206. TO HIS FAMILY
18 December 1855

                                  Decr. 18. Boston.
          Continue to address care of Ticknor & Fields here.
    At last has come the hand writing of my dearest women & Granny, and I know (what I have never for one moment made myself uncomfortable about) that they are all well and jolly and busy—And I have come back from Providence to day, and have wrote other 5 letters, and have had other 10 visitors, and have read little Dorrit in the cars: and have dined at 3 o'clock and feel a trifle apoplectic but must scribble on as I have to lecture to night and afterwards to go to Edy Story's childs party where I suspect a delightful surprize is in store for me—of little children acting Giglio & Bulbo though of course I know nothing about it. The lecturing is no part of the hardship of this business: it is the suppers & representation afterwards wh. must be done—Next Monday I leave this kind place spend Xmas at Troy, go

to Buffalo where I daresay I shant see Niagara after all, & then shall go to New York for a day, to Philadelphia & Southward—perhaps to New Orleans—most probably—working up the Mississippi in March to Saint Louis—lecturing at Cincinnati & Western Places arterwards and finding myself back hereabouts in April—May—that is, if health endures, but Lord bless us who can count on tomorrow? Last week I was obliged to give up a lecture on account not of shiver & shakes but my old friend—not a bad attack of him—I think I rather enjoyed a mild stomach-ache and 2 days of quiet in bed; reading the Life of Goethe that old rogue—he had an unnappy attachment at 75 and the young lady who shared it was *sent back to school;* let us hope the poor young people both consoled themselves.   Sally Baxter's marriage went off very smartly on the 12th. & I hope she will get over *her* passion for an old fogey who shall be nameless—It began to be a newsance at last to the old party, & very likely to the young one. My girls I suppose must undergo the common lot; but I hope they wont Sallify—Indulge *in amours de tête* I mean. Indeed I dont like to think of their entering into that business at all unless upon good reasonable steady grounds—with a Tomkins who is likely to make them happy and has enough to keep them—and who above all falls in love with them first—for Say he is the best of young fellows but cannot keep himself—who is to do it?—the old father to keep the family?—that wouldn't be generous nor fair. No my dearest old Fat you mustnt hanker after a penniless young clergyman with one lung. It is as much as I can do to scrape together enough to keep my 3 daughters (your mother being one): and you must no more think about a penniless husband, than I can think about striking work—these luxuries do not belong to our station. Besides has he ever thought about you? Girls are romantic, visionary, love beautiful whiskers & so forth—but every time a girl permits herself to *think* an advance of this sort she hurts herself—loses somewhat of her dignity, rubs off a little of her maiden-bloom. Keep yours on your cheeks till 50 if necessary. Creyke has nothing—an incurable illness—& all the habits of a rich man—his illness prevents him from earning (I'm very fond of him you know & think him a fine fellow)—but you might as well ask me to give you a diamond necklace as to accom[m]odate you with this luxury of a husband, of little darlings, of bills to pay, house to keep &c &c—You must marry a man that can keep you—and you've just pitched precisely on the gentleman that cannot. I dont say banish him from your mind—perhaps it is a fatal pashn ravaging your young bussom—perhaps only a fancy wh. has left already a head that has taken in a deal of novels—but settle it in your mind that it would be just as right for you to marry Charles Pearman (what do I say? Charles is healthy & can make his 40£ a year) as poor Creyke—and so despair & peridge, or resume your victuals and be jolly—determining that this thing never can be. Don't you suppose everybody in life wants something he cant get? Sorry we can't give you this Tomkins—Good bye Tomkins—God bless my dearest old Fat.

I write to Lubbock to send G P. 100£—to night is the last lecture here. Yesterday for a moment I did not remember the No. of the house in Onslow Square—Suppose my brains fail and I cant work who's to take charge of me?—let's work whilst we can and gather up our modest little harvest whilst the sun yet shines. God bless my dearest Granny & G P, & my dearest Children and see us all together sometime in the happy New Year

W M T.

little Dorrit: Number 1, for December 1855, of Dickens' novel (1856-57). *Edy Story:* Edith Story, daughter of William Wetmore Story. *Giglio & Bulbo:* characters in Thackeray's Christmas book for 1854, *The Rose and the Ring,* which he had read to Edith Story in Rome from the manuscript. *the Life: The Life and Works of Goethe* (1855) by George Henry Lewes, who identifies the young lady as Minna Herzlieb. *amours de tête:* (Fr.) loves of the head (not the heart).

207. TO MRS. GEORGE TICKNOR
13 January 1856

Washington. Jan 13. 1856.

My dear Mrs. Ticknor. I dont know why I feel a particular desire to shake you by the hand this morning. I have nothing funny or pleasant to say: I ought to be at Church; but how my dear Madam could I go through the snow and slush, when there are no coaches out and people fall and break their legs + ? Nothing has happened to me except that I am getting more and more weary of that lecturing: and if I were at Boston on Wednesday morning next, I dont know what I might not be tempted to do—It will end that way I am sure. Outraged nature will revolt and jump on board ship and say have done with this quackery. I have had a pleasant and profitable time at Buffalo: at Philadelphia: at Baltimore the weather was almost too bad and the counter-attraction of an opera for 2 nights drew off no doubt a portion of my audience. One day that of the New Year I spent in N. York (mournfully revisiting the cari luoghi from wh. *Somebody* went forth to her Southern home)—I have not been snowed up, but missed that excitement, happily by a day—came on yesterday to shake hands with old friends here—dined with Mr. Crampton and met Chas Sumner and 'How do you do Mrs Ticknor that is all I have to say.' (v. Lecture II. page 30) I have read Prescotts 2 volumes and Macaulays third. I think the latter's hand is a little languid, dont you? I should have liked the guns to roar louder at the battle of the Boyne: but they banged away very pleasantly, and o what a howl there will be amongst the Irishry at his account of them their King their bravery and their behaviour! Talking at dinner at Crampton's yesterday we agreed that Prescott's was the pleasantest book to read through—It is a shame of these historians taking the bread out of the mouths of us *other* romancers. Give me Hallam—*he* does not degrade history by making her amusing. He is an author that should be in every library as the critics say—and never taken down. Dear kind old Mr. Hallam! I little thought when I began this note I should be making flippant remarks about him!   My mourning for Rogers has not yet come home, and I bear up as well as I can. Often & often I think of Walter Scott whom I first learned to know in Mr. Ticknors library Boston. Mass. I wish I was there now.

Although this is nonsense—yet my dear Mrs. Ticknor, it is meant in very good part. If you are kind to me, can I help feeling pleased? If Burgundy is grateful to me, ought I not to be grateful for Burgundy? They give us too much white wine here—a great deal too much white wine—I like old ways and good old Boston houses—with good old cellars and old talk afterwards. Mr. Ticknor Sir, I drink your health Sir, and Mrs. Ticknor's, and the young ladies, and the gentleman on your dexter hand Sir. I have not the least idea where I am going after Baltimore tomorrow, and Richmond Va subsequently, but wherever I am, it is certain I shall be yours my dear Mrs. Ticknor

very truly
W M Thackeray.

+ I beg pardon for this unguarded expression.

cari luoghi: (Ital.) dear places.   *Somebody . . . home:* Sarah Baxter Hampton, who had gone to her husband's home in South Carolina.   *Crampton:* John (later Sir John) Fiennes Twisleton Crampton (1805-86), British Minister to the United States.   *Sumner:* Charles Sumner (1811-74), American political figure.   '*How . . . say*': an allusion to Thackeray's lecture on George II, where he quotes from one of the letters addressed by Mary Bellenden to Henrietta Howard, Countess of Suffolk: "How do you do, Mrs. Howard? that is all I have to say."   *Prescotts 2 volumes and Macaulays:* the American historian, William Hickling Prescott's (1796-1859) *A History of the Reign of Philip the Second*, the first two volumes of which had been published in 1855, and Macaulay's *The History of England from the Accession of James II*, volumes 3 and 4 of which had been published in 1855.   *Hallam:* Henry Hallam, best known for *The Constitutional History of England* (1827).   *Rogers:* Samuel Rogers had died on 18 December 1855.   *young*

208. TO KATE PERRY
14-16 February 1856

Savannah, Georgia,—
Feast of St. Valentine.

This welcome day brought me a nice long letter from K. E. P., and she must know that I write from the most comfortable quarters I have ever had in the United States—in a tranquil old city wide streeted tree planted with a few cows and carriages toiling through the sandy road, a few happy negroes sauntering here and there; a red river with a tranquil little fleet of merchantmen taking in cargo; and tranquil warehouses barricaded with packs of cotton—no row, no tearing Northern bustle no ceaseless hotel racket, no spitting in the hall, no crowds drinking at the bar—a snug little languid audience of 3 or 400 people far too lazy to laugh or applaud; a famous good dinner breakfast &c—and leisure all the morning to think and do and sleep and read as I like—THE ONLY place I say in the States where I can get these comforts, all free gratis in the house of my friend Andrew Low of the great house of A Low & Co. Cotton dealers, brokers, merchants, whats the word? Last time I was here he was a widower with 2 daughters in England about whom & other 2 daughters there was endless talk between us. Now there is a pretty wife added to the establishment and a little daughter no 3 crowing in the adjoining nursery. They are tremendous men these cotton merchants—for one summer he says during 6 weeks he calculated he was [...] room & snug bath-room such as I have not enjoyed this many a day. What an awfully stupid letter that was I wrote to J E from Charleston last week! I was bored to death there even though Sally B—whom you love was in the house. O me! since she has left off making love to me I no more care for her than for the Queen of Sheba—nor for any one else of the race of women excep 6. 3 in Paris & 3 in London town.

When I had finished at Charleston I went off to a queer little rustic city called Augusta—a great broad street 2 miles long—old quaint looking shops, houses with galleries, warehouses—trees—cows and negroes strolling about the side walks, plank roads, a happy dirty tranquillity generally prevalent—It lies 135 miles from Charleston. You take 8 1/2 hours to get there by the railway—about same time and distance to come here over endless plains of swampy pine-lands—a village or 2 here & there in a clearing—I brought away a snug little purse from snug little Augusta—though I had a rival a wild man lecturing in the very same hall. I tell you it is not a dignified métier that wh. I pursue. What is this about the Saturday Review? After giving V. Harcourt 2/6 to send me the 5 first numbers and only getting No 1, it is too bad they should assault me, and for what? My lecture is rather extra-loyal whenever the Queen is mentioned, and the most applauded passage in them I shall have the honor of delivering to night in the lecture on George II where the speaker says, 'In laughing at these old world follies and ceremonies shall we not acknowledge the change of to day? As the mistress of St. James's passes me now, I salute the Sovereign wise moderate exemplary of life, the good mother, the good wife, the accomplished lady, the enlightened friend of art, the tender Sympathizer in her people's glories and sorrows' Whack Whack Whack—I can't say more, can I? And as for George III I leave off with the people just on the crying point. And I never for one minute should think that my brave old Venable would hit me, or if he did that he hadn't good cause for it.   Forsters placification delights me. It's right that men of such ability and merit should get Government recognition and honorable public employ. It is a compliment to all of us when one receives such promotion. As for me I have pestered you with my account of dollars and cents; and it is quite clear that kings or laws cannot do anything as well for me as these jaws & this pen, please God they are allowed to wag a little longer. I wish I did not read about your illness and weakness in that letter. Ah me many and many a time every day do I think of you all. As I go this journey, I remember other thoughts scattered along the journey 3 years ago; & griefs wh. used to make me wild and fierce, and wh. are now sweet and bearable. We get out of the stormy region of longing passion unfulfilled—we dont love any the less—please God—Let the young folks step in and play the game of tears & hearts. We have played our game: and we have lost. And at 45 we smoke our pipes and clear the drawing room for the sports of the young ones.— All except young Sir Erskine of course, over whose hymeneal path may the fresh roses be scattered. Enter a Servant (black) with the card of Bishop Elliott with two T's. Elliot & T—o shouldn't I like 'em both! If you are taking a drive some day do go and pay a visit of charity to my good Cook and Housekeeper Gray and say you have heard of me and that I am very well and making plenty of money & that Charles is well and the greatest comfort to me—it will comfort the poor woman all alone in poor 36 yonder. What charming letters Anny writes me! a little loose & straggling in expression, but with exquisite pretty turns now & then. St. Valentine brought me a delightful letter from her too, & from the dear old mother—and, and whether its the comfort of this house or the pleasure of having an hours chat with you, or the sweet clean bed I had last night and undisturbed rest and good breakfast—Altogether I think I have no right to grumble at my lot and am very decently happy, don't you?

16 Feb. My course is for Macon Montgomery & New Orleans No Havannah, the dollars forbid. From N O. I shall go up Mississippi D V. to St. Louis & Cincinnati and ye who write will address care of

J. G. King's Sons New York—Wont you? And so God bless 3 women in Belgravia says your affte

WMT.

Andrew Low: (1812?-86), a wealthy Savannah merchant. *[...]:* a portion of text is missing from the original. *métier:* (Fr.) trade, profession. *Harcourt:* Vernon Harcourt (1827-1904), a journalist, lawyer, and political figure. *assault me... Venables:* although George Stovin Venables wrote for *The Saturday Review,* its article of 15 December 1855 attacking Thackeray's lecture on George IV on the basis of American newspaper reviews was written by Henry Sumner Maine. *Forster's placification:* his recent appointment as Secretary to the Commissioners of Lunacy. *kings or laws:* a reminiscence of Samuel Johnson's couplet in Goldsmith's *The Traveller:* "How small, of all that human hearts endure, / That part which laws or kings can cause or cure!" *Sir Erskine:* Sir Thomas Erskine Perry, Miss Perry's brother, who on 6 June 1855 had married as his second wife Elizabeth Margaret Van den Bempde-Johnstone. *Bishop Elliott:* Stephen Elliott (1806-66), Episcopal Bishop of Georgia.

209. TO MRS. THOMAS FREDERICK ELLIOT AND KATE PERRY
10 March 1856

New Orleans. March 10.

Though letters are stupid parties in England are kind. There is a party whose birthday will happen about 4 days before this letter reaches Chesham Place—to whom I pray God to send happier birthdays than she has had for some years past: and who will please, when the intelligence of the arrival of this letter is brought to her, will please to imagine me safe at the City of St. Louis only about a thousand miles from N. York, and thinking that the time for going home is drawing very near. I wish I had gone to Cuba instead of pursuing this ignoble dollar-hunting in the languid dreary Southern towns between here &

Savannah This is a picture of 1000 miles of railway that I have passed over—pines marshes—flats—flats pines marshes—wretched huts now and again with squalid negroes sauntering about or holding up great pine torches as we pass through the dreary darkness at 12 miles an hour. Then I had 3 days up the Alabama from Montgomery to

Mobile—o dreary yellow river! o dingy companions of my travels—o you knife swallowers—o you bl-w-rs-of-n-s-s in f-ng-rs! o hair brush hung up for the use of the whole company of passengers! what an odd dirty scene it was—with dark troops of slaves landing here and there and marching up the dismal bank into the dingy wilderness beyond: with planters waiting to come on board with their cotton bales with starved ragged planters houses shuddering upon the steep river sides with darkies bearing turkies for sale with ague stricken woodmen at whose wharves we stop and take in pine wood—Somehow I cant write a descriptive letter any more—If Anny were here I could dictate one, but to sit down and describe scenery to ones friends seems trifling and hypocritical doesn't it? *We* never have any useful conversation when we meet, do we? We talk nonsense or about each others pains & aches or &c &c &c dont we? Other people have other tastes and gifts, but didactic friendship I dont value.

Mobile was very pleasant with an admirable clean hotel and pleasant folks to fall among. This is pleasant too—like Europe in part—vast varied busy picturesque—but I am fallen into a very kind hospitable dreadfully stupid set of cotton merchants, who dine me every day when I could be much better off at the hotel, and force me to eat and drink far more than is good for me. Yesterday I crossed the great river, and had a long Sunday walk. I spend great sums among the negro children, who have an imp like beauty that somehow touches & amuses me—I saw a negro praying in a hut—another negro—but haven't I told all this to the girls in another letter, and is it worth the repetition? If I could but wait till Wednesday there would be something to tell—As I came from breakfast, I saw a card dangling from a lamp opposite the Ladies' Drawing room with the announcement 'Hop on Wednesday'

Here comes in a famous letter from dear girls who say they have had such a kind letter from Chesham Place, and I wish that I had one too. Did I tell you to direct care of Messrs. J. G. King's Sons New York? Perhaps it is to the Clarendon you are writing. And Madams, the sight of your hand writing is good for these eyes. Mayn't any one else write even a single line? God bless her. Do you know what I augur from that silence? Can you guess? We won't go on—We see 3 ladies looking at each other—We see 2 smiling—We see one hanging down her head—We wish we could see them all now. Do you still go on listening faithfully to the Inspectoral sermons? My poor old friend my heart feels very gentle towards him at times—......

Now I daresay you know that I have laid the pen down and been thinking ever so many thousand miles away, and ever so many years back. This has been but a dull letter, mes bonnes sœurs—I think I say that always dont I? We don't get amusinger as we get older, we grow prosy and repeat ourselves and talk about our complaints and selfish grievances: but our old friends bear up with our dullness for old times' sake; and we go and get sober cups of tea with them, and potter and prattle; &, dull as we are, they like us—and we don't care for making any new friends, and for young amusements or companions or conversations We remember that we are nearly five and forty years old. We care for no woman under thirty, except our daughters, & we like the sober grey-headed twilighty kind of life pretty well. At least it befits our age and we can't, though we would choose, take another. Good bye Lowndes Square and Chesham Place and ye lodgings wheresoever ye are! Why in the month after next I shall be on my way to see you. Come quickly month after next says Yours

W M T.

210. TO MRS. THOMAS FREDERICK ELLIOT AND KATE PERRY
24-26 March 1856

Cairo. St. Louis. March 24-26.
I did not write to you from New Orleans, but a pleasanter thing I heard from mes bonnes sœurs, and what you said about Higgins melted my heart so that I wrote straightway off to him as kind and good willing a letter as I could in hopes of softening that wayward generous touchy soul. We cant at our age ladies make many more friendships, and I don't want to lose any that remain to me. I wish to God we were reconciled for all the harm I've said of him does not amount to 1/4 and he owes me 10000£ of kind words and grateful feelings—I had a pretty pleasant time at New Orleans a deal too much pleasure dinner parties every day in a society that might as well have been at Liverpool—all cotton brokers—the talk all about wine and the passages in ships, each man outdoing the other in the splendor of his entertainment—I had 3 distinct bottles of brandy sent me for my voyage up the Mississippi and a dozen of claret wh. latter I was forced to bring and presented 9 bottles wh. I could not drink to the black waiters on board the Thomas Small Steamer.   I am just off the Thomas Small steamer Dont you see how my hand trembles? The boat in her passage up the river throbbed and trembled so that I thought she would shake her cranky sides off her ribs. And the river or the trembling of the boat gave me a fit of my old chill and fever wh. served pour passer le temps and occupied one day out of the 5. 'Look there Sir!' says a cheerful friend of mine on the Levee at N. O. as we looked at a hundred enormous steamers moored there—

[']There aft the White Mansion do you see? that post was knocked out by a piece of the boiler of the John Jones wh. burst here Sir—here on this spot where we are standing—and the heads and mangled limbs of the people were scattered and a mule by G— Sir was cut in two in a dray and I saw it lying where you stand now!' The morning I came away I read that a ferry steamer had taken fire on the Delaware and 25 persons were killed—that the Alabama steamer on the Red River had bursted her boilers & afterwards taken fire the number of the killed not known—pleasant wasn't it? for a man just setting out on a river journey—but its over and we didnt blow up and we only took fire twice and burned down our upper cook house and 2 hours ago I was quite sorry to leave the T. Small. She was very clean and the servants civil and I had Marryatt's novels wh. kept me in amusement through Alabama & Mississippi too. He is a vulgar dog but he makes me laugh and very few can now. Certainly not your's truly the author of Vanity Fair.

Where do you think this is written from? the place they say that was Martin Chuzzlewit's Eden Cairo at the confluence of the Ohio & Miss. such a dreary Heaven abandoned place! but it will be a great city in 5 years spite of overflows and fever and ague—Twelve hours to night DV will take me to St. Louis and then I shall feel as if I am on my road home again to see my children and my bonnes sœurs.

I thought the chill was coming on again and went for some whiskey to the bar—it is 2 feet below the level of the ground wh. appears to me to be 7 or so below the level of the water—A man with a pipe in his mouth looks into the room from the street spits into the *former* and walks away. I lay down my book in the boat a man walks up takes the book spits reads lays down the book spits again at me and

rises. And to see the pocket handkerchiefs! I mean these

—and the knives down the throats—by Heavens at the ladies' table yesterday every single woman had her knife down her throat (we all have to stand and clutch hold of our chairs until the ladies are seated if you please)—and a poor Giantess who was going to show at Memphis & dined by herself—I looked at her and she was putting her knife down her poor old throat too. Besides we had the whiskered lady on board, the Swiss warbler (a man so called because he imitates animals) 2 actors, a choctaw chief a mad woman screaming & calling to people from her stateroom a gentleman from the deck with delirium tremens who made incursions into the cabin with his coat off—If I had been young as once I was I could have made some fun out of these people or if I had the sperrits wh. once I had—but the sperrits is not strong in my old bottle: & there are very few laughs left in me. Spite of kindness everywhere pleasant people now and again and dollars in sufficiency this Southern country is hardly bearable to me. Why need I go on making a quack of myself any more? But if when I come home after speaking of Queen Vic in the very handsomest manner after making thousands of folks that hated him feel kindly for old George I am attacked for speaking my mind about George IV (mind I left out the Q. Caroline scandal entirely)—by Jupiter!—It will do me good. I want a fight, I have always told you I can hit harder than any man alive, and I never do—but o! I think a little exercise would do me good!—And now I have got some money—enough to keep me almost—you cant think what a grand independence I feel. A man with 10000 readers and 500£ a year is a puissance, quoi! Well, it would be good fun wouldn't it a fight, and warm up my sluggish old blood.

I wrote didnt I? how this country whiggifies me. The rabble supremacy turns my gorge. The gentlemen stand aloof from public affairs, and count no more than yonder Irish bog trotter who is driving a pig before the window or those two illiterate blaspheming ruffians who were cutting their gums with their penknives in the bar—I couldn't bear to live in a country at this stage of its political existence—In fine I want to get home more and more every day. To do what? to dawdle about Europe again and write another novel?—Who can say for tomorrow? But I want to kiss my dear children and see my bonnes sœurs and speak to people whom I *can* speak to. Two months more of the *tréteaux* and mayn't we hope for these things? Yes if winds and waves and Heaven permit I wonder after being how many whole weeks in London I shall want to be on the move again? God bless you I keep this little piece for tomorrow and this is the 24 of March and isn't tomorrow my lady's day?

St. Louis. Mo.

26. Although it was my ladys day I didnt fill the corner: but each day near and far away I love and bless and mourn her. Upon my lady's Eve the cars a weary wight did carry He wakeful looked upon the stars the pine wood and the prairie. And as the weary travel ceased the sun arose in splendor And sure he looked towards the East where dwells his lady tender He blessed the East he blessed the morn (methinks 'twas midday yonder) That saw his gentle lady born—and O me! I couldnt finish the rhyme havent I had 10 visitors? and isnt it post time now and mustnt I put up with a kind kind greeting to mes bonnes sœurs.

---

pour passer le temps: (Fr.) to pass the time.   *puissance, quoi!:* (Fr.) a power, what!   *tréteaux:* (Fr.) mountebank's stage.

211. TO WILLIAM DUER ROBINSON
7-9 May 1856

On board last day. May 7. 1856.
My dear old Robinson I tell you that writing is just as dismal and disgusting as saying good bye—I hate it and but for a sense of duty I wouldn't write at all—confound me if I would. But you know after a fellow has been so uncommonly hospitable and kind and that sort of thing—a fellow ought you see to write and tell a fellow that a fellow's very much obliged and—in a word you understand. Sir you made me happy when I was with you you made me sorry to come away and you make me happy now when I think what a kind generous friendly W D R you are. You have Davis back in the Bower of Virtue—you'll fill that jug one day and drink to my health wont you? And when you come to Europe you'll come to me & my girls mind, and we'll see if there is not some good claret at 36 Onslow Square.

Your neighbour's tinkering has lasted me through the voyage: and I propose to set to work straightway and get my water pipes cistern &c in complete order—We have had a dreary rough passage yesterday the hardest blow of all I have been ill with one of my old intermittent attacks after wh. my mouth broke out with an unusually brilliant eruption and I am going into Liverpool with a beard 8 days long—It is not becoming in its present stage. I have not been sea-sick but haven't been well a single day—Wine is ojus to me, segars create loathing—Couldnt I write something funnier and more cheerful? Perhaps I may when we are fairly into Liverpool—perhaps we may be there to night perhaps not till tomorrow morning for it blew a hurricane into our face last night and the odds are we shall not have water enough to pass the bar.

HOME. (wiz 36 Onslow Square Brompton London) May 9. We did pass the bar, and didnt I have a good dinner at the Adelphi, and wasn't I glad to get back to town yesterday, and wasn't there a great dinner at the Garrick Club (the annual Shakspeare dinner wh. ought to have come off on the 23 ult. but was put off on acct. of a naval review) and didn't I make a Yankee Speech, and oh lor Robison! havnt I got a headache this morning? I'm ashamed to ask for Sober-water thats the fact.—And so heres the old house, the old room the old teapot by my bed side, the old trees nodding in at the window—it looks as if I'd never been away—and that it is a dream I have been making Well, in my dream I dreamt there was an uncommonly good fellow by name W D R. and I dreamed that he treated me with all sorts of kindness, and I send him and J C B D. and D D (and whats L's name down stairs?) my heartiest regards, and when my young women come home I shall tell them what a deal of kindness their Papa had across the water— So good bye my dear Robinson & believe me always gratefully yours

W M T.

Tell Jim Wallack that we hadn't a single actor at the Shakspere dinner and that F. Fladgate and C. Dance send their best remembrances to him. How did that Sunday dinner go off? Was it as bad as the dreary Friday?

Davis: John Chandler Bancroft Davis. *the Bower of Virtue:* Thackeray's name for the house at 604 Houston Street, New York, inhabited by Robinson and Davis. *D D:* William Denning Duer. *L:* Samuel E. Lyon, lawyer, who also lived at 604 Houston Street. *Wallack:* James William Wallack (1791?-1864), actor. *Fladgate:* Francis Fladgate (1799-1892), barrister. *Dance:* Charles Dance (1794-1863), dramatist.

212. TO MRS. FRANK HAMPTON
12-13 July 1856

36 Onslow Sqr. Brompton. London
12-13. July

Do you remember this hand writing? Since circumstances have occurred, you have not seen it much. I write to nobody now, that's the fact, except a dozen or two of brief business letters during the week That is the best—no sentimentalities—Dont you think more of the little personage whose likely advent has been announced to me than of scores of old friends pleasures & what not? We take up with the business of our lives when the time comes—May your nursery be thronged & merry!

I am writing on my back rather ill in bed—Have been ill ever since I came home forced to give up the pomps & vanities of this wicked world and all the sinful lusts of the season—am greatly better though, and fancy that I am going to be better still. All that melancholy you remember that glum carelessness of life &c came from bodily ailment and not mental as we used romantically to fancy. I am greatly improved of my ailment and with the illness the melancholy goes—next year I shall be as jolly as 20—perfectly reconciled to life—interested even in trivialities let us hope—trumps, politics, what there is for dinner, or what our neighbour has—I have been 2 1/2 months in London now without doing the littlest bit of work except doctoring myself Poor Anny has lost her season and we have been able to go but to 2 fine parties—I had an ague attack after both so that she is reconciled to staying away. Indeed she is so good & unselfish that even without this penalty to me she would give up her own pleasure for mine. And that I seriously think is all my news. I am dead: go nowhere, do, think, write, nothing Shall I not best burn this letter instead of sending it all the way to the Second Avenue?

Shall I ever come back to see you again? Not as a public performer. I won't go through the degrading ordeal of press-abuse again. Those scoundrels managed last time to offend and insult the most friendly stranger that ever entered your country or quitted it—I like my dear old friends just as well as ever mind you—but the public *non pas*.

At this juncture yesterday the Dr. made his appearance; and now it is Sunday morning 13 July, and though it's only 10 o'clock I have had my breakfast these 3 hours, and read 3 papers, and 3 pamphlets about the Prince of Wales (my favorite George IV) and what on earth have I got to say to fill up these 2 pages? The George lectures are much better liked here than they were with you that is if I may judge from a petit comité to whom I have read 3 of them—The terrible Venables came to the first and Minny of whose criticism I am more afraid than of any one's—V. spoke very highly of No 1. Old Lady Morley cried at No 3,—Ld. Morley who belonged to the Court was not in the least scandalized—it was evident in a word that the people were amused. I read the lectures straight out from the American M.S. wh. your people said I should not dare to read in England, & should have given them in public but that I was not sure of my health, and thought the best thing I could do was to go into hospital. I am now all but set up again: and when we're well Laud! wont we be happy & have a lark! Those girls are the comfort of my life that's a fact—that affair I once talked to you about was all nonsense. The young man was in London the other day, I asked him to dinner,—& first told Minny who laughed & then told Anny who laughed too—their romantic old Granny was the founder of the story—Do you laugh & think I am humbugged? No—if there had been any thing in it, I am sure my girl wd. have told me. Little Amy Crowe lives with us still and is so good and gentle that actually nobody in my family is jealous of her—poor Eyre gets no work, paints no better, half starves, has himself to thank for his poverty—Mr. Charles Pearman has not resumed his livery on his return to his native country but dresses in black and is [a] much greater man. The Ticknors are here, its very hard that I cannot make a feast for them—but the Dr. wont let me, and I save in dinners what I pay in fees. Indeed our little house is very pretty. I dont see a gayer one any where and if a man is to be ill why there cant be a pleasanter room than this in wh. I'm writing, quiet, bright, with a beautiful garden and green avenue before it, such as W B. Astor couldn't have in New York, with all his money. And these are my news Madam. I hope you liked the teapottykin &c—they

were so nice to my mind that I thought there was no use in going farther for them than Broadway. I send my very best regards to your husband, and my love to my dear kind friends yonder—Whilst I am writing, the girls come in, and I say 'Whom do you think I am writing to?['] Miss Min. tosses up her head & says 'to Sally Bax---['] Good bye my dear S S H. says

Yours afftly. always
W M T.

pomps . . . lusts: The Catechism, *Book of Common Prayer:* "Renounce . . . the pomps and vanity of this wicked world, and all the sinful lusts of the flesh." *non pas:* (Fr.) not at all.   *petit comité:* (Fr.) little group.   *Old Lady Morley . . . Ld. Morley:* the Dowager Lady Morley and her son, Edmund Parker Morley (1810-64), second Earl.   *the Dr.:* Henry (later Sir Henry) Thompson (1820-1904), urologist.

213. TO MRS. THOMAS FREDERICK ELLIOT AND KATE PERRY
10 September 1856

Hotel Bristol. Place Vendome. Wednesday.

Are your travels over? are you back in Chesham Place? Has K P taken her poor little holy day and sent her young people on their tour? Ours has been but a very small one—to Calais wh. is very good fun and a great deal more French than Paris; to Spa wh. was very pleasant too but for the quantity of acquaintances and 1/2 acquaintances that as père de famille I did not care to make whole acquaintances; to Dusseldorf where we passed a couple of agreeable days among the painters; and then to Aix la Chapelle wh. disagreed with me as it always does. Here we heard of the death of Mrs. Robert Carmichael Smyth, my step-father's brother's wife and thinking the family would be in trouble, and my mother (who was away touring too, we did not know where) would be sure to come to Paris, we came on last Friday. But there was no Granny for the girls She is to stay the month out at Heidelberg—the daughters are gone to stay with a cousin of ours Rue Godot where they are all very jolly together, and I am for a few days 'in boy' at the Hotel Bristol; haunted by No. 1. of Mr. Thackeray's new Serial, wh. won't leave me alone wh. follows me about in all my walks, wakes me up at night, prevents me from hearing what is said at the play, and yet seems farther off than ever. It seems to me as if I had said my say, as if anything I write must be repetition, and that people will say with justice 'he has worn himself out, I always told you he would &c &c.['] But 6000£ is a great bribe isn't it? Suppose I do wear myself out, & that posterity says so, why shouldn't she? and what for care to appear to future ages (who will be deeply interested in discussing the subject) as other than I really am?

My poor friend A Beckett's death has shocked me. He has left no money and hasn't insured his life—Down from competence and comfort goes a whole family into absolute penury. One boy 1/2 through the University, & likely to have done well there I believe—another at a public school daughters with masters and mamma with tastes for music and millinery—What is to happen to these people? Had I dropped 3 years ago my poor wife and young ones would have been no better off. Yes, we must do the Forthcoming Serial Work and never mind if it should turn out a failure. We went to see Mrs. Norton yesterday who has burned her neck severely while shielding her little grandchild—a little black eyed curly pated lazzaronykin Brinsley's daughter—That fellow would be a good character for a book—and his mother too if one could but say all one thought—but in England we are so awfully squeamish—Ah—if one's hands were not tied, there might be some good fun in that forthcoming Serial—You see I always come back to it—in fact this very sheet of paper was pulled out for the purpose of writing a page only somehow it has taken the direction of Chesham place and will be read I hope tomorrow by my bonnes sœurs. Are you all in London? Ah me! what letters I have written in this very room at this table some 5 years since. It is a nice quiet room—away from the noisy street. I daresay the Zouaves are playing their music in the Place Vendome at this present moment. Blow away trumpets! We saw the men yesterday. They are magnificent-looking warriors that's certain. The town is getting too handsome for me. I miss my old corners—my dining-places have disappeared & palaces stand in their stead: but the Palais Royal looking seedy & deserted consoles me: and one gets a good time among the pictures at the Louvre, and with the pleasure of the girls. What shall I do, if any scoundrel of a husband takes away Anny's kind cheerfulness from me?

I have been twice to the theayter but can't sit out the plays the Dame aux Camelias I could not bear beyond the second act: it is too wicked: and so is the Juif Errant—I had intended to go to a screaming farce last night, but came home instead to think about the—Plague take it! Here is the Forthcoming Serial come up again! Well, you let me say whatever is in my mind, and you know of some people who are always there. God bless them all says.

W M T.

I shall be here a few days more. Will anybody write a line or two?

père de famille: (Fr.) father of the family.   *Mrs. Robert Carmichael Smyth:* the former Agnes Hervey, wife of Major Carmichael-Smyth's younger brother. *cousin:* Charlotte Ritchie.   *'in boy':* (Fr.: *en garçon*) as a bachelor.   *new Serial: The Virginians* (1857-59).   *A Beckett:* Gilbert Abbott À Beckett (1811-56), a *Punch* colleague, had died on 30 August.   *Mrs. Norton:* the Honourable Caroline Norton, née Sheridan (1808-77).   *lazzaronykin:* (Angl. diminutive of Ital.: *lazzarone*) little beggar.   *Brinsley's daughter:* Carlotta (b. 1854), the daughter of Mrs. Norton's son, Thomas Brinsley Norton (1831-77), later fourth Baron Grantley.   *Dame aux Camelias:* play (1848) by Alexandre Dumas *fils*. *Juif Errant:* play (1849) by Eugène Sue.

214. TO BRADBURY AND EVANS
18 November 1856

3 Randolph Crescent. Edinburgh.
Novr. 18. 1856.

My dear B & E.

I know you think this is Thackeray dunning for money again—but it's no such thing. He has plenty of money: he has his hands full of lectures until Xmas; wh. will bring plenty more: he is gorged with champagne claret and the very best of wittles every day: nevertheless he wishes he was a coming to dine with you fellows tomorrow in Bouverie St. and sends a kyindly greeting to all assembled round that deal table.

Thats all upon my word.

Yours ever
W M T.

215. TO AMY CROWE
November 1856

My dear little Dorrit

I think it is not unlikely that my dear old Mother will send over to you on her own private hook and beg and implore you to replace the girls when they come back to their Papa. Now, this must not be. You are most useful I may say Hindispensable to us—There must be a companion with my gals, with my girl when one of them goes out and I dont know a woman in all the world I could live with except little Dorrit. So if you are written to say you think you ought to ask my consent (as you ought Miss) and write and ask it and then I will refuse it. The old G P. ought to come to England, but he won't move. As he won't, he has no right to break up my household—and the refusal I think will oblige him to come across the water—to settle at Brighton or somewhere where we can be near and go to them from time to time.

I have written to the girls to be at home on the 20th. December: about wh. time I too shall be back to go lecturing about the country in February again for a month or two and to bag some more money for those young people. My dear old mother is nervous, she hardly has her head at times—I don't want Minny—*my wife's daughter* you understand—to be subject to the sight of that excitement—and I can't write that to her or to my mother You may refuse on account of your own family matters—the unpleasantness of your being near some one who shall be nameless. Show this letter to Mrs. Eugenie and colloque over it. The situation is very painful—If I remonstrate with my poor old G P. he will break out in some furious fit of senile anger. My mother will go off into hysterics The girls will catch the excitement. He must go his own way, and I must go mine. I wish I knew how to make matters comfortable but it cannot be during poor dear old G P's invincible dislike to England. I am quite well thank you. The lectures are even more popular here than in America, and I am Eugénie's and Amy's affectionate old friend

    Always
    W M T.

I saw Chr-stie at Edinburgh. He is still constant. I hope Mr. Wynn wont be jealous of him. At breakfast at Glasgow t'other day, he dashed into a playful French sentence wh. was curious in a grammatical point of view.

Chr-stie: the Scottish painter, Alexander Christie (1807-60). *Mr. Wynn:* Robert Wynne, husband of the former Eugènie Crowe.

216. TO MRS. THOMAS FREDERICK ELLIOT AND KATE PERRY
November 1856

3 Randolph Crescent. Edinburgh.

My dear J E. K P. Only a little line, but I think you'll be glad to know that the Lectures are a great success They have been repeated here to 3 per cent of the whole population—If I could but get 3 per cent of the population of London! At Glasgow 3000 people come and feed nightly and the wretches make 500£ whilst I only get

100. Never mind. The ball goes along merrily I am in pretty good health most kindly treated every where. It isn't a bad profession is it?—to be feasted every day to have to work an hour per diem and get 150 or 200£ at the end of the week! Mes bonnes sœurs I hope you are as well as your young friend who at present addresses you. I have no news. I am whirling back and forward every day from Glasgow, writing letters all the morning and talking at night. I see I must play this play out and take in this odd harvest wh. seems springing up every day at my feet—Why the girls will be little heiresses if we go on in this way. Let us not be vain nor overproud but be thankful for what God sends us. I get famous letters from the girls. They wouldn't have had much of their Pa after all in the skurry and bustle of this lecturing and they are doing their duty by their Granny—and dont we intend to be jolly in January in London?

    Do you know there are 9 other letters lying on the table before me and more to write. Do you ever write to any body at Nice and say a God bless you—Farewell mes bonnes sœurs. Bon jour Monsieur Fred.

W M T.

Write me a nice letter to Hull next week care of Literary Philosophical Society.

217. TO MRS. THOMAS FREDERICK ELLIOT AND KATE PERRY
2 December 1856

Station Hotel.
Hull. Monday. Decr. 2. 1856

Well, I thought as sure as sure could be, I should find a letter from kind J. E. Pray why doesn't she write to me? I'd like to know, and if not she, where's her sister Miss K. P. one or other is surely free to send a line to doubleyou tea. What is the reason? I've often said—Are Kate or Jane both ill in bed? Is that little shivering grey hound dead? or has any thing possibly happened to Fred? or have they taken a friend instead of that old fellow they've often fed (along with Venables Clem: & Sped) with a broken nose and a snowy head? Tell me how shall this riddle be read?

    What a busy month it has been! Nightly prating of king and Queen—Edinburgh Glasgow Paisley I've seen, with dinners suppers and breakfasts between—I cant go on with poetry but why Maam dont you send me a little of your prose? I finished at Dumfries on Saturday night in a funny little theatre crammed full of kind people—the night before I had more than 3000 people in the City Hall at Glasgow (but a miscreant Society makes all the profits) the night before that was in a Church at Paisley, the night before that farewell at Edinburgh—and perhaps I am going a fresh Scottish campaign.   It agrees with me wonderfully the ceaseless racket—Dont you see how I am going back to my natural old handwriting, and giving up that mean literary man's fist?. Let this go on, and one more novel, and we absolutely shall be INDEPENDENT. Hip Hip Huzzay.   Then, what shall we do afterwards, we who have the ear of the public, and a thousand a year of our own, and who needn't care for any body? Police-magistrateships forsooth! We will look to better things than Beakships. What title do you think I should take? Wd. Lord Brompton do? It would be affected modesty.   O me! I think I bragged in this way once before from the States. Well I know you will like to hear that I am well and prospering and that everybody is kind to me.   I get famous letters from the girls and it is as well perhaps that they did not come the Northern Tour with me as I had so much more work than I expected. All the time at Edinburgh was spent at J. Blackwood's house—the most hospitable and magnificent inn I ever put up in—the company not altogether so polished as Sir Charles Grandison or David Dundas but good shrewd fellows, the 4 Blackwood brothers liking each other hugely and sitting jovially together night after night over bottle after bottle of the most prodigious Good Claret. At Glasgow was very pleasant company indeed in the College—Mrs. Blackburn whose wonderful genius strikes me more and more, and nicer people still a very great Natural Philosopher whom Fred will know by name Professor Thomson, with a sweet kind invalid wife lying for ever on a sofa (and making me think of Somebody in old times) and pretty sisters in law.—At Paisley Mr. Peter Coats the great thread-maker entertained me—You never saw such splendor the Duchess of Sutherland's room was nothing to the best bed-room. We had 16 to dinner at 6, and eighteen to supper at 10—none of your kickshaws but regular Ham and turkey and all this splendid succession of victualling administered by one maid and a hired waiter to whom Charles graciously condescended to give a little aid. These kind simple people are worth a million of money I daresay and keep 1100 girls working in their factory at thread. I saw the girls, and healthy jolly kindly girls they looked. All with good characters too says Mr. Peter Coats and why should I doubt about the 1100 virgins?   The wretches at Glasgow cheated me, but they are welcome. The honest folks were on my side and Heaven knows I am paid well enough. At Dumfries whither I went in the bitter Snow, I was entertained by a little Editor with a pretty little sister in a nice cheery old fashioned house: and at dinner was a parson and a Doctor and we brewed a cheery toddy in Burns's tumbler—and at night the poor Doctor had to set off miles on miles through the snow to see a patient for 5 shillings and I thought with a sort of shame how lucky I was. After perfooming I came on to Carlisle and spent a quiet Sunday morning there and at night to Newcastle and on Monday to Hull and O what a jolly long sleep I had! From 9.30 to 9.30. the first good long rest this month. And here is such a comfortable Inn—and such a pleasant quiet day by the fire looking out at the Snow.

Whatfor do I tell you all this? Because it's good to have a talk with Bonnes Sœurs from time to time; and I almost fancy we are chattering over the tea—it is just 5 and indeed I should like to be there.

What a pro-digious long letter! Good bye my dear J & K (and—what Initial am I thinking of now do you think?) Remember me if you can to friends and wont I be glad to come and see you in 3 weeks? asks without the least necessity for a reply, your faithful
W M T.

Clem: & Sped: "Clem" is unidentified. "Sped" is James Spedding. *literary man's:* the two words are written in Thackeray's upright script. *Sir Charles Grandison:* the title figure of Samuel Richardson's novel (1754). *Dundas:* David Dundas (1799-1877), lawyer and political figure. *the 4 Blackwood brothers:* Alexander, Sir Archibald, James, and John. *Mrs. Blackburn:* the painter, Mrs. Hugh Blackburn. *Professor Thomson:* the scientist, William Thomson (1824-1907), later first Baron Kelvin. *Coats:* Peter (later Sir Peter) Coats (1808-90). *Duchess of Sutherland:* the former Lady Harriet Howard (d. 1868), wife of George Granville (1786-1861), second Duke of Sutherland. *the 1100 virgins:* a play on the 11,000 virgins allegedly martyred with St. Ursula at Cologne.

218. TO MRS. THOMAS FREDERICK ELLIOT AND KATE PERRY
6-7 December 1856

Hull. Saturday. 6 December.
For a wonder the Post has only brought me two letters this morning—yesterday, though, after the receipt of Madam J. E's letter, I was for firing off an answer immediately, yet I had to write 14 letters on duty love or business, and by 4 o'clock my hand was so tired and my spirits likewise so beat that I could not sit down to a long one such as you want. My dear old folks keep me in endless perplexity—indeed when didn't they? It's small comfort I get out of the anxious loves jealousies glooms despondencies of that poor old mother; to whom we're always going, and who is always miserable at parting from us, or in grief for one cause or another. That most faithful uxorious

exacting old gentleman weighs down her life with his dullness—cares for no amusement but his fireside, and to talk stupid articles out of the newspaper, doesn't like much talking or too many candles even in his room—keeps us all mum and dismal.—I don't want to live to be 76, if 76 is to be no better fun than that. 'Bon Dieu! What a miserable old age you are preparing for yourself!' a Frenchman said to another who owned that he did not know how to play at cards. What a blessing a rubber or a game of backgammon would be in our dreary paternal mansion in place of that stupid talk about the designs of that rascal the Emperor of Russia, or that villain Napoleon! We must take the ups and the downs—That philosopher Minny writes in her last letter—'There's always something agreeable and something disagreeable in everything, so we must do the best we can.' Bravo Minny! What a comfort it will be to see her funny little face in a fortnight. Very likely we shall have the elders too. That will be small fun—for us and for that poor old Bird who has paired with my maternal Hen these forty years, and feels that he has no business in our nest at all. I fear actually for my mother's reason. Her nerves have broken right down. She is sleepless unless amused, and he wont let her be amused. This isn't very cheerful talk is it? It could scarce have been more glum had I begun yesterday when the evening was drawing in, and I was tired all day writing, writing. What a comfort your letter was though! My dear dear J O B. So her health does not allow her to walk and there's actually a little No 3 in preparation! That pretty well finishes matters. Suppose the way ever so clear. Her children, if they are brave children, would hate a sham father. There's something immodest in the marriage of an elderly woman with children even to a charming lovyer like me. How disgusted I have felt at hearing my old G P. snoring in my mother's room! When Fred dies, Dont you marry any body else. Rather have a neat funereal firework built up—let us see in Cadogan Garden would be a nice open space—I & Kate and your friends will walk down with you to the Terminus. The Deans of Bristol and Carlisle (as was to be) shall read the service *des agonisans*—You distribute your jewels take Fairy in your arms (from those of the weeping William) mount the pile and fizz! there is a *roti*, and you and Fred are walking in the Elysian Fields.—I think this is rather Walpolean or SydneySmithian isn't it? Had I been writing a novel at this time, I could not have afforded to be so funny in a mere letter. But writing—heaven bless us!—It is impossible in this whirl of business and calls and travels and letter writing. What a pleasure to have the old house again, and Kate at her desk painting away at her little pictures, or writing kind notes, kind humbugging notes to Eliza Smith and pretending she likes her still! To whom was it I wrote about Miss Block? to Mrs. Fanshawe I suppose. I found her (Miss B) out on a second or 3d interview, and thought her a little humbug. But that does not prevent her singing a very good ballad. Your news from your dear Nice was very welcome, but you mustn't mention me I suppose because of course that Dean is prowling round the premises by this time. Did I say to you, in all the egotisms of the last communication, that I am glad I am roaming about; and seeing new people, & new aspects of the world? This is a mean ugly petty place but there's very good company in it. The ceremony-dinner of 20 was awfully bad to be sure and John upset a glass of Port accurately into my sleeve—but the dinner of leg of mutton with Dr. Cooper (Sir Enry Cooper he is called, having been Mayor and knighted last year) was pleasant and there was a very pleasant well-educated Jew, who has some '20 Port wh. we are going to drink on Sunday. He showed us a queer thing the Israelite I mean—how long do you suppose did Jacob wait after marrying Leah, before he married Rebecca? Seven years say all the little flannel-petticoats in your school, & their mistress.—No such thing. He only waited a week. And then he married Becky, and *afterwards* served his seven years with Laban—*nobbling* him at the end, as I need not inform your young friends in th[. . .] petticoats. He He He! It cannot be denied that Impiety adds a little zest to conversation, and I am glad Lord Shaftesbury is not in the room when you read this out. I think I must go back to Punch really. That man is getting too much influence. Those narrow-eyed Evangelicals must not be allowed to go on swindling the Church of England as Isaac swindled Jacob. Come! This is page 8. You'll be having too much of me, if I go on chattering in this way. Let us light a cigar, and read the Illustrious News—for you know the Post doesn't go out till tomorrow.

Sunday. I thought I could have done another 4 pages to day and smothered you quite with sheets of MS.—but the evening shades are beginning to prevail, and think! I have written other 11 letters since breakfast.

Good bye mes bonnes Sœurs
[signature cut away]

Emperor of Russia: Czar Nicholas I.   *Napoleon:* Louis Napoleon (Napoleon III).   *Deans of Bristol and Carlisle:* Gilbert Elliot (1800-91), Dean of Bristol 1850-91, and Francis Close (1797-1882), Dean of Carlisle 1856-81.   *des agonisans:* (Fr.) of the dying.   *roti:* (Fr.) roast.   *Cooper:* Sir Henry Cooper (1807-91), Mayor of Hull 1853-55, knighted 1854.   *[. . .]:* the hiatus has been caused by the cutting away of the signature on the verso.   *Lord Shaftesbury:* Anthony Ashley Cooper, seventh Earl of Shaftesbury, a noted philanthropist whom Thackeray apparently viewed as a self-appointed guardian of public morals.

219. TO MRS. FRANK HAMPTON
10-12 December 1856

Bradford .. Manchester. Decr. 10-12.
I remember how near a certain Anniversary is and must wish you many happy anniversaries. The letter wh. you wrote to me just before the birth of your boy was such a *damp* one that I didn't care to reply to it. Why, if I am grown cold, younger folks are grown colder, if I don't care younger people are equally pococurante—That was before the birth of the boy Let us hope life has other interests and quite a new charm for you. What have I been doing since October? (when I returned home & found your letter & your mothers)—have scarcely been at home since that time, kept in perpetual motion by the illness of my dear old mother and the botherations attendant on it—and since November never quiet with the lectures—wh. are a much greater success here than in America—as great even pecuniarily. People knowing the subject better more familiar with the allusions &c like the stuff—I am glad for my part that this should be the opinion—for I know in America it was thought I had brought them an inferior article—glass beads as it were for the natives—But no newspaper in this country will say like Bennett that any young man could sit down in their office and write such lectures in an evening—I'm obliged to skip over because I've no blotting paper—and O such numbers of letters daily to write—90 a week at the very least—thats why I have returned to the old slanting hand in place of the familiar upright—Slanting is much quicker—

My mother has been very unwell and even more frightened than hurt. Hence my dear girls who were just ready to start to the North with me, were obliged to forego their pleasure, & stay with her & nurse her their best—(We were telegraphed over—out of a pleasant party at Russell Sturgis's who has a palace of a house near London.) and we were to have gone to a half dozen fine houses and Miss Min rather prematurely to have made her entrée into this wicked world but things have been otherwise ruled. There is my history for months past. My spirits are very much better—though I get those fierce attacks of illness still—am just out of bed from one of them wh. prevented my lecturing last night & to night. Think that at the end of next year if I work I shall be worth 20,000£!—Its as much as I want—10000 a piece for the girls is enough for any authors daughters—and then when I am independent what shall we do? Hush—perhaps have a shy at politics for wh. I dont care now—but one must do something and when you begin to play you get interested in the game—I have taken share in the Transatlantic Telegraph—I felt glad somehow to contribute to a thread that shall tie our two countries together—for though I don't love America I love Americans with all my heart—And I daresay you know what family taught me to love them.

What a hideous place this is I am staying at—what kind people every where! What a beautiful woman came to see me to day with her Usband! The faithful evidently multiply—and—I find as usual that I dont care one single phigg. Praise does not produce the least elation—censure a little captiousness but thats all. At Edinburgh I was hissed about Mary Queen of Scots—and rather amused—I was not familiar with the Scotch as I could not be except in certain families with you—as soon as I got back to England began to sympathize with my company again, and passed all last week at Hull amongst traders in a very hearty homely comfortable society. A Jew there on Sunday gave me such a quantity of Port wine that though I did not like it and knew the end of it I drank & am ill in consequence. Wonderful consequence of Port wine! I could not help telling the son of the house that one of the guests a Jew too was an infernal Snob in wh. the lad agreed and wh. was utterly true but why say it?

One good that has come out of the poor dear mothers illness has been that it has drawn us all pretty close together—She & the—and here there came in strangers and then more strangers and then a friend to dinner and then bed time and then early morning to Lpool, and dinner lecture supper there and now it is 12 December—she is receiving company in the brown house in diamonds & lace and what a fine supper there is in the dining room and what flowers on the stairs and what a smart new dress mamma has got on, and how pale poor Lucy looks as she peeps out of her room and just goes back to chill & fever! Well, well, all this was a year ago—but didnt I think of it this morning as I lay awake and heard the wind roaring in the same house from wh. I embarked for America both times! Good bye my dear—God bless you—Ive only time and spirits to say that Havent I written 10 letters already—and aint I unwell still and isn't there the lecture to do to night—and o it will be pleasant to see the girls next week! Mamma may read this first & send it on think of the Cunarder having to put back! I've took 1000£ share in the telegraph line we'll hold each other by the hand then. Good bye again my dear Sarah & God speed you & your husband & child

Anniversary: of her marriage on 12 December 1855.   *your boy:* Frank Hampton [Jr.] (1856-1926).   *pococurante:* (Ital.) indifferent.   *Bennett:* James Gordon Bennett (1795-1872), editor of *The New York Herald*, a frequent critic of Thackeray's lectures.   *upright:* for this word Thackeray returned to his upright hand.   *Cunarder:* the Royal Mail steamship *America,* which had sailed from Liverpool for New York on 6 December 1856, was severely damaged in a gale on 9 December and put back at Liverpool two days later.

220. TO MRS. JOHN BLACKWOOD
14 December 1856

Apperley. Bradford. 14 Dec.
(I know it's Sunday: but if I dont write now when shall I ever find the time?)

My dear Mrs. Blackwood. Of course with my knowledge of human nature I can just fancy what you & J. B. and Baby have been thinking—'After the way in wh. we kept that fellow for a month, he might have the grace to write a line or two.'—and when I got Johns letter yesterday without a word of reproach—of course I felt the silence all the more cruel. But you saw—on your own Stationary and envelopes—the letters I wrote in Randolph Crescent—It has been worse since—my days are past in railroads or letter writing—and when the business of the day is done I have no heart left to write a jolly pleasant lively amiable rattling letter—such as one would like to—such as a fellow, who would wish to make himself agreeable and wants to be asked to that house again, would desire to—you understand in a word.—I've dropt all my correspondence, except the 14 letters per diem wh. I write regularly on business, send hurried scraps to the girls, and write to my 2 or 3 old friends 6 words in the inside of envelopes—to say [']How dye do. Have been ill. Am very well thank you. Hope to see you in town at Xmas.' And by the time that & the business letters are done it is dinner at Mr. Jones after wh. comes lecture after wh. comes supper at Mr. Browns—sleep—soda water, breakfast railway, more letters, dinner at Mr. Hobbs, lecture, supper at Mr. Dobbs's—EXPLOSION Doctor 10 grains bl—k D—se—2 days lie for it—Up again, lecture—railway—letters—dinner at Mr. Jobbs's, lecture, supper at Mr. Snobbs & so on & so on—And I can't avoid my fate as you know Could I avoid it in Randolph Crescent? Didn't I dodge up stairs? plead illness? sneak out of the way? Was it *my* fault that I smoked and drank brandy & water superposed on claret & Madeira? I am a Victim—Write over my bloated corpse that I am MURDERED. That is what people are doing to me, and I have 3 months more of the agony to go through. When I tell John Blackwood for instance that at Liverpool at the friend's house where I am staying there is Port Wine FIVE TIMES better than the Randolph Crescent Port—he will know that there is nothing for me but to do my duty and perish at my post—My last severe attack was all Port—a gentleman at Hull had some '20 and I say cheerfully I will dine with him. Very good. I go to dinner this day week. He was a Jew a worthy & clever man. Well, when the time for Port comes he gives me a glass of excellent wine—that is 1840 says he—O 40! Says I. The bottle is finished Now try *this* says he—Capital I say winking at glass 1 of Bottle 2. That is 1826 says my host, and we finish the bottle.

Then we have the '20—and very good twenty it is. But dont you see that I am obliged to do this every day, and my host only once in a month—6 months—a year?—No wonder I'm a blighted being. If I hadn't drunk the mans wine he would have been hurt.—I protest I could go on covering reams of paper with my griefs.

How jolly it will be to see the girls next week and to have a little quiet and dear delicious water-gruel! About 18 February I start northwards. 1 March am in Scotland again performing every lawful day—and winding up on the 21 at Edinburgh—and then it will be pretty well time, wont it? to give up this business for it is not wholesome or dignified or pleasant—only lucrative, and so let us do it and end it—

I am very glad to hear that the Major's evils are so well over, and as he is not marked of course as John says he is not to be pitted. And I should like with all my heart to see my dear little Babsy again—and though I know it's wrong I should like to sit at that kind table surrounded by the brothers, and drink that famous &c, and &c, and &c. (with just *one* small glass of whatsthenameofit? brought round by Baker in the intervals)—although I know they are hurrying me to an untimely tomb.—I get quite soft and sentimental as I think about you all and your kindness—Good bye my dear friends—a merry Xmas to all Blackwoods present and to come—says   Yours & Johns and Babys

Very   sincere
W M Thackeray.

O stop! by the way!—Will you ask James to ask the Captain to ask John if—that uncommonly pretty—ahem—ahousemaid is still in Randolph Crescent?

221. TO MRS. HENRY CARMICHAEL-SMYTH
9-12 January 1857

[Bath]

This is begun in the beautiful city where Miss Ann Becher first danced with Captain G P. It is only 4 hours from London now by the slow train, as I came yesterday I thought of the supper at Marlborough and the York House coach. It was dark when I arrived I had to go to dinner and directly afterwards to my lecture-room—The room was crammed with 400 genteel folks and 350 of the wulgar The genteel could not understand what I was talking about I looked into their genteel blank faces and saw they were dullards[;] the vulgar took the jokes understood the points laughed & cheered at the right places.

Among the polite were many parsons. They rule here and tyrannize as all parsonic bodies do—A man who has been with me about more lectures this morning told me for taking a walk of a Sunday evening after Church where his clergyman had seen him, he was rebuked by his Reverence who said 'You had better have remained at home.' Between our side & their's ought there not to be war?   To day I get invitations from Ireland declined with thanks, from Devonshire, from Bath again and Bristol, from Yorkshire for the summer, where is this going to stop? What I said about 'a great career' is not swagger but a fair look at Chances in the face. Just when the novel-writing faculty is pretty well used up here is Independence a place in Parliament and who knows what afterwards? Upon my word I dont seem much to care, and fate carries me along in a stream somehow—Shall I float with it or jump on shore? I shant be happy in politics and they'll interfere with my digestion—but with the game there, it seems faint-hearted not to play it. 'Retire and paint pooty little pictures' says Ease perhaps Conscience: 'Retire and work at literature at history[']—But that game is very tempting. I wonder will it come off or whether this is mere idle vaporing & dreaming? Did I tell you about the Whigs whipper in sending to me about a seat in parliament? Sir says I with 15000 subscribers to my books (all this is entre nous), and hundreds of thousands of hearers all over England I'm not going to be a Whig under strapper?—I think I did tell you—One of the obstacles to getting on perhaps is this dreadful want of memory. What is the use of forming plans & castles in the air? A hundred things may happen to knock down this one. Well, I shan't care.

Bob has just been here in pretty good spirits and I am to go and see his Baby between 3 & 5, poor fellow. And then to Mrs. Forrest's and then to Impeys and then to dine again with the Thackeray cousins who won't hear of my eating at my own hour and send me choking into lecture.   I hear sad accounts of the Morning Herald—What a comfort it is to be a popular performer at such moments!—I know where there always are 50£ for honest Paddy.

Monday—My dear old womans comfortable letter has just come in—the pleasantest I have seen for many a long day—& I send off my scrap with good news about all of us—I went to see Bob & his baby and the child is a perfect wonder—the finest child ever seen finer than Mrs. Story's—the most jolly handsome broad chested fair-skinned little hero with a look of G P in the Hessian boot picture—and I saw Mrs. Forrest & Emmy, and came away very much pleased with kind handsome Bath—where the Miss Thackerays have a house twice as big & handsome as mine wh. costs 700£.

It rains money—This morning I have arranged for 2 sets of lectures at Willis's & Brighton—the 8 hours will bring me four hundred pounds!—I have engaged for the month of April for twenty four lectures for wh. I am to be paid 1200 guineas!—perhaps we may have 2 or 3 months of this sort of money-making. Great Powers! it's prodigious—Meanwhile I don't think I've above 100£ at Lubbocks or I would send Granny some—Mum about the price of the lectures. It seems a fable. If they come off I have promised Amy 100£. Have anything you like Dont stint God bless you my dear old Granny & G P. What a comfort to see your hand not shaking!

W M T.

Bob . . . Mrs. Forrest: Captain Robert Forrest, son of Mrs. William Forrest, the former Georgiana Carmichael-Smyth. *Paddy:* John Frazer Corkran, Paris correspondent of *The Morning Herald. child . . . Mrs. Story's:* Waldo Story, son of Mrs. William Wetmore Story. *Willis's:* Willis's Rooms, King Street, St. James's.

222. TO FREDERICK SWARTOUT COZZENS
8 February–5 April 1857

36 Onslow Sqe. London.
Feb 8—(It's a Sunday evening) and Im waiting for dinner & thats how you come by an answer
My dear Cozzens. Thank you for a sight of your hand writing, and the kindly reminiscences of those jolly Centurions whose hospitality and affectionateness this ♡ never intends to forget.

What pleased me most in your letter is to have it under your own hand & seal that you are well—I should like to see those pretty little chicks again—that snug cottage—those rosy-tinted palissades that dining-room cupboard up wh. victuals came with clangor—that snug bedroom where the celebrated Thacker left the razor strap and could hear for hours Judge Daly talking talking into the midnight. My dear old Judge—I havent forgot what I owe him—I dont like to send it until I hear whether he is married or not;—there was a hitch men told me—the course of true love didn't run smooth—Enlighten me some of you about this and let me pay my debts to my kind host & friend. Where Bayard may be now the Loramussy only knows We liked his pretty sisters, we had brief glimpses of a jolly time together—We hope to meet in April or May when I bragged about taking him into the fashionable world. But I hear that I am in disgrace with the fashionable world for speaking disrespectfully of the Georgyporgies—and am not to be invited myself, much more to be allowed to take others into polight Society. I writhe at the exclusion.

The Georges are so astoundingly popular here that I go on month after month hauling in fresh bags of Sovereigns, wondering that the people are not tired & that the lecturer is not found out—Tomorrow I am away for 2 months to the North—have found a Barnum who pays me an awful sum for April & May and let us hope June—shall make 10000£ by my beloved Monarchs one way or the other—and then and then & then—well I don't know what is going to happen—If I had not to write 20 letters a day on business I would have written to George Curtis, and given him an old man's blessing on his marriage—But I cant write—no, only for business or for money can this pen bite this paper—As I am talking nonsense to you—all the fellows are present in my mind, I hear their laughter & talk, and taste that 44 Chateau Margaux—and that Champagne do you remember?—And I say again I would like to see those pretty little chicks.   So the Athenæum assaulted you—lo you now! I never heard of the circumstance—the shot is fired, the report is over, the man not killed—the critic popgunning away at some other mark by this time—and you I hope you are writing some more of those papers. Your book & Bayard Taylors helped me over the voyage—How curious it is writing! I feel as if I was back again in New York and shaking hands with 100 of you—the heart becomes warm—God bless all good fellows say I. Shall I ever see you all again? Providebit Dominus   I forget whether you know Bancroft Davis—The folks here are hospitable to him. He has a pleasant time. Yesterday we elected him into the Garrick—and on the mantelpiece in my dining room is a bottle of Madeira wh. he gave it me and wh. I am going to hand out to some worthies who are coming to dine—They have never tasted anything like it—thats the fact—As I go on twaddling I feel I MUST come back & see you all. I praise Mr. Washington five times more here than I did in the States—Our people cheer—the fine folks look a little glum but the celebrated Thacker does not care for that natural ill-temper. Only 2 newspapers here have abused me, & I have been quite on their side.

April 5.   To think this was written on Feb 8 and left in my portfolio! I went out of town the next day only returned April 3—have been killing & eating the Georges ever since. I do not know what this letter is about—I am not going to read so much M. S. if I can help it—but I remember, when I wrote it, how I had a great desire to commune with my old chums at New York and hereby renew the kindest greetings to them. Tell me, Judge Daly, are you married & ahappy? If so I will send you them books I owe you. Poor Kane! I grieved to think of that hero carried so soon out of our world. There—I can no

more—Good bye my dear Cozzens—I salute you my excellent Century—G Curtis & Young & Daly I am
                                    Yours always
                                    Will. Thackeray

Cozzens: Frederick Swartout Cozzens, a New York wine merchant.   *Centurions:* members of the Century Club in New York.   *the celebrated Thacker:* a phrase applied to Thackeray in St. Louis during March 1856 by an Irish waiter who knew of his fame but not his correct name or accomplishments. Thackeray enjoyed telling the story to his friends.   *Daly:* Judge Charles Patrick Daly (1816-99).   *married:* Judge Daly did in fact marry Maria Lydig in 1856.   *the course . . . smooth:* A Midsummer Night's Dream, I, 1, 132.   *Bayard:* Bayard Taylor (1825-78), American traveller and author.   *a Barnum:* Thomas Willert Beale (1828-94), Thackeray's manager for the lectures.   *Curtis . . . marriage:* George William Curtis married Anna Shawe in 1856.   *the Athenæum assaults you:* in a review of Cozzens' *The Sparrowgrass Papers* (1856) that appeared in the 20 September 1856 issue of *The Athenæum*.   *book . . . Taylors:* probably Taylor's *Poems of Home and Travel* (1856).   *Providebit Dominus:* (Lat.) may the Lord provide for it.   *Kane:* Elisha Kane, the arctic explorer, died on 16 February 1857.   *Young:* William Young (1809-88), editor of *The New York Albion*.

223. TO MRS. THOMAS FREDERICK ELLIOT AND KATE PERRY
21-22 February 1857

Sheffield. Saturday
C. E. Ellison Esq. 3 George St. East. Newcastle.
Sunday. 21 Feb.

If I had not been ill last week, and if I had not had 10 letters a day to write as business this week, besides journies to Leeds and York, lecture every day, and one day twice,—I make no doubt I should ere this have written to my bonnes soeurs especially as Anny writes me that one of them has been ill who I hope is up and about now again and rid of her cold and fever. I don't think illness is very bad fun. In a dismal dirty inn at Halifax I found myself pretty comfortable last week reading Mahon's History of England—the mildest kind of amusement and instruction combined, and the Times steadily when it arrived, and knocking off between whiles those scores of business letters wh will follow one about. Altogether it is a good time I am having—The kindness and welcome of people touches me. I peep into new pleasant interiors, and see good folks eager to show me hospitality, some rough, some clever and literate—as for instance a Doctor here who had a supper for me the other night roast fowls, a great pork-pie, mince pies and jellies rather difficult to swallow 3 hours after dinner: but I managed a merrythought and we had a cozy pipe after dinner, and a pleasant talk about books—It is the quiet country-folks who read books—not we busy Londoners whose life is a scramble of clubs and parties. Books are æras in these people's lives, and such as give them pleasure are remembered for years and years. That's what Elwin of the Quarterly Review always tells me, and surely it's true. Whose portrait do you think was hanging in the Dr's drawing-room? that of the Revd W. H. B. H. M. I. of S. he is a native of Sheffield and his nephew, a clever young lawyer of the place, a caricature likeness of the Inspector joined the tobacco-soirée in the evening. The Dr's wife asked me whether I had not heard that a Sermon on the Temptation by W. H. B. had made a great sensation? and mentioned with great pride that she had read the Sermon! I told some good that I knew of him especially of the good fellow's bringing me £100 when I was hit by the railway and he a poor curate; I was glad to speak kindly of him and feel so God help us. Mrs Dr. asked about Mr. B's Wife's family—It was evident from her tone, that those aristocratic and 'aughty Eltons are no favorites in Sheffield. Last night was the last—I took my 100 guineas, ran out of doors and did not hear the vote of thanks proposed and carried by acclamation. The same disgraceful conduct characterised the celebrated Thacker at York the night before. I wanted to save the train so as to be back here and get to bed, and was in agonies whilst gentlemen were passing eujoliums, and each explaining how they must be brief as Mr. Thackeray wanted to save the train. Ha! there goes 11—at 11.30 I must be in the Newcastle train where D. V. I preach to night and will resume the pen to mes bonnes dames.

Sunday. This is Newcastle, I am in a comfortable house with a nice young married couple, he an old acquaintance of mine and Police Magistrate here. From 11.35 till 5 was in the railway then came dinner, and then George I. Those hours of lecture begin to pass the stage of disgust even now, and remain a blank afterwards. I bawl out the text with proper emphasis I suppose read the verses, and make no blunders and utterly forget what has happened during the hour. After 4 such hours a man comes, and gives me a hundred and a five pound note. Why couldn't one read 6 lectures a day, and have done with 'em?

   Are you going to Andalusia? The girls write she has asked them and could you take them? I like my women to have what little pleasure they can. I kneel down in spirit and thank Heaven and Rowland Hill for the penny postage which enables me to write and get a line every day almost. You see Mum, one becomes very soft hearted Mum when one's away on one's travels Mum, and as I shall be on and about here for a week, leaving this next Saturday for good, why perhaps I shall have a little letter from Chesham Place. Good bye and Good luck go with all there says

W. M. T.

Ellison: Cuthbert Edward Ellison (d. 1883), a police magistrate. *Mahon's History: History of England from the Peace of Utrecht to the Peace of Aix-la-Chapelle* , 7 vols. (1836-54), by Philip Stanhope (1805-75), fifth Earl Stanhope (called Viscount Mahon 1821-55). *Elwin:* The Reverend Whitwell Elwin (1816-1900), editor of *The Quarterly Review.* *W. H. B. H. M. I. of S.:* William Henry Brookfield, Her Majesty's Inspector of Schools. *Andalusia:* presumably the daughter of Lady Molesworth (*née* Andalusia Grant). *Rowland Hill:* later Sir Rowland Hill (1795-1879), who was responsible for the introduction of penny postage on 10 January 1840.

224. TO JOHN EVERETT MILLAIS
26 February 1857

Newcastle on Tyne. Feb. 26.
My dear Millais.
    I thank you very much for your proffered hospitality. I wonder can I accept it and how I am to get from Kirkcaldy where I lecture on the 10th. to Perth where I am set down for lecturing the next day—On the 12th. I am to be at Dundee: and about that horrible Kirkcaldy can make out nothing after the most desperate study of Bradshaw. You at Perth will be best able to judge what will be the best plan for me—whether, by the nature of things, I shan't arrive late—whether I shan't have to set off early the next morning to keep my Dundee engagement, and whether under these circumstances I had not best go to an Inn where beds are always ready porters and cabs are always in attendance &c—Likewise I am obliged to travel with a servant owing to obstinate attacks of Roman (bilious) fever wh. has had hold of me these 4 years past, and seizes and prostrates me every month or so. If, considering these things, you think a Hotel the best place for me, perhaps you will decide *against* my coming to you. But the offer of hospitality is equally kind on your part and Mrs. Millais' & I am very much obliged to you for proposing to have me as your guest.

Always sincerely yours
W M Thackeray.

Millais: John (later Sir John) Everett Millais (1829-96), painter, whose wife was the former Euphemia Gray (1828-97). *Bradshaw: Bradshaw's General Railway Directory.*

225. TO THE GEORGE BAXTERS
31 October-27 November 1857

36 Onslow Square.
November 1.
but begun yesterday at the
Athenæum where I found your letter.

These are pretty reproaches indeed Ladies!—I should like to know who wrote last to both of you? I flatter myself its I who am the injured party—though that it may be months ago since I wrote I confess. And I have been thinking of you all the time of this panic and actually was too frightened to write. Last Monday I came home to the girls and announced that the carriage and one must be sold (we keep a carriage and one a very pretty open carriage and a brougham if you please.) that Jeames must certainly go, if not chawls too (Mr. Chawls is such a great man now that he cant do without a young man in livery to help him) that all the American savings were gone to smash, including the 500£ from Harper Brothers for the Virginians. It is astonishing how well we took our ruin. Next day however things began to brighten again: and it appears we are not done for, as yet at least. What shall I tell I have just come back from Oxford after that little electioneering freak. I should have won but for the Sabbath question, and on that point I wont truckle or change to get any possible promotion or glory—and am quite as well out of Parliament as in. Tell Sally my fits of blue devils continue—that I have fallen in love with nobody else and intend to dont—that nobody is come after my homely girl who is the delight of her father when he sees her. I have had the parents with me for the last 3 months: or with the girls rather my visits being only occasional. I dont think the Virginians is good yet though it has taken me an immense deal of trouble but I know it will be good at the end. I tremble for the poor publishers who give me 300£ a number—I dont think they can afford it and shall have the melancholy duty of disgorging. Sure I think this is all my news; but I think about America a many & many times and in so friendly a manner that I am perfectly certain I shall be walking Broadway again ere long. Do write and tell me that you are not severely hurt in the panic. I took a share in the Transatlantic Telegraph (deeming it a sort of duty) but the Oxford Election cost me so much that I was obliged to sell the Transatlantic-share, so that that money was so much saved—

Only 2 people of all those I canvassed had ever heard of my name. It wouldn't be so in America, would it? It was a good lesson to my vanity.

My summer trip was confined to a house at Brighton and a little excursion to Homburg & Paris. The girls rode hack horses and bathed and were happy. My mother who has been ailing for more than a year has improved very much during her 3 months visit to us. I am rather better in health I think but becoming more silent & selfish every day. Women know how to dissemble when they are bored, and appear cheerful though they are yawning in spirit. I wish I could be a little more of a hypocrite sometimes. Your daughter S. H. writes glumly that she is a wreck:—a wreck with a pooty ittle boy floating on it is always an interesting object—Let us carry the young ones safe to shore. Ha! There is a large tear wh. my pen has shed. It is one of a box of pens wh. I bought in Washington. D. C. What about the boys? Is Wyllie working hard and as good as ever Has George begun to grow a moustache? Is that tiresome fever and ague out of the house? I have not had a touch since the 4 of July when I was sitting quite happy and unprepared, after a good dinner, listening to Lord Brougham & Lord Lyndhurst telling wicked old stories, and lo! I felt the enemy creeping down my back. Mysterious chill & fever!—Prattling wh. nonsense my paper has come to an end. Was it a grand marriage of Miss Libbie? Mind, I consider it is my privilege to send each of those young ladies a tea-pot. The girls and I will go into town to day to look for one: & when Madame Jaudon uses it she will please remember her & your

Here it is the 2[7] November and the letter begun on the 1st. still lying in my box. Do you know why it was not sent?—First we went out to look for a T. pot—then we couldnt find a pretty little one such as befits a young bride who wishes to console herself with Bohea in the absence of her hearts darling. Then when in about a week I had got scent of a pretty little old tea pot it is a fact I had NO MONEY—that is to spare—That is times are so bad and every man so hard pressed that 1, 2, 3, 4 up to 14 people have been to me for gold and silver in the course of the month, and I couldnt refuse them in their distress and didn't dare to buy even a two penny halfpenny present whilst all these unfortunates were calling out for help. As I came in just now Charles says Mr. C's servant just called with a note wh. he was to leave [']in case you were at home' Do you suppose I dont know what that means? Mr. C. will call himself tomorrow morning before 11 (the wretch!) and say My dear fellow the times are so bad that if you can lend me &c. and how on airth with all this can I go and get that teapot? Never mind. Wait a while, Libbie, It must and SHALL be bought, meanwhile take the benediction of your affectionate Uncle—wh. is I think my relationship to you.   What has happened since the 1st.? Nothing particular. My good old parents are gone away after a good long visit—The old Major grows to be more and more like Colonel Newcome every day. My mothers health has greatly improved She enjoyed her visit here. We are very smart. You should see our new Brougham if you please, &c &c &c. God bless you all—a very merry Xmas to you, to brides to bridegrooms to spinsters piccaninnies grandmothers grandfathers grand and common uncles, and to S S H from yours ever

the panic: a panic caused by the collapse of a number of financial institutions. *electioneering freak:* Thackeray spent nearly £900 as an unsuccessful candidate for Parliament in Oxford during July 1857. *Lord Brougham:* Henry Peter (1778-1868), first Baron Brougham and Vaux, liberal reformer and Lord Chancellor. *Lord Lyndhurst:* John Singleton Copley (1772-1863), first Baron Lyndhurst, Lord Chancellor. *marriage of Miss Libbie:* to Frank Jaudon in October 1857.

226. TO JOHN BLACKWOOD
21 December 1857

Monday. Decr. 21. 1857.
My dear J. B.
    I write you a line of thanks for your capital kind letter of ever so many days agone: wh. reached me when I was agonizing of no III—so little way have I made in the last weeks. All last month not a word. My good old parents took possession of the house, as they have a right to do, but by this and that managed to bother me so that I couldnt write or think or do anything but fume and fret and wonder when they'd go. O J. B! when your children grow up, Dont you go & stay four months in their house! I have announced to Anny & Minny that *I* never will do such a thing when they are married. Well, I got through the number in a dreadful nervous way and want if I can to do another number this month—We are going to the Sturgises for Xmas the whole party of us Amy Crowe and all. They have a famous house and claret almost as good as Randolph Crescent. O Lor what a drink I had yesterday at H. Waddingtons & the day before that & tomorrow at Tom Barings and so on & so on—It's a wonder how I stand it that it is.
    What to tell you about our news? We dont sell 20000 of the Virginians as we hoped, but more than 16000 and should have done better but for the confounded times. I have thought proper to knock 50£ a month off my pay from Bradbury & Evans till we get up to a

higher number—For you see Sir my publishers have always acted honestly & kindly by me and I dont want any man to lose by me. I never hear the book mentioned except in stray kind notices from country friends, from you, from Prescott at Boston who is delighted—And I am delighted that you are so—A few days ago on coming home just about dinner time whom should I find in the drawing room but young SMETH. I said 'Smith I am very sorry I cannot ask you to dinner to day'. He burst out laughing but totally declined to go away and so, strange to say, he stayed and told us how kind you & Mrs. Blackwood had been to him and what a many times he dropped into Randolph Crescent about meal time: in wh. I must say Smeth showed his good sense.

When shall I come, I wonder? Let me get a couple of numbers on a head and see—I dont like this going to Mount Felix knowing that little work is done in a country house, but who could afford to disappoint the girls and such dear good girls as mine? We are giving and going to lots of dinner-parties—the Swells are beginning to forgive me & ask me again: but I dont want them now I am paterfamilias, and give them a wide berth—Saturday I dined with Dickens a mans party to poor W. Russell who sails for India on the 26 and is very low about it. To day Mr. Forster dines with me & 2 boys from Oxford and ever so many more and we would fain be merry. Sir, I have invested 100£ in '48 claret, and hope to be alive to drink it with some good fellows 4 years hence when it is to be the finest wine in the world. Do you begin to smoke how you come by this letter? It wanted 1/2 an hour of dinner. Thinks I let us send off a shake of the hand to Randolph Crescent before the Coompanee comes and wish a God bless you & a happy Xmas to all kind folks round that kind table. Accept that benediction then young people, and little people, from

Your sincere old friend

no III: Number 3 of *The Virginians* for January 1858.   *Waddington:* Horatio Waddington (1799-1867), civil servant.   *Baring:* Thomas Baring (1799-1873), financeer and M. P.   *knock . . . pay:* Thackeray's initial rate of income from *The Virginians* was £300 per installment.   *Mount Felix:* a seat in Surrey adjoining Walton-on-Thames.   *poor W. Russell:* the newspaper correspondent William Howard Russell (1820-1907), who had been ordered by *The Times* to India to report on the atrocities committed during the Mutiny of 1857, was reluctant to leave his wife, who was seriously ill.

227. TO WILLIAM DUER ROBINSON
23 January-25 February 1858

Saturday. Jan 23. 1858. 36 Onslow Sqre
A sudden gust of friendship blows from this boosom in the direction of Houston Street and my Wobinson. The fact is, Sir, I was in the drawing room just now, and out of a portfolio on one of the elegant rosewood tables, there peeped a photograph, wh. represented the honest old mug of W. D. R. How is he? Can he afford to drink Claret still? are there any cocktails about 604? I would give a guinea to be there—and now and then get quite a bust of feeling towards folks on your side. Davis's marriage came upon me quite inopportunely; I have had to give presents to no less than 4 brides this year and I can't positively stand no more. The last was Libbie Strong, whose votive teapot is at this present moment in my house, waiting for an opportunity to X the water. What can I tell you about myself? Nothing very good, new, or funny. That complaint you wot of is never cured quite, and I have the doctor always about my hydraulic engine. Virginians are doing pretty well thank you, but not so very well as we expected so that I only draw 250£ per month instead of 300£ as the agreement is. But I like every body who deals with me to make money by me So I cede those 50£ you see until better times. I have just paid the last of the Oxford Election bills, and got how much do you think out of 900£—13£ is the modest figure returned. Then you know J G King's Sons have somehow forgotten to send me any dividends upon Michigan Centrals & N Y Centrals. So I am not much richer in Jan 58 than I was in Jan 57, that's the fact. But then in compensation I live very much more expensively. Charles, much injured by going to America, has been ruined by the company he keeps next door. Next door has a butler and a footman in livery. Charles found it was impossible to carry on without a footman in livery: so when the girls dine off 2 mutton chops they have the pleasure of being waited on by 2 menials who walk round & round them. We give very good dinners. Our house is full of pretty little things. Our cellar is not badly off. Sir I am going in a few days to pay 100£ for 18 dozen of '48 Claret that is not to be drunk for 4 years. That is the price Wine has got to now. 'Tis as dear as at New York. No wonder a fellow can't afford to send a marriage token to his friend when he lives in this here extravagant way.   I fondly talk of going to America in the autumn and finishing my story sur les lieux. I want to know what was the colour of Washingtons livery—Where the deuce was George Warrington carried after he was knocked down at Braddock's defeat. Was he taken by Indians, or into a French fort? I want him to be away for a year and a half, or until the siege of Quebec. If you see Fred. Cozzens or George Curtis, ask them to manage this job for me, and send me a little line

stating what really has happened to the eldest of the 2 Virginians. (This is genteeler paper than the other, wh. I use for my 'copy' paper.) I only got my number done last night, and am getting more disgustingly lazy every day. I *can't* do the work until it's wanted. And yet with all these attacks of illness wh. I have, I ought, you know I ought. Sir I came up stairs now to do a little work before dinner; only I thought how much pleasanter it would be to have a chat with old Robinson! Do you see in the Times this morning the death of Beverley Robinson late a Captain of the R. Artillery? He must be one of you. And now it is 5 minutes to 7: and it is time to go dress for dinner. Hark at the Brougham-horse snorting in the frost!

Not that WT is grown any fatter wearing still the same coat waistcoat & britches wh. he sported in N. *York*

This is Wednesday 27. What do you think I did yesterday? gave one of the old 51 lectures in a Suburb of London. It was quite refreshing. Went there with my (hydraulic) doctor who attended me all last year without a fee—gave him the 25£ cheque wh. they gave me for the lecture. It was easily earned money wasn't it?

HE DRESSES FOR DINNER

How shall I fill up the rest of this thin paper? Ever since the Georges I have been in disgrace with the Bo Monde. My former entertainers the Earls and Marquises having fought very shy of me. This year they're beginning to come back

Thursday 25th. Yes, but the 25th. February. What a time this letter has been a-composing! I have written a number two numbers since it began have had 3 confounded attacks of spasms have spent ever so much money grown ever so much older and not a bit wiser— am just at my desk again after attack No 3. Yes. Claret drunk not wisely but too well, an immoderate use of the fleshpots are beginning to tell upon the friend of W. D. R. If I dont write this letter off now I shall never send it thats flat. It must go, Robinson, and I want you to ask Duer THIS IS THE ONLY IMPORTANT PART of the letter, whether (I cannot spoil my own mug on the other side) whether the Michigan Centrals and New York Centrals are ever going to pay, and what becomes of the absent dividend of last year? What are my Michigan Bonds worth now? Will you get me a philosophic answer to these questions please? What more? I often look at your beauteous image. Next week I am going to Macready in the country to read one of those demd old Georges. He offers me 50£ to read in 2 little towns close by and I wont. Why do for nothing what I wont do for 50£? because I am sick of letting myself out for hire—I have just bought a famous little cob that carries me to perfection. Adieu Robinson, Davis, Duer

---

Davis's marriage: Bancroft Davis married Frederica Gore King on 19 November 1857. *sur les lieux:* (Fr.) on the spot. *not wisely but too well:* Othello, V, ii, 344.

228. TO JOHN REUBEN THOMPSON
25 February 1858

36 Onslow Sqre.
Brompton.
Feb 25.

My dear Thompson
    I was away from home when your melancholy news came last year, and have left a longer interval than I intended before writing to you and begging you to tell Mrs. Stanard how sincerely I deplore her loss and esteemed and respected the friend who has been called away from among you. I have been much in Virginia since as you know who have followed my books, and that friendly kind honest good Stanard has been constantly in my mind as I thought of your dear little friendly place. I have all his hospitality in my recollection the pictures on his walls, the flavour of his wine, the tone of his voice, and the generous welcome.
    Mrs. Stanard knew how much I liked him. I counted on more than one other pleasant meeting with him—Your City will hardly be the same to me without him.   And to you others who lived with him every day—to the wife whom he cherished with such extraordinary tenderness, and who knows his intimate and sacred good qualities a thousand times better than we do, what must his loss be! No stranger has a right to speak in the presence of such a great domestic affliction, but we may say an honest word of regard and respect for a good man departed, and I beg you my dear Thompson to tell Mrs. Stanard and her boy how very warmly and gratefully I think of Robert Stanards kindness to me, and how heartily I liked and respected him.
    I am myself so constantly unwell now that I begin to think my turn to be called cannot be delayed very long. These Virginians take me as much time as if I was writing a History. I often hope that I may

come over and finish it on the ground itself, and certainly mean to do so if health & circumstance will let me. I would give a guinea to sit in the Rocking Chair again, and shake a few hands in Richmond. Give my regards to any who remember me to Gibson and Myers and your good father; and please to tell Mrs. Stanard how very sincerely I am hers

and yours my dear Thompson
W M Thackeray.

We are in a great political excitement here, but I was cured of my political fever by the bleeding I had at Oxford last year. I can't spend 1000£ at every election.

Thompson: John Reuben Thompson (1823-73), editor of *The Southern Literary Messenger.* *Mrs. Stanard . . . her loss:* Mrs. Robert Craig Stanard, the former Martha Pierce, whose husband had died in June 1857. *your good father:* John Thompson.

229. TO MRS. GEORGE BAXTER
10-23 April 1858

April 10, 23.
36 Onslow Sqre.

My dear Mrs. Baxter. Isn't it a horrible thing that Libbies tea pot is still in the cupboard yonder under Washington's bust? Is it a year since she was married? A set of weeks become a month and a set of months a year before I know where I am now, and every day of the year has its turmoil, trouble, illness, parties, letters, printers'-devils, duns botherations, and so we go on and on until the end of troubles and pleasures—Do you know heres the 10th. of the month and only 3 pages of my number done? I have had 2 attacks within the last fortnight of my enemy: each attack throwing me back a week or so. I have been with the girls to a deal of parties and dinners. That graceless Charles Pearman has left my service after five years, but has left a remembrance of himself behind with the house maid who has been with me 12 years a respectable honest ugly elderlyish person who must forsooth forget 35 years of decent life and respectable parentage, in order to read the old story with Mr. Charles. O fie!—But to return to Libbie's tea pot, Captain Comstock wrote to me some time ago that he was coming to London and would take it with him—I not liking to trust the precious article to the common carriage or possible miscarriage of a steamer Hence the delay in the transmission of this domestic little article. Have I ever written to you before on this ugly paper? I find it pleasanter far to the pen than your beautiful cream-laids and gilt edges.

23. And here the letter again stopped 12 days ago; and, on Friday night after awful trouble, I only got my number done, just in time to send it by post to Liverpool & America. The book's clever but stupid thats the fact. I hate story-making incidents, surprizes, love-making, &c more and more every day: and here is a third of a great story done equal to two thirds of an ordinary novel—and nothing actually has happened, except that a young gentleman has come from America to England—I wish an elderly one could do 'tother thing, and have the strongest wish to come and see you all. Are there any more Hamptonkins come or coming?   What have we been about these 10 days? tramping the round of parties, giving dinners, and eating brandy peaches from New York—quite plain dinners, not ostentatious, but o dear me how much pleasanter the men's parties are than those with ladies, that's the fact.—Tomorrow Miss Anny gives her first drum—I have set my face hitherto against these entertainments from the peculiar nature of Our Society—we know great people & small, polite & otherwise: the otherwise are not a bit comfortable in company of the others but get angry if they are not asked. I know this horrible teafight will bring down all sorts of odium upon the givers: but they will have it, and though I'm not quite such a soft Papa as G B of 2d. Avenue, if my young women set their hearts on anything they are pretty sure to get it. I am afraid the 2 Lambert girls in the Virginians are very like them, but of course deny it if any body accuses me.

We have been in the midst of immense political fluster. I have seen my name as a candidate for no less than 4 places in event of a dissolution of parliament, but dont want one now for a while. Let us have some more lectures and some more money first. My expenses (have I ever grumbled to you about them?) are awful. I have a one horse chay and spend 2600£ a year *at least.* Two families each with a carriage could live for that money—but then they dont give away 500£ as somebody somehow does. Also at the end of the month when the number is done, I go and buy pooty things—6 such byootiful spoons as I brought home yesterday! And what do you think? I have had a new coat the first in four years. I have a famous little horse to ride and get on him once a fortnight. I have good daughters, good wine in the cellar, easy work, plenty of money in my pocket, a fair reputation—I ought to be happy oughtn't I? Eh bien! I dont think I am above 4 days in the month. A man without a woman is a lonely wretch. Hark at the bells dingdonging for Church! Shall I go? No I forgot—Mr. & Mrs. Blackwood, Mr. & Mrs. Pollen (o Sally Hampton such a pretty woman!) 4 Selves, Lord John Hay, Sir Charles Taylor, Mr. Bidwell, Mr. Motley (of U.S.A) Mr. Creyke, and Mr. Edwards are coming to dinner at 7. A Frenchman is my butler and valet, in the place of the seductive Charles—and poor Eliza went away 3 days ago —going into the room and giving a last fond look at her young ladies, whom she has faithfully and affectionately tended since Childhood. It's pitiable isn't it? Meanwhile, comme à l'ordinaire I know who will have to pay the Doctor—Last year the lady with whom my wife lives, made a great outcry because her house was robbed of goods to the value of 25£ & her plate. I gave her 25£ and 6 table spoons 6 tea ditto 6 forks—So it was *I* in fact who was robbed: but she goes on crying about it to this present day. Here have I been chattering till it is time for dinner! My dear kind old friend—once and again it is a pleasure to come and sit down and talk to you—Give my best regards to all, & God bless you—Perhaps you'll let S S H have this and my dooty to her. You see I dont like to stop but keep chattering on till I'm in the hall, down the steps and actually out of doors—Good bye.

W M T.

Eh bien!: (Fr.) Ah well!   *Pollen:* Mr. and Mrs. John Hungerford Pollen. *Lord John Hay:* (1827-1916), son of the eighth Marquis of Tweeddale.   *Sir Charles Taylor:* (1817-76?), second Baronet.   *Motley:* John Lothrop Motley (1814-77), American historian and diplomat.   *Edwards:* Henry Sutherland Edwards (1828-1906), journalist.   *comme à l'ordinaire:* (Fr.) as usual.

230. TO MRS. HENRY CARMICHAEL-SMYTH
May 1858

My dearest Mother. My letter wont be as neatly written as usual, for I write all askew lying on my back these 4 days under Thompson's inevitable operations. The first 2 days to add to the pleasure I had the spasms as well as the other malady But the last 3 attacks have been decidedly lighter, and I sleep through most part of 'em. So the poor girls' drum went off, and the people who are not asked are all angry as I expected and they agree now that it will be wise never to drum again. The rooms looked very pretty the fire places being crammed with 20/ worth of hired flowers and I delighted Lady Airlie by telling her Mrs. Fladgates artless compliment Who is that handsome woman in the door with the black lace Behind? Everybody praised Pauline but but BUT, I know she's not tall enough for the place In spite of the pain & bother, the rest up here has not been unpleasant. When do I ever get 4 days to myself without printers devils engagements petitions for money—O stop Ive forgotten poor Mr. Langley to whom I give 1£ a week for a sham job! I must ring and ask about Mr. Langley—yes he has been here sure enough poor fellow yes he is coming again. We pack him up his sovereign. May we always have one to spare for a poor fellow!

Well what to say? Here is sad news in the literary world—no less than a separation between Mr. & Mrs. Dickens—with all sorts of horrible stories buzzing about. The worst is that Im in a manner dragged in for one—Last week going into the Garrick I heard that D is separated from his wife on account of an intrigue with his sister in law. No says I no such thing—its with an actress—and the other story has not got to Dickens's ears but this has—and he fancies that I am going about abusing him! We shall never be allowed to be friends that's clear. I had mine from a man at Epsom the first I ever heard of the matter, and should have said nothing about it but that I heard the other much worse story whereupon I told mine to counteract it. There *is* some row about an actress in the case, & he denies with the utmost indignation any charge against her or himself—but says that it has been known to any one intimate with his family that his and his wifes tempers were totally incompatible & now that the children are grown up—it is agreed they are to part—the eldest Son living with her the daughters &c remaining under the care of Miss Hogarth who has always been mother, governess, housekeeper, everything to the family. I havent seen the statement but this is what is brought to me on my bed of sickness, and I'd give 100£ it could [. . .] To think of the poor matron, after 22 years of marriage going away out of her house! O dear me its a fatal story for our trade.

Langley: Samuel Langley, Thackeray's secretary.   *an actress:* Ellen Ternan (1839-1914).   *[. . .]:* the writing has faded at this point.

231. TO ADELAIDE ANN PROCTER
4 June 1858

36 Onslow Sqre. June 4.

My dear Adelaide
      Thank you for the little book with the kind little inscription on the first page. There will always be an a . . . . r . . . . . between us, won't there? and we shall like each other out of our books and melancholies and satires and poetries & proses. Why are your verses so very very grey and sad? I have been reading them this morning till the sky has got a crape over it—other folks' prose I have heard has sometimes a like dismal effect.—one man's especially I mean with whom I am pretty intimate, and who writes very glumly though I believe he is inwardly a cheerful wine-bibbing easy-going person, liking the wicked world pretty well in spite of all his

grumbling. We can't help what we write though; an unknown Something works within us and makes us write so & so—I'm putting this case *de me* (as usual) and *de te*. I don't like to think you half so sad as your verses. I like some of them very much indeed: especially the little tender bits. All the allusions to children are full of a sweet natural compassionateness; and you sit in your poems like a grey nun with 3 or 4 little prattlers nestling round your knees, and smiling at you, and a thin hand laid upon the golden heads of one or two of them: and having smoothed them, and patted them, and told them a little story, and given them a bonbon the grey nun walks into the grey twilight, taking up her own sad thoughts, and leaving the *parvulos* silent & wistful. There goes the Angelus! There they are lighting up the Chapel. Go home, little children, to your breadandbutters and teas: and kneel at your bedsides in crisp little night gowns.

 I wonder whether this has anything on earth to do with Adelaide Anne Procter's poems? I wish the tunes she sang were gayer: but *que voulez vous?* The Lord has made a multitude of birds and fitted them with various pipes; (there goes *my* Anny singing in her room, with a voice that is not so good as Adelaide Sartoris's, but wh. touches me inexpressibly when I hear it) and the chorus of all is Laus Domino.

 I am writing in this queer way, I suppose, because I went to St. Pauls yesterday—Charity Children's day, Miss, and the sight and sound immensely moved & charmed

Yours affectionately dear Adelaide
W M Thackeray.

book: Miss Procter's *Legends and Lyrics* (1858).   *a...r...:* Thackeray evidently meant "affectionate regard."   *de me...de te:* (Lat.) regarding me... regarding you.   *parvulos:* (Lat.) little ones.   *que voulez vous?:* (Fr.) what do you expect?   *Laus Domino:* (Lat.) Praise to the Lord.

232. TO THE GEORGE BAXTERS
25 August 1858

36 Onslow Sqe. August 25.

 I wonder whether I shall have the energy to get through this sheet—this sheet? this page. But try we wool though I owe ever so many people letters before you Madam, and this is safe to be dreadfuly stupid. Dont you see that I cant even spell?—I am constantly unwell now—a fit of spasms—then get well in about 5 days; then 5 days grumbling and thinking of my work; then 14 days work and spasms da capo—and what a horribly stupid story I am writing! Dont tell me.

I know better than any of you. No incident, no character no go left in this dreary old expiring carcass—There Miss Sally—you howl on your sea-shore and I will roar from mine. Come let us placidly take leave of our friends (not telling them anything I mean) go each to the top of a rock, and jump over and end our troubleoubleoubles in the midst of the sad sea waves' bubbleubblubbles—I am serious—You fancy I am joking. I tell you I am done, & I don't care. My dear it is all liver. We have been away on a (for the girls) jolly little Swiss tourkin of 5 weeks and I find the kind letters among the heap on my return home. As for my dear Mrs. Baxters, it steps silently into the room, and soothes me like a sweet refreshing calming anodyne—Fact is I'm quite beat and unwell and can scarce see the paper on wh. I write.

Is Libbies teapot ever going? Yes Andrew Arcedeckne Esqe. (the original of Mr. Foker dont say so though) will take it over in a foo days. It has got black and is so small & shabby that I am ashamed to send it. But o my dear Libbie—Times are dark and will be dark so dark that no man shall be able to work—Make haste and get married Lucy my dear, if you want a sillivyer tea pot or you will have none from your unfortunate W. M. T. My dear kind mothers heart, I am so glad it is elated at Wylly's getting such honours. When he comes to England he will talk to 2 orphans in a shabby genteel house about their maniac father. Nobody in the least is coming to marry them—and nobody I am sure is wanted, by their selfish parent—Annys happiness makes almost me happy—*unblases* me when I am under the influence over it—When I am lying up stairs in bed you know dreadfully ill with those spasms, and yet secretly quite contented and easy, I say to myself 'Good God what a good girl that is!['] Amen.

I have nothing to tell you as usual—I went away having got into trouble with a young fellow who told lies of me in a newspaper, wh. I was obliged to notice as we are acquaintances, and meet together at a little Club—You have read something about it in the papers, I daresay—The little papers are still going on abusing me about it I hear—and dont care as I never read one. The public does not care about the story nor about the Virginians nor I about either—nor do I know what there is in these 3 pages, nor whether I shall send them. Yes I think I shall send them because I can pay the post you know, and because once and away I like to growl out that I love you ever so many of you very sincerely—   I think taraxacum might do something for Sally who is still (comparatively) young. If I wanted to see the children I would say so: but I don't. I suppose for form's sake I must send my love to them though. There. Bless you bless you my little dears. Take em away Nurse. Wowwoowow Rawwawwaw. Chickaly Chickaly Chickaly. O zoo pooty little darlings—O you unfeeling Broo-oo-oot! says Aunt Lucy walking out of the room quite haughty. Well—he is really unwell that is the fact Grandmamma says. I think I'm ever so little better now I am got to the end of this absurd paper. God bless you all—Papa and the boys and the gals and Uncle Oliver says

                Your affte
                W M T.

da capo: (Ital.) over again from the beginning.   *so dark . . . able to work:* paraphrased from John 9: 4: "the night cometh, when no man can work." *unblases me:* makes me no longer *blasé*.   *into trouble . . . young fellow . . . newspaper:* the controversial "Garrick Club affair," which began with a snide article on Thackeray published by Edmund Yates in *Town Talk*, and concluded with Yates being expelled from membership in the Garrick Club at Thackeray's request. *taraxacum:* a drug made from dandelion root and used as a tonic.   *Uncle Oliver:* Oliver Smith Strong (1806-74), Libby's widowed father.

233. TO LADY POLLOCK
20 September 1858

      Hotel Bristol. Place Vendôme. Paris.
Monday But what is the day of the month?+ of September 1858.

My dear Lady Pollock
  The other day, as I was groaning on my sick bed at home, came the postman's daily packet, which I scarce had courage to open; and amongst the letters, a pretty envelope with 2 pretty glazed cards embracing each other within, announcing the pairing and departure of the first of your young birds from the happy Hatton nest.
  I have not had time to write till the honeymoon is well nigh over; for 2 or 3 attacks of illness in the last few weeks sent me dreadfully behindhand with my work; but it was finished this morning (when Mr. George Warrington of Castlewood Va came to life again) and the first letter must be to congratulate Mrs. Chitty's mamma, and hope she will be a happy Grandmamma, and that all good fortune, good health, and good temper may attend her young people. Mothers I know, like their daughters to be married; but I am prepared to hate the man who shall take away either of mine: so I congratulate you, and heartily condole with the Chief Baron. This reads rather stiff and prim, and as if it was taken out of a book, doesn't it? but it is meant very sincerely, I do hope and believe; for, you see, a man can't have so much kindness and hospitality and friendship as I and mine have had

from you and yours without feeling a little grateful (though I daresay my books say otherwise) and interested in all that befals you. So I wish the young folks heartily well, and their parents ever so many years to enjoy the junior's prosperity.

My girls are here with their GMother: your humble Servant at this hotel, and just going down stairs from the 4me. to the 1er. to dine with the Attorney General and Lady Kelly. And so please to believe me

Ever yours sincerely
W. M. Thackeray.

P.S. After dinner. Nice little dinner. Ay. Gl. very agreeable. I find on reference to my pocket-book that today is Monday 20th.
+ That absurd question shows I didn't go to church yesterday.

from the happy Hatton nest: on 7 September 1859 Clara Jessie, the eldest daughter of Lord Chief Baron and Lady Pollock, married Joseph William Chitty, a barrister. Hatton was the Pollock's residence in Middlesex. *Warrington . . . again:* in chapter 48 of Number 12 for October 1858. *Kelly:* Sir Fitzroy Kelly (1796-1880), husband of the former Ada Cunningham.

234. TO DR. JOHN BROWN
4 November 1858

Hotel des 2 Mondes. Rue d'Antin. Paris
November 4.

My dear Dr. John.

Your kind note has followed me hither. I have many a time thought of you and of writing to you: but it's the old story: work, dinner spasm, and da capo. I have nothing specially cheerful to say about myself, and dont like the Virginians 1/2 as much as you do. Very good writing, but it ought to have been at its present stage of the story at no X—I dawdled fatally between V & X—those spasms were knocking me about; or I am old, or I am tired, or some other reason. All remains yet doubtful about my poor mother. She has had more than 6 weeks bed: but we dont know yet whether the fracture is to join or what is quite the nature of it. Poor dear it was in returning from coming to see me in one of my fits that some boys ran against her near her own door, & occasioned the mishap. She bears it wonderfully: her health has rather improved—her mental health certainly, and neither she nor her husband quite knows how serious the accident is. I send no condolements about the departure of your good old Father. He was ready I suppose, and had his passport made out for his journey. Next comes our little turn to pack up and depart. To stay is well enough: but shall we be very sorry to go? What more is there in life that we haven't tried? What that we have tried is so very much worth repetition or endurance? I have just come from,—a beefsteak and potatoes 1f.—a bottle of claret 5f. both excellent of their kind: but we can part from them without a very severe pang—and nota that we shall get no greater pleasures than these from this time to the end of our days. What *is* a greater pleasure? Gratified ambition? accumulation of money? What? Fruition of some sort of desire perhaps—when one is twenty, yes, but at 47 Venus may rise from the sea and I for one shd. hardly put my spectacles on to have a look—Here I am snarling away on the old pococurante theme. How good-natured you are not to be tired of me!

The girls & I have been to Versailles to day. We rather liked it. They went to my mother afterwards I to solitude & beefsteak before mentioned. The spasms are certainly not so bad as formerly The last 2 attacks I have had—one a week since, one 6 weeks ago, I have taken no medicine at all and find myself as well at the end of the perfo[r]mance. Hydraulics in moderate working order—always to be got under control any day. The worst of the spasms is there must be no more lecturing for I never can calculate upon being well. Have never heard Dickens but hope & believe he will make a great bit of money for the 8 children. Must entirely concur in your opinion about poor Aytoun: and cant conceive how the fellow has got to be such an utter affectation as he is. O how cold my back is! how cold the weather is! how stupid the letter is! How much better it would be to be sitting by the fire reading that stupid book, than writing this stupid note! From the tone of this note dont you think I had better take a grain of blue pill to night? Good night Doctor, good night Madam, good night children

Wednesday. mg. But *is* Miss Mackenzie going to marry milor? Bath House will be restored to us in that case. Since her death, I have not been within the door. Have been sleeping in the most innocent manner for 10 hours, have got such beautiful apartments here, am living at an awful expense though. 1£ a day for rooms is nothing here. It is the dearest capital in Europe: how respectable folks in your Athens would tremble at the extravagance here! Come. There is no more room in the paper

PS. My mother goes on remarkably well so well that I think I may soon go home.

da capo: (Ital.) over again from the beginning.   *your good old Father:* John Brown, Senior, who had died on 13 October 1858.   *pococurante:* (Ital.) indifferent.   *heard Dickens:* heard Dickens give a public reading from his works.

Aytoun: William Edmondstoune Aytoun (1813-65), lawyer and poet. *Mackenzie:* Louisa Mackenzie, who became the second wife of William Bingham Baring, second Baron Ashburton, on 17 November 1858. *her death:* since the death of Lord Ashburton's first wife, the former Lady Harriet Montagu, on 4 May 1857.

235. TO CAPT. GEORGE FRANKLIN ATKINSON
27 December 1858

Hotel Bristol. Place Vendome.
December 27. 1858.

My dear Captain Atkinson
  I received your beautiful book whilst I was in London, but was in such a state of bewilderment and botheration with my own little volume that I hadn't heart to perform the proper duties of gratitude and society and thank you for your present and dedication. It was very interesting to me to see what my native country is like now—I have far off visions of great saloons and people dancing in them, enormous idols & fireworks, rides on elephants or in gigs, and fogs clearing away and pagodas appearing over the trees, yellow rivers and budgerows &c—I'm always interested about the place, and your sketches came to me as very welcome, besides being exceedingly pretty cheerful & lively. I hope the book will succeed: It must have been an awful bill to pay.

  As for that little hint about Printing House Square, I know the Editors and most of the writers; and, knowing, never think of asking a favor for myself or any mortal man. They are awful and inscrutable, and a request for a notice might bring a slasher down upon you, such as I once had in the Times for one of my own books (Esmond) of wh. the sale was absolutely stopped by a Times article. I wish your volume every success, and thank you for putting my name on its first page.

Ever yours
W M Thackeray.

Atkinson: Captain George Franklin Atkinson (1822-59), East India Company army officer and author. *your beautiful book:* *Curry and Rice* (1858), dedicated to Thackeray. *budgerow:* a keelless Indian barge. *Editors:* of *The Times*. *Times article:* a negative review of *Esmond* by Samuel Phillips (d. 1854) that appeared in *The Times* of 22 December 1852.

236. TO LADY HARDINGE
13 March 1859

36 Onslow Sqr. S. W.
Sunday. March 1[3].

Dear Lady Harding
Thanks for the Wolfe orders. They are, I think, very characteristic of the man who drew his sword and swaggered so oddly in Pitt's dining room. I like the Quixotism in his character, wh. helped him perhaps to be a hero; and fancy a sort of gasconading and military strut not in the least unbecoming a good and brave man. But I daren't draw the character quite as I fancy it: for I may be utterly in the wrong, and have no right to take liberties with such great names. I am sure Pitt Sr. was a prodigious quack and think he did an immense mischief but who am I to dare to say as much, or to fling mud at the tall Statue wh. History has chosen to elevate to him? Some day or other I may perhaps try & treat this subject quite seriously, or find it too high for me, and leave it alone.

Very faithfully yours
W M Thackeray.

Lady Harding: the former Lady Emily Jane Stewart, who had married the first Viscount Hardinge. *drew his sword and swaggered:* the night before General James Wolfe's departure for America the elder Pitt invited him and Lord Temple to dinner, at which Wolfe spoke with bravado of what he would do, drew his sword, and flourished it around the room.

237. TO MRS. MARIA HAAS
15 May 1859

36 Onslow Sqe. S. W.
May 15. 1859.

Dear Madam
I have been ill and very busy, or I should sooner have acknowledged your note. I am very thankful to have such testimonies of good will as your letter contains, and am occupied this early Sunday morning in answering no less than four wh. the last number of my story has brought me. I have been called misanthrope and cynic so long and so often, that I can't help being pleased when people find out that my heart is not altogether stone. The truth is I think in art as in life that Sentiment should be most carefully and sacredly used: and mistrust the man who is always crying in his books or in his daily dealings. That I can give my readers comfort or pleasure is a sincere

pleasure and comfort to me: and the thought of being able sometimes to do so, is one of the most precious rewards wh. my profession brings me. I am glad that you & Theo are both out of your troubles, and am yours dear Madam very faithfully

W M Thackeray

238. TO MRS. JOHN BLACKWOOD
28 May 1859

36 Onslow Sqre. May 28.

Madam. On Friday 3 June Can you & Monsieur Blackwood come and dine if you please with yours

W M T & Co.

O what a narrow escape I have had this month!
Twice ill. 4 days each time. Obliged to
come out without my plates.
What a national calamity!
only done at 6
Yesterday
evg!
Hip Hip
Huzzay

239. TO ANNE AND HARRIET THACKERAY
23 August 1859

XXXVI. O.S. S.W.
XXIII. VIII. MCCCCCCCLXIX

Once more I'm out again, and going about again, should be sorry to have such another bad bout again. Only think of that unlucky Charles whom I told to stop at Haden's on his way saying that he rang 3 times & couldn't get in. Hence I wasted 6 hours. The sickness came on the medicine wouldnt stay in my stomach—and I'm only better this morning. Also. The brandy wh. Cole gave me & wh. I had 1 glass had leaked to a glass & a half: he says 'some one must have another key to the cupboard[']; also the once-round ties about wh. I made a hubbub have come back into residence in my drawers. I'm afraid the poor fellow is a roguypoguy. But then the poor fellow took an excursion-train 5/ there & back and only spent 8d. for his dinner.

Nothing has happened except that I have a letter from an anonymous gentleman in Germany who says that unless I can help him to something to do, he shall shoot himself on the night of the 8th. September next in St. James's Park!—a German evidently, but writing excellent English.

The news with Smith & Elder is this. For the new Magazine we are going to turn the Comedy into a story in 6 numbers to be followed by the 4 Georges in 4 numbers—and not begin the long story until July. Haden strongly recommends me to try Harrogate or Aix les Bains—And Im at a loss between the 2. It will be late for the latter when my next number is done.

And tell Mrs. Southern with my compliments that I hope the married couple will go out of my room tomorrow as we shall scarcely be comfortable three in a bed.

And give Sir Wm. an old man's blessing for taking care of my daughters—I shan't make any promises about coming down *à cause:* but I hope tomorrow will be the happy day & shall have spent 6 days in London, on only the first of wh. any work was done. Perhaps it mayn't be tomorrow after all. There are still 12 pages to do.

And so farewell my sweet young creatures says

Your respectable père
W M T.

Of course give the poor boys anything you like.

Haden: Dr. Francis Seymour Haden (1818-1910), surgeon and etcher.   *Cole:* Sir Henry Cole.   *new Magazine: The Cornhill Magazine,* which began publication with its January 1860 issue.   *the Comedy:* Thackeray's play, "The Wolves and the Lamb."   *a story: Lovel the Widower.*   *Sir Wm.:* Sir William Plunkett de Bathe (1793-1870), third Baronet.   *à cause:* (Fr.) because.

240. TO ALFRED TENNYSON
September — 16 October 1859

Folkestone. September
36 Onslow Sqre. S. W. October

My dear old Alfred.

I owe you a letter of happiness and thanks. Sir, about 3 weeks ago, when I was ill in bed I read the Idylls of the King, and I thought 'o I must write to him now, for this pleasure, this delight, this splendour of happiness wh. I (a poor creature [. . .]) have been enjoying.['] But I should have blotted the sheets—'tis ill writing on one's back. the letter full of gratitude never went as far as the post office—and how comes it now?

D'abord—A bottle of claret. (The landlord of the hotel asked me down to the cellar and treated me.) Then afterwards sitting here, an old magazine, Frasers's Magazine 1850, and I come on a poem out of The Princess wh. says 'I hear the horns of Elfland blowing blowing'—no it is 'the horns of Elfland faintly blowing—' (I have been into my bed room to fetch my pen, & it has made that blot.) and, reading the lines, wh. only one man in the world could write, I thought about the other horns of Elfland blowing in full strength, and Arthur in gold armour and Guenevere with gold hair, and all those knights & heroes and beauties and purple landscapes and misty grey lakes in wh. you have made me live. They seem like facts to me, since about 3 weeks ago (3 weeks or a month was it?) when I read the book. It is on the table yonder, and I dont like, somehow, to disturb it, but the delight and gratitude! You have made me as happy as I was as a child with the Arabian nights: every step I have walked in Elfland has been a sort of Paradise to me. (The landlord gave *two* bottles of his claret and I think I drank the most.) and here I have been lying back in the chair and thinking of those delightful idylls—my thoughts being turned to you, what could I do but be grateful to that surprizing Genius wh. has made me so happy?. Do you understand that what I mean is all true, and that I should break out were you sitting opposite with a pipe in you[r] mouth? Gold and purple and diamonds, I say, Gentlemen and Glory & Love and Honour—if you haven't given me all these why should I be in such an ardor of gratitude? But I have had out of that dear book the greatest delight that has ever come to me since I was a young man—to write & think about it makes me almost young—and this I suppose is what I'm doing—like an after-dinner speech.

P.S. I thought the Grandmother quite as fine. How can you at 50 be doing things as well as at 35?.

October 16 (I should think 6 weeks after the writing of the above.)

The rhapsody of gratitude was never sent, and for a peculiar reason—just about the time of writing I came to an arrangement with Smith & Elder to edit their new magazine—and to have a contribution from A was the publisher's & editors highest ambition. But to ask a man for a favor, and to praise and bow down before him in the same page seemed to be so like hypocrisy, that I held my hand—and left this note in my desk, where it has been lying during a little French-Italian-Swiss tour wh. my girls & their Papa have been making.

Meanwhile S & E & Co have been making their own proposals to you, and you have replied not favorably I am sorry to hear: but now there is no reason why you should not have my homages, and I am just as thankful for the Idylls, and love and admire them just as much as I did 2 months ago when I began to write in that ardor of claret and gratitude. If you can't write for us you cant. If you can by chance some day, and help an old friend, how pleased and happy I shall be! This however must be left to fate & your convenience: I dont intend to give up hope, but accept the good fortune if it comes.   I see one two three quarterlies advertized to day as all bringing laurels to laureus—He wont refuse the private tribute of an old friend, will he? You dont know how pleased the girls were at Kensington t'other day to hear you quote their father's little verses—and he too I dare say was not disgusted.   He sends you and yours his very best regards in this most heartful and artless

(note of admiration) !

Always yours my dear Alfred
W M Thackeray.

[. . .]: the ink has almost completely faded at this point.   *D'abord:* (Fr.) first of all.   *a poem:* quoted in Charles Kingsley's "Tennyson," a review article in the September 1850 issue of *Fraser's Magazine* devoted to *Poems* (1842), *The Princess* (1847; rev. 1850), and *In Memoriam* (1850).   *Grandmother:* "The Grandmother's Complaint" (1859).

241. TO MRS. GEORGE BAXTER
21 September — 18 October 1859

Genoa. Hotel d'Italie. Sepr. 21. 1859.
My dear Mrs. Baxter.   Two days ago at Nice, I saw many boys with brown faces and great eyes wh. put me in mind of a boy in a brown house in a Second Avenue in New York where I used to see many kind faces a few years ago: and just now looking out of window into the harbour here, I see passing a ten-oared man-of-war's boat with a flag of Stars and Stripes flying at the Stern and the Captain says with his speaking trumpet says he 'Why dont you write to New York?' 'Very good, Captain' says I 'you are quite right, and I will.' I havent touched a pen for a whole fortnight (o wonder!) and I may as well sit down and remind old friends that I remember them and am alive. We shut up the dreary old Virginians at 2 o'clock on the morning of the 7th. I took the last pages up to London with me, and returned straight to Folkestone, and we crossed to Boulogne, and of course I was more sick than in 4 voyages across the Atlantic—and next day we whisked off to Tours, only passing through Paris, from

one Station to another; and from Tours we went to Bordeaux, Toulouse, Marseilles, Nice a charming place to my fancy, and thence came on hither by the steamer. I was thankful to the 🦟 (I killed 5, but only send you portraits of 2) wh. wouldnt let me sleep below and sent me on deck to see a moonrise ten times as big and lucent as our moons, and a sunrise over the mountains round this bay—As for the sun *set*, it is a positive fact that I never see one without thinking of America.

What to tell you since I wrote last? When did I? I fear it is months ago: & my letters, when they do come (filled, like every other literary man's letters, with himself,) are not pleasant. In these last 2 years I have had at least 20 attacks of confounded spasms, wh. are death-like whilst they last—I mean I hardly know what happens what with pain, laudanum, & so forth) and then 2 or 3 days of recovery, and then the printer's devil at the door again, and the unavoidable chapter to be done—The unhappy book is all the worse for the ill health of the author, and from about the 10th. to the 30th. October we shall see in the newspapers and reviews some pretty remarks on this subject—About the 4th. number, being then very ill, I got all my people into a fatal groove through wh. I was obliged to see them; and so spoiled my book. The last number contains the incidents wh. should have been filled out into 6. It is a failure thats the fact, and I intended to have made a great victory—Farewell Virginians. Bonjour 2 years labour. But when I came to put the real personages on the stage—I had the queerest scruples of Conscience—'How dare you,['] it was always saying, 'mention the names of real respectable gentlemen & ladies and tell lies about them?['] Battles, adventures, and escapes and such like are equally repugnant to me—I constantly turn from them, and have said to Mrs. Secretary Anny, on coming to some such incident and with one, no several, of my frightful oaths — & — me & — — let me ring the bell, and tell John to do this chapter—so the incident has ended in a brief sentence or two, wh. a real novelist and one not above his business would put into 30 or 40 glowing interesting pages. And seeing how my health had failed, and my style was languid, I had determined to rest and fortify both and was going not to put pen to paper for 6 months—but—BUT it is arranged otherwise. We begin a new magazine on the first January, of wh. I am to be conductor—You see, in spite of failing health, and perhaps powers, the sun is shining brighter than ever, the hay-crop must be taken in—I've not got enough yet to live upon without labor—and if I drop at it, why not? Hush! If I live for 3 years, more I calculate I shall make—well—I wont tell you the number of hundreds of thousands of pounds: but a good bit of money: and enough to give us comfortable maintenance for the days when work is past. You see, Mr. Baxter, about those New York Centrals wh. I bought (and of wh.

I bought a few more last year at 92!)—a family man mustnt put his trust in them alone—and the next eggs my Goose lays for me must be placed in another basket.

But how kind the goose has been! We have been travelling with 4 post horses: don't care whether we spend 20$ a day or 50—and every time we come to a very beautiful view, or pleasant place, I cry out with my accustomed pleasantry 'Heaven bless you, O my public!' and the girls laugh, as I expect them to do when I say anything, & whenever I say it afterwards. 'Why Papa,' cries Anny from the opposite table of our ducal Saloon (theres not such a sized room no not in 5th. Avenue, let alone Second)—'to see you sitting there writing to Mrs.Baxter—it's as if you were quite young again!'—and so one is for the little holyday—no care for the confounded next number—no spasms and abominable physic—no greater trouble than that musquito wh. has just given me the mildest little nip under my right eye—and if I could do nothing for 6 months, no doubt I should be immensely better—but here is the crop: and now is the time to cut it. When our poor fellows went into action at Peiho the other day—no doubt they knew that a ball if it hit 'em, wouldn't agree with them—But—O what a smell of salt fish comes in at our ducal-palazzo windows!—and just as I was going off into a phrase about DUTY.

We had been staying at Folkestone for a month before we left England to be near my mother who I think is coming to settle in England. Since her accident in September last, she shows that she is 67 years old, and walks very very slowly on her stick. Her husband is 80 and pretty well, and as good and gentle as old Colonel Newcome in his last days. We want to persuade them to a house at Brighton where we can be within reach, and she can get sermons of any required strength & length. What is this I read about Bellows and a new religion? And I buy a penny paper and find a bit of a novel by G. Curtis: is it Hadji? Ye gods, but I should like to see you all again—When did I have a letter from Mrs. Sarah? It was a sad one: and an unanswerable one too. Nobody thinks of coming to marry my girls—and so much the better for their father—An old friend of mine, a Frenchman, said last year—Theres my Paul. He is just of an age! How much do you give your girls? Its not enough. Ah what *dommage!*

One of them sits on the opposite side of the room drawing the other who I believe is drawing me—and so we are a sitting in our droring room a droring each other all round.

O blessed indolence! There is nothing, no nothing like doing nothing! And the abominable Care being away from the door, and the weary brains at rest, we are at leisure to talk to old friends—and to have a chat with my dear kind Mrs. Baxter, to whom and to all whose belongings W M T sends his best and most affectionate regard.

October 18. Only think of my bringing this all the way back to London! I have brought back my poor Anny who fell ill in Switzerland, my parents from Paris who are growing very old & infirm, myself who am but a cranky vessel, and am getting into harness again, & busying myself with the new magazine with wh. the New Year begins—may it be happy for us and ours

says yours ever
W M T.

Peiho: the battle of the Peiho River in China, part of a British attempt to install a Minister at Peking.   *Bellows:* the Reverend Henry Whitney Bellows (1814-82), pastor of the First Unitarian Church of New York.   *Hadji:* the "G. Curtis" was apparently not George William Curtis.   *what dommage!:* (Fr.: *quel dommage*) what a pity!

242. TO ANTHONY TROLLOPE
28 OCTOBER 1859

36 Onslow Sqre. S. W.
October 28

My dear Mr. Trollope
    Smith & Elder have sent you their proposals: and the business part done, let me come to the pleasure: and say how very glad indeed I shall be to have you as a Cooperator in our New Magazine. And, looking over the annexed programme, you will see whether you can't help us in many other ways besides tale-telling. Whatever a man knows about life and its doings that let us hear about. You must have tossed a deal about the world, and have countless sketches in your memory or your portfolio Please to think if you can furbish up any of these besides the novel: When events occur on wh. you can have a good lively talk, bear us in mind. One of our chief objects in this Magazine is the getting out of novel-spinning, and back into the world—Dont understand me to disparage our craft, especially *your* wares. I often say that I am like the pastry cook, and dont care for tarts, but prefer bread and cheese—but the public loves the tarts (luckily for us) and we must bake & sell them. There was quite an excitement in my family one evening when Paterfamilias (who goes to sleep over a novel almost always when he tries it after dinner) came up stairs to the Drawing Room wide awake, and calling for the Second Volume of the Three Clerks. I hope the CornHill Magazine will have as pleasant a story: and the Chapmans, if they are the honest men I take them to be, I've no doubt have told you with what sincere liking your works have been read by

                           yours very faithfully
                           W. M. Thackeray.

as a Cooperator: Trollope began his contributions to *The Cornhill Magazine* with his novel, *Framley Parsonage* (1860-61).   *Three Clerks:* Trollope's novel, *The Three Clerks* (1858).   *the Chapmans:* the publishers Edward and Frederic Chapman.

243. TO JOHN H. BEWLEY
31 October 1859

36 Onslow Sqr. S. W. London
October 31. 1859.

Dear Sir

I mislaid your note last week when I received it, and wrote by last Friday's mail to a friend at New York, requesting him to see you and thank you for writing to me. None of us ever knew any of poor Glynn's relations. The most intimate friend he had is away in South America. I met him first at Mr. Eliot Warburton's rooms whose fate was even more melancholy than Glynn's He had lived for many years in Paris before his emigration to the States: Mine I think was the last house he was in in London, and his almost the last face I saw as I left New York. He found more than one very kind friend there. I never saw him to greater advantage than at New York in a shabby coat toiling away at a lithographic press, perfectly cheerful, pleasant and cordial. A character something like his I put into one of my stories. Of course he recognized it: & laughed and told me he thought the Captain of my story was a very fine fellow. So had the original many admirable qualities, bravery, generosity, hopefulness, kindliness but Fortune is not to be taken by a *coup de main*, and poor Glynn had a chance or two, of wh. I know, and of wh. he failed to take advantage. At the outbreak of the Hungarian War I got him a situation of War-Correspondent to a Morning Paper. It seemed the very thing for him He departed with uniforms and all sorts of recommendations. He did everything—but the correspondence—All this of course is private between us—Nothing could be more kindly than the obituary notice of him wh. you sent me. Have there been any expenses attendant on his funeral? I shall be very glad to divide them with you, who have shown so much care and kindness for his remains. Will you be so good if you think fit, to make out a little account of the cost of burial &c & permit me to pay the half of it? My friends Messrs. J. G. King's Sons of New York will, I have no doubt, on your presenting this letter, pay the sum whatever it may be. Believe me Dear Sir

Your obliged faithful Servt
W M Thackeray.

Glynn: Captain Harry Glynn, who was a model for Captain Strong of *Pendennis.*
coup de main: (Fr.) surprise attack.

244. TO "A CONTRIBUTOR"
1 November 1859

[Private]

"The Cornhill Magazine," Smith, Elder & Co.
65, Cornhill, 1st November, 1859.

TO A CONTRIBUTOR.

Dear ———

Our Store-House being in Cornhill, we date and name our Magazine from its place of publication. We might have assumed a title much more startling: for example, "The Thames on Fire" was a name suggested; and, placarded in red letters about the City and Country, it would no doubt have excited some curiosity. But, on going to London Bridge, the expectant rustic would have found the stream rolling on its accustomed course, and would have turned away angry at being hoaxed. Sensible people are not to be misled by fine prospectuses and sounding names: the present Writer has been for five-and-twenty years before the world, which has taken his measure pretty accurately. We are too long acquainted to try and deceive one another; and, were I to propose any such astounding feat as that above announced, I know quite well how the schemer would be received, and the scheme would end.

You then, who ask what "The Cornhill Magazine" is to be, and what sort of articles you shall supply for it; if you were told that the Editor, known hitherto only by his published writings, was in reality a great reformer, philosopher, and wiseacre, about to expound prodigious doctrines and truths until now unrevealed, to guide and direct the peoples, to pull down the existing order of things, to edify new social or political structures, and, in a word, to set the Thames on Fire; if you heard such designs ascribed to him—*risum teneatis?* You know I have no such pretensions: but, as an Author who has written long, and had the good fortune to find a very great number of readers, I think I am not mistaken in supposing that they give me credit for experience, observation, and for having lived with educated people in many countries, and seen the world in no small variety; and, having heard me soliloquize, with so much kindness and favor, and say my own say about life, and men and women, they will not be unwilling to try me as Conductor of a Concert, in which I trust many skilful performers will take part.

We hope for a large number of readers, and must seek, in the first place, to amuse and interest them. Fortunately for some folks, novels are as daily bread to others; and fiction of course must form a part, but only a part of our entertainment. We want, on the other hand, as much reality as possible—discussion, and narrative of events interesting to the public, personal adventure and observation, familiar reports of scientific discovery, description of Social Institutions—*quicquid agunt homines*—a Great Eastern, a battle in China, a Race Course, a popular Preacher—there is hardly any subject we *don't* want to hear about, from lettered and instructed men who are competent to speak on it.

I read the other day in "The Illustrated London News," (in my own room at home,) that I was at that moment at Bordeaux, purchasing first class claret for first class contributors, and second class for those of inferior *cru*. Let me continue this hospitable simile; and say that at our contributors' table, I do not ask or desire to shine especially myself, but to take my part occasionally, and to invite pleasant and instructed gentlemen and ladies to contribute their share to the conversation. It may be a Foxhunter who has the turn to speak; or a Geologist, Engineer, Manufacturer, Member of the House of Commons, Lawyer, Chemist,—what you please. If we can only get people to tell what they know, pretty briefly and good-humouredly, and not in a manner obtrusively didactic—what a pleasant ordinary we may have, and how gladly folks will come to it! If our friends have good manners, a good education, and write in good English, the company, I am sure, will be all the better pleased; and the guests, whatever their rank, age, sex be, will be glad to be addressed by well-educated gentlemen and women. A professor ever so learned, a curate in his country retirement, an artisan after work-hours, a schoolmaster or mistress when the children are gone home, or the young ones themselves when their lessons are over, may like to hear what the world is talking about, or be brought into friendly communication with persons whom the world knows. There are points on which agreement is impossible, and on these we need not touch. At our social table, we shall suppose the ladies and children always present; we shall not set rival politicians by the ears; we shall listen to every guest who has an apt word to say; and I hope, induce clergymen of various denominations to say grace in their turn. The kindly fruits of the earth, which grow for all—may we not enjoy them with friendly hearts? The field is immensely wide; the harvest perennial, and rising everywhere; we can promise competent fellow-labourers a welcome and a good wage; and hope a fair custom from the public for our stores at "THE CORNHILL MAGAZINE."

W. M. Thackeray.

risum teneatis: (Lat.) could you refrain from laughing? (Horace, *Ars Poetica*, l. 5).
quicquid agunt homines: (Lat.) all the activities of man (Juvenal, *Satires*, I, 85).
cru: (Fr.) locality of vineyards, upon which their classification is based.

245. TO THE REV. SAMUEL REYNOLDS HOLE
26 January 1860?

January 26.
36 Onslow Sqre.

My dear Hole
Did I ever write and comply with your desire—To have a page of autograph? You're welcome to a quire. Tell your friend the lady I have no pleasure higher than in writing pretty poetry and striking of the lyre in compliment to a gentleman whom benevolence did inspire to send me pheasants and partridges killed with shot or wire (but whatever the way of killing them I equally admire) and who of such kind practices I trust will never tire. May you bring your birds down every time you fire This, my noble sportsman, is the fond desire of W. M. Thackeray Editor and Esquire.

Hole: The Reverend Samuel Reynolds Hole (1819-1904), clergyman and huntsman.

246. TO SIR HENRY DAVISON
4 May 1860

4 May.

How dy do my dear old Davus? Read the Cornhill Magazine for May the article little Scholars is by my dear old fat Anny—She sends you her love So does Minny—We re going out to drive—
We ve got 2 hosses in our carriage now. The Magazine goes on increasing and how much do you think my next 12 months earnings & receipts will be if I work?

$$10,000 \pounds$$

Cockadoodleoodoodloodle.
We are going to spend 4000 in building a new house on Palace Green Kensington. We have our health. We have brought Granny & G P to live at Brompton Crescent close by us—and we are my dear old Davus's

Faithful
W M. A. I. & H M. T.

Davison: Thackeray had dedicated *The Virginians* to Davison, who was serving as a judge in India.

247. TO THE GEORGE BAXTERS
25 December 1860

The autumn has passed away in wh. you were to have come to England and here is a bitter cold Christmas day and no news of you. I am unwell. I am hard at work trying to get the new Story on a head—I have been quill driving all the morning, but I must say a word of God bless you to my dear kind friends at Brown House Street and wish you a Christmas as merry as may be. Aren't you in a fright at the Separation? Is Sally going to be a Countrywoman of your's no longer, and will her children in arms fight Libby's? It's a horrible thing to me to read of. Have you ever seen a coloured print called the Belle of the West I have it hanging up because it is like a young woman whom I used to admire very much. (perhaps other little partialities are hung up too and are now only so many painted memorials on a wall) Is it this horrid Separation that has prevented your all coming to Europe—Or are you waiting till next year when my fine new house will be built—at Palace Green, Kensington—opposite the old palace. If I live, please God, I shall write the history of Queen Anne there. My dear relations are furious at my arrogance extravagance & presumption in building a handsome new house, and one of them who never made a joke in his life said yesterday to me 'You ought to call it Vanity Fair.'

I wonder whom you have got at dinner to day? Our house is all hollyfied from bottom to top. We have asked a poor widow from India with her *five* children, and two or 3 men friends, and we have got a delicate feast consisting of

>Boiled Turkey.
>Roast Goose
>Roast Beef.

and I am going to make a great bowl of punch in the grand silver bowl you know—the testimonial bowl.

No one has come to marry either of my dear girls. I am surprized they dont. But I hardly know any men under fifty, and cant be on the look out for eligible bachelors as good dear London mammas can. I have not made their fortunes as yet, but am getting towards it and have saved a little since I wrote last; but I am free handed, have to keep my wife, to help my parents, & to give to poor literary folks—in fine my expenses are very large I am supposed to make 10,000£ a year Write 5 and it is about the mark. Health very so so. Repeated attacks of illness. Great thankfulness to God Almighty for good means, for good children. And thats all. Hadnt I better go on with Philip? Here is the very last sentence I wrote.

'When I was a girl I used always to be reading novels, she said but la! they're mostly nonsense! There's Mr. Pendennis, I wonder how a married man can go on writing about love and all that stuff!' And indeed it is rather absurd for elderly fingers to be still twanging Dan Cupid's toy bow & arrows. Yesterday is gone, yes— but very well remembered. And we think of it the more now we know that Tomorrow is not going to bring us much.

Good bye my dear Yesterdays. And believe me affectionately yours

When I ... us much: see *Philip,* ch. 6.

248. TO THOMAS FREDERICK ELLIOT
11 January 1861

Jan. 11. 36 O Sqre.

My dear Fred,
I have lost the best friend left me in the world. I write a line to Kate. What can the girls do for Jones' school? It seems to me a comfort that we can look after that and do something that will please the dear Soul in Heaven. God bless you, my dear friend. Since I have known you and her I have had nothing but kindness and sympathy and tenderness from both of you.

Affectionately yours,
W. M. T.

best friend: Mrs. Elliot had died suddenly on 9 January 1861.

249. TO FREDERICK LOCKER
22 January 1861

My dear Locker
I hope you bear your ♣ of Saturday equanimously. I ought to have been here to prevent it for you were only b-k b-ll-d because there was nobody to speak for you and there should have been such a friend. But I was in bed Thursday Friday & 1/2 Saturday with one of my spasm fits & too sick to think of anything but the basin. I had to go out on Saturday to see Fred Elliot, and just as I was driving

away his sister in law poor Miss Perry said she would like to see me—When I arrived here, all was over. Bear up like a man. You are none the worse, & 28 guineas the richer.

Yours
W M T.

Locker: the poet, Frederick Locker (1821-95), later Locker-Lampson.   *here:* the Garrick Club.

250. TO JOHN FREDERICK BOYES
10-19 March 1861

March 10. 1861.

My dear F. B.

Only 2 days ago, in one of my own attacks of illness wh. are now so frequent, I was lying in bed thinking of old times and my illness at School and your Mother's dear kind face standing over me—and when I got up I thought I would go and see her, and shake a hand with the kind old times wh. are now ended. I only found your note amongst my heap of letters this morning, Sunday, when I'm able to read—not quite to remember and arrange—for the first time these 5 days—Im so weak and nervous now from illness (and other circumstances wh. become immensely annoying when the corpus is not yet quite sanum) that I can only write you a word of hearty condolence and sympathy and promise you that I retain always a warm tender recollection of old kindness, old days, old *youth*—now gone whither? Are we young people still walking about at this minute with your dear Mother, or sitting round the old supper-table? Why shouldn't the good old Father be walking down to the New River with us boys now? Perhaps we are all kneeling down somewhere, and hearing Pritchard praying away—What a turn it gave me, when I went to see you, to recognize the old books—Thalaba, Martyr of Antioch and so on!—Those recollections were not dead, only sleeping—and so, pray God, nothing dies love least of all—wh. your dear Mother assuredly has for you in Heaven, as you here below have for her. So we all hold on by love to the past, and by just a little turn of the circle, it becomes the future. All the way up the countless ages preceding us, Mother and Children reach in wonderful tender tradition, and off our earth pass into the world beyond—I have had a child there for 20 years now, and love her still. Good bye. I am writing with such horrible ink, pens, paper, disturbance, desk, conversation (just after Church) going on, and weakness of illness, that I scarce know how my sentences begin or end—but I am your[s] my dear old friend always

                                                                                   W M T.

    March 19. This incoherency you see is more than a week old. It was scarce done when I had to struggle to my unfinished months work and get it done somehow or other—and looking at this paper thinks I—it is all about myself and not about my old friend. Never mind—the meaning is, that I sympathize with your grief, and kindly remember old times. Our best regards to your wife. We hope to come and see you ere long and I am always yours

                                                                                   W M T.

    But that point is odd to speculate about, isn't it? The soul being immortal—The have been is eternal, as well as the will be. We are not only elderly men, but young men, boys, children.

F. B.: John Frederick Boyes (1811-79), whom Thackeray had known at Charterhouse. From 1825 to 1828 Thackeray had boarded with Boyes's parents, Mr. and Mrs. Benjamin Boyes.   *your Mother:* Mrs. Boyes had recently died.   *corpus . . . sanum:* (Lat.) body . . . healthy. A reminiscence of Juvenal, *Satires*, X, 356: *Orandum est ut sit mens sana in corpore sano* (You should pray to have a healthy mind in a healthy body).   *Pritchard:* William Pritchard (b. 1812), a schoolfellow at Charterhouse.   *Thalaba:* Robert Southey's *Thalaba the Destroyer* (1801).   *Martyr of Antioch:* (1822), by Henry Hart Milman.

251. TO WILLIAM STIRLING
1 May? 1861

                                          Windsor Castle. April 31.

My dear Stirling
    I had something of importance on my mind last night wh. I have wished to communicate to you for some days past but as usual when we met the most treacherous memory in the world played me false, and I came away without having mentioned the subject upon wh. I was anxious not to say eager to speak to you—
    What I have to say is not much but at least I can count on your courtesy for a plain answer to a simple question. That question is 'When is an apothecary always supplied with vaccine matter?[']
    The query may strike you as absurd but the solution of the ridiculous question is at least *ingenious*.

He is supplied with vaccine matter because he is an Apothecary and a Cow sure.

Your obedient Servt
The Lord Bishop of Durham.

P.S. When my Son in law Cheese was married I remarked in my Cathedral that he was a *Cheese pairing*. The harmless little *jeu de mots* (I am not an enemy to innocent mirth) elicited fits of laughter from both my Chaplains.

jeu de mots: (Fr.) play on words.

252. TO HENRY HOLLAND
17 May 1861

Dear Holland.
Yes. It's delightful; your new house. But you havent seen mine since the *new Study* has been built. That is the Roc's egg. Next time you take your walks abroad go and look at that room and be miserable ever after.
The remembrance of the Study has just come over me and given me inexpressible consolation: as I know you will be inclined to break the last of our excellent commandments & covet the house of

Your neighbour
Palace Gardens.

Holland: Henry Thurstan Holland, later first Viscount Knutsford. *the Roc's egg:* an emblem of the rare and fabulous; see "The Second Voyage of Sinbad" in *The Arabian Nights' Entertainment.*

253. TO MRS. GEORGE BAXTER
24 May 1861

24 May. 36 Onslow Sqre.
I think you hardly know me in this hand-writing I return to it by fits and starts and when I write with quill pens. Your little package of photographs came and touched us all—How I should like to see the originals, and the one who *isn't* represented, Madam. Why is there not one of you? I suppose Papa did not care to have his wife shown with a wrinkle in her face, and always thinks of her as that young lady in

white muslin and a frill, who to my mind is not half so good looking as the Mrs. Baxter I knew. How the boys have grown! Wyllys moustache is quite elegant. I daresay George has one by this time on his solemn face. Do you know, but then I should not like to tell her, I think Sarah has grown handsomer: and we are divided here about wh. of the children we like best—the dark little maiden with the round eyes or the little man with the Saxon face. There's a very fine kind melancholy letter from Sarah Hampton wh. I have been reading—It is stretching a hand out into the past and shaking hands with a ghost there. I suppose you wont have the courage to leave home now that it is made so comfortable to you by war. If Wylly doesn't come till December or so we shall most likely be able to house him in Vanity Fair House. If he comes sooner we must get him a lodging round the corner. At the pastry cook's you know, there are very decent rooms: and it's not farther off than the brown house from the Clarendon. That wretch W. H. Russell! On the night before he left London we dined at the Garrick Club: and what did I do but cut off a beautiful lock of snowy hair and write in an envelope Be kind to the bearer of this. And he never bore it to you; though he went to the Clarendon. And I dont at all envy him the errand upon wh. he is gone to the states.

AWFUL REPRISALS. Thackeray invested the money wh. he received for his lectures in America, in American railway stocks. If they cease to pay dividends, he threatens to come back to America, and give more lectures.

I wonder shall I go and call upon your Minister? I have well nigh broken with the world the grand world and only go to the people who make my daughters welcome. The fine ladies won't: or is it that the girls are haughty, and very difficult to please? They won't submit to be patronized by the grandees at all, that's the fact: and I think I rather like them for being rebellious and independent—more so than their Papa, who is older and more worldly.

I think I kept back this notekin in order to sketch the new house at Kensington—but fond memory supplies the place of actual survey: and this is what you will see when you come to London—

the reddest house in all the town. I have already had 1000£ offered me for my bargain: but I want if I can afford health & time to write the life of Queen Anne in that room with the arched window wh. has a jolly look out on noble Kensington Garden Elms, and is no farther from the centre than what? than 25th. Street let us say. But the house is very dear It costs 6000£ and 100£ a year ground rent. Where we are now only costs 3000—But its a famous situation & will be a little competency to the girl who inherits it.   Anny has been ailing of late, and has gone to the country for change of air—

I think Trollope is much more popular with the CornHill Magazine readers than I am: and doubt whether I am not going down hill considerably in public favor. It doesn't concern me very much Were I to let yonder red house We could live almost without writing but then you know Wife and parents are expensive. They want more money here than at Paris: and Thank God up to the present there's no lack. But my mother gets very rebellious and wants to go back. There's a little clique of old ladies there who are very fond of her and with whom she is a much more important personage than she is in this great city. If any thing happens to the Major she will go to Paris and give us the slip and grumble when she is there and presently come back.

Well. This is not much to tell is it?. To write twopenny news of domestic gossip to people enjoying a revolution. I have never got to believe in it as serious as yet: and my impression of the U. S. is so incurably friendly that I can't fancy you quarrelling and hating each other. I cant think the fight will be a serious fight. In what will it benefit the North to be recoupled to the South? In the old wars we used to talk of the ruin of England as ensuing on the Separation of the Colonies—and aren't both better for the Separation?

Come let me shut up this little twaddling letterkin, and pay a shilling for it wh. is 11 1/2 more than its worth, and send it with a handshake to dear friends from their faithful

W M T.

maiden . . . little man: Georgia Anna Hampton (1858-65) and her brother, Frank. *Russell . . . errand:* W. H. Russell had been sent by *The Times* in March 1861 to report on the American Civil War.   *your Minister:* Charles Francis Adams (1807-86), American Minister to Great Britain 1861-68.

254. TO GEORGE SMITH
May 1861

My dear S
   I'm very sorry for this mishap regarding Low's payment. The loss ought to be mine not your's. I shall have done the number please goodness tomorrow night, and shall go on straightway with another. Couldn't go to Paris—my hydraulics were too much out of order. Well. I've often been to Paris before, and am not very sorry.
   I believe if Lovel were brought out in a little book people would like it. It amused me when I read it: and others—a few others have spoken well of it besides

Yours always
W M Thackeray

Low: Sampson Low and Sons, London agents for Harper and Brothers. *Lovel:* Smith, Elder republished *Lovel the Widower* in one-volume book form during 1861.

255. TO THE REV. WHITWELL ELWIN
24-31 May 1861

24 May.
Ever so many days after birth.

My dear Primrose.
   I think I have just been proposed and *refused* as a member of the Literary Club, so that I cant well dine with you there. Walpole proposed me: and I told him that an adverse fate wd. very likely befal me. All people dont like me as you do. I think sometimes I am deservedly unpopular and in some cases I rather like it. Why should I want to be liked by Jack and Tom? Not long ago I went to the stalls at Drury Lane with Robert Bell, and to us came in the next stalls Dickens and Wilkie Collins. Dickens & I shook hands and didn't say one single word to each other. And if he read my feelings on my face as such a clever fellow would he knows now that I have found him out. Forster was the man who cut me because he fancied I meant him in one of the Roundabout papers, when the truth is I was no more thinking of him than of you: and I relish putting the joke in print: and know that my dear friend has read it, and won't let him cut me when he tries. I know the Thackeray that those fellows have imagined to themselves a very selfish heartless artful morose and designing man—and poor Yates in the famous Garrick Club row, was only the

mouthpiece of his masters. Did you see the penny papers, the American papers, wh. were set to work to abuse me at that time? What gall and wormwood is trickling from my pen!—Well, there's no black drop in *you*, Mr. Parson—but, mind you primroses are very rare flowers by the side of Thames.

This scrap was written a week ago: don't you think it were best burned? Many letters were best burned—for example love letters—and specially *hate* letters. But if I dont send this one off to you, how on earth shall I communicate with my Vicar of Wakefield? You know I am too lazy to begin a new page. Those hatreds in our profession are very curious. My old friend James White has been in London several weeks and at 200 yards from this and never let me know of his being here. He has a great alliance with Dickens and Forster. But why should that prevent him from seeing an older friend?. Ah if I dared but put all those fellows into a book! And suppose they put me into Another—giving their views of your humble servant? Those books would be queer reading.

I wonder shall I have life and health to write Queen Anne? I long to get to it in my old age, feeling that the days of novels romances and love making are over. Some one told me that you praised at Forster's some verses of mine written in an album—'Voices familiar once no more he hears' &c—The voice was that wh. you heard on that day at Forster's table. I hear it scarcely ever now: and shall never hear another I like so well; except that of my own children.—Come Come!

This note had certainly better be burned. You do that for it, please. What about books? You know we dont read 'em in London. I admire but cant read Adam Bede and the books of that author. Motley and the Spanish Armada amused me very much: and sure Buckle is very diverting. How savage the Scotch will be! So they will be with Yours truly in a Roundabout Paper in July I think. What a wonderful speech was Aumale's at the L. F. dinner! a perfect specimen of princely oratory—wise dignified noble and wickedly severe. I was very angry at being put up to speak against my will and in spite of my distinct refusal. The funds did not fall in consequence of my wrath.

Wont you come to London and see the new house I am building? Such a good comfortable cheerful one—And the daughter who gets it will have a snug little four hundred a year for life—It's all built out of CornHill money and I shall put 2 wheat-sheaves on the doors. There's a delightful study and I must and will do Queen Anne there. D. V:—but that is always a subaudition. Writing a gossiping letter! Well, upon my word this is a rarity! Good bye my dear Vicar. Mind & come see me when you come up for that dinner.

Yours always
W M T.

Literary Club: founded in 1764 by Sir Joshua Reynolds and Samuel Johnson. *Walpole:* Spencer Horatio Walpole (1806-98), historian and political figure. *one . . . papers:* "On a Joke I Once Heard from the Late Thomas Hood." *putting . . . print:* in "On Being Found Out." *primroses:* Thackeray called Elwin "Dr. Primrose," from the character in Goldsmith's *The Vicar of Wakefield* (1766). *'Voices . . . hears':* from Thackeray's "The Pen and the Album," written in Kate Perry's autograph-book. It had been published in *The Keepsake* of 1853, and reprinted in *Miscellanies,* Volume I (1855). *White:* the Reverend James White. *Motley:* John Lothrop Motley, author of *The Rise of the Dutch Republic* (1856). *Buckle:* Henry Thomas Buckle (1821-62). The second volume of his *History of Civilization in England,* which had recently been published, contained five chapters on Scotland in which Buckle's analysis of Scottish society and "the Scotch intellect" is frequently enlivened with comical anecdotes and satire. *Roundabout Paper:* "Small-Beer Chronicle," which mocked the Melville column in Edinburgh and the "tendency in North Britain to over-estimate its heroes." *Aumale . . . L. F. dinner:* Henri d'Orléans (1822-97), Duc d'Aumale, presided on 15 May 1861 at a dinner of the Royal Literary Fund.

256. TO MRS. THOMAS MILNER GIBSON
21-26 July 1861

> Pavilion Folkestone. Sunday.
> (and this is Friday, and I thought the letter
> was gone 5 days ago and I believe your
> young bride has actually been through here)

Dear Mrs. Gibson
    Now that the wedding is over, and the slipper has been flung after your young bride, I have a dismal satisfaction in thinking that, had we accepted your kind invitation to be present at the ceremony, two of us would not have been able to keep our engagement. I have brought my eldest daughter ailing down to this place. She has been unwell for some weeks past, and forbidden to go out. Her father has spent 2 days in bed, and only got out of it yesterday. Only one of our detachment has been in health this week; and she is wanted to look after the other two. But I can drink prosperity to the bride and bridegroom in a glass of invigorating quinine in place of champagne; and always remember the kindness I have had from you and your kind old father.

> Very faithfully yours
> W M Thackeray.

Gibson ... bride: Mrs. Gibson's daughter, Alice Mary, married William Wybrow Robertson on 20 July 1861.   *kind old father:* the Reverend Sir Thomas Cullum.

257. TO GEORGE SMITH
30 September 1861

36 O. S.
September 30.

My dear S.   Some people think long faces very becoming Mine will lengthen: but it is because your speculation is not so good as it might be: not for the personal loss to

Yours always
W M T.

In respect of Tauchnitz (as in some other cases) to be thankful for what I can get is my maxim.

Why consider. In the 2 years I have lived comfortably helped the old folks lent a good bit to friends and paid 4000£ on the house. Ought I to grumble? No thank you. In 1862 we come down of course.

P.S. I suppose Hood may publish his verses? Will you write to him yea or nay.

Tauchnitz: the Leipzig publisher who issued English works on the Continent. *Hood:* Thomas Hood, Jr. (1835-74), who published several poems in *The Cornhill Magazine.*

258. TO JOHN FREDERICK BOYES
1 October 1861

36 Onslow Sqr. October 1.
S. W.   1861.

My dear J. F. B.
    I dont know how long your packet has been lying here. I thought it contained old books purchased by me, and only opened it yesterday, when I recognized the little old Lives wh. I remember reading when we were boys in CharterHouse Square. Now we are half a century old and the kind hand wh. wrote the name in the books in that fine well-remembered writing is laid under the grass wh. will cover us old gentlemen too ere long, after our little life journey is over. And the carriage is going down the hill, is n't it? Mine is: after having had some pleasant travelling, after being well nigh upset, after being patched up again, after being robbed by footpads &c &c. The terminus can't be far off—a few years more or less. I wouldn't care to travel over the ground again: though I have had some pleasant days and dear companions.
    I have just come back from Scotland where I have been burying my good old step-father; who had but a few hours illness, and was quite well and cheerful the night before he was sent for. So they pass away. And now comes the turn of our generation: and Amen. We send our best regards to your wife and thank you for the little books.

Yours always
W M T.

step-father: Major Carmichael-Smyth had died on 9 November 1861.

259. TO GEORGE VIRTUE
13 December 1861

Decr. 13. 1861.

Dear Mr. Virtue

I lent Maginn 500£ in his life time and he paid me 20£ back. I think I have done enough in giving him bread—let other philanthropists give him a stone.

Faithfully yours
W M Thackeray

Virtue: George Virtue (1794-1868), publisher. *bread . . . stone:* a play on Matthew 7: 9: "Or what man is there of you, whom if his son ask bread, will he give him a stone?" Thackeray was being asked to help pay for a memorial.

260. TO WILLIAM STIRLING
1861

Sir—

I am desired by the Lord Bishop of this Diocese to ask if you have any idea why a Hive is like a Church Dignitary?

You probably imagine that the answer is indecent but you little know the purity of his Lordship's mind.

A hive is like a Church Dignitary because it is a Bee-shop to be sure and I am Sir

Your most obedient Servt.
Simeon Stylites
Chaplain to his Lp.

Stylites: St. Simeon Stylites (d. 459), the famous ascetic who is said to have lived for thirty years on top of a pillar near Antioch. He is the title figure of a satirical poem published by Tennyson in 1842.

261. TO EDWARD FORDHAM FLOWER
7 January 1862

36 Onslow Sqr. S. W
Jan. 7.

My dear Mr. Flower

Many thanks for the Ale. Is it because you have heard I am a Cynic that you send me a barrel? I shall empty your's with comfort,

and a good health to the giver. Good gifts never come single. I have just had a barrel of ale sent all the way from Albany, New York: and shall broach the Warwickshire present as soon as we have done with your generous New York rival. The former quite equals my XXpectations. I know yours is good of old time, and am the donor's
                              Very gratefully
                              W M Thackeray

Flower: Edward Fordham Flower (1806-83) was a brewer living in Stratford-on-Avon.   *Cynic . . . barrel:* an allusion to the Greek Cynic philosopher Diogenes, who is said to have lived in a barrel.

262. TO CONTRIBUTORS AND CORRESPONDENTS
THE CORNHILL MAGAZINE
25 March 1862

                                          March 25, 1862

Ladies and Gentlemen (who *will* continue, in spite of the standing notice below, to send papers to the Editor's private residence)—perhaps you will direct the postman to some other house, when you hear that the Editor of "The Cornhill Magazine" no longer lives in mine.

My esteemed successor lives at Number———, but I will not intrude upon the poor man's brief interval of quiet. He will have troubles enough in that thorn-cushioned editorial chair which is forwarded to him this day by the Parcels (Happy) Delivery Company.

In our first number, ladies and gentlemen, I, your humble servant, likened himself to the captain of a ship, to which and whom I wished a pleasant voyage. Pleasant! Those who have travelled on shipboard know what a careworn, oppressed, uncomfortable man the captain is. Meals disturbed, quiet impossible, rest interrupted—such is the lot of captains. This one resigns his commission. I had rather have a quiet life than gold-lace and epaulets: and deeper than did ever plummet sound I fling my speaking trumpet. Once in a voyage to America I met a Sea-Captain who was passenger in the ship which he formerly had commanded. No man could be more happy, cheerful, courteous than this. He rode through the gale with the most perfect confidence in the ship and its Captain; he surveyed the storm as being another gentleman's business: and his great delight was to be called at his watch to invoke a blessing on the steward's boy who woke him, and to turn round in his crib and go to sleep again. Let my successor command the *Cornhill,* giving me always a passage on board; and if the Printer's boy rings at my door of an early morning with a message that there are three pages wanting or four too much, I will send out my benediction to that Printer's boy and take t'other half-hour's doze.

Though Editor no more, I hope long to remain a contributor to my friend's Magazine. I believe my own special readers will agree that my books will not suffer when their Author is released from the daily tasks of reading, accepting, refusing, losing and finding the works of other people. To say No has often cost me a morning's peace and a day's work. I tremble *recenti metu.* Oh, those hours of madness spent in searching for Louisa's lost lines to her dead Piping Bullfinch, for Nhoj Senoj's mislaid Essay! I tell them for the last time that the (late) Editor will not be responsible for rejected communications, and herewith send off the Chair and the great *Cornhill Magazine* Tin-box with its load of care.

Whilst the present tale of *Philip* is passing through the press, I am preparing another, on which I have worked at intervals for many years past, and which I hope to introduce in the ensuing year; and I have stipulated for the liberty of continuing the little Essays which have amused the public and the writer, and which I propose to contribute from time to time to the pages of *The Cornhill Magazine.*

W. M. T.

thorn-cushioned editorial chair: an allusion to Thackeray's Roundabout Paper, "Thorns in the Cushion," which had appeared in the July 1860 issue of *The Cornhill Magazine. In our first number:* at the end of the January 1860 issue, in Thackeray's Roundabout Paper, "On a Lazy Idle Boy." *deeper than did ever plummet sound:* an adaptation of *The Tempest,* V, i, 56-57. *recenti metu:* (Lat.) with fear still fresh (Horace, *Odes,* II, xix, 5). *another . . . years past:* "The Knights of Borsellen," which remains incomplete.

263. TO MR. AND MRS. GEORGE BAXTER
6?-9 May 1862

Friday. May 9.

My dear friends. I am glad to have a word of news of all of you, and that you should have wished to hear of me. I didn't write though I have thought of you many a time; and feared for you, lest the war should have brought it's calamity down upon you. Before that grief wh. I know must be in your house: what to say or to do? I know what your feelings are; loyal Northerns though you may be, with the daughter and grandchildren in the South who look at us out of our photograph book so innocent & pretty and then there's the bread winner, the warehouse—does the warehouse bring any rent now? I know & feel that trying times are come on you all.

Some one called me away the other day when I wrote those last words and then I have been ill for 2 days and I was called away just as I was going to say something—Now tell me my dear kind good Baxter and wife—There may be troubles at home—no dividends—the deuce to pay. I know a fellow who is not rich, for he has spent all his money in building this fine house: all but a very little—but who knows? Draw on me for 500£ at 3 months after date: and I am your man. You wont be angry? You may be worth millions; and laugh at my impudence:—I dont know but I dont mean no harm. Only I remember and shall all my life the kindness and hospitality of the dear old brown house.

This one is delightful. I have paid 5000£ on it in 2 years out of income—but theres ever so much more to pay I dont know how much. When done however it will be a little income to the girl who inherits it and do you know I dont much care when she does. I am constantly ill—A Doctor told me at Paris t'other day that I had a fatal complaint and I wasn't very sorry. It turns out not to be true—but, but, but .... Well upon my word it is one of the nicest houses I have ever seen—as good as Mr. Haight's let us say—There is an old green and an old palace and magnificent trees before the windows at wh. I write. I have the most delightful study, bedroom, and so forth; can get 10£ for as much writing as there is on these 4 little sides; have a strong idea that in the next world I shan't be a bit better off—Well—since her husband's death my poor old mother is wandering about happy no where. I inherit from her this despondency I suppose—but have the pull over her of a strong sense of humour wh. gets plenty of cheerful laughs out of your glum old friend. Nobody comes to marry the daughters. Every body is fond of them. I think they have been the happier for my having gone to America, where a good father & mother I know of used to tell me they liked their children to have 'a good time'

I saw the Bigelows at Paris last week—he as jolly as ever. Good bye God bless you Never mind if I dont write I may be lazy or moody but always affectionately yours

W M T.

264. TO ROBERT BELL
May 1862

O Bell what a time you have chosen—I and Trollope have been engaged this week in lending a man an awful sum of money—On that Friday when your note arrived—just as I was going into dinner with some friends to dine I had actually given the man *six hundred pounds*—and I dropped your note like a hot coal and ran into dinner and lost the note and never found it till this minute when I am quill-driving for the dear life. What is to be done? Last year I lent other six hundred pounds and have received back + + + I cant and mustnt go on. I will give 20 but by George I am almost crazy—and I actually wrote to America three weeks ago to offer 400£ to some very dear friends there who I think may be in distress and I havent their answer but fully expect they will come down on

the unhappy
W M T.

265. TO GEORGE SMITH
1 July 1862

Palace Green. July 1
1862.

My dear S.

I think 'Philip' *tout court* is better than the Adventures of &c. and that a running title on every other page as in Esmond will give a little freshness to the reprint. I shall have done D. V. to day or tomorrow.

Sitting in this beautiful room, surrounded by ease and comfort and finishing the story, I stop writing for a minute or two, with rather a full heart.

Will you let Laurence make another drawing of you? I should like to hang it here.

Always yours
W M Thackeray.

tout court: (Fr.) simply.   *reprint:* "Philip" and a series of changing words and phrases appeared as the alternating running heads in the three-volume edition of 1862.   *Laurence:* Samuel Laurence.

266. TO MRS. HENRY CARMICHAEL-SMYTH
5 July 1862

July 5.

My dearest old Mother gets the budget from the girls, and the history of all our doings. On Thursday at 6.15 p.m after working all day I wrote Finis to Philip: rather a lame ending. Yesterday I spent all day in great delectation & rest of mind making a very bad drawing.

Young Walker who is 20 does twice as well: and at 20 you know we all thought I was a genius at drawing. O the mistakes people make about themselves!—Then at 5 we drive down like persons of quality in our pretty new (paid for) carriage with our 'gens' on the box to the Aumale Fête at Twickenham, where I daresay the Dukes & Duchesses would have admired my new lavender gloves (price 2/) very much—only I forgot 'em and left them in my great Coat pocket. Never mind it was a beautiful fête and I am all the better this morning, because I could only get a crust to eat and a scrap of galantine left in a lady's plate, and a bottle of excellent claret. And did the girls tell you how I had no dinner the day before having to take them to the Barbiere (a new opera by Mr. Rossini)—and where I had a most refreshing sleep in the back of the box—And this is our life: and now there is a little lull after a constant care and occupation. No, by the way, not yet, quite. Mr. Smith says 'Do, pray write a Roundabout Paper.' And that, you see, is churning in my brain whilst I am writing off a scrap to my dear old mother. Mesdemoiselles who were up actually till 12 last night could not be ready for prayers, so I was parson, and I can tell you one person of the Congregation was very thankful for our preservation and all the blessings of this life wh. have fallen to us. Think of the beginning of the story of the Little Sister in the Shabby genteel Story twenty years ago, and the wife crazy, and the Publisher refusing me 15£ who owes me £13..10 and the Times to wh. I apply for a little more than 5 guineas for a weeks work, refusing to give me more—and all that money-difficulty ended—God be praised—and an old gentleman sitting in a fine house, like the hero at the end of a Story!— The actual increase of health and comfort since we got into the Palazzo is quite curious—I am certainly much better in body—I think the novel-writing vein is used up though, and you may be sure some kind critics will say as much for me before long. Anny's style is admirable, and Smith and Elder are in raptures about it. But she is very modest and I am mistrustful too. I am sure I shant love her a bit better for being successful. They are both of them beginning to bewail their Virginity in the mountains: and seem to be much excited because Ella Merivale who is only 17 has had 3 or 4 lovers already and is doubting between 2 who are imploring her.—

Here comes Mr. Langley with the proofs wh. must be read, and there is a good morning's work over them—And then that Roundabout Paper—A plague on it—But it will [be] 60 or 70£ and I must have money to go on, now Philip is over and the supplies are stopped.

'Mr. Langley, where is the Cicero? in 2 volumes quarto. I want a quotation out of it'—Mr. Langley maunders about the room helplessly. He wont find it: I shall: and he will be persuaded that he found it, and that I can't possibly get on without him.

I wonder shall we make out the Petersburg journey?. I have a fancy for it because it will pay itself in a couple of papers that will be as easy to write as letters, and wont wear and tear the brains. Then we must do some more work. I think the story wh. I began 20 years ago—and then, and then, &c—Did you read about poor Buckle, when he got the fever at Damascus crying out 'O my book, my book.' I dont care enough about mine to be disquieted, when that day comes. Shall I live to do the big history? Who knows? But I think I shall like to work on it if the time is left me. God bless you, dear old Mother, I dont write to you by post: but I am writing through the printer all day long, and the song is always Ego. Ego. God bless us all—And now come Mr. Langley and let us go through those proofs, and all the blunders

W M T.

Walker: Frederick Walker (1840-75), painter and engraver, who helped Thackeray to illustrate *Philip*.   *'gens':* (Fr.) servants.   *raptures about it:* Anne's novel, *The Story of Elizabeth,* which appeared in *The Cornhill Magazine* from September 1862 through January 1863.   *bewail . . . mountains:* Judges, 11: 38.   *Ella:* daughter of Herman Merivale (1806-74), barrister, civil servant, and writer.

267. TO THE GEORGE BAXTERS
25 December 1862

Christmas Day. 1862

My dear friends.   The sad letter has been here for many days I had the news before from Mr. John Dillon, who has friends in the South I have not had the courage to write to you about it. I know there's no consolation. I lost a child myself once. That's enough to say that I understand your grief. That journey of Lucy and her father is the saddest thing I have read of for many a long day. I look at Sarah's face in the photograph book and then at a print wh. I have had for many years because it was like her when I first saw her. My friend Miss Perry was telling me how she had just read an old letter of mine to her dear sister (who is dead too, and who was one of the dearest friends I ever had) and how there was a description of this New York girl. What a bright creature! What a laugh, a life, a happiness! And it is all gone: and you dear people sit bewailing your darling. The letters she sent to me at rare times were awfully sad. In that photograph how sad she looks! As for those little children those two we know—we three in this house love them both. Ever since they came to us they have been in the girls' sitting room, and the Belle of the West is yonder in mine. How well I remember that first look of her, with the red ribbon in her hair! and next is that sad matron, and next your letter. What a warm welcome, what a kindly fireside, what kind faces round it—and her's the brightest of all! Amen. Dear mourning father, mother, sister we can only shake you by the hand, and pray God comfort you . . . I have been thinking in this pause of that hospitable table in your dining room, and the Spirits moving about: and looking up wistfully in this big lone room, lest a form should make itself visible. .

Christmas Day is gone and over. We had a gathering but my poor mother was too sad to come; and our relation Lady Elizabeth was too melancholy: and Miss Perry wouldn't come having her mourning to keep: and I was glad enough when they were all gone. Have you read Anny's story of Elizabeth? I have read only one number and thought the style admirable. The reading it tears my entrails somehow: and I understand what my mother says that she cant read my books. Poor dear Soul! She is very sad & lonely. She finds a doubtful consolation in her favorite parson Mr. Molyneux, who gives her 3 sermons a week. As soon as I was gone to America, leaving my girls with her, she whisked them off to a French Calvinist, for wh. her cruel son has never forgiven her. Had they followed his preaching, we should have been strangers to another: and the greatest comfort of my life would have been taken from me. In our country, religion often brings not peace but a sword—It seems to me we have talked about this in old old days. O! Have you heard how Amy Crowe has married my cousin Edward Thackeray, a fine fellow. V. C. of the Bengal Engineers. I got him his appointment. And we had a weddingkin: and they have been to Scotland, and back again: and go to India straightway.

I have cleaned out my pockets in building this fine house: and am decidedly falling in the market. My las[t.] If the next has no better success . . Well. There is bread and cheese secured: and if the coach and horses disappear I know three people who will be very cheerful and one (who thinks her whole soul is set on heaven) who will be mortified. But this is a secret. Our house is delightful. It looks like 10000£ a year; but costs to keep little more than the old one. This morning I was lying awake in the grey looking out at the elms, and thinking of your dear Sarah. God be with us. I dont feel much care about dying. As we love our children, wont our Father love us?

Dear friends I have been so happy in my home, and in your's that I can feel for the grief wh. now bears you down. God bless you all.

         Yours affectionately always
          W M Thackeray.

I dont talk a word of politics to you. I was touched by Young saying kind words of me in his paper

sad ... news: of the death of Sarah Baxter Hampton on 10 September 1862. *Dillon:* John Blake Dillon. *Lady Elizabeth:* the former Lady Elizabeth Carnegie (1798?-1886), who had married the military officer, Frederick Rennell Thackeray (1775-1860). *Molyneux:* probably the Reverend Capel Molyneux, who was the Incumbent of St. Paul's Church, Onslow Square, several blocks from Mrs. Carmichael-Smyth's residence at 52 Brompton Crescent. *French Calvinist:* Adolphe Frédéric Théodore Monod. *Edward:* Edward Talbot Thackeray (b. 1836), a military officer who served in India. *Young:* William Young, editor of *The New York Albion.*

268. TO DR. JOHN BROWN
23 September 1863

Palace Green. Kensington
Sepr. 23.

My dear J. B.
I am very glad you like my little Min. With her and her Sister I have led such a happy life, that I am afraid almost as I think of it, lest any accident should disturb it. She seems to be enjoying herself greatly: but when she has done with the Lows, I think she ought to come back to her Papa & sister. We three get on so comfortably together, that the house is not the house, when one is away. I know how kind you and your children would be to her. But Anny wants her companion, and a month will give her as much change of air as please God will be good for her. I have done no work for a whole year and must now set to at this stale old desk, or there will be no beef and mutton. I have spent too much money on this fine house, more than 8000£ one way or t'other besides gimcracks, furniture, china, plate, the deuce knows what. This was at the time of the golden days of the CornHill Magazine: but I couldn't keep the Editorship under the terms proposed to me; and so I am rather poorer than I was in Onslow Square, with a fine house wh. to be sure is worth its money & more and will be worth more still 5 years hence. If I dont mistake there was a man who lived at Abbotsford overhoused himself. I am not in debt thank my stars—but instead of writing to you why am I not writing the history of Denis Duval Esqre., Admiral of the White Squadron?

Because I don't know any thing about the sea and seamen, and get brought up by my ignorance every other page—above all because I am lazy, so lazy that a couple of dozen would do me good. Good bye my dear J B. My love to the children from

Your grateful old friend
W M T.

the Lows: the family of Andrew Low, whom Thackeray had known in America, but who spent much of their life in Great Britain. *Abbotsford:* the home of Sir Walter Scott.

269. TO DR. HENRY THOMPSON
15 December 1863

Palace Green.
Tuesday. 3 p.m.

My dear Thompson

I went to bed with 1 on Sunday night and have been there since until now 30 hours say, with no 4 inside me for the last 3. I might perhaps have staid other 20 hours for I was not uncomfortable, but I want very much indeed to have my story of 8 numbers done before I go seriously to work 3 3/4 numbers are done. I shall keep myself open as well as I can meanwhile, and wont put myself under discipline tomorrow as we talked of doing. I couldnt follow your plan on Sunday I shut up several times and used no 1/2.

Yours unfaithfully
W M T.

The hot water bottle has been my great comfort & kept off rigors.

story of 8 numbers: Denis Duval, which remained incomplete but was published in *The Cornhill Magazine* after Thackeray's death of a cerebral effusion during the night of 23/24 December 1863.

270. TO JOSEPH PARKES
[1844-50]

My dear Parkes—

I am always engaged of a Monday at our weekly dinner with Mr.

Parkes: Joseph Parkes (1796-1865), liberal politician.

271. TO LADY MORLEY
[1846-55]

But, permit me to say dear Lady Morley—Merciful powers! what must have been the astonishment of the reigning Duchess on entering her grand daughters apartment long before daybreak on the

bridal morning (with her maids of honour called up from their couches to attend the anxious parent & Sovereign) what I say must have been her H's astonishment to find the Princess's couch deserted!—

Yes deserted!—The virgin night-cap lay crimped and undisturbed on the unruffled pillow, the pillow on the swelling featherbed—wh. that night—enfin, wh. had not been slep upon that night. The room was vacant. The window was open. The bird had flown. Dear Lady Morley, Adelgisa had fled!

With best respects to your family circle believe me ever faithfully yours

Samuel Rogers

enfin: (Fr.) in short.

272. TO THE MISSES POWER?
[1847-49?]

At seven o'clock in
the morning the Poet was lying

on his bed and he sang the following
strain. Praise be to Allah.

———

Could I recal the past I would implore the Prophet to give me back yesterday.
Yesterday when many houris contended who should administer delights to this Son of Allah: and beauty beckoned to him from a hundred casements.

'The bulbul sings sweetly in the summer-moonlight[.] Come' said Sartorissa 'and I will sing more sweetly than the Bulbul.' But she took her dulcimer and sang, and I never heard her.

'I will dance before you and make you a feast' said that moonfaced one, that charmer Milneery-Gibsoon: and she danced with the tamboureen and the castanets but this Poet was blind to her agility.

[']You shall have muffins and tea before sunset['] said a Mollah's wife who lives in the Park of the Regent—[']Come to us and the butter shall trickle down your beard'. But I never regaled myself with the buttered-cakes of the Mollah's wife; and her dainties did not tempt this bard.

[']Come['] said two young song-birds in the joy-gardens of Kensington [']come and listen to us in the moonshine!—Are the Peris more beautiful than we? and are there brighter eyes than ours in the Shah's zenena? Come thou fat old poet and we will dance and sing for thee and make thy beard to wag.' But the poet never got the token wh. was sent to him by the little slave of the young song birds and knew not that those lovely ones were waiting.

There is an Imaum of a little Mosque near the Etmeidan and he said to this son of Allah, 'Friend come in and eat a kabob and smoke a Narghile. My hut is a humble tenement, but my wife Zuleikhah shall make thee a sherbet and lap thy soul in delight'. I went and sate down with the Imaum and his wife. Ah! I drank in other things besides the Sherbet, and my heart was skewered like the Kebobs with wh. she fed me. O Imaum's wife thou pearl of beauty. O Imaum's wife who makest roast meat of my heart, why ever did you roast me with your burning burning eyes?

So could I recal all the past I would implore thee Prophet to give me back yesterday—And were I to choose again among all those beauties wh. would I choose? That which is gone is gone.

the Misses Power: Ellen and Marguerite Power, nieces of Lady Blessington. *Sartorissa:* Mrs. Edward Sartoris. *Milneery-Gibsoon:* Mrs. Thomas Milner Gibson. *zenena:* (Pers.) women's quarters. *Narghile:* a tobacco water-pipe.

273. TO LADY LOUISA DE ROTHSCHILD
[1848-49]

Kensington, December 28.

Dear Lady de Rothschild— It has not been Annie's fault but mine that the two most beautiful bon-bon baskets I ever saw have come into the house and given the greatest delight to the children whom you remembered so kindly, and that you have had no word of acknowledgment for such a charming present. Annie brought me a letter ten days ago which has grown dingy already in among my papers. I wanted to write myself and thank you for your remembrance of us, but waited until my work should be done for the month before I began to pay my debt of gratitude. The printer's devil has only bid farewell to the house an hour ago. I had hardly time to think about kindness or gratitude or Xmas until he was gone, and now he is quit of the premises. I hope it's not too late to tell you that I was very pleased when your presents came to think that you were so good as to remember the children. It would have pleased you to have seen their pleasure: and what further pleased me in this pleasant transaction was that the young ones, who thought the two baskets the most beautiful and splendid treasures they ever had in their lives, nevertheless, and with a severe pang, resolved to give one of them away to some little friends of their own who had been very kind to them. This act of self-denial rejoiced the paternal heart, and I like to tell it in confidence to your ladyship, so you see you have made a great number of young folk and a middle-aged gentleman happy. Could bon-bons ever be expected to do more? Wh[y], if one could but be sure that they would always bring the same result about, wouldn't one be eating pralines and chocolate all day? This, however, reads like a remark out of *Pendennis* or some such book, and I don't wish to figure in that as an author any more now that the month's work is done; or only as the author of the two children to whom you have been so kind.

Dear Lady Rothschild, accept my thanks and best wishes for the New Year for you and your family, and believe me, ever most faithfully yours,

W. M. Thackeray

Rothschild: Lady Louisa de Rothschild (1821-1910), wife of Sir Anthony de Rothschild (1810-76), first Baronet.

274. TO SIR JONATHAN FREDERICK POLLOCK
[1848-54]

To Mylord Chief Baron
        bidding me to dine with him on ye last day of May.

By Fate's benevolent award
        Should I attain the day
I'll drink a bumper with my Lord
        Upon the last of May.
That I may reach that happy time
        most fervently I pray
For ducks and pease are in their prime
        upon the last of May.
At thirty boards 'twixt this & then
        my knife & fork will play
But better wine and better men
        I shall not meet in May.
And though, good host who bid me dine!
        your honest beard is grey,
And, like this powdered head of mine,
        has seen its last of May's
Yet with a heart thats frank & kind
        a boyish spirit gay
You've spring perennial in your mind
        and round you make a May.

275. TO LADY OLLIFFE
[1853-63]

Dear Lady Olliffe.
    The cake wh. you were so unkind as to send me has made me very unwell. I could not help eating a great deal too much of it and I know very well that I shall go on eating and eating as long as any of it remains. How many enjoyments are there in this life of wh. we will partake although we know they are injurious how many temptations (especially those bits of sweetmeat) wh. we cannot resist; how many things on the other hand wh. we are obliged to digest wh. are not near so agreeable as Lady Olliffes plum cake!

I am with sincere regret your most faithful Servt
Thomas Fraser.
Archbishop of Dublin.

Lady Olliffe: the former Laura Cubitt (d. 1898), wife of Sir Joseph Olliffe.

276. TO WILLIAM MAKEPEACE THACKERAY SYNGE
[1860-1863]

Jan 7.

My dear William Makepeace Thackeray
 I just saw this nice fish in a shop, and thought it would be a nice gift for my god-son. Dear boy, you have some friends to dine: give them this; and when they have quite done, and the shell is clean, I think you may make boats of the tail, and boots of the claws.   I wish the man had not cut the claw off: he did with his great knife, and at the same time hit me on the nose. I did not cry: and I am
Your true friend and
GOD–PA–PA

PS. I can not eat any of it. I am glad.

Synge: son of William Webb Follett Synge (1826-91), diplomat.   *glad:* Thackeray printed the body of the letter and the postscript.

277. TO DR. JAMES REEVES TRAER
[1862-1863]

Wednesday evg.

If Mr. Traer can make it convenient to call at the above address tomorrow early he will hear of something to his advantage.

Traer: Dr. James Reeves Traer, surgeon.

FURTHER READING

The Oxford Thackeray, ed. George Saintsbury. 17 vols. London, New York, and Toronto: Oxford University Press, 1908.

Annotations for the Selected Works of William Makepeace Thackeray. The Complete Novels, the Major Non-Fictional Prose, and Selected Shorter Pieces, ed. Edgar F. Harden. 2 vols. New York and London: Garland Publishing, Inc., 1990.

The Letters and Private Papers of William Makepeace Thackeray, ed. Gordon N. Ray. 4 vols. Cambridge, Mass.: Harvard University Press, 1945-46.

The Letters and Private Papers of William Makepeace Thackeray, ed. Edgar F. Harden. 2 vols. New York and London: Garland Publishing, Inc., 1994.

Thackeray. The Uses of Adversity. 1811-1846, by Gordon N. Ray. New York, Toronto, and London: McGraw-Hill, Inc., 1955.

Thackeray. The Age of Wisdom. 1847-1863, by Gordon N. Ray. New York, Toronto, and London: McGraw-Hill, Inc., 1958.

INDEX

INDEX

À Beckett family, [Gilbert Abbott] 300
À Beckett, Gilbert Abbott 300
Achilli, Giovanni 223
Adams, Charles Francis 353
Addison, Joseph 269, 270
    Sir Roger de Coverley 39
Adelaide, Queen 186
Adelphi Hotel 296
Adelphi Theatre 2, 20
Ainsworth's Magazine 102, 113, 128
Ainsworth, William Harrison 127, 139, 146, 167
    Jack Sheppard 49, 58, 146
Airlie, David Graham Drummond Ogilvy, 7th Earl of 208, 265
Airlie, Lady [Henrietta Blanche Stanley, m. 7th Earl] 208, 265, 327
Albert, Prince Consort 201
Alboni, Marietta 140
Alison, Sir Archibald
    Marlborough 276
All Souls College, Oxford 163
Allah 266, 267, 372
Allen, Capt. Bird 98
Allen, John 54
    Letter to 272
Allen, May 272
Allen, Mrs. John 61, 272
Allingham, William
    Letter to 222
America, The 309
Amphitrite, The 26
Appleton and Co. 231, 237
Appleton, Thomas 282
Arabian Nights' Entertainment 85, 352
    "The Barber's Fifth Brother"
        Alnaschar 34, 59, 66, 214, 233
Arcedeckne, Andrew 330
Aretz, M. 270

382 INDEX

Arthur's School 1
Arthur, Mr. [of Southampton] 192
Ashburton, Lady [Lady Harriet Mary Montagu, 1st w. of 2nd Baron] 189, 270, 279, 333
Ashburton, Lady [Louisa Mackenzie, 2nd w. of 2nd Baron] 333
Ashburton, William Bingham Baring, 2nd Baron 189, 211, 212, 228, 270, 333
Astor, William Backhouse 240, 298
Athenæum Club 186, 272, 318
Athenæum, The 31, 231, 314
Atkinson, Capt. George Franklin
    Curry and Rice 334
    Letter to 334
Atkinson, Mr. 125
Aubigné, Jean d' 226
"Audenard, The Battle of" 276
Augustine, St. 191
Aumale, Henri d'Orléans, Duc d' 356, 365
Austin family 86
Aytoun, William Edmondstoune 333
Bacchus 20
Baker, Mr. 311
Bakewell, Mr. 127, 272
Bakewell, Mrs. 125, 127, 272, 327
Balfour, Mr. 8
Bancroft, George 233
Bannantyne Controversy 66
Baring Brothers 236
Baring, Thomas 320
Barnum, Phineas T. 314
Bartholomew Fair 25
Barwell, Mr. 129
Bath, John Alexander Thynne, 4th Marquess of 250
Bathe, Sir William Plunkett de 337
Baxter family [George] 280, 309, 320, 326, 339, 342, 362
    Letters to 246, 318, 329, 348, 366
Baxter, George 284, 326, 331, 340, 352, 364, 366
    Letter to 362
Baxter, George [Jr.] 261, 319, 331, 353
Baxter, Lucy 237, 245, 247, 256, 281, 309, 330, 366
    Letters to 243, 260
Baxter, Mrs. George [Anna Strong] 235, 249, 250, 260, 261, 281, 308, 309, 330, 331, 341, 364
    Letters to 237, 245, 284, 325, 339, 352, 362
Baxter, Wyllys 261, 319, 330, 331, 353

Bayley, Mrs. 261
Beale, Thomas Willert 314
Beauclerc, Topham 147
Beaumont, Thomas Wentworth 40
Becher, Anne 1, 127
Becher, Charles 1
Becher, Mrs. John [Anne Fleyeham] 1
Bedford, Francis Russell, 7th Duke of 178
Bedingfield family 144
Bedingfield, Richard
    Blind Lover 122
    Letter to 122
Beethoven, Ludwig van
    Fidelio 273
Bell, Robert 355
    Letters to 154, 363
    rev. of *Vanity Fair* 154
Bellini, Vincenzo
    Il Pirata 23
Bellows, Rev. Henry Whitney 341
Belshazzar, King 170
Bennett, James Gordon 308
Bentley, Richard 80, 83
    Letters to 46, 90
Beowulf 40
Berkeley, Grantley 66
Berry, Agnes 192, 258
Berry, Mary 192, 215, 221, 258
Berryman, Miss 246
Berwick, Jacques Fitz-James, Duc de 276
    Mémoires 276
Bewley, John H.
    Letter to 344
Bible, The 10, 69, 123, 226, 352
    2 Chronicles 227
    2 Kings 227
    Abraham 123
    Acts 201
    Christ, Jesus 29, 44, 51, 123, 145, 226
    Corinthians 195
    Ecclesiastes 30
    Elisha 123
    Ephesians 139
    Exodus 237
    Ezekiel 123

384 INDEX

 Genesis 70
 Isaac 123
 Isaac, Jacob 307
 Iscariot, Judas 51
 Jacob, Isaac, Sarah 254
 Jacob, Leah, Rebecca, Laban 307
 Jeremiah 68, 154
 Job 70, 171, 176, 198
 Jonah 220
 Joshua 123
 Judges 365
 Kings 241
 Lucifer 4
 Malachi 70
 Methuselah 88
 Moses 226
 Proverbs 133, 255
 Psalms 65
 Queen of Sheba 289
 Revelation 6, 53, 215
 St. John 29, 330
 St. Joseph 134
 St. Luke 6, 37, 44, 51, 80, 144, 262
 St. Mark 37
 St. Matthew 37, 44, 144, 262, 360
 St. Stephen 191
Bidwell, Mr. 61, 326
Bigelow family 363
Bitcherdear, Mrs. 102
Black, Mr. 110
Blackburn, Mrs. Hugh 304
Blackwood children [John] 320
Blackwood family [John] 321
Blackwood, "Puck" 310, 311
Blackwood, Alexander 304
Blackwood, James 304, 311
Blackwood, John 271, 304, 310, 311, 326, 336
 Letter to 320
Blackwood, Maj. Archibald 304, 311
Blackwood, Maj. William 311
Blackwood, Mrs. John 321, 326
 Letters to 310, 336
Blackwood's Edinburgh Magazine 54, 271
Blanchard, Samuel Laman 35, 113, 167
Blechynden, Mrs. James [Sarah Redfield] 92, 94, 146

Bleecker, Mr. 245, 256
Blenheim Palace 162
Blenheim, battle of 221
Blessington, Countess of [Marguerite Power, m. 1st Earl] 151
    Letters to 167, 174
Block, Miss 306
Blomfield, Charles James [Bishop of London] 81
Boissy, Mme. de [Teresa Gamba, m. Marquis] 151
Bonneval, Lady de [Caroline Gallwey, m. Count Lionel] 279
Bonneval, Lionel, Comte de 279
Book of Common Prayer 185, 224, 255, 297, 308
Borbonico, Museo 267
Bower, Elliott 224
Bower, Mrs. Elliott 224
Bowes, John Bowes 91, 92, 170
Boyes, Benjamin 350
Boyes, John Frederick
    Letters to 350, 359
Boyes, Mrs. Benjamin 350, 359
Boyes, Mrs. John Frederick 351, 359
Boyne, battle of the 105, 287
Brackenridge, Henry Marie
    Letter to 239
Bradbury and Evans 118, 140, 158, 268, 318, 320
    Letters to 132, 301
Bradshaw's General Railway Directory 317
Bridgman, Laura 239
Brighton and Sussex Club 167, 257
Brimley, George 231
British and Foreign Review, The 40
British Critic, The 66
British Museum 53, 108
Brodie, Jessie 48, 53, 61, 68
Brontë, Charlotte 142, 223
    Jane Eyre 141, 142
Brooke, Miss 29
Brookfield family [William Henry] 209
Brookfield, Arthur Montagu 258, 259, 306
Brookfield, Magdalene 193, 195, 198, 200, 206, 258, 259, 306
    Letter to 187
Brookfield, Mr. 198
Brookfield, Mrs. William Henry [Jane Octavia Elton] 113, 127, 134, 179, 186, 187, 196, 198, 206, 207, 211, 213, 224, 232, 233, 245, 250, 251, 258, 259, 265, 268, 289, 291, 292, 295, 304, 305, 306, 316

Letters to 150, 152, 156, 159, 161, 166, 169, 176, 193, 194, 199, 201
Brookfield, Rev. William Henry 153, 156, 157, 163, 166, 170, 171, 177, 179, 186, 187, 193, 195, 196, 200, 201, 206, 208, 211, 233, 245, 250, 258, 292, 316
Letters to 114, 134, 189, 198
Brougham and Vaux, Henry Peter, 1st Baron 319
Brown children [John] 333
Brown family [John] 368
Brown, "Jock" 212, 271
Brown, Dr. John 212, 333
Letters to 224, 271, 332, 368
Brown, Dr. John [Sr.] 332
Brown, Ellen 271
Brown, Helen 212
Brown, Mrs. John 225, 333
Letters to 212, 271
Browning, Elizabeth Barrett 264
Browning, Robert 264, 282
Buckle, Henry Thomas 366
History of Civilization in England 356, 366
Buckstone, John Baldwin
Wreck Ashore 157
Buller, Charles [Jr.] 65, 166
Buller, Mrs. Charles, Sr. [Barbara Isabella Kirkpatrick] 45, 54, 166
Bulwer, William Henry Lytton Earle [Baron Dalling and Bulwer] 168
Bulwer-Lytton, Lady [Rosina Doyle Wheeler, m. 1st Baron] 58
Bulwer-Lytton, Sir Edward George Earle Lytton [1st Baron Lytton] 21, 49, 53, 58, 84, 97, 139, 167, 178, 233, 271
Caxtons 248
Eugene Aram 21
Lady of Lyons 263
Letter to 248
My Novel 255
Sea Captain 48
Bunyan, John
Pilgrim's Progress 86
Burns, Robert 171, 304
Burton, John
Life and Correspondence of David Hume 129
Butler, Mrs. E. W. ["GM," Harriet Becher] 28, 30, 32, 35, 45, 47, 54, 58, 62, 66, 68, 69, 71, 77, 81, 83, 101, 117, 128, 137, 139
Butler, Mrs. Pierce, *see* Kemble, Frances Anne 97
Byron, George Gordon, 6th Baron 86, 283
Childe Harold 8

Caesar, Augustus 123
Caesar, Julius 123
Café Anglais 43
Cairnes, Col. 107
Calcutta Star, The 110
Caldwell, Mr. 20, 21
Cambridge University 14
Cambridge University Union 4
Canada, The 224, 228, 229
Candy, Mr. 194
Canova, Antonio 268
Caracci, Agostino 268
Caracci, Annibale 268
Caracci, Ludovico 268
Cardigan, James Thomas, 7th Earl of 76
Carlisle, George William Frederick Howard, 7th Earl of 124
Carlyle, Mrs. Thomas [Jane Welsh] 54
    Letters to 79, 82, 203
Carlyle, Thomas 49, 54, 79, 83, 145, 146, 185, 225
    Critical and Miscellaneous Essays 49
    Frederick the Great 225
    French Revolution 83
    Heroes and Hero-Worship 59
    Letter to 203
    Life of John Sterling 209
    "Repeal of the Union" 146
Carmichael, Col. Charles 77, 81, 94, 100, 102, 144, 169
Carmichael, Mrs. Charles [Mary Graham] 11, 12, 14, 24, 36, 45, 48, 62, 71, 72, 77, 81, 94, 100, 102, 125, 127, 140, 169, 171, 196
Carmichael, Sir James 24, 110
Carmichael-Smyth, Maj. Henry ["GP"] 1, 3, 12, 14, 17, 24, 26, 31, 33, 35, 36, 59, 69, 75, 77, 89, 93, 96, 97, 101, 107, 116, 118, 121, 128, 129, 132, 139, 140, 152, 161, 173, 211, 215, 217, 219, 230, 231, 235, 246, 250, 256, 258, 259, 263, 270, 281, 287, 301, 305, 306, 311, 312, 318, 320, 332, 341, 342, 347, 348, 354, 358, 359, 363
Carmichael-Smyth, Mrs. Henry [Anne Becher (Thackeray)] 17, 20, 31, 33, 35, 36, 37, 41, 44, 45, 48, 77, 89, 91, 92, 93, 94, 96, 97, 120, 143, 146, 157, 159, 161, 165, 166, 171, 173, 176, 196, 204, 216, 217, 219, 225, 226, 230, 231, 235, 246, 250, 258, 260, 264, 265, 272, 289, 290, 298, 299, 301, 302, 303, 305, 306, 308, 318, 320, 330, 332, 333, 341, 342, 347, 348, 354, 358, 363, 367
    Letters to 1, 2, 3, 4, 5, 7, 9, 12, 14, 23, 25, 27, 32, 46, 48, 50, 52, 57, 61, 65, 67, 69, 72, 73, 74, 100, 105, 110, 115, 118,

121, 122, 124, 126, 128, 131, 137, 138, 151, 209, 214, 239, 244, 262, 280, 282, 285, 311, 327, 364
Carmichael-Smyth, Mrs. Robert [Agnes Rosa Hervey] 299
Carne, Joseph 3, 4
Caroline, Queen 295
Castlereagh, see Londonderry 178
Cattermole, George 41, 54
Cattermole, Mrs. George 54
Cavaignac, Godefroy 79, 83
Century Club 313, 315
Cerubini, Luigi
    Medée 11
Cervantes, Miguel de
    Don Quixote 252, 257
Chamberlayne, Edward
    Angliae Notitia 276
Champmartin, Charles Émile Callande de 31
Chapman and Hall 66, 67, 71, 72, 74, 78, 102, 118
    Letter to 121
Chapman, Edward 343
    Letters to 138, 163
Chapman, Frederic 343
Charles II 276
Charles [a servant] 336
Charterhouse School 2, 4, 15, 17, 43, 137, 197, 359
Chartism 53, 65
Chasles, Philarète 171
Cherry, Andrew, and John Davy
    "Bay of Biscay" 118
Chitty, Joseph William 331
Chitty, Mrs. Joseph William [Clara Jessie Pollock] 331
Chorley, Henry Fothergill 63, 64, 81, 86, 88
Christ's Church, Oxford 163
Christie, Alexander 302
Cicero, Marcus Tullius 365
    Epistolae ad Familiares 190
Civil War, see United States 348
Clarendon Hotel 231, 235, 280, 292, 353
Clarke, Edward William
    Library of Useless Knowledge 99
Clevedon Court 162, 163, 194
Close, Francis 306
Clough, Arthur Hugh
    Bothie of Taber-Na-Vuolich 165
    Letter to 165

Coats, Peter 304
Cobden, Richard 124
Cole, Charles Augustus 93
Cole, Sir Henry 201, 336
Coleridge, Samuel Taylor 101
Collignon, M. 98
Collignon, Mme. 98
Collins, Wilkie 355
Collins, William
    "The Passions" 1
Colmache, Mme. Édouard 127
Colosseum, the 267
Comic Almanac, The 49
Comstock, Captain 325
Constitutional, The 35, 36, 38, 39, 40, 270
Contributor to *The Cornhill Magazine*, A
    Letter to 345
Contributors and Correspondents of *The Cornhill Magazine*
    Letter to 361
Conyngham, Lord 105
Cook, Rev. John 230
Cooper, Sir Henry 307
Corbin, Mr. 261
Cornhill Magazine, The 337, 338, 340, 343, 345, 347, 354, 356, 361, 362, 368
Corpus Christi College, Cambridge 3
Cortona, Pietro da 171
Cottin, Elizabeth 113
Courvoisier, François Benjamin 63
Cousin, Victor 22
    Cours de l'histoire de la philosophie 22
Covent Garden Theatre 74, 88
Cozzens, Frederick Swartout 322
    Letter to 313
    Sparrowgrass Papers 314
Crampton, Sir John Fiennes Twisleton 287, 288
Craven, Augustus 268
Craven, Mrs. Augustus [Pauline de la Ferronays] 268
Crawford, James 24
Crawford, Mrs. James [Charlotte Shakespear] 20, 24, 66
Creighton, Mr. 261
Creyke, Mr. 286, 298, 326
Crimean War 271
Cromwell, Oliver 106, 146
Crowe, Amy, *see* Thackeray, Mrs. Edward Talbot 298

Crowe, Eugènie Marie, *see* Wynne, Mrs. Robert 302
Crowe, Eyre 215, 224, 230, 235, 238, 239, 298
Crowe, Eyre Evans 43, 92, 139, 210
Crowe, Mrs. Eyre Evans [Margaret Archer] 43, 92, 139
    Letter to 168
Crowe, Mrs. [of Edinburgh] 271
Crowe, Sir Joseph 210
Cruikshank, George 49, 58
Crystal Palace 200
Cullum, Lady
    Letter to 158
Cullum, Rev. Sir Thomas 210, 357
Cunningham, Hugh 61, 66, 90
Cunningham, Peter 137
    "Chronicles of Charter House" 137
Cupid 254, 349
Curtis, George William 251, 314, 322, 341
    Nile Notes 250
    "Thackeray in America" 251
Curtis, Mrs. George William [Anna Shawe] 314
Daily News, The 210
Daly, Judge Charles Patrick 313, 314
Daly, Mrs. Charles Patrick [Maria Lydig] 313
Dance, Charles 297
Dante Alighieri
    Divine Comedy 80
Davis, John Chandler Bancroft 261, 296, 314, 322, 324
Davis, Mr. [of Boston] 235
Davis, Mrs. John Chandler [Frederica Gore King] 322
Davison, Sir Henry 147
    Letter to 347
Déjazet, Pauline Virginie 87
Delaroche, Paul
    Jane Grey 29
Delmonico's 281
Dering, Mrs. Nicoll Havens [Sarah Huggins Strong] 250
Derry, Mr. 268
Devonshire, William George Cavendish, 6th Duke of 207
    Letter to 148
Devrient, Ludwig 273
Dexter, William Sohier 288
Dick, Mrs. William Flemming [Emily Thackeray] 2, 54
Dick, William Flemming 110
Dickens children [Charles] 333
Dickens family [Charles] 328

Dickens, Charles 66, 113, 116, 121, 139, 175, 189, 202, 203, 205, 233, 240, 264, 271, 280, 321, 328, 333, 355, 356
    American Notes 239
    Barnaby Rudge 46
    Christmas Carol 116
    David Copperfield 175, 202
    Little Dorrit 285, 301
    Martin Chuzzlewit 294
    Master Humphrey's Clock 58, 66
    Nicholas Nickleby 87, 99
    Oliver Twist 46
    Pickwick Papers 45
Dickens, Charles [Jr.] 328
Dickens, Mrs. Charles [Catherine Hogarth] 113, 146, 189, 328
Diderot, Denis 169
Dillon, Henry Augustus Dillon-Lee, 13th Viscount 220
Dillon, John Blake 241, 366
Dillon, Lady [Henrietta Browne, m. 13th Viscount] 220
Diogenes 79, 360
Disraeli, Benjamin [1st Earl of Beaconsfield] 233
Dobb, Mr. 21
Donizetti, Gaetano
    Elisire d'Amore 85
Dowling, Mr. 109
Downing, Mrs. Harriet
    "Monthly Nurse" 42
Doyle, Richard 200, 237, 257, 264, 265
Drury Lane Theatre 152, 355
Drury, Henry 19
Drury, Miss 138, 140, 144, 146, 151, 152
Duer, William Denning 283, 296, 323
Duke, Sir James, 1st Baronet 181
Dumas, Alexandre [fils]
    Dame aux camélias 300
    Demi-Monde 279
Dumas, Alexandre [père]
    Count of Monte Cristo 258
Dundas, Sir David 304
Dupuis, Adolphe 279
Durham, John George Lambton, 1st Earl of 65
Duvernay, Marie-Louise 24, 27, 29
Dying Gladiator 263
Eastlake, Lady [Elizabeth Rigby, m. Sir Charles]
    Letter to 197
Eastlake, Sir Charles Lock 29, 197

Edgeworth, Maria 48
Edinburgh Review, The 145
Edward I 276
Edwards, Mr. 20, 326
Ehrenbreitstein 8
Eliot, George [Mary Ann Evans Cross]
    Adam Bede 356
Eliza [a servant] 327
Elliot children [Thomas Frederick] 251, 258, 259, 267, 268
Elliot family [Thomas Frederick] 290, 317
Elliot, Gilbert 306
Elliot, Mrs. Thomas Frederick [Jane Perry] 177, 186, 201, 265, 289, 349, 366
    Letters to 180, 207, 213, 219, 232, 251, 258, 278, 291, 293, 299, 302, 303, 305, 315
Elliot, Rev. Gilbert 194, 196
Elliot, Thomas Frederick 186, 215, 220, 221, 233, 259, 303, 304, 306, 349
    Letter to 349
Elliotson, Dr. John 183
Elliott, Bishop Stephen 290
Ellis, Sir Henry 108
Ellison, Cuthbert Edward 315, 316
Ellison, Mrs. Cuthbert Edward 316
Elmore, Alfred 39
Elmore, Dr. 39
Elton family 316
Elton, Arthur Hallam 195
Elton, Laura Beatrice 194
Elton, Mary Agnes 194
Elton, Mrs. Arthur Hallam [Rhoda Willis (Baird)] 159, 195
Elton, Sir Charles 195
Elwin, Rev. Whitwell 316
    Letter to 355
English, Miss 1
Ernest, Duke of Cumberland and King of Hanover 53
Eros 167, 180
Errington, Mrs. John Edward 252
Esquirol, Jean 76
Eton College 283
Eton Latin Grammar 17
Etty, William 30
Euclid 4
Europa, The 244, 247
Evans, Mary Ann, see Eliot, George 356

Examiner, The 146, 204, 269
Fanshawe, Mrs. Charles S. 192, 207, 306
    Letter to 188
Fanshawe, Rev. Charles S. 188
Fanshawe, Rosa ["Totty"] 188, 192
Farquhar, George 97
Faucher, Léon 40
Ferozeshah, battle of 127
Fielding, Henry 53, 147, 166, 186, 257
    Tom Jones 155
Fillmore, Millard 242
FitzGerald, Edward 20, 21, 26, 33, 36, 45, 48, 53, 110, 113, 178, 185, 272
    Letters to 16, 19, 28, 37, 76, 95, 98, 103, 145, 167, 228
FitzGerald, Edward Marlborough 126, 146
FitzGerald, family [Edward Marlborough] 126
FitzGerald, John Purcell 140
FitzGerald, Mrs. Edward Marlborough
    Letter to 142
FitzGerald, Mrs. John Purcell [Mary Francis] 140, 146, 272
FitzGerald, Mrs. Peter 106, 117
FitzGerald, Peter 105, 117
Fitzjames, Duc de 9
Fladgate, Francis 297
Fladgate, Mrs. Francis 327
Flower, Edward Fordham
    Letter to 360
Fonblanque, Albany 160, 210
    Letter to 239
Foreign Quarterly Review, The 46, 102, 116
Forgues, Paul Émile Daurand
    Letter to 269
Forrest son [Robert] 312
Forrest, Capt. Robert 312
Forrest, Lt. Col. William 69
Forrest, Mrs. William [Georgiana Carmichael-Smyth] 312
Forster, Christopher 121
Forster, John 64, 80, 83, 121, 139, 155, 157, 182, 186, 204, 210, 237, 239, 264, 290, 321, 355, 356
    Goldsmith 147
    Letters to 147, 189, 204
Francis of the Indies, St. 219
Frascati's 5, 23
Fraser's Magazine 42, 46, 57, 72, 93, 102, 111, 116, 118, 137, 154, 274, 338

Fraser, James 61, 66, 80, 83, 88, 93
    Letters to 42, 78
Friedrich Karl, Prince of Prussia 11
Frith, Robert William 7
Frost, John 53
Fullerton, Lady Georgiana Charlotte 223, 253
    Grantley Manor 253
Galignani's Messenger 98
Galignani's shop 22
Garrick Club 25, 52, 116, 200, 296, 314, 328, 350, 353
Garrick Club affair 330, 356
Garrick, David 257
Gazette des Tribunaux 92
Gent, Mr. 22
George I 222, 295
George IV 295, 298
Gerrard, Capt. 23
Gibbon, Edward 279
    Decline and Fall 23, 279
Gibson, Mr. [of Richmond] 325
Gibson, Mrs. Thomas Milner [Susanna Arethusa Cullum] 372
    Letter to 357
Glasgow Argus, The 68
Glenelg, Charles Grant Glenelg, 1st Baron 252
Gloyne, Mrs. 127, 138
Glykon
    Farnese Hercules 268
Glynn, Capt. Henry 344
Goethe, Alma von 274
Goethe, Frau August von [Ottilie von Pogwisch] 10, 273, 274
Goethe, Johann Wolfgang von 10, 13, 14, 16, 202, 273, 274, 286
Goldshede, Mr. 21
Goldsmith, Oliver 147, 234
    Deserted Village 148
    History of the Earth and Animated Nature 148
    Vicar of Wakefield 356
Goldsworthy, John 54, 58, 72, 76, 141
Gore, Cecilia Anne Mary, *see* Thynne, Lady 193
Gore, Mrs. Charles Arthur [Catherine Moody] 250
    Cecil 82
    Letter to 172
Gossaint, M. 226
Gramp, Mr. 100
Gray, Mrs. [a housekeeper] 290
Great Eastern, The 346

Great Exhibition of 1851 200, 201
Great Liverpool, The 129
Grey, Lady Jane 155
Grey, William George 215
Griffin, Mr. 5
Grisi, Giulia 27
Guild of Literature and Art 205, 270
Haas, Mrs. Maria
    Letter to 335
Haden, Dr. Francis Seymour 336
Haight, Richard K. 363
Hallam, Henry 186, 190, 194, 196, 288
Hallam, Henry Fitzmaurice 194, 196
Halliday, Mrs. [Augusta Thackeray (Elliot)] 24, 61, 94
Hamerton, Elizabeth 86, 107, 110, 116, 139
Hamerton, Maria 86
Hampton children [Frank] 330
Hampton, Frank 281, 285, 286, 299, 308, 309
Hampton, Frank [Jr.] 297, 308, 309, 319, 353, 362, 366
Hampton, Georgia Anna 353, 362, 366
Hampton, Mrs. Frank [Sarah Baxter] 236, 237, 238, 245, 247, 281, 285, 286, 287, 289, 318, 319, 326, 327, 330, 341, 348, 353, 362, 366, 367
    Letters to 234, 249, 254, 297, 308
Hankey, Mrs. 116
Harcourt, Sir William Vernon 289
Hardinge, Arthur 127
Hardinge, Henry, 1st Viscount 127
Hardinge, Lady [Lady Emily Jane Stewart (James), m. 1st Viscount] 127
    Letter to 335
Harper and Brothers 231, 318
Harris family 116
Harrow School 140, 283
Hay, Lord John 326
Haydn, Franz Joseph 246
Hayes, Catherine 190
Hayward, Abraham
    Letter to 186
Hedges, Sir Charles 177
Hemans, Felicia
    Homes of England 59
Heraud, John Abraham 88
Herbert, John Rogers 223
Herbert, Sir Charles 45

Herrick, Robert 21
Herzlieb, Minna 286
Hewlett, J. T. J.
   Peter Priggins 88
Hickman, Mr. 110
Higgins, Matthew James ["Jacob Omnium"] 150, 182, 233, 259, 293
Hill, Sir Rowland 316
Hine, James 3
Hobhouse, Sir John Cam [Lord Broughton] 195, 196, 211, 213
Hogarth, Georgina 146, 328
Hole, Rev. Samuel Reynolds
   Letter to 347
Holland, Henry Edward Fox, 4th Baron 268
Holland, Lady [Lady Augusta-Mary Coventry, m. 4th Baron] 268
Holmes, Dr. Oliver Wendell 235
Holmes, Mary 215
   Letter to 223
Homer
   Iliad
      Hector 276
      Paris 127, 276
Hooch, Pieter de 29
Hood, Thomas [Jr.] 359
Hook, Theodore Edward
   Peter Priggins 88
Horace [Quintus Horatius Flaccus]
   Art of Poetry 240, 345
   Odes 135, 197, 224, 239, 362
Horneck, Catherine 147
Horneck, Mary ["the Jessamy Bride"] 147, 234
Hotel Bristol 299, 331, 334
Hudson, Sir Geoffrey 29
Hugo, Victor
   Hernani 11
   Le Rhin 99
Hume, David 129
Hume, Joseph 40
Hume, Mr. 110
Hummell, Johann 11
Hunt, William Henry 41
Hunt, [James Henry] Leigh 60, 84
   Jar of Honey from Mount Hybla 141
   Letters to 141, 204
Huyshe, Alfred 2
Huyshe, Mrs. Francis 140

Huyshe, Wentworth 140
Illustrated London News, The 307, 346
Impey family 312
Institut de France, L' 170
Irvine, Mrs. Archibald [Marianne Shakespear] 61
Istrie, Duchesse d' 279
Jackson, Andrew 156
James I 105
James II 288
James, Samuel 192, 211
Janin, Jules 169, 279
Janin, Mme. Jules 169
Jaudon, Frank 319
Jerrold, Douglas 136, 139, 264
Johnson, Dr. Samuel 186
    couplet in Goldsmith's *The Traveller* 290
Johnson, Mr. 39
Jones, Harry Longueville 23
Jones, Mr. 349
Josephine, Empress of the French 221
Journal des Debats 169, 170
Jullien, Louis George Antoine Jules 159
Justinian
    Pandects 13
Juvenal [Decimus Junius Juvenalis]
    Satires 346, 350
Kane, Elisha Kent 281, 314
Karl August, Grand Duke of Weimar 10, 13, 273
Karl Friedrich, Grand Duke of Weimar 10, 13
Kay, Mr. 21
Keane, David Deady
    "Illustrations of Discount" 111
Keats, John 255
Kelly, Lady [Ada Cunningham, m. Sir Fitzroy] 332
Kelly, Robert 233
Kelly, Sir Fitzroy 332
Kelvin, Lady [m. 1st Baron] 304
Kelvin, William Thompson, 1st Baron 304
Kemble family [Charles] 19, 22, 54
Kemble, Charles 19, 40
Kemble, Frances Anne ["Fanny," Mrs. Pierce Butler] 40, 97, 212, 263
Kemble, John Mitchell 34
    Letters to 18, 40
Kemble, Mrs. Charles [Marie Thérèse Decamp] 40, 54, 265

Kemble, Mrs. John Mitchell [Natalie Wendt] 40
Kennaway, Sir John [1st Baronet] 11
Kenney, Charles Lamb 198
Kenny, Miss 117
Kensett, John Frederick 283
Kerrich family [John] 98
Kerrich, John 77, 98
Kerrich, Mrs. John [Mary-Eleanor FitzGerald] 77, 98
Kinderley, Mr. 21
King's College, Cambridge 3, 178
King, Charles 283
King, J. G., and Sons 291, 292, 322, 344
King, Rufus 283
Kinglake family [Alexander William] 126
Kinglake, Alexander William 141, 177, 213, 233, 259
    Letter to 125
Kinglake, Mrs. William [Mary Woodforde] 126, 259
Kirwan, Andrew Valentine 116
Knowles, James Sheridan 86
Knutsford, Henry Thurstan Holland, 1st Viscount
    Letter to 352
Koran, The 227
Körner, Karl Theodor 11
Kotzebue, August von 16
L'Illustration 138
Laclos, Choderlos de
    Les Liaisons dangereuses 148
Lady Mary Wood, The 119
Laïs 279
Landseer, Sir Edwin Henry 30, 278
Langford, Harriet 29
Langley, Samuel 327, 365, 366
Langslow, Mrs. Robert [Sarah Jane Thackeray] 138
Langslow, Robert 34, 54, 138
Lardner, Dr. Dionysius 58
Laurence, Samuel 228, 283, 364
Leader, The 196, 231
Leech, John 146, 197
Leigh, Percival
    Mr. Pips his Diary
        T's imitation of 200
Leipzig Gazette 108
Lemann, Mr. 24
Lemon, Mark
    Letter to 136

Lemprière, John
    Classical Dictionary 162
Leslie, Charles Robert 147
Lettsom, Mrs. William Garrow 69
Lettsom, William Garrow 10, 52, 54, 57
Lever, Charles James 107, 164
    Roland Cashel 164
Lewes, George Henry
    Letters to 144, 273
Lewes, Mrs. George Henry [Agnes Jervis] 196
Lewis, John Frederick 41
Lille, siege of 276
Lillo, George
    George Barnwell 190
Lindsay, Mrs. John 265
Literary Club, The 355
Locker-Lampson, Frederick
    Letter to 349
Lockhart, John Gibson 66, 264
Loftus, Lady Augustus [Emma Maria Greville] 253
London Library 178
Londonderry, Charles William Stewart, 3rd Marquess of
    Tour in the North of Europe 46
Londonderry, Frederick Stewart, 4th Marquess of 178
Londonderry, Lady [Lady Elizabeth Frances Jocelyn (Powerscourt), m. 4th Marquess] 178, 221
    Letter to 184
Long, St. John 96
Longman, Thomas Norton 66
Louis Napoleon [Napoleon III] 306
Louis of Gonzaga, St. 219
Louis Philippe 144, 276
Louvre 22, 29, 31, 171, 300
Low family [Andrew] 368
Low, Andrew 289
Low, Mrs. Andrew 289
Low, Sampson and Sons 231, 355
Lowther, Mrs. William 268
Lowther, William 268
Lubbock, Forster, and Co. 46, 71, 116, 118, 287, 313
Luscombe, Michael Henry 35
Lushington, Franklin 195
Luther, Martin 10
Lyndhurst, John Singleton Copley, 1st Baron 319
Lyon, Samuel E. 296

Macaulay, Kenneth 150
Macaulay, Thomas Babington, 1st Baron 185
    History of England 287
Macbean, Aeneas 263
Macdonald, Norman 163
Macleod, Capt. 129
Maclise, Daniel 31, 41, 274, 279
Macready, William Charles 88, 97, 152, 200, 257, 323
Maginn, William 21, 22, 42, 147, 360
Mahon, Charles 139
Mahon, Philip Henry Stanhope, Viscount, *see* Stanhope, 5th Earl 315
Mahony, Francis Sylvester ["Father Prout"] 31, 41
Maine, Mrs. Henry Sumner [Jane Maine] 178
Maine, Sir Henry Sumner 290
Mannert, Konrad
    Kompendium der deutschen Reichsgeschichte 16
Manning, Henry Edward, Cardinal 265
Maria of Weimar, Princess of Prussia 11
Maria Paulowna, Grand Duchess of Weimar 13, 273, 275
Marie Louise, Empress of the French 221
Marks, Mr. 65
Marlborough, John Churchill, 1st Duke of 162, 276, 277
Marochetti, Carlo, Baron 259
Marriott, Mr. 62
Marryat, Capt. Frederick 294
    Joseph Rushbrook 91
Mars 167
Martineau, Arthur 19
Martineau, James 225
Marvy, Louis 168
Mary, Queen of Scots 279, 309
Masson, David
    Letter to 202
Mathews, Charles 74
Matthew, Henry 16, 177
Matthew, Miss 177
Matthew, Mrs. Henry 177
Matthew, Rev. John 17
Maturin, Charles Robert
    Melmoth the Wanderer 274
Mayhew, Horace 233
Mazzinghi, Thomas John
    Letter to 199
Mazzini, Giuseppe 203
Meagher, Thomas Francis 241

Melos, Mme. 12
Mérimée, Prosper 279
Merivale, Ella 365
Merriman, Dr. John Jones 181
Merton College, Oxford 163
Meurice's Hotel 23, 43
Michigan Central Railroad 322, 323
Mildmay, Henry Bingham 238, 247, 254
Mildmay, Humphrey 238
Millais, John Everett, 1st Baronet
    Letter to 317
Millais, Mrs. John Everett [Euphemia Gray (Ruskin)] 317
Mills, Mrs. 37
Milman, Henry Hart [Dean of St. Paul's] 186
    Martyr of Antioch 350
Milnes, Mrs. Richard Monckton [Annabel Crewe] 209
Milnes, Richard Monckton [Lord Houghton] 63, 77, 87, 209
    Letter to 130
Milton, John
    L'Allegro 88
    Paradise Lost 49, 191, 236
Mohammed 227, 372
Molesworth daughter [Andalusia] 316
Molesworth, Lady [Andalusia Carstairs, m. 8th Baronet] 153
Molesworth, Sir William, 8th Baronet 153, 220
Molyneux, Rev. Capel 367
Monod, Adolphe Frédéric Théodore 235, 367
Monro, Mr. 21
Montagu, Mrs. Basil [Benson (Skepper)] 68
Montefiore, Sir Moses 70
Montgomery family [Alfred] 178
Moore, Thomas 8, 105
Morgan, Lady [Sydney Owenson, m. Sir Thomas Charles] 61
Morier, James Justinian 160
Morier, Mrs. James Justinian 160
Morley, Dowager Lady [Frances Talbot, m. 1st Earl] 177, 298
    Letter to 370
Morley, Edmund Parker, 2nd Earl of 298
Morning Chronicle, The 124, 127, 144
Morning Herald, The 312
Morning Post, The 92
Morris, Mowbray 150, 278
Morton family [Saville] 224
Morton, Saville 63, 97, 130, 146, 215, 224
Motley, John Lothrop 326

Rise of Dutch Republic 356
Mozart, Wolfgang Amadeus 246
　Magic Flute 11
Murphy, Francis Stack 147
Myers, Mr. [of Richmond] 325
Napoleon I [Bonaparte] 4, 49, 77, 221, 227
Nasmyth, Mrs. 125
National Standard, The 24, 25, 26
Nazarenes, The 97
Neate, Charles
　Dialogues des Morts 165
Neptune 1
Neri, St. Philip 193
New Monthly Magazine, The 88
New York Albion, The 368
New York American, The 283
New York Central Railroad 322, 323, 340
New York Herald, The 231, 233, 308
Newgate Prison 63
Newman, John Henry, Cardinal 264
Newton, John 226
Nicholas I, Czar of Russia 306
Nickisson, George William
　Letters to 93, 111, 137
Nokes, John 35
Normanby, Constantine Henry Phipps, 1st Marquess of 252
Normanby, Lady [Hon. Maria Liddell, m. 1st Marquess] 252
North British Review 202
Norton, Carlotta 300
Norton, The Hon. Mrs. Caroline 300
Norton, Thomas Brinsley [4th Baron Grantley] 300
nursery rhymes
　"Goosey, goosey, gander" 62
Nursey, Perry 16
O'Brien, Miss 1
O'Brien, Mrs. 1
O'Connell, Daniel 75
O'Connell, Morgan John 142
O'Donnel, Arnout 83, 88, 92
O'Gorman, Richard 241
Octavia [a servant] 263
Odry, Jacques Charles 81
Oglethorpe, Gen. James Edward 147
Olliffe, Lady [Laura Cubitt, m. Sir Joseph] 374
Olliffe, Sir Joseph Francis 250

Orsay, Alfred, Count d' 150, 175
Ovid [Publius Ovidius Naso],
    Tristia 274
Oxford election 318, 322, 325
Packman, Dr. F. W. S. 160
Palais Royal 22, 300
Palmerston, Henry John Temple, 3rd Viscount 210, 212
Pan 169
Panizzi, Anthony
    Letter to 108
Pappenheim, Jenny von 11, 12
Parker, Mrs. 71
Parkes, Joseph
    Letter to 369
Parr, Thomas 195
Pattle daughters [James] 127
Pattle family [James] 27
Pattle, Mrs. James 27
Pattle, Theodosia 27
Pattle, Virginia, *see* Somers, Lady 157
Pauline [a servant] 327
Paxton, Sir Joseph 207
Pearman, Charles 250, 252, 262, 266, 281, 283, 286, 290, 298, 304, 317, 318, 319, 322, 325, 327
Pearsall and Jorden 76
Peel, Sir Robert 124, 283
Peiho River, battle of 341
Percy, Thomas
    Reliques of Ancient English Poetry 56
Perkins, Mrs. 285
Perrault, Charles
    Histoires
        "Bluebeard" 190, 207
Perry, Flora 267
Perry, Kate 177, 265, 289, 349, 350, 366, 367
    Letters to 180, 206, 207, 213, 219, 232, 251, 258, 266, 278, 289, 291, 293, 299, 302, 303, 305, 315
Perry, Lady [Elizabeth Margaret Van den Bempde-Johnstone, 2nd wife of Sir Thomas Erskine] 290
Perry, Sir Thomas Erskine 234, 252, 290
Phillips, Thomas 221
Phryne 279
Pichot, Amédée 269
Pierce, Franklin 242
Pitt, William, the Elder 335

Pius IX, Pope 265
Poittevin, Edmond le 27
Pollen, John Hungerford 264, 265, 326
Pollen, Mrs. John Hungerford 326
Pollock family [Sir (Jonathan) Frederick] 332
Pollock, Gerald 214
Pollock, Lady [Sarah Langslow, m. Sir (Jonathan) Frederick]
    Letters to 213, 331
Pollock, Sir [Jonathan] Frederick 213, 331
    Letter to 374
Polycarp, St. 124
Pomeroy, Charles 254
Poole, John
    Paul Pry 26, 157
Porter, Jane
    Scottish Chiefs 157
    Thaddeus of Warsaw 157
Post, Mrs. 256
Powell, Mr. 68, 75
Power, Ellen 175
    Letter to 371
Power, Marguerite 175
    Letter to 371
Powerscourt, Richard Wingfield, 5th Viscount 221
Prescott, William Hickling 321
    Philip II 287
Price, Mr. 47
Prinsep family [Henry Thoby] 127
Prior, Matthew
    "The Thief and the Cordelier" 219
Pritchard, William 350
Procter children [Bryan Waller] 82, 134
Procter family [Bryan Waller] 237
Procter, Adelaide Ann 84, 229, 257, 265
    Legends and Lyrics 328
    Letters to 173, 180, 328
Procter, Bryan Waller ["Barry Cornwall"] 81, 84, 86, 88, 90, 114, 130, 133, 142, 152, 181, 185, 229, 265
    Essays and Tales in Prose 257
    Letters to 63, 257
    "The Sea" 229
Procter, Mrs. Bryan Waller [Anne Skepper] 63, 68, 142, 152, 174, 181, 257, 259
    Letters to 55, 59, 63, 81, 84, 86, 114, 130, 133, 134, 152, 157, 183, 228, 236, 263

Punch 92, 102, 110, 116, 130, 136, 140, 163, 167, 178, 185, 202, 307, 369
Purcell family, [Peter] 117
Purcell, Mrs. Peter 117
Purcell, Peter 105
    Letter to 117
Putnam's Monthly Magazine 251
Puzin, M. 111, 118
Quarterly Review, The 49, 316
Quebec, siege of 322
Quin, Dr. Frederick 137
Rabelais, François 53
Rachel, Mme. [Elisa Félix] 87
Radcliff, Ann
    The Italian 102
Raglan, FitzRoy James Henry Somerset, 1st Baron 127
Raikes, Thomas
    City of the Czar 46
Ramsay, Allan
    Poems 66
Raphael [Raffaello Santi] 9, 162
Rauch, Christian Daniel 274
Reeve, Henry 81, 82, 185
    Letter to 135
Reform Bill [1832] 149
Reform Club 57, 58, 62, 66
Regulus 25
Reich, Dr. 92
Rembrandt Harmensz van Rijn 16
Renaudin, Capt. 83
Reni, Guido 268
Reviss, Theresa 54
Revue des deux Mondes 170, 269, 270
Reynolds, Capt. Richard Anthony 76
Reynolds, Sir Joshua 31
    Oliver Goldsmith 148
Ribblesdale, Lady [Emma Mure, m. 3rd Baron] 252
Richardson, Samuel
    Clarissa Harlowe 169
    Sir Charles Grandison 304
Rigby, Dr. Edward 160
Ristori, Adelaide 279
Ritchie family [John] 34, 54
Ritchie, Charlotte 61, 95, 118, 299
Ritchie, Jane 33, 95

Ritchie, John 2, 94
Ritchie, Mrs. John [Charlotte Sarah Thackeray] 2, 24, 27, 34, 48, 61
    Letters to 37, 94, 143
Ritchie, Mrs. William [Augusta Trimmer] 277, 278
Ritchie, William
    Letters to 33, 277
Robbins, Capt. George 195
Robertson, Mrs. William Wybrow [Alice Mary Gibson] 357
Robertson, William Wybrow 357
Robespierre, Maximilien de 227
Robinson, Beverley 323
Robinson, William Duer
    Letters to 296, 322
Rodd, Lady [Jane Rennell, m. Sir John] 54, 182
Rodd, V.-Adm. Sir John Tremayne 54
Roden, Lady [Juliana Orde, m. 2nd Earl] 221
Roden, Robert Jocelyn, 2nd Earl of 220
Rogers, Samuel 105, 185, 274, 288
Ronsard, Pierre de
    Sonnets pour Hélène 235
Roqueplan, Joseph 31
Rossini, Gioacchino
    Barber of Seville 11, 265, 365
    Stabat Mater 98
Rossiter, Mr. 200
Rothesay, Charles Stuart, 1st Baron Stuart de 221
Rothesay, Lady de [Lady Elizabeth Yorke, m. 1st Baron] 221
Rothschild family [Sir Anthony de] 373
Rothschild, Lady de [Louisa Montefiori, m. Sir Anthony]
    Letter to 373
Rowland, S. N.
    Letter to 276
Royal Academy 216
Royal Literary Fund 176, 356
Rubens, Peter Paul 162
Russell, Dr. John 2
Russell, John, 1st Earl 124, 215, 233
Russell, Lady [Lady Frances Elliot, 2nd w. of 1st Earl] 215
Russell, William Howard 321, 353
Sablonière Hotel 21
Salisbury, Mr. 268
Salt, Mr. 50, 52, 55
Sand, George [Aurore Dupin, Baronne Dudevant] 69
Santley, Lady [Gertrude Kemble, m. Sir Charles] 48
Sartoris, Edward John 264

    Letter to 154
Sartoris, Mrs. Edward John [Adelaide Kemble] 97, 113, 264, 329, 372
    Letter to 154
Saturday Review, The 289, 290
Saunders, Dr. Augustus Page 215
Schiller, Friedrich von 13, 273, 275
    Maria Stuart 87, 279
    Räuber 273
Schneider, Miss 21
Schröder-Devrient, Wilhelmine 273
Schulte, Franz 16
Scott, Mary 116
Scott, Sir Walter 66, 288, 368
    Anne of Geierstein 102
Scott, Thomas 226
Sedley, Sir Charles 149
Shaftesbury, Anthony Ashley Cooper, 7th Earl of 307
Shakespear, Sir Richmond 277
Shakespeare, William 59, 296
    As You Like It 52, 83, 246
    Falstaff 273
    Hamlet 273
    Henry VIII 152
    King Lear 149
    Macbeth 198
    Merchant of Venice 273
    Midsummer Night's Dream 313
    Othello 13, 125, 227, 323
    Tempest 361
    Two Gentlemen of Verona 69
Shawe, Arthur 57, 58, 61, 138
Shawe, Jane 36, 55, 58, 73, 262
Shawe, Lt. Col. Merrick 35, 36, 45, 58
Shawe, Mrs. 281
Shawe, Mrs. Arthur 138
Shawe, Mrs. Matthew [Isabella Creagh] 35, 36, 37, 43, 55, 58, 71, 72, 73, 74, 107
    Letter to 44
Sheil, Mrs. Richard Lalor [Anastasia Power] 160
Sheil, Richard Lalor 160
Shelley, Percy Bysshe 8
Sheridan, Richard Brinsley
    Rivals 151, 152
Smith, Albert 146

Smith, Alexander
    Life Drama and Other Poems 255
Smith, Elder, and Co. 337, 338, 343, 345, 365
Smith, Eliza 159, 306
Smith, George 228, 365
    Letters to 211, 231, 355, 358, 364
Smith, James
    Rejected Addresses 26
Smith, Misses [d. of Horace] 159
Smith, Mr. 321
Smith, Sydney 306
Smyth, Charles 2
Snelling, Mrs. Andrew [Eliza Templeton Strong] 261
Society of Painters in Watercolour 34, 41
Somers, Lady [Virginia Pattle, m. 3rd Earl] 157, 159, 160, 161
Somerset, Maj. Arthur 127
Somerville, Mr. 58
Southern, Mrs. 337
Southey, Robert 49
    Thalaba the Destroyer 350
Souvestre, Emile 92
Soyer, Alexis Benoît 200
Soyres, Mrs. Francis de [Andalusia FitzGerald] 16, 98
Spanish Succession, War of 276
Spectator, The 64, 68, 204, 231
Spedding, James 146, 272, 303
    Letter to 185
Spencer family 91
Spencer, Caroline 74
Spencer, Mrs. 75
Spiegel, Hof Marschall von 273
Spiegel, Louise von 273
Spiegel, Melanie von 11, 12, 273
St. Nicholas Hotel 247
St. Paul's Cathedral 329
St. Peter's Basilica 262, 264
Stanard family [Robert Craig] 324
Stanard, Mrs. Robert Craig [Martha Pierce] 324
Stanard, Robert Craig 324
Standard, The 21
Stanhope, Philip Henry, 5th Earl
    History of England 315
Stanley, Edward John, 2nd Baron 210
Stanley, Lady [Lady Henrietta Dillon-Lee, m. 2nd Baron] 220
    Letter to 208

Sterling Club 185
Sterling, Anthony Coningham 80
Sterling, Edward 80, 113
Sterling, John 36, 113
Sterling, Mrs. Edward [Harriet Coningham] 45, 80, 83, 113
Sterling, Mrs. John 113
Sterne, Laurence 101, 169, 238, 249
    Letters to Eliza 235
Stevens, Augustus 92, 114
Stirling-Maxwell, Sir William [Stirling of Keir] 278
    Letters to 351, 360
Stoddart, William Wellwood 210
Stone family [of Boston] 281
Stone, Frank
    Letters to 30, 41
Story family [William Wetmore] 264
Story, Edith 285
Story, Mrs. William Wetmore [Emelyn Eldridge] 312
Story, Waldo 312
Strasburg Cathedral 252
Streatfeild, Mrs. Sidney Robert 215
Streatfeild, Sidney Richard 215
Streatfeild, Sidney Robert 215
Strong, Elizabeth ["Libby," later Mrs. Frank Jaudon] 237, 319, 322, 325, 330, 348
    Letter to 260
Strong, Mrs. Charles 256
Strong, Oliver 331
Stuart, James Francis Edward 276
Sturgis, Mrs. Russell 256, 320
Sturgis, Russell 308, 320
Stylites, St. Simeon 360
Sue, Eugène
    Juif errant 300
    Mathilde 92
Sumner, Charles 287
Surgères, Hélène de 235
Surtees, Robert Smith
    Letter to 197
Sutherland, Duchess of [Lady Harriet Howard, m. 2nd Duke] 242, 304
Swift, Jonathan 105, 233
    Journal to Stella 276
Synge, William Makepeace Thackeray
    Letter to 375

Tacitus, Cornelius 252, 257
Talfourd, Sir Thomas Noon 205
Tamburini, Antonio 98
Taprell, William 21
Tauchnitz, Firma 208, 358
Taylor, Bayard 313
    Poems of Home and Travel 314
Taylor, Sir Charles 326
Taylor, Sir Henry 220
Taylor, Tom
    Diogenes and his Lantern 183
    Letter to 183
Tchelchagoff, Adm. 9
Tennent, Sir James Emerson 118
Tennyson, Alfred, 1st Baron 54, 89, 171, 186, 199, 255, 282
    "Grandmother" 338
    Idylls of the King 337, 339
    Letter to 337
    Princess 141, 338
Ter Borch, Gerard 29
Ternan, Ellen 328
Thackeray, Anne Isabella ["Anny," later Lady Ritchie] 44, 45, 47, 48, 50, 52, 54, 55, 57, 61, 62, 66, 68, 69, 71, 72, 73, 75, 76, 77, 83, 87, 91, 98, 101, 102, 106, 107, 111, 113, 117, 118, 121, 125, 127, 128, 131, 134, 135, 137, 138, 143, 146, 151, 152, 157, 158, 159, 165, 166, 171, 177, 182, 188, 193, 195, 197, 199, 201, 204, 206, 210, 212, 213, 214, 219, 222, 223, 224, 225, 229, 235, 236, 239, 244, 246, 249, 250, 251, 252, 254, 255, 256, 257, 258, 259, 260, 262, 263, 265, 266, 267, 268, 271, 272, 273, 277, 279, 280, 284, 289, 290, 292, 294, 295, 296, 297, 298, 299, 300, 301, 302, 303, 304, 305, 308, 309, 310, 311, 315, 316, 318, 319, 320, 322, 325, 326, 327, 329, 330, 332, 333, 336, 338, 339, 340, 341, 342, 347, 348, 349, 351, 353, 357, 364, 365, 366, 367, 368, 373
    Elizabeth [1862-1863] 367
    Letters to 109, 115, 192, 196, 216, 217, 225, 229, 280, 285, 336
    "Little Scholars" [1860] 347
Thackeray, Charles 94
Thackeray, Edward Talbot 367
Thackeray, Francis 32, 54
Thackeray, Harriet Marian ["Minny," later Mrs. Leslie Stephen] 61, 62, 66, 68, 69, 73, 75, 76, 77, 83, 87, 91, 98, 102, 106, 107, 110, 111, 113, 117, 118, 121, 125, 127, 128, 131, 134, 135, 137, 138, 143, 146, 151, 152, 157, 158, 159, 165, 166, 171, 177, 182, 188, 193, 195, 196, 197, 199, 201, 204, 206, 210, 212, 213, 214, 219, 222, 223, 224, 225, 229, 235, 236, 239, 244, 246, 249, 250, 251,

252, 254, 256, 257, 258, 259, 260, 262, 263, 266, 267, 268, 271, 272, 273, 277, 279, 280, 289, 292, 294, 295, 296, 298, 299, 301, 302, 303, 304, 305, 306, 308, 309, 310, 311, 316, 318, 319, 320, 322, 325, 326, 327, 330, 332, 333, 336, 338, 339, 341, 342, 347, 348, 349, 351, 353, 357, 363, 364, 365, 366, 367, 368, 373
    Letters to 115, 192, 216, 217, 229, 285, 336
Thackeray, Jane 44, 47, 61, 214, 267, 366
Thackeray, Lady Elizabeth [Margaret Carnegie, m. Frederick] 367
Thackeray, Martin 43
Thackeray, Misses [of Bath] 312
Thackeray, Mrs. Edward Talbot [Amy Marianne Crowe] 281, 284, 298, 313, 320, 326, 367
    Letter to 301
Thackeray, Mrs. Elias 106
Thackeray, Mrs. Martin [Augusta Yenn] 43
Thackeray, Mrs. William Makepeace [Isabella Shawe] 33, 37, 38, 39, 40, 41, 42, 44, 47, 48, 53, 57, 58, 61, 64, 66, 68, 69, 71, 72, 73, 74, 76, 77, 78, 80, 83, 85, 87, 91, 92, 93, 94, 95, 96, 98, 101, 102, 111, 117, 118, 125, 126, 127, 129, 157, 166, 171, 225, 228, 236, 272, 286, 300, 302, 327, 348, 354
    Letters to 35, 43, 112, 119
Thackeray, Rev. Elias 106
Thackeray, Rev. Francis 34, 276, 277
Thackeray, Richmond 277
Thackeray, Thomas James 61
Thackeray, William Makepeace
    "An Exhibition Gossip" [1842] 102
    Ballads [1855] 228
    Barry Lyndon, Memoirs of [1844] 97, 116, 118
    Book of Snobs, The [1846-47] 136
    "Burton's 'Life and Correspondence of David Hume'" [1846] 129
    Catherine [1840] 53, 58
    "Chronicle of the Drum" [in *Second Funeral of Napoleon*] 82
    Comic Tales and Sketches [1841] 80, 84
    Denis Duval [1864] 368, 369
    "Dickens in France" [1842] 99
    "Dionysius Diddler, History of" [1840] 58
    Dr. Birch and His Young Friends [1848] 167
    English Humourists of the Eighteenth Century [1853]
        U. S. rights 231
    "Fielding's Works" [1840] 72, 166
    "Firebrand Correspondence, The" [1841] 92
    "Fitz-Boodle Papers" [1842-43] 102
    "George Cruikshank's Works" [1840] 58
    "Gisquet's Memoirs" [1841] 79

Great Hoggarty Diamond, The History of Samuel Titmarsh and the [1841] 90, 93
Henry Esmond, The History of [1852] 207, 209, 210, 211, 214, 216, 218, 221, 224, 228, 229, 231, 234, 236, 237, 239, 245, 252, 259, 270, 276, 334, 364
Irish Sketch Book, The [1843] 66, 68, 72, 103, 106, 107, 109, 110, 112, 113
Kickleburys on the Rhine, The [1850] 197
Lectures
    English Humourists 200, 203, 204, 205, 209, 211, 214, 216, 223, 224, 231, 233, 236, 238, 242, 244
    Four Georges 280, 281, 284, 285, 287, 289, 290, 295, 298, 301, 302, 303, 304, 308, 309, 310, 311, 313, 315, 316, 317, 323, 337
Lovel the Widower [1860] 337, 355
"Madame Sand and the New Apocalypse" [1839] 70
"Manners and Society in St. Petersburg" [1839] 46
"May Day Ode" [1851] 199, 201
"Memorials of Gormandizing" [1841] 79
"Men and Coats" [1841] 92
Miscellanies (Appleton) [1852-53] 248
Mr. Brown's Letters to a Young Man About Town [1849]
    American preface 248
"Mr. Tims and a Good-natured Friend" [1848] 163
Mrs. Perkins's Ball [1846] 131, 138, 190
"New Accounts of Paris" [1844] 116
Newcomes, The [1853-55] 249, 251, 252, 255, 256, 257, 264, 265, 268, 271, 279, 320, 341
Notes of a Journey from Cornhill to Grand Cairo [1846] 118, 121, 127
"Notes on the North What-d'ye-callem Election" [1841] 92, 93
Our Street [1847] 153
Paris Sketch Book, The [1840] 49, 57, 61, 62, 63, 65
"Peg of Limavaddy" 186
Pendennis, The History of [1848-50] 153, 158, 159, 160, 161, 165, 167, 169, 175, 177, 178, 180, 182, 190, 192, 193, 197, 270, 281, 330, 344, 373
Philip, The Adventures of [1861-62] 348, 349, 362, 364, 365
Projects
    editing of Walpole 259
    Foolscap Library 58
    History of Queen Anne 348, 354, 356, 366
    Life of Talleyrand 118, 121
    "Knights of Borsellen" 77, 82, 362, 366
"Punch's Prize Novelists" [1847] 164

"Raikes's 'City of the Czar'" [1838] 46
"Ranke's 'History of the Popes'" [1840] 67
Rebecca and Rowena [1849] 184
Rose and the Ring [1854] 285
Roundabout Papers [1860-63] 362, 365
    "On a Joke I Once Heard from the Late Thomas Hood" 355
    "On a Lazy Idle Boy" 361
    "On Being Found Out" 355
    "Small-Beer Chronicle" 356
    "Thorns in the Cushion" 361
Second Funeral of Napoleon, The [1841] 77, 78, 82, 83
"Shabby Genteel Story, A" [1840] 72, 365
"Some More Words About the Ladies" [1849] 178
"Sultan Stork" [1842] 102
"The German in England" [1842] 102
"The Last Fifteen Years of the Bourbons" [1842] 102
"The Legend of Jawbrahim Heraudee" [1842] 102
Vanity Fair [1847-48] 128, 132, 136, 138, 139, 140, 143, 144, 145, 148, 151, 152, 153, 154, 155, 160, 170, 178, 188, 202, 208, 225, 279, 294, 348
Virginians, The [1857-59] 231, 299, 300, 318, 320, 322, 323, 324, 326, 330, 331, 332, 334, 336, 337, 339, 340
Wolves and the Lamb, The [1855] 337
"Yellowplush Papers" [1837-40] 42, 43, 49, 53, 248, 264

Théâtre des Variétés 170
Thiers, Louis Adolphe 233
Thirlwall, Connop [Bishop of St. Davids] 190
Thomas, Mr. 179
Thompson, Dr. Henry 298, 323, 327
    Letter to 369
Thompson, John 325
Thompson, John Reuben
    Letter to 324
Thresher, Mr. and Mrs. 1
Thwait, Mr. 131
Thynne, Lady [Cecilia Gore, m. Lord Edward] 172, 193, 250
Thynne, Lord Edward 250
Ticknor and Fields 231, 285
Ticknor family [George] 298
Ticknor, Anna 288
Ticknor, Eliza 288
Ticknor, George 238, 288
Ticknor, Mrs. George [Anna Eliot] 238
    Letters to 244, 287

Times, The 49, 57, 65, 72, 79, 80, 113, 150, 166, 198, 199, 282, 315, 334, 365
Tinling, Rev. Edward Douglas 194
Titian [Tiziano Vecelli] 29, 162, 171
Torcy, Jean Baptiste Colbert, Marquis de
    Mémoires 276
Torlonia Bank 121
Tower, T. 125
Traer, Dr. James Reeves
    Letter to 376
Transatlantic Electric Cable 308, 318
Trinity College, Cambridge 3, 178
Trois Frères Provençaux 247
Trollope, Anthony 354, 363
    Framley Parsonage 343
    Letter to 343
    Three Clerks 343
Trollope, Mrs. [Frances Milton]
    Vicar of Wrexhill 46
Trueba y Cozio, Don Telesforo de 26
Trulock, Alice Jane 192, 215
Turner, Miss 42
Turner, Mr. 102
Turner, Mrs. John 1
Turpin, Mrs. 176
Tyndall, Thomas 195
United States of America
    Civil War 348, 354, 362
    T.'s reactions to 233, 282, 289, 291, 293, 295
Ursula, St., and the 11,000 Virgins 7, 304
Vaudricourt, Mme. 50
Vaughan, Dr. 265
Vault, François Eugène de, ed.
    Mémoires militaires 276
Vedy, Mrs. 88
Venables, George Stovin 99, 132, 290, 298, 303
Venedey, Jacob 108
Vengeur, The 83
Venus 127, 167, 333
Venus de Milo 171
Véry's 247
Vestris, Mme. [Lucia Elizabeth Mathews] 87
Victoria, Princess 201
Victoria, Queen 49, 53, 152, 201, 241, 290, 295
Vieuxbois, M. 58

Vinci, Leonardo da 29
Virtue, George
    Letter to 360
Vizetelly, Henry
    Letter to 131
Waddell, Eliza 116, 168
Waddell, Mr. 168
Waddell, Mrs. 168
Waddington, Horatio 320
Wailly, Armand François de 214
Wales, Albert Edward, Prince of [later Edward VII] 201
Walker, Frederick 365
Wallack, James William 297
Walpole, Horace 259, 306
Walpole, Spencer Horatio 355
Warburton children [Eliot] 213
Warburton, Eliot [Bartholomew Elliott George] 213, 229, 344
    Letter to 190
    Memoirs of Prince Rupert 191
Warburton, Mrs. Eliot 191, 213
Ward, Samuel 281
Warenne, William de 235
Warren, Judge 235
Warren, Samuel
    Ten Thousand a Year 54
Washington, George 156, 322, 325
Webb, Amelia 276
Webb, Col. John Richmond 276
Webb, Gen. John Richmond 276, 277
Weber, Karl Maria von
    Freischütz 21
Weincke, Dr. 92
Weissenborn, Dr. Friedrich 10
Wellington, Arthur Wellesley, 1st Duke of 201, 233
Wesley, John 137
West, Mr. and Mrs. Temple 220
Westminster School 284
Whately, Richard [Archbishop of Dublin] 107
White, Rev. James 125, 356
Wieland, Christoph 13
Wightwick, George
    Blue Friars 42
Wilkie, Sir David 30
William Henry, Duke of Clarence [later William IV] 83
William II, King of Holland 105

William IV 105
William the Conqueror 235
Williams, William Smith
    Letters to 141, 142
Williams-Wynn, Charlotte 264, 265
Willis's Rooms 200, 312
Wiseman, Nicholas, Cardinal 106
    Lectures 106
Wolfe, Maj.-Gen. James 335
Wood, Mr. 20
Woolgar, Sarah Jane 157
Wordsworth, William 199
    "Intimations of Immortality" 48
Wynendael, battle of 34, 276
Wynn, Mr. 265
Wynne, Mrs. Robert [Eugènie Marie Crowe] 168, 302
Wynne, Robert 302
Yates, Edmund 330, 355
Yates, Frederick Henry 99
Yates, Mrs. Frederick Henry 2
Yorke, Mrs. Grantham Munton [Marian Emily Montgomery]
    Letter to 179
Yorke, Rev. Grantham Munton 179
Young, Edward 56
Young, James Reynolds 3
Young, William 315, 368
Zampieri, Domenichino
    Cumæan Sybil 263
Zonny 34